SHAKESPEARE STUDIES

EDITORIAL BOARD

David M. Bevington
  The University of Chicago

Catherine Belsey
  University of Wales College of Cardiff

Michael Bristol
  McGill University

S. P. Cerasano
  Colgate University

Barry Gaines
  The University of New Mexico

Lena Cowen Orlin
  The Folger Shakespeare Library

John Pitcher
  St. Johns College, Oxford

Maureen Quilligan
  The University of Pennsylvania

Alan Sinfield
  The University of Sussex

Peter Stallybrass
  The University of Pennsylvania

SHAKESPEARE STUDIES VOLUME XXIII

EDITED BY
LEEDS BARROLL

BOOK-REVIEW EDITOR

Susan Zimmerman

Madison • Teaneck
Fairleigh Dickinson University Press
London : Associated University Presses

© 1995 by Associated University Presses, Inc.

All rights reserved. Authorization to photocopy items for internal or personal use, or the internal or personal use of specific clients, is granted by the copyright owner, provided that a base fee of $10.00, plus eight cents per page, per copy is paid directly to the Copyright Clearance Center, 222 Rosewood Drive, Danvers, Massachusetts 01923 [0-8386-3640-3/95 $10.00+8¢ pp, pc.]

Associated University Presses
440 Forsgate Drive
Cranbury, NJ 08512

Associated University Presses
25 Sicilian Avenue
London WC1A 2QH, England

Associated University Presses
P.O. Box 338, Port Credit
Mississauga, Ontario
Canada L5G 4L8

The paper used in this publication meets the requirements of the American National Standard for Permanence of Paper for Printed Library Materials Z39.48-1984.

All editorial correspondence concerning Shakespeare Studies should be addressed to the Editorial Office, Shakespeare Studies, Department of English, University of Maryland (Baltimore County), Catonsville, Maryland 21228. Send two copies of submitted articles and return postage. Correspondence concerning orders and subscriptions should be addressed to: Associated University Presses, 440 Forsgate Drive, Cranbury, New Jersey 08512.

International Standard Book Number 0-8386-3640-3 (vol. xxiii)
International Standard Serial Number 0582-9399

PRINTED IN THE UNITED STATES OF AMERICA

Contents

From the Editor   9

List of Contributors   11

Articles

"So beloved that men use his pictures for their signs": Richard Tarlton and the Uses of Sixteenth-Century Celebrity
    ALEXANDRA HALASZ   19

Spheres of Influence: Cartography and the Gaze in Shakespearean Tragedy and History
    PHILIP ARMSTRONG   39

Androgynous "Union" and the Woman in *Hamlet*
    JAMES STONE   71

Interlinear Trysting and "household stuff": the Latin Lesson and the Domestication of Learning in *The Taming of the Shrew*
    THOMAS MOISAN   100

"Are We Being Historical Yet?": Colonialist Interpretations of Shakespeare's *Tempest*
    BEN ROSS SCHNEIDER, JR.   120

"The name and all th'addition": *King Lear*'s Opening Scene and the Common Law Use
    CHARLES SPINOSA   146

"She is fast my wife": Sex, Marriage, and Ducal Authority in *Measure for Measure*
    ALBERTO CACICEDO   187

Lucrece's Gaze
    STEPHEN CARTER   210

Contents

Reviews

Francis Barker, *The Culture of Violence: Essays on Tragedy and History*
  KIERNAN RYAN — 225

Linda Charnes, *Notorious Identity: Materializing the Subject in Shakespeare*
  HARRY BERGER, JR. — 229

R. A. Foakes, *Hamlet versus Lear: Cultural Politics and Shakespeare's Art*
  ALEXANDER LEGGATT — 237

Margo Hendricks and Patricia Parker, eds., *Women, "Race," and Writing in the Early Modern Period*
  VALERIE TRAUB — 241

Jean E. Howard, *The Stage and Social Struggle in Early Modern England*
  MARY BETH ROSE — 247

Wallace T. MacCaffrey, *Elizabeth I*
Susan Frye, *Elizabeth I*
  MAURICE LEE, JR. — 251

Gordon McMullan and Jonathan Hope, eds., *The Politics of Tragicomedy: Shakespeare and After*
  JILL L. LEVENSON — 257

Marianne Novy, ed., *Cross-Cultural Performance: Differences in Women's Re-Visions of Shakespeare*
  BARBARA E. BOWEN — 261

Lena Cowen Orlin, *Private Matters and Public Culture in Post-Reformation England*
  RICHARD HELGERSON — 268

Alan Sinfield, *Faultlines: Cultural Materialism and the Politics of Dissident Reading*
  TERENCE HAWKES — 275

Meredith Anne Skura, *Shakespeare the Actor and the Purposes of Playing*
  LOIS POTTER — 280

Brian Vickers, *Appropriating Shakespeare: Contemporary Critical Quarrels*
   Robert S. Miola   284

Index   289

From the Editor

IN FORTHCOMING ISSUES, beginning with Volume XXIV, to be published in fall 1996, *Shakespeare Studies* will introduce a number of features suggested by our new editorial board. These will include "current interventions," that is, articles which evaluate the status of recent scholarship with respect to a particular field or topic (for Volume XXIV, for example, we are planning essays on recent work in semiotics, and on studies concerning sexuality and gender); multi-authored forums on controversial issues; short (c. 4000 words) provocative theoretical pieces; and short reports on significant archival discoveries. We will also be expanding our customary range of reviews to include relevant theoretical texts that may not directly address Shakespeare (for example, we will feature a review article on Judith Butler's work in Volume XXIV); appropriate texts in disciplines relevant to literary and theatrical studies, such as history, women's studies, anthropology; advance reviews of important new works available at the time of review in galleys only (in this issue, Richard Helgerson's review of Lena Cowlin Orlin's book); and "cluster" reviews of multiple texts dealing with the same area of inquiry. The Editor welcomes the responses of our readers to these innovations.

The Editor

Contributors

PHILIP ARMSTRONG teaches in the Department of English at the University of Auckland. He is currently researching the structures of visual perception in Shakespearean tragedy.

HARRY BERGER JR. is Professor of Literature at the University of California at Santa Cruz.

BARBARA E. BOWEN is Associate Professor of English and Women's Studies at Queens College and the Graduate Center, City University of New York. She is the author of *Gender in the Theater of War: Shakespeare's "Troilus and Cressida"*, and currently working on the use of Shakespeare in radical political movements.

ALBERTO CACICEDO is Associate Professor of English at Albright College. He is currently working on a book concerned with biological and intellectual conception in Shakespeare.

STEVEN J. CARTER is a Seminar Instructor of Communications and Film at York University. He is currently completing a monograph on linguistic transcendence and the narrativized "other" in African-American cinema and articles on narratology in the works of R. K. Narayan, Mieke Bal, and Jean Baudrillard.

ALEXANDRA HALASZ is Assistant Professor of English at Dartmouth College. She is currently completing a book on pamphlets and the marketplace of print at the turn of the sixteenth century in England.

TERENCE HAWKES is Professor of English at the University of Wales, Cardiff, UK. He is the author of *Meaning By Shakespeare* (1992).

RICHARD HELGERSON is Professor of English at the University of California, Santa Barbara. His most recent book is *Forms of Nationhood: The Elizabethan Writing of England*.

Contributors

MAURICE LEE, JR. is Margaret Judson Professor of History at Rutgers University. His most recent book is *Great Britain's Solomon: James VI and I in His Three Kingdoms*.

ALEXANDER LEGGATT is Professor of English at University College, University of Toronto. His publications include *Shakespeare's Comedy of Love*, *Shakespeare's Political Drama*, and *Jacobean Public Theatre*.

JILL L. LEVENSON is Professor of English at Trinity College, The University of Toronto.

ROBERT S. MIOLA is Professor of English and Lecturer in Classics (adjunct) at Loyola College, Baltimore. He has recently published *Shakespeare and Classical Comedy* with The Clarendon Press, Oxford.

THOMAS MOISAN is Professor and Chair of English at Saint Louis University. He is currently at work on a book on the relationship of poetic practice and culture in the poetry of Robert Herrick.

LOIS POTTER is Ned. B. Allen Professor of English at the University of Delaware. She recently completed the Arden edition of *The Two Noble Kinsmen*.

MARY BETH ROSE is Director of the Newberry Center for Renaissance Studies. She is also the editor of *Renaissance Drama*, and is currently completing a book on gender and the heroic in English Renaissance literature.

KIERNAN RYAN is fellow and Director of Studies in English at New Hall, University of Cambridge. He is currently working on a study of Shakespearean comedy and romance.

BEN ROSS SCHNEIDER, JR. is Professor Emeritus of English at Lawrence University, Appleton, Wisconsin. He is currently completing a book on the ethos of Shakespeare's plays.

CHARLES SPINOSA is Assistant Professor of English at Miami University of Ohio. He frequently writes on Shakespeare and the common law and is currently completing a book with Hubert L. Dreyfus on Heidegger's understanding of gods and divinities.

JAMES W. STONE is a graduate student at the University of California at Berkeley. He is currently completing a dissertation on chiastic gender confusion—"Crossing the Mirror: Androgyny and Transvestism in the English Renaissance."

VALERIE TRAUB is Associate Professor in the English Department at Vanderbilt University. She is author of *Desire and Anxiety: Circulations of Sexuality in Shakespearean Drama* (1992). She is currently working on discourses of female erotic pleasure in the early modern period.

SHAKESPEARE STUDIES

ARTICLES

"So beloved that men use his picture for their signs": Richard Tarlton and the Uses of Sixteenth-Century Celebrity

Alexandra Halasz

IN THE 1615 edition of Stow's *Annales* there is a brief mention of Richard Tarlton in an entry appended to the record of 1583 that recounts the formation of Queen Elizabeth's Men:[1]

> Comedians and stage-players of former time were very poore and ignorant in respect of these of this time, but being now grown very skilfull and exquisite actors for all matters, they were entertained into the service of great lords, out of which companies were xii of the best chosen and at the request of Sir Francis Walsingham, they were sworne the Queenes servants, and were allowed wages and liveries as groomes of the chamber: and until this year the Queene hadde no players. Amongst these xii players . . . [was] . . . Richard Tarlton for a wondrous plentifull pleasant extemporall wit, hee was the wonder of his time.

Printed in the margin of the 1615 *Annales*, next to the passage I've just quoted is the following comment: "Tarlton so beloved that men use his picture for their signs." The signs meant are alehouse signs (at least one tavern named after Tarlton survived well into the eighteenth century) and presumably the picture was a crude version of the performer with tabor and pipe.[2] "Tarlton so beloved" is a figure of affection and trust who functions to signify a site of pleasure and entertainment indisputably popular, non-exclusive—the alehouse, a place of community gathering, storytelling, merriment. The text, in contrast, speaks of an exclusive, elite position: a highly skilled performer, with access to the court, regular wages and benefits, patronage from the queen and her closest advisors.

Taken together, text and margin present Tarlton as a figure of national interest whose reputation rests on his speech performance, specifically his quick wit, and whose potency as a figure emerges from his dual class positioning—at once of the people and part of the elite. But the text and margin are not continuous; that is, they supply no coherent account of Tarlton's position. Rather the text asserts that Tarlton's special skills facilitate, if not necessitate, his entry into elite circles and make him an object of "wonder." "Wonder" refers both to the rarity of his skill and to a distancing effect produced by his elevated status. The marginal comment, however, defines Tarlton as a kind of common currency; his image circulates, available for anyone's use. In the conjunction of rarity and ubiquity that the *Annales* registers we can recognize the now familiar condition of celebrity. I will return to the *Annales* mention of Tarlton, but for the time being I want to note only that Tarlton's celebrity neither emerges from nor culminates in the *Annales*. Though the *Annales* was published in 1588 (the year of Tarlton's death), 1592, 1600, 1601, and 1605, it is not until twenty-seven years after his death that he is mentioned. In other words, the *Annales* affirms a celebrity image already in productive circulation.

Celebrity images have become a staple of contemporary cultural analysis: sites where the interaction of market functions, media practices, and various forms of labor and subjectivity can be traced. Critics have focused primarily on nineteenth and twentieth century instances—as if the celebrity image were a creature of the mass media and fully developed capitalism.[3] But what celebrity might have meant, how it was constructed, and what interests it represented or served in an early modern context is far from clear. In the case of Richard Tarlton, I will argue, the layering of meanings onto his reputation suggests that celebrity, rather then being created by the media, actually participates in the development of the media and the (proto)capitalist organization of both daily life and national identity. Tracing the process by which the figure of Tarlton accumulates representational force will involve locating the reputation he acquired by his performance practice in his lifetime and the appropriation of that reputation by the book trade in its effort to expand and create a market for printed texts. The book trade's particular use of Tarlton's reputation, I will argue, had an effect far beyond its market interests, for the image of Tarlton came to mark altered relations in leisure activity, in the circulation of discourse, and in class and geographical difference.

Disentangling Tarlton from the significations attached to his name is not an easy or obvious task. The entry on Tarlton in the *Dictionary of National Biography* runs to five columns and provides enough anecdotal evidence to reconstruct at least three lives:

he was born in Shropshire and worked as a swineherd until he was discovered by the servant of a prominent courtier who, hearing his "happy unhappy wit," rescued him and brought him to London; he was born in London and worked as a water bearer; he was an apprentice in London, then later kept a tavern or an inn; he was married; he wasn't married—rather, he died in the house of a notorious prostitute; he was a favorite of the queen, alone capable of bringing her out of what the sixteenth century called "the dumps." In fact, we have only scant "documentary" evidence about Richard Tarlton. He was an actor, especially renowned as a clown, or comedian, and as a performer of jigs. He was a member of Queen Elizabeth's Men from 1583, the date of its incorporation, until his death in 1588. He left a six-year-old son and his will was disputed by his mother. We also know that in 1587 he became a Master of Fence.[4]

The wealth of material in the *Dictionary of National Biography* emerges from the fact that Tarlton is mentioned in scores of late-sixteenth and early-seventeenth century texts and designated as the author of ballads, stories, and pamphlets written both before and after his death. In other words, the *DNB* entry that attests to Tarlton's cultural importance does so tautologically, for it was his cultural importance that produced the material out of which the *DNB* constructs his life. Tarlton, it would seem, was always a mythic representation—a name and a persona around whom allusions gathered that came to function as an icon. Why Tarlton? What did his name signify? What was at stake in using his name as a signifier—and for whom?

From the late-nineteenth century perspective of the *DNB* writers, the answer is fairly straightforward. Tarlton is a figure of "merry old England"—part of the context of Shakespeare's work which gentlemen/scholars had reconstructed earlier in the century as they gathered the ballads and pamphlets roughly contemporaneous with Shakespeare's plays and published them for the first time since the seventeenth century. The connection to Shakespeare is not entirely adventitious—the pamphlets attributed to Tarlton but published after his death present him as the spiritual father of William Kempe and Robert Armin, the two actors with whom and for whom Shakespeare wrote his clown parts.[5] At the same time, however, the Shakespeare "filter" through which Tarlton and other figures and texts associated with early modern English popular culture are viewed is preemptive and distorting. Tarlton's association with Shakespeare or Shakespeare lore functions to support a conflation of Shakespeare and English national identity; it does not answer the question of what and how Tarlton's name signified in the late sixteenth and seventeenth centuries.

The texts attributed to Tarlton in the late sixteenth century are equivocally positioned between establishing and exploiting his reputation.[6] Some of the early texts seem incongruous—a ballad recounting a disastrous flood published in 1570, for example, or a pamphlet called *Tarlton's Tragical Treatises* published in 1578. Such texts establish that he had sufficient London reputation that his name was used, but they do not specify the contents of that reputation. Indeed, in the flood ballad, he is simply the reporter—"quod Tarlton"; as such he figures the crossing between oral and printed forms of discourse. While the initial use of Tarlton's name as a signifier by the book trade does not depend on a specific reputation, other evidence makes it clear that the later reputation as a quick wit was already established. In a manuscript written about 1580, for example, Gabriel Harvey, one of England's preeminent learned men, worries that his extempore speech (based on his training in classical rhetoric) will be indistinguishable from Tarlton's improvisations on the stage.[7] Harvey's invocation of Tarlton simultaneously recognizes the wit and attempts to mark it in class-inflected ways. Unlike Harvey's own, Tarlton's wit is popular; that is, it is widely known and appreciated (even by Harvey who elsewhere reports having been personally invited to a performance) and nonexclusive—it does not depend on privilege or access to the kind of cultural authority a university man like Harvey possessed.[8]

After Tarlton's death humorous quick wit comes to define his reputation. Indeed, it might be argued that Tarlton's death allows the stabilization of his reputation and thus provides the ground of mythmaking: a persona then can be constructed in accord with a singular and no longer contestable image.[9] In any case, Tarlton's death makes his name available as a signifier for the activities in which he once supposedly engaged. The representation of Tarlton or the use of his name is imbued with a nostalgia for his performance at the same time as that representation becomes the means of advancing other interests. We can trace this process in a series of intertextually related pamphlets that use the figure of Tarlton for quite conscious ends, specifically to articulate their place as a literature of popular entertainment, a literature that, like Tarlton's performance, is widely appreciated and does not depend on exclusivity or privilege. By appropriating Tarlton's image as an entertainer, these pamphlets inscribe their own practice as another kind of popular entertainment.

"So beloved that men use his picture for their signs" 23

In the first of these, *Tarltons Newes out of Purgatory*, published in 1590, the narrator offers "a toy of Tarltons, called his newes out of Purgatory".[10] Tarlton comes to the narrator in a dream; his "newes" consists of a brief account of his journey to Purgatory into which are set six fabliaux or comic stories. The narrator's story of the dream opens with an account of the loss of Tarlton:

> sorrowing ... for the death of Richard Tarlton. ... the wonted desire to see plaies left me. [I] mourned in conceite and absented myself from all plaies; ... yet at last, as the longest sommer day hath his night, so this dumpe had an end, and forsooth upon a Whitson Monday I would needs to the Theatre to a play. (53–54)

The dream happens because the narrator does not enter the Theatre but instead falls asleep under a tree. Tarlton's appearance causes the narrator to break into a sweat and Tarlton offers his "newes" as a calming gesture:

> yes, yes, my good brother, there is *quoddam tertium*, a third place that all our great grandmothers have talkt of, that Dant hath so learnedly writ of, and that is purgatorie.... take Dick Tarlton once for thine author, who is now come from purgatory. (56–57)

Tarlton's gesture is more than calming; the two antecedents he supplies for his narrative, the tales of old women and Dante's poem, locate the narrator's story discursively as well. The "third" purgatorial space lies between the learned poetic and masculine tradition of Dante and the oral, feminized stories of "our great grandmothers." If, from the perspective of an authoritative poetic tradition (represented by Dante), *Tarltons Newes* might be dismissed as an ephemeral publication, the invocation of a feminized orality (old wives' tales) prevents that dismissal, for the ephemeral position is already (and always) occupied. By means of this triangulation, the pamphlet claims a "masculine" place and also tacitly asserts its difference from the ephemerality and ambiguous gendering of theatrical performance.

The narrator of *Tarltons Newes* situates his dream temporally as well as spatially; he goes to the Theatre on Whitson Monday, the second day of the feast of Pentecost. The reference to Whitson Monday not only suggests a parody of the descent of the Holy Spirit and the gift of tongues, but also recalls the medieval ale festivals held on that Monday. Like the antecedents Tarlton identifies for his account of Purgatory, the narrator's reference to Whitson Monday recalls both an oral and a textual tradition, again indicating a "third space." The Pentecostal allusion identifies the narrator's vocation as apostolic; by his dream he is infused with the spirit of Tarlton and he acquires the power to spread the word of Tarlton. The new discursive space is potentially available to all (like the biblical narrative) and profane (like the ale festival).

Tarlton's narrative, which takes the place of a performance, ends with an affirmation of his reputation as a performer: his purgatorial task, he tells the narrator, is to play his tabor and pipe forever. In the dream, as he starts to play, the narrator awakens.

> and with that [the narrator continues] I knew the play was doon; wherupon, rising up, and smiling at my dream, after supper took my pen, and neer as I could set it down. (105)

"Tak[ing] Dick Tarlton once for [an] author," involves removing Tarlton from the oral context of the ale festival and the Theatre and making his performance into a text that reworks the entertainment Tarlton once provided. The printed pamphlet becomes a competitor with the theater. It offers the spirit of Tarlton in a form that defies both the finality of death and the ephemerality of oral performance, a parodic, secular version of "the living word."

Later the same year (1590), a second pamphlet represents the reception of *Tarltons Newes*, disallowing some of its claims and advancing others. *The Cobler of Canterbury* tells of a journey on the Thames under traveling conditions so easy that the occupants of the boat had only to pass the time.[11]

> As thus every man was striving to passe away the time pleasantly, a Gentleman puld out of his sleeve a little pamphlet, and begun to reade to himselfe: amongst the rest, my selfe was so bold as to aske him what booke it was: mary quoth he a foolish toy, called *Tarltons Newes out of Purgatorie*: at this they all fell to descanting of the booke some commended it highly, and sayd it was good invention and fine tales: tush, quoth another, most of them stolne out of *Boccacc Decameron*: for all that quoth the third, it tis pretie and wittie. As they were thus commending and discommending, there sate by an ancient man that was a cobler in *Canterbury*: Maisters, quoth he, I have read the booke, and 'tis indifferent, like a cup of bottle ale, half one and halfe the other: but tis not merrie enough for Tarltons vaine, nor stuffed with his fine conceits: therfore it shall pass for a booke and no more. (5–6)

Tarltons Newes does not successfully substitute for Tarlton's performance, claims the cobbler, calling attention to the interestedness of using Tarlton's name to advertise the book. He then recalls Chaucer's *The Canterbury Tales* and suggests that since they too are bound for Canterbury, they occupy their time in telling tales. There follow six fabliaux told by the various passengers, including the gentleman (who is evidently not allowed to read to himself in public). *The Cobler of Canterbury* initially seems to assert that it is neither the association with Tarlton's performance nor the high poetic tradition of Dante that defines pamphlet entertainment, but rather the link to the earlier tale-telling tradition of Boccacio and Chaucer. That tradition already occupies a middle position between orality and high literacy; the classic status of progenitors like *The Decameron* and *The Canterbury Tales* thus warrants pamphlet stories.

Yet, like *Tarltons Newes*, which substitutes a narrative for theatrical performance, *The Cobler of Canterbury* participates in a displacement, representing the oral exchange of tales as a substitute for the reading of *Tarltons Newes*. The first framing fiction of *The Cobler of Canterbury* is that storytelling is reclaimed from printed texts by its "original" producers and made oral and social again. When, at the end of the day's journey, the passengers retire to an alehouse and review their tales, the cobbler resolves to publish them:

> I can (quoth the Cobler) remember them all, and very neere verbatim collect and gather them together: which by the Grace of God gentlemen, I meane to do, and then to set them out in a pamphlet, under mine owne name, as an invective against *Tarltons News out of Purgatorie*. (83)

The second framing fiction of *The Cobler of Canterbury* undoes the first: the cobbler severs the connection between storytelling and Tarlton's performance not to restore the oral exchange of tales but so that he can offer the same kind of material under his "owne name." His assertion of reportorial accuracy ("very neere verbatim") is immediately ironized by the claim that he publishes under his "owne name," for he does so in an anonymous text.

As an invective against *Tarltons Newes*, *The Cobler of Canterbury* at once exposes the appropriation of Tarlton's name and appropriates for itself the space of storytelling in print, but without a proper name. What neither pamphlet acknowledges is that its "own" tales are in fact already appropriated, retold. Moreover, if not interchangeable between pamphlets, each of the tales could be replaced by a number of similar others found in the various collections written and compiled in the fourteenth, fifteenth and sixteenth centuries. This recycled material is framed by another story, ostensibly the story of how the stories came to be told. In *Tarltons Newes*, Tarlton's name is appropriated because it signifies, quite literally, an acting subject, and thus supplies an attested storyteller position, an agent of the entertainment provided. By severing the connection between Tarlton and pamphlet storytelling, *The Cobler of Canterbury* offers a double substitution that reveals a continual process of appropriation. First, by representing the oral exchange of tales, the narrative suggests that it is impossible to contain stories within the boundaries of a medium or text. Anyone can tell stories and thus facilitate their circulation. Second, when the cobbler publishes the same material under his "owne name," he fabricates a boundary, fixing the stories in print.

The practice that produces *The Cobler of Canterbury* is an editorial one. An editorial practice does not require an identification between a known performer and narrative; rather the narrator, editor, "I," emerges as a full substitute for the performer as the text does for performance. But when the cobbler announces his plans to publish and tells the tale-tellers that "if [they] please to send to the Printer . . . every one . . . shall have a booke for his labor" (83), he also highlights the duplicity of his textual performance by parodying payment in kind to writers. If, in *Tarltons Newes* Tarlton's persona as a performer functions to familiarize the commodified entertainment of the pamphlet, the burden of *The Cobler of Canterbury*'s invective is to demystify that function by revealing the social relations involved in the production of pamphlet storytelling. The agency of pamphlet entertainment as described by *The Cobler of Canterbury* is collective. In the alternative scenario offered by *Tarltons Newes* (and other pamphlets ascribed to Tarlton), the use of Tarlton's name subsumes the collaborative work involved in pamphlet storytelling into the persona of Tarlton. Any authorial name creates a fiction of individual production that belies the circumstances and practices involved in producing a printed text. When the cobbler announces his plans to publish and then parodies the printer's payment in kind to writers, he makes the agencies involved in production clear. (In the case of an authorial name that refers to the actual writer, at least the agent of the representation is indicated.) Tarlton's name, however, would seem to mask the agencies involved. Though *The Cobler of Canterbury* exposes the appropriation of Tarlton's name, it also depends on the signification attached to his name in *Tarltons Newes* even as it relocates

"So beloved that men use his picture for their signs" 27

that performative quality in the practices of ordinary men and women and in the editorial efforts of anonymous pamphlet writers. Tarlton's name and persona are more effective in promoting pamphlet entertainment that the cobbler or his demystification precisely because Tarlton signifies a singular performance.

In a provocative essay on stardom, Barry King argues that "the formation of the persona of the star accomplishes, from the side of labour power, the same suppression of the fundamentally collective character of all productive activity that enables the capitalist to appear as the demiurge of production" (158).[12] In other words, the star provides "a metonymy for labour power in general" (153). King's materialist theorization of stardom derives from an analysis of the twentieth century film industry and offers a corrective to those accounts of stardom that focus on the production of stars for consumption or the consumption of star images. The case of Tarlton seems to fit easily and obviously in King's model, for his persona supplies an agency that situates the pamphlet in (imagined) conditions of labor and performance, in the process of producing entertainment. But the case of Tarlton also subtly differs from the stardom King investigates, for unlike the movie star, Tarlton does not actually labor in the production of the commodity his name and persona advertise. Rather his persona is appropriated and adapted from the practices associated with the historical personage. Set into motion by the book trade, the persona operates metaphorically as well as metonymically, simultaneously translating the theatricality of the historical performances to pamphlet storytelling and standing for the labor involved in the production of the commodity pamphlet. The appropriation and substitutive use of Tarlton's persona thus allows the full ambiguity of the star's position in relation to a capitalist (commodity) economy to be explored in the very process of its emergence. Someone took Tarlton's name to establish the value of a text. That text, as Copy, has value as a form of property; as a copy, it has value as a commodity; and it is purchased because it has potential value as entertainment. Tarlton's name signifies in relation to each of the disparate values that can be attributed to a text bearing his name. Indeed, it might be said to unify them, suppressing their difference much as it masked the collective effort involved in the production of the printed text itself.

I use Copy to indicate the legal fiction that establishes ownership of a text—what is now copyright. In the late sixteenth and early seventeenth centuries, Copy was a property developed by and limited to the trade, members of the Stationers' Company.[13] Copy is an abstract form of the text; it consists in the right to reproduce the text (or sell it to someone else for reproduction). As such, it is a form of capital. The stories in *Tarltons Newes* and *The Cobler of Canterbury* are taken from public "unowned" circulation. Gathered into a particular pamphlet, the stories become the protected property of the Copy owner (usually the publisher) even as their narrative frames directly address the circumstances of their circulation and appropriation. Tarlton's name (among others) implies a claim of ownership on behalf of the person entitled to reproduce the text. In other words, not only does Tarlton's persona signify the labor involved in the production of the text, but his name also marks the alienation of that labor and its accumulation as a form of capital. The book trade has an interest specifically in Tarlton's name because it functions as a signifier for the performative quality of pamphlet entertainment, indicating its potential use. Thus the figure of Tarlton is a mediating representation, one that makes the diverse interests and agencies of production, consumption, and ownership appear as one and as a given, as "natural."

The book trade's proprietary interest in Tarlton ideally requires that the qualities once associated with his performance become associated with the pamphlet literature it produces and distributes. But as *The Cobler of Canterbury* makes clear, storytelling is a common activity and entertainment a common pursuit; neither requires the pamphlet. In 1592, two years after *Tarlton's Newes* and the *Cobler of Canterbury*, a third pamphlet, *Kind Harts Dreame*, uses Tarlton to examine the varied and competing interests invested in the space and means of entertainment.[14] Tarlton is one of five figures who appear sequentially to the narrator, Kind Hart, in a dream. In accord with Tarlton's reputation, he appears as a clown, presenting a speech and concluding as would a performer on tabor and pipe: "with a turn on the toe I take my leave" (44). Tarlton begins by calling attention to his renown: "Now Maisters, what say you to a merrie knave, that for this two years day hath not beene talkt of?" (39). By complaining that he has not been "talkt of" in two years, Tarlton calls attention to the circulation of his name in the pamphlets that offer themselves as substitutes for his performance. Identifying Tarlton as he appeared in the dream, Kind Hart says: "I knew him to be either the body or the resemblaunce of Tarleton" (12). Embodied in a printed text, the "resemblaunce of Tarleton" signifies not only a specific dramatic practice but also a general social one: "Sith it is thus," Tarlton says, "Ile be a time-pleaser" (39). Detached from the spatiotemporal locus of his practice, the name and the persona it implies become an icon, the representational market of time (and space) not bound by work or necessity.

Tarlton's speech in *Kind Harts Dreame* is a satiric defense of playing that proceeds by impersonating individuals who are or have invested in "time-pleasing." In other words, it textualizes the performative practice for which Tarlton was known. Playing had been prohibited in London in June of 1592 (due to the plague) and Tarlton notes that the prohibition was "to the no smal profit of the Bouling-alleyes in Bedlam and other places" (49) and suggests that bowling alleys might "joine with the Dicing houses to make sute again for their [plays'] longer restraint, though the sickness cease" (40). A man with time and money to spend in an afternoon must decide where he wishes to spend it. In one place he might find ale and card games, in another food, drink and music, and in a third a story performed, retold; each place offers to make time pleasing and all are in competition for the spender's choice.

> But I have more to say than this; Is it not greate shame, that the houses of retaylers neare the Townes end should be by their [plays'] continuance impoverished? Alas good hearts, they pay great rentes, and pittie it is but they be provided for. While playes are usde, halfe the day is spent by most youthes that have libertie uppon them, or at least the greatest company drawn to the places where they frequent. If they were supprest, the flocke of yoong people would bee equally parted. But now the greatest trade is brought into one street. Is it not as faire a way to *Myle*-end by *White-chappel*, as by *Shoreditch* to *Hackney*? (40)

The word that describes the spender's enacted choice is "usde." The spender uses the play, that is, he passes, or spends his time by means of it. Conversely and simultaneously, it mediates or fills his time. What his money buys is entrance to the particular place where (the) play is available to him. In *Tarltons Newes* the word "use" describes the performative skill Tarlton acquires by playing ceaselessly: "[it] hath brought me into such use, that I now play far better than when I was alive" (105). The performer's "use" is also a time-filling or mediating activity like that of the spender. The player's "use " is what he has to sell and what the spender might use; their respective uses can meet and satisfy each other and therefore themselves, Tarlton argues, only in a particular place, in the house of a retailer.

Tarlton details the position of the retailer by momentarily assuming it:

> I am a man now as other men be . . . come up to London. . . . no other occupation have I but to be an ale-draper, the Landlord wil have fortie pound fine and twenty marke a year, I and mine must not lie in the street: he knowes by honest courses I can never paye the Rent. (41)

The retailer's "house" is not his own and the worth of what he retails must be balanced not only against its wholesale or production cost but also against the "great rents" he pays. That is, the retail position marks the intersection of interests in a market relationship. Tarlton's speech in *Kind-Harts Dreame* reveals how the common space of entertainment is, in fact, intersected by particular interests arranged according to the logic of the retail position. He produces an analysis of the retail trade in entertainment—in time-pleasing, one that addresses the existence of competing sites (theaters, dice halls, taverns, etc.) and argues that they have a common structure—they all make people into consumers who pay to pass the time pleasantly.

Entertaining practices, whether they occupy the space of an alehouse, a theater or a book, are mediated by the investments of property owners, retailers and "users." The player and the writer occupy a version of the retail position: they retell stories. But what they have to sell depends for its utterance on the calculations of property owners whose investment in that property—theater buildings, costumes and "properties" (including scripts), or print shops, paper and ink, Copy—determines the value of the time-pleasing a player or writer offers. Entertaining practices, that is, are subject to a calculus of interests that mediates the "use" of performers/producers with that of audience/consumers. Thus, entertainment is not simply a common pursuit or mutual endeavor but a "use" of time and space that has an exchange value determined by that calculus of interests. In *Kind-Harts Dreame* Tarlton represents "time-pleasing" as a commodity or service the marketplace offers. And it is, finally, the marketing impulse in the book trade that made Tarlton into an icon that circulated for four or five generations.

By appropriating Tarlton's name, by textualizing the practices for which he was known, and by making him into a representational icon, pamphlets advertise their capacity to provide the kind of experience associated with Tarlton's performance. Clearly the book trade produced an image of Tarlton and used it to develop its own interests, to mark out discursive territory it then could occupy, to expand its audience and market. But that production of Tarlton as a representation depended on the prior existence of Tarlton's reputation. In other words, it was the appropriated image that enabled an expansion of print culture and an articulation of its relation to other media of entertainment and discourse. The icon of Tarlton marks the pamphlet as a site where someone else's work is available for purchase as a vehicle of pleasure.

A pamphlet called *Tarlton's Jests* published at least by 1609, possibly before 1600, indicates the last stage in the book trade's development of the figure.[15] Jest books were a fairly common genre in early print culture and often attached to historical figures. When attached to such figures, the jest book produces a pseudobiography that can be extracted from the narrative material.[16] In the case of Tarlton, one of the effects of *Tarlton's Jests* is the creation of a fullblown celebrity image. The identification of Tarlton with quick wit is obviously preserved, but that identity is enacted in various contexts that represent a life, rather than simply a performance practice. At least three quarters of the jests can be traced to earlier books—in other words, they are not specifically Tarlton's jokes. At the same time, Tarlton may well have told them. If printed jest books mediate the cultural repertoire of joking, simultaneously diffusing it and subjecting it to the relations of the marketplace, attributing the jests to Tarlton's wit underscores the emphasis on ownership that emerges in a market context.

Like older jest books, the material in *Tarlton's Jests* raises significant class issues—humor being a protected mode of challenging hierarchy and authority. Unlike older jest books, the pamphlet also raises significant questions about the meaning and relations of place. It is divided into three sections: "Tarlton's Court-Witty Jests" (17), "Tarlton's Sound City Jests" (25), and "Tarlton's Pretty Country Jests" (31). The spatial/geographic organization of *Tarlton's Jests* participates in the same market logic as the earlier pamphlets attributed to Tarlton. That is, together with the various class positions and issues traditionally found in jest books, the spatial/geographic range envisions a wide and varied potential audience. *Tarlton's Jests* offers funny stories for and/or about anyone, anywhere. The division into court, city and country sections plots Tarlton's reputation on a spatial/geographic axis that implies the nation, moving from the center of political power to the economic center to the country at large. The intersection of class issues with geographic ones produces what might be called a representational grid held together around the figure of Tarlton who alone crosses the vertical boundaries of class and the horizontal ones of space. Tarlton's significance is widened: he becomes at once a celebrity image and a representative figure. As a celebrity he is apparently the possessor of unique talents that enable him to do and say things other people are inhibited from doing and saying. Yet insofar as he mixes with all kinds of people in all kinds of places without differentiating his behavior according to the status or place of his interlocutors, he could be anyone, anywhere. Paradoxically then, he becomes available as a site of identification abstracted from any particulars save those of his mythic image, while at the same time, the mythic image is precisely the sufficient condition of his representativeness.

Richard Tarlton produces his speech performance at the intersection of his own talents and various discursive and performative traditions—the Vice, the Lord of Misrule, the clown. His own social rise, such as it may have been, resulted directly from that performance/labor.[17] He becomes a celebrity image, however, by the work of others who make the representation of that speech performance simultaneously an icon of the pleasures available in the marketplace, particularly the marketplace of print, and a generally accessible repertoire of jokes and witty ripostes. Consumers acquire that repertoire of entertaining speech and its imitability as well as the more situated celebrity image of the speaker who jokes as easily with courtiers as country folk. In other words, the figure of Tarlton offers an image of free, that is endlessly circulating *and* uninhibited, speech.

Tarlton's association with an oral performative tradition and particularly with quick wit determines the appropriation of his proper name to articulate the space and potential of a literature of popular entertainment, for only a name and a reputation like his could simultaneously signify a familiar image of entertainment, a fantasy of uninhibited speech, and the notion that the pleasures of quick wit are bound to time and must be had again and again in new forms. The construction of Tarlton as a figure whose speech circulates throughout the country also obviously serves the interest of the book trade not only by implying a national market but, more important, by thematizing the circulation of printed material as if it were an unconstrained act. Thus, the image of Tarlton functions to naturalize pamphlet entertainment in particular and print culture in general as a phenomenon of the marketplace. Though each successive appropriation and production of Tarlton by the book trade was consciously motivated, the cumulative result—the celebrity image of Tarlton and the significations explicitly or tacitly attached to that image—is overdetermined precisely because the

"So beloved that men use his picture for their signs" 33

book trade's interest was particular, that is, was concerned with promoting pamphlet sales rather than with the aftereffects of their successful marketing strategies.

* * * * *

Tarlton's News, The Cobler of Canterbury, and *Tarlton's Jests* became relatively valuable properties; they were transferred between publishers and reprinted several times in the next four decades.[18] Circulating alongside the texts attributed to Tarlton (or prominently featuring him) were frequent mentions of him in a variety of texts—invocations of his wit and anecdotes about him in letters and books, printed epitaphs and epigrams.[19] These too begin after his death and intensify as the sixteenth century turns to the seventeenth. The brief, seemingly objective mention of Tarlton in the 1615 *Annales* part of this circulation and as such inseparable from the image consolidated by the book trade. If, for the book trade, as we have seen, Tarlton's name successfully figures or refunctions the production of entertainment in the commodity pamphlet, the *Annales* entry, by its apparent objectivity and its compactness simultaneously reveals the accumulated interest/value attached to his name and shifts his account to another register in the circulation of discourse, to a quasi-official record of the nation. That is, the *Annales* entry converts the commodity-capital form of Tarlton to symbolic capital in the service of national identity. The conversion the *Annales* entry effects was satirically anticipated by John Donne sometime between 1603 and 1611 in a mock library catalogue listing Tarlton as the author of a book called *On the Privileges of Parliament*.[20]

An anecdote surviving among the state papers of Elizabeth's reign involves Tarlton making jokes (inevitably sexualized) about the queen's lap dog and telling stories about the things that really make women happy in the presence of the queen and two of her privy councillors.[21] The point is not that this anecdote, or others like it, is historically accurate, but that such stories coincide with the celebrity image of Tarlton and come to have currency. Just how much currency can be seen in an retrospective summary account written by Thomas Fuller in his *History of the Worthies of England* in 1652:

> When Queen Elizabeth was serious, I dare not say sullen, and out of good humor, he would *undumpish* her at his pleasure. Her highest favorites would, in some cases, go to Tarlton before they would go to

the Queen and he was their usher to prepare their advantageous access unto her. In a word, he told the Queen more of her faults than most of her chaplains, and cured her melancholy better than her physicians.[22]

In Fuller's account, Tarlton is not an entertainer/performer but a facilitator of state business and uniquely privileged in his access to the queen. Like the traditional figure of the jester or fool, he can say what he thinks without fear of consequences, but he differs from the fool in that his role is not reactive, for he apparently initiates and controls the exchanges. What Fuller, a moderate royalist in the Civil War, really dare not say is that his account tacitly makes Tarlton the queen's equal. Yet the unconscious of Fuller's text, I would suggest, is produced by the insistent pairing of Tarlton and the queen and the use of Tarlton as a representative figure. Elizabeth herself was extremely savvy about associating herself, indeed her body, with the nation and she did so not only in authoritative royal poses like the Ditchley portrait in which she stands on top of the map of England, but in self-representations designed to make her seem "one of the people": she would feel the same about bringing Mary Queen of Scots to trial, she told parliament, were they two milkmaids.[23] In Fuller's text, the ideological impact of Tarlton's image is clear: he functions as an "usher," to borrow Fuller's word, of national identification. From a late-twentieth-century perspective, Stowe's (Howe's) and Fuller's Tarlton is an easily recognizable figure of popular fantasies of access to power and prestige: the common person whose particular talent serves the state, in this case, by maintaining the health of both body politic and monarch at once. The conflation between the performance of quick wit and the facilitation of state business in the figure of Tarlton seems to promise both the recognition and reward of talent with status and an ongoing bond between alehouse and court, ordinary people and powerful ones.

The interestedness of using Tarlton as a figure of an imaginary unity—whether class-based or nation-based—is evident in a story told by Thomas Nashe. Writing in 1592, he tells the story of a "cholericke wise justice" who

> having a play presented before him and his township by Tarlton and the rest of his fellowes, her majesties servants, and they were now entering into their first merriment (as they call it), the people began exceedingly to laugh, when Tarlton first peept out his head. Whereat the justice, not a little moved, and seeing with his beckes and nods he could not make them cease, he went with his staffe, and beat them

round about unmercifully on the bare pates, in that they, being but farmers and poore country hyndes, would presume to laugh at the Queen's Men, and make no more account of her cloth in his presence.[24]

The justice, acting on behalf of the queen's name and dignity and himself representative of her authority, forcibly severs the identification between Tarlton and "the people," silencing those who presume to laugh. In Nashe's story, the violence is a response to laughter/identification with Tarlton perceived as a political threat—the identification might work against the queen's interest, rather than for it. That violence proleptically suggests the underside of Tarlton's celebrity image. It is the circulation of his image by the book trade that allows the identification between Tarlton, the queen, and the people to be recuperated. Tarlton's "free" speech becomes associated with entertainment and with discourse as a commodity and thus tamed, becomes available for constructing a nostalgic image of national identity. Such a recuperation is symbolically violent. It displaces both political speech and social difference and it inhibits the potential recognition of vested interests in the marketplace mediation of entertainment and national identity.

The construction of Tarlton as a figure of national identity depends on a nostalgia that was part of his celebrity image from the beginning, but by the later seventeenth century it is a nostalgia for an image of England rather than for Tarlton's performance as a comedian. That image of England ruled by a queen who listens to and is comforted by a man of the people ("If you don't know whose grave this is," says a Latin epitaph on Tarlton published in 1607, "ask any child") functions reparatively in the years of the disintegrating commonwealth and anticipates a restoration in which the pleasures of consumption in the marketplace are indistinguishable from subscribing to an historic Englishness.[25]

Notes

1. Stowe's *Annales*, continued by Edmund Howe (London, 1615), 697.
2. One of Joseph Hall's satires published in 1598 refers to Tarlton's association with alehouse signs: "O honour farre beyond a brazen shrine / To sit with Tarleton on an Ale posts signe! (VI.1.203–4; *The Collected Poems of Joseph Hall*, ed. A. Davenport [Liverpool: The University Press, 1949]). In his edition of *Tarleton's Jests* (note 10 below), J. O. Halliwell quotes Sir Henry Ellis: "his portrait, with tabor and pipe, still serves as a sign to an alehouse in the Borough" (*The History and Antiquities of . . . Shoreditch* [London: John Nicholls, 1798], 209). Two ver-

sions of a drawing of Tarlton are fairly widely reproduced. Both are easily accessible in R. A. Foakes, *Illustrations of the English Stage 1580–1642* (Stanford, Calif.: Stanford University Press, 1985). The surviving "original" of the drawings comes from a manuscript alphabet book produced by a writing master in Norwich, John Scottowe, and provocatively suggests an association between the figure of Tarlton and writing literacy. Since it is not known for whom or what occasion the manuscript was produced and its luxuriousness suggests that it was not intended for regular classroom use, the point cannot be pushed much further. See *John Scottowe's Alphabet Books*, ed. Janet Backhouse (Menston: Scholar Press, 1974) for a description and brief commentary.

3. For a general historical and analytic overview of the work on celebrity in relation to the movie industry and a lengthy bibliography, see Richard Dyer, *Stars* (London: British Film Institute, 1986). For a general theory of stardom, see Francesco Alberoni, The Powerless Elite: Theory and Sociological Research on the Phenomenon of the Stars" in *Sociology of Mass Communication*, edited Denis McQuail (Harmondsworth: Penguin, 1972). Alberoni explicitly denies stars any political influence and thus disables the ideological implications of his analysis.

4. His death is attested by the record of his burial at Shoreditch; the Mastery of Fence by a manuscript register of a School of Defense (British Library, Sloane MS 2530); and the will is in the prerogative Court of Canterbury. The will is printed in *Playhouse Wills, 1558–1642*, ed. E. A. J. Honigmann and Susan Brock (Manchester: Manchester University Press, 1993). The papers involved in the dispute over the will are preserved in the State Papers Domestic and were printed by J. O. Halliwell, *Papers Respecting Disputes which Arose from Incidents at the Death-Bed of Richard Tarlton, the Actor, in the year 1588* (privately printed, 1866). Tarlton's mother disputed the will by offering as evidence on her behalf a putatively later will, which, the epitomizer of the State Papers tells us, "was signed in three places by Tarlton, the last time evidently in the throes of death." The dispute over which piece of writing signed by Tarlton represents his true will, what the value of his estate was, and who was the appropriate executor unwittingly sets out in miniature the phenomenon of Tarlton: his inheritance had multiple claimants and contested value.

5. The importance of Tarlton to Shakespeare's development of the clown/fool is discussed by Robert Weimann in *Shakespeare and the Popular Tradition in the Theater* (Baltimore: Johns Hopkins University Press, 1978) and David Wiles in *Shakespeare's Clown* (Cambridge: Cambridge University Press, 1987). Both locate Tarlton's practice in terms of the performance traditions of the late middle ages. Wiles (but not Weimann) builds his analysis on "deductions" from the printed material I discuss below. In *Forms of Nationhood* (Chicago: University of Chicago Press, 1992), Richard Helgerson draws on both Weimann and Wiles to discuss Tarlton's clown as a figure of the rustic and popular, that is, as a status marker as well as a figure of the carnivalesque and performative traditions. See chapter 5, "Staging Exclusion."

6. *The Short-Title Catalogue of Books Printed in English, 1471–1640* lists the following titles: Ballad, 1570; *Tarltons Toyes*, 1576; *Tarltons Tragical Treatises*, 1578; *Tarltons Device*, 1579; *Tarltons Farewell*, 1588; *Tarltons Recantacion*, 1589; *Tarltons Repentence*, 1589, *Tarltons Newes Out of Purgatory*, 1590; *Tarltons Jests*, before 1600.

7. The statement occurs in a scenario Harvey is scripting about the supposedly "unauthorized" publication of some of his writing. "Ye have prejudiced my good name forever in thrustynge me thus on the stage to make tryall of my extemporall

faculty and to play Wylsons or Tarltons parte" (*Letterbook of Gabriel Harvey*, ed. Edward John Long Scott [Westminster: Nicholls and Sons, 1883], p. 67).

8. In Harvey's published writings Tarlton is frequently mentioned, almost always as a signifier of discourse contaminated by the market place. "Tarltonizing," for example is the term that Harvey uses to describe the degradation of Robert Greene's writing. But such mentions of Tarlton all appear after his death and the publication of the material I discuss below. See the index to Alexander Grosart's edition, *The Works of Gabriel Harvey* (London, 1885). Harvey's report of the personal invitation and brief exchange with Tarlton appears in *Foure Letters* (1592) (Grosart, 1:194).

9. Such an argument is a commonplace of what Barry King calls the populist version of stardom; James Dean and Marilyn Monroe supply obvious examples. In "The Star and the Commodity: Notes Toward a Performance Theory of Stardom" (*Cultural Studies* 1 (1987): 145–161) King sketches a materialist theory of stardom to which I am indebted. I discuss King's argument below.

10. *Tarltons Newes Out of Purgatory* (STC 23685) is available in a nineteenth-century edition from which I quote. *Tarltons Jests and Newes out of Purgatory*, ed. James Halliwell (London: for the Shakespeare Society, 1844).

11. *The Cobler of Canterbury* (STC 4579) was also edited in the nineteenth century. That edition was recently reprinted: *The Cobbler of Canterbury: Frederic Ouvry's Edition of 1862 with a New Introduction by H. Neville Davies* (Totowa, N.J.: Rowman and Littlefield, 1976).

12. I quote from King's summary of the argument that the star personifies the agency of labor power (as opposed to the personification of capital in owners or monopolists that Marx discusses in *Capital*).

> In sum, the formation of the persona of the star accomplishes, from the side of labour power, the same suppression of the fundamentally collective character of all productive activity that enable the capitalist to appear as the demiurge of production. But the place of the star is on the side of labour, as visibly an employee within the process of representation, even if the star is also his or her own employer (not forgetting that the celebrity of the star always rests in the last analysis on popular approval). These conditions mean that stardom can be seen as returning to the level of the collective account as a signifier of the potency of labour. In reality, the persona of the star is the moment of the performance commodity. (158)

13. For a brief discussion of Copy, see Lyman Ray Patterson, *Copyright in Historical Perspective* (Nashville, Tenn.: Vanderbilt University Press, 1968).

14. Henry Chettle, *Kind-Hartes Dreame* (STC 5123), ed. G. B. Harrison (New York: Barnes and Noble, 1966). Chettle was a compositor and a member of the Stationers' Company. The pamphlet addresses various issues involved in the production and circulation of printed material such as the difficulty of controlling circulation and the threat that the wide dissemination of texts posed to learned men, the erstwhile custodians of textuality. Tarlton's section focuses specifically on the competitors to print entertainment.

15. *Tarltons Jests* (STC 23683.3) is reprinted with *Tarltons Newes* in the edition prepared by Halliwell (note 10). It is also reprinted in *Shakespeare's Jestbooks*, ed. W. Carew Hazlitt (London: Willis and Sotheran, 1864).

16. A considerable portion of the *DNB* entry I discussed earlier is drawn from *Tarlton's Jests*. Two earlier jest books that used a historical figure as an organizing device were *Merie Tales of Skelton* (1567) and *Jests of Scoggin* (1565–66), both printed in Hazlitt's edition (note 15). See P. M. Zall's introductory essay in *A*

Hundred Mery Tales (Lincoln: University of Nebraska Press, 1963) for a brief history of the genre.

17. According to a petition supposedly written by Tarlton to Francis Walsingham and associated with the controversy over Tarlton's will (see note 4), in 1582 Philip Sidney stood as godfather to Tarlton's son, also named Philip, making it clear that Tarlton was associated with courtly circles before the formation of the Queen's Men. Sidney himself was named after Philip II of Spain, at the time of Sidney's birth consort to Queen Mary. In both gestures of naming and establishing affiliative ties can be seen an effort to affirm, if not secure, status.

18. See the respective listings in *STC*.

19. Both Halliwell (note 10) and Hazlitt (note 15) include a generous sampling of such material and indicate where more might be found.

20. John Donne, *Catalogus Librorum Aulicorum incomparabilium et vendibilium* (The Courtier's Library of Rare Books Not for Sale) was circulated in manuscript but not published until 1650. See *The Courtier's Library*, ed. Evelyn Mary Simpson, trans. Percy Simpson (London: The Nonesuch Press, 1930).

21. *The Calendar of State Papers Domestic, 1581–1590* (London: Longmans, 1865).

22. Quoted in Halliwell's edition (note 10), p. xxvii.

23. The speech is reprinted in *Women Writers of the Renaissance and Reformation*, ed. Katharina Wilson (Athens: University of Georgia Press, 1987).

24. *The Works of Thomas Nashe*, ed. by R. B. McKerrow (Oxford: Basil Blackwell, 1958) 1:188.

25. The epitaph is from George Stradling's *Epigrammata* (1607). Hazlitt includes it in his edition (note 15). I am indebted to my colleague Monica Otter for precise translation of this and other material. I am also grateful to Jonathan Crewe, Elizabeth Hanson, James Siemon, Henry Woudhuysen and Abby Zanger for their comments on earlier versions of this essay.

Spheres of Influence: Cartography and the Gaze in Shakespearean Tragedy and History

PHILIP ARMSTRONG

1. "I Have Forgot the Map!"

FROM THE FIFTEENTH to the seventeenth centuries, a powerful cartographic paradigm emerges alongside early modern developments in linear perspective, mathematics, and optics. The fundamental principles of this cartography derive from Euclidean geometry and its Ptolemaic applications, as modified by practitioners such as Abraham Ortelius and Gerard Mercator in the Netherlands, and John Dee, John Davis, Richard Hakluyt, and Edward Wright in Britain. It is possible to glimpse, inextricably caught up in the development of this visual and representational economy, one ancestor of that "modern" subjectivity typified by and reliant upon its occupation of a single, fixed and centralized viewpoint.

Jacques Lacan insists that this subjectivity, as manifest in Europe and European-influenced cultures since Descartes and Pascal, constructs an ego which speaks, thinks or sees—these being its most characteristic functions—according to the displacements, elisions, and distortions of precisely those principles at work in, and derived from, early modern experiments in perspective painting: hence his lengthy discussion of the operation of linear perspective in Holbein's *Ambassadors*, or his repeated exhortations to his listeners to study optics.[1] The subject, situated opposite and fixated upon the vanishing point of the painting (or, I will suggest, the map), functions as "itself a sort of geometrical point, a point of perspective".[2] I would argue that the same principles are at work, instituting the same ego according to the same operations, in the dissemination throughout Elizabethan culture of an innovative cartographic idiom, and that this idiom has a critical influence upon the rhetoric and dramaturgy of Shakespearean theatre.

King Lear offers the prime example, peremptorily demanding "the map there" (*King Lear*, F, 1.1.37), and proceeding to reduce the political and phenomenal world to a cartographic representation.[3] Lear translates a land "with shadowy forests and with champaigns riched, / With plenteous rivers and wide-skirted meads," into a set of geometrical divisions, "these bounds even from this line to this" (F, 1.1.63–65).[4] The mastery of his gaze over this realm appears explicit in Lear's imperious dissection of the map and, by extension, the kingdom itself. Such scenes actually occurred in Renaissance Europe with increasing frequency, as land was carved up and served out by politicians with no knowledge of the territory outside of its representation on maps and globes: one famous example being the arbitrary line of demarcation drawn by Pope Alexander VI in 1493 to divide Columbus's recently "discovered" New World between Spain and Portugal.[5]

For Lear, however, it soon becomes apparent that his stable, potent and central symbolic position in this opening scene is illusory, dependent upon an imaginary correlation between his own unified image as king, and its reflection, the unified image of the kingdom. By dividing one, he inadvertently fragments both.[6] Towards the middle of the play, this dehiscence of king and kingdom reaches its climactic expression in Lear's madness and the storm. Interestingly, however, although Lear seems to embrace this double disintegration, he does so in terms that seek to reconstitute the world precisely according to that device of cartographic representation which he employed to perform the initial division:

> thou all-shaking thunder,
> Strike flat the thick rotundity o'th' world,
> Crack nature's moulds, all germens spill at once
> That makes ingrateful man
>
> (F, 3.2.6–9)

Lear demands that the three-dimensional world, with all its wealth of sensory and perceptual composition, be "struck" flat, like an engraving, text, or map, like an image on a coin, an engraver's mould, or a printer's type. This translation from three dimensions into two would put the phenomenal world, in all its "thick rotundity" once more under the sway of (his own) sovereign geometrical vision, as it was in the first scene when he unrolled, read, and redrew his map. The three-dimensional here acts as an unsettling irruption, into imaginary and symbolic space, of what Lacan would call the "real," that which resists representation and disrupts the illusory correlation between ego and ideal image, king and map.

In another famous scene of map reading, the leaders of the factions rebelling against the king in 1 *Henry IV* discuss the trisection of the realm (sanctioned, like the division of the Americas between Spain and Portugal, by the church):

> *Glyndŵr.* Come, here's the map. Shall we divide our right,
> According to our threefold order ta'en?
> *Mortimer.* The Archdeacon hath divided it
> Into three limits very equally.
> England from Trent and Severn hitherto
> By south and east is to my part assigned;
> All westward—Wales beyond the Severn shore
> And all the fertile land within that bound—
> To Owain Glyndŵr; *(To Hotspur)* and, dear coz, to you
> The remnant northward lying off from Trent.
> (3.1.67–76)

Once again, however, what frustrates or conflicts with the representation of the map are the geographical contours of the land itself, what Lear calls its "thick rotundity." In this case, the course of the river Trent elbows into the picture, marking an intrusion by something the map would rather ignore:

> *Hotspur.* See how this river comes me cranking in,
> And cuts me from the best of all my land
> A huge half-moon, a monstrous cantle, out.
> (ll. 95–97)

Moreover, instead of the cartographic representation adapting itself to provide an accurate and innocent representation of the land it purports to reflect, the country itself is to be carved up by the redirection of the river. The map institutes strict lines of geometrical propriety ("three limits very equally") with which the geographical reality must be forced to comply:

> *Hotspur.* I'll have the current in this place damned up,
> And here the smug and silver Trent shall run
> In a new channel fair and evenly.
> It shall not wind with such a deep indent,
> To rob me of so rich a bottom here.
> (2. 98–102)

The arbitrariness of such transactions—for Hotspur changes his mind back within thirty lines—again recalls the division of the New World according to cartographic abstractions, as it was taking place in the palaces of Europe at the time.

Marlowe also dramatizes the violence of these transactions when Tamburlaine boasts that with his sword as a pen, he will "reduce" those regions as yet unconquered, the New World, "to a map," and remarks that "here at Damascus will I make the point / That shall begin the perpendicular" (pt. 1, 4.4.75–84).[7] The perpendicular or prime meridian, originating at the "point" from which he surveys the area to be conquered, signifies both his own privileged viewing position and the central vanishing point around which he will reorganize the lines of perspective on the map of his empire. By the end of part 2, Tamburlaine's imminent death reflects the disintegration of the world he has subjected. "Give me a map, then let me see how much / Is left for me to conquer all the world" (pt. 2, 5.3.123–124). With the same command used by Lear to signify his mastery over the realm and to inaugurate its dissection, the dying Tamburlaine enumerates his conquests, constructing a verbal map of an empire that disintegrates as he speaks. Again, "symbolic" geography seeks to dominate the "real": Ethel Seaton has shown that Tamburlaine's world map follows the contours of Ortelius's *Theatrum Orbis Terrarum* (1570), faithful even to its errors, inconsistencies, and omissions.[8]

Such scenes, therefore, provide more than just powerful allegories of the way in which the phenomenological structures instituted by cartographic representation came to dominate the political perception and treatment of geographical terrain during this period. Maps did not simply influence political decisions or facilitate their coordination. Rather, in a very practical sense, countries, nations and empires—and, implicitly, their inhabitants—*became* maps, and were read and rewritten as such.

2. "Call for Some Men of Sound Direction"

If a chart could be drawn showing the relationships between the various figures involved in the dissemination of maps and mapmaking technology in Shakespeare's England, a central place would be occupied by the work of Gerard Mercator as the most famous exponent of those cartographic innovations which were to revolutionize the shapes of world maps for the next few hundred years.

Mercator relied upon and reformed the models and principles of Ptolemy's *Geographia,* which provided clear applications of Euclid's geometrical propositions to the drawing of map projections. Ptolemy's procedures involved the cartographer envisaging the globe from a single central viewing position, in which the eye was diametrically opposite to the chosen prime meridian, what Marlowe refers to as the "point / That shall begin the perpendicular." The "thick rotundity" of the globe could then be "struck flat," as the latitudes and longitudes were stretched out from this spot to produce a two-dimensional representation.

Mercator produced his projection by straightening the meridians—which, on a globe, would meet at either pole—until they extended parallel to one another. Because he was concerned to provide a projection usable by navigators, Mercator also needed to lengthen the meridians, in order to counteract the east-west stretching produced by straightening them. The resulting arrangement—which has been the dominant template for maps of the world until very recently—is remarkable for the increasing distortion of landmasses approaching the polar regions, while the Arctic "circle" itself actually becomes a strip along the top edge. Mercator's map, moreover, required many further adjustments and calculations before it could be used by navigators. For although directions could now be accurately charted, distances—especially those further from the equator—were wildly inaccurate, so a series of mathematical scales needed to be provided to remedy this fault. The map was eventually modified by Edward Wright, a Cambridge mathematician, and John Davis, a mariner. Their version was published in 1599, along with an account of the latter's voyage to the New World, in Richard Hakluyt's *Principal Navigations . . . of the English Nation.*[9] It is here, most probably, that Shakespeare saw it.

In *Twelfth Night,* Maria remarks that, having fallen in love with Olivia, Malvolio "does smile his face into more lines than is in the new map with the augmentation of the Indies" (3.2.74–75). The three most obvious features of Wright's map are highlighted here: the novelty of the Mercator projection, the additions to the western coastline of the Americas, made during Drake's circumnavigation of 1577, and the peculiarly dense network of rhumb lines drawn all over the map, fanning out from several compass roses placed at strategic positions around the world (see accompanying map).

Rhumb lines were drawn on a map in order to facilitate its use by mariners. The navigator, having drawn a line between the ship's position on the map and its intended destination, would find the

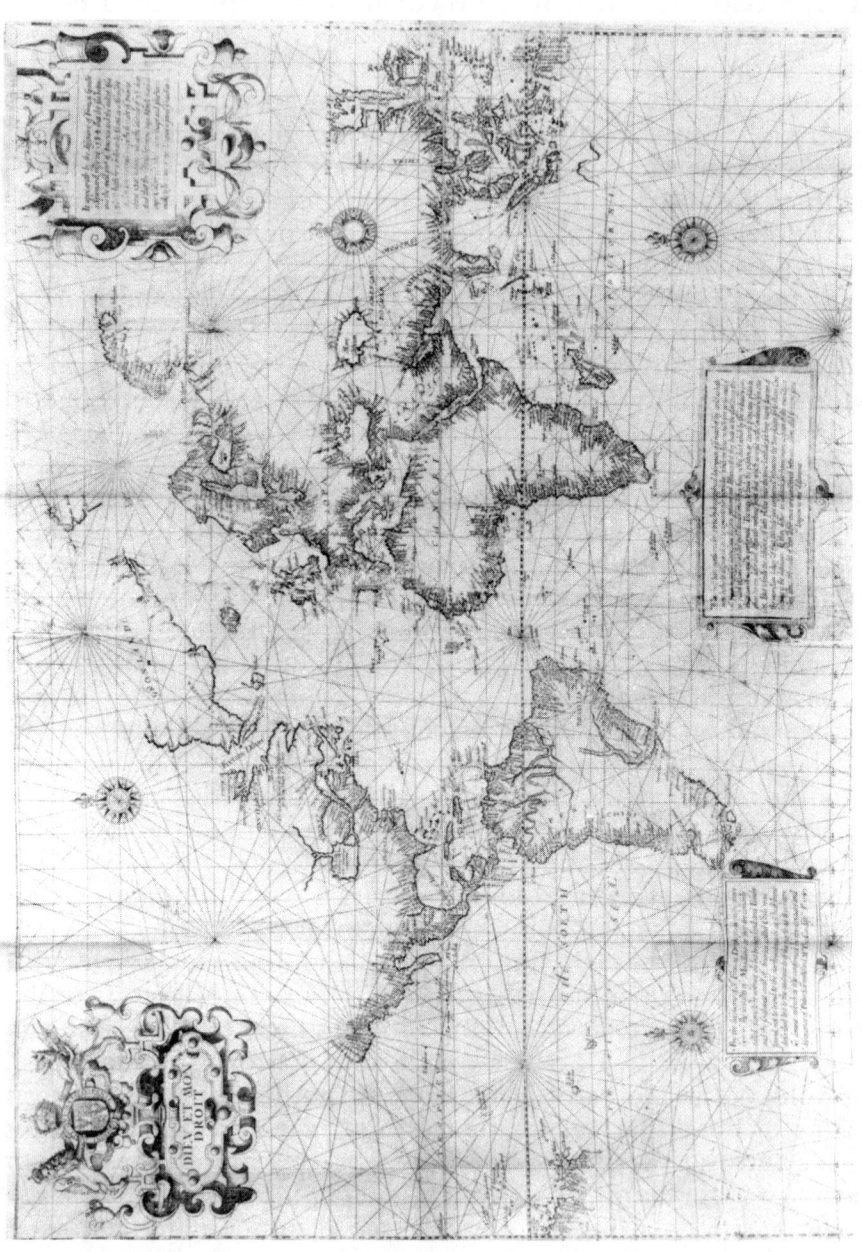

Edward Wright and John Davies: Map of the World (Hakluyt, Vol. 1, p. 358)

rhumb parallel to this and, tracing this back to the appropriate compass rose, thereby discover the necessary direction to follow. Wright's "new map," then, positions the gaze of the reader in several important ways. First, according to the principles of Ptolemy and Mercator, as outlined above, it demands the fixed viewing point characteristic of Renaissance linear perspective. From this spot, the map flattens the world, stretching it out along a grid of latitudes and longitudes reticulated from the central vanishing point located on the prime meridian. The actual central point of the map, the geometrical locus around which the parallels and perpendiculars are organised, remains a blank, located somewhere (or, in effect, nowhere) in the mid Atlantic, indicated on Wright's map only negatively, as the spot from which the middle star of compass rays fans out.

Faced by the nothingness of this vanishing point, the eye of the map reader is pushed inexorably outwards, along the rhumb lines—radiating out from the central visual field like the crow's feet spreading out from Malvolio's eye—to the edges of the map. It is, of course, toward these areas—northeast and northwest, the west coast of North America and the Far East, those parts of the map most extravagantly and anamorphically distorted—that the acquisitive eyes of Elizabethan merchants, explorers and colonists were mainly directed at this time, in the search for colonies and trading routes to Cathay and the Spice Islands. As the English cartographer Robert Thorne wrote to Henry VIII,

> out of Spaine they have discovered all the Indies and seas Occidentall, and out of Portingall all the Indies and Seas Orientall: . . . So that now rest to be discovered the . . . North parts, the which it seemeth to mee, is onely your charge and duety.[10]

These hyperbolic margins of the world map had been the target of English voyages of exploration for some time, from Sebastian Cabot's discovery of Newfoundland in 1497, to the quests in search of the Northeast Passage by Sir Hugh Willoughby and Anthony Jenkinson in the 1550s and 1560s.[11] All these efforts were commemorated by maps of their own. Cut by Clement Adams, Cabot's map showed the imagined location of the Northwest Passage and also displayed his North American discoveries. It was hung on the wall of the Privy Gallery at Whitehall Palace from 1549, where it was "regularly described by visitors for the next century and a half".[12] As this was the chamber in which foreign dignitaries awaited their audience with the monarch, it is not difficult to imagine the propagandist power of such maps, which led the gaze naturally and inevitably out from the center to trace the contours of past English discoveries and projected English possessions. On Wright's map, again, the route followed by Sir Francis Drake—whose voyage of 1577 merits a special descriptive cartouche in the lower left-hand corner—draws the calculating Elizabethan eye to the exaggerated extremities, down through the Straits of Magellan, and northwards to the invitingly unfinished western coastline of North America, culminating there in the suggestive name "NOVA ALBION." This point, in turn, becomes the origin for another set of rhumb lines, inviting both eye and navigator to wander further still. The exaggerated landmasses produced at the edges of the known world create a centrifugal effect, for which the compass lines radiating out from the center offer a striking diagram, which cannot but contribute to the desire to conquer, colonize and exploit the new worlds currently being drawn into European maps.

The cartographic developments exemplified by Wright's map also play a crucial part in the dissemination of Euclidean geometrical principles into many areas of early modern knowledge. Samuel Edgerton has traced the influence of Ptolemy's *Geographia*—with its institution of the central viewing axis, from which the grid of parallels and perpendiculars reticulates—upon the early practitioners of Quattrocento linear perspective. Among these, he focuses upon the architecture of Filippo Brunelleschi and the applications of Euclidean geometry to painting by his friend Leon Battista Alberti in *De pictura* (c. 1435).[13] These developments influenced the dominant modes of optical representation throughout the ensuing centuries. In Britain, John Dee's "Preface" to the English translation of Euclid's *Elements of Geometry* (1570), provides a family tree of the prodigious multiplication of sciences and arts issuing from these geometrical principles: including perspective, astrology, cosmography, hydrography, and chorography, architecture and music, astronomy and navigation, and the measurement of distance, depth and breadth on land or water. Above all, however, Dee emphasises the role of cartography in the mathematical sciences, pointing out that geometry implies "(according to the very etimologie of the word) Land measuring."[14] Dee's promotion of English colonial activity influences much of his mathematical writings, which contain the first extant use of the term "British Empire." He also proposed the maintenance of a permanent navy, and in 1580 submitted to Elizabeth a map supporting the legitimacy of her claims in North America.[15]

Unsurprisingly, therefore, this complicity between political and mercantile opportunism, navigation and cartography pervades many of the metaphors by which Shakespearean characters describe their nation and its relation with the rest of the world. In *King John*, Salisbury's speech performs just such a graphic redrafting of the map of Europe:

> O nation, that thou couldst remove;
> That Neptune's arms who clippeth thee about
> Would bear thee from the knowledge of thyself
> And gripple thee unto a pagan shore...
>
> (5.2.33–36)

Salisbury's rhetoric wrestles his nation from its present shameful position and performs a drastic cartographic revision, imagining the British Isles maneuvered into a new geographical alignment. The underlying nautical metaphor—"gripple," as a variant of "grapple"—recalls the expanding maritime activity which in Shakespeare's time was playing such an active role in redrawing political maps: Raleigh's voyage to Virginia, Drake's discoveries, the Spanish Armada. This "tickling commodity," the "smooth-faced gentleman" of political and commercial expediency, features earlier in the play in the Bastard's famous speech as "the bias of the world":

> The world, who of itself is peised well,
> Made to run even upon even ground,
> Till this advantage, this commodity,
> Makes it take head from all indifferency,
> From all direction, purpose, course, intent
>
> (2.1.574–581)

Two developments in Renaissance cosmography sustain this conceit. A Copernican universe displaces the Ptolemaic centrality of the earth, which can thus "run" rather than stand still. But at the same time, the relationship between the personified commodity and a world reduced to a globe the size of the bowling ball, on which "all direction, purpose, course, intent" have been altered, also reflects the economy of the new cartographic relationship between the reader and the world map, as forged by the likes of Mercator modifying Ptolemy. Simultaneous with the displacement of the medieval religious cosmology, with "man" at its center under the gaze of God, comes the installation of the new subject, ruled by commodity, who takes "his" bearings from an astronomical cosmos centered on the sun, and who places the earth under a powerful gaze of "his" own.

The Machiavellian Richard III shows an awareness of the need for the sovereign to align himself with this centralized and privileged gaze of the map reader, when he first expresses his desire for the crown:

> I do but dream on sovereignty
> Like one that stands upon a promontory
> And spies a far-off shore where he would tread,
> Wishing his foot were equal with his eye,
> And chides the sea that sunders him from thence
> (3 Henry VI 3.2.134–138)

The components of this verbal panorama are familiar from our preceding discussion of cartography. The establishment of a direct line of sight between the privileged viewing position—"one that stands upon a promontory"—and the distant locus of desire matches the organization of the map around a central vanishing point diametrically opposite the subject's eye. The elision between this optical positioning and the means of its translation into practice—"wishing his foot were equal with his eye"—evokes the fantasy of an effective power. And the desire for a "far-off shore" from which the subject is separated by the sea parallels the exhortations of Dee, Drake, Hakluyt and the like to their monarch to acquire possessions abroad. The visual economy utilized by Renaissance tragedy to situate each of the central figures cited so far—Lear, Tamburlaine, and Richard—functions as a new-found means for contemporary politicians, merchants, explorers, patriots, and cartographers to pursue their acquisitive drives and capacities.

Commentators agree that the knowledge of navigation displayed in Shakespearean drama derives from Richard Eden's translation of the Spanish *Art de navigar* (1561).[16] The stars by which mariners conventionally fixed their course were those in the constellation of Ursa Minor, particularly the two "Guards" and the Pole Star. This expert knowledge is displayed by the Second Gentleman in *Othello*, when he describes a tempest of such ferocity that these crucial navigational coordinates are eclipsed:

> The wind-shaked surge with high and monstrous mane,

Seems to cast water on the burning Bear,
And quench the guards of th'ever-fixed Pole

(2.1.13–15)

The astrolabe (or one of its variants, the quadrant, sextant or octant) was employed by mariners to fix their position vis-à-vis these stars, and by Elizabethan cartographers to plot latitude on land, situating their position according to the height of the sun or the Pole Star above the horizon at the place of observation.[17] An accurate point on the map could be plotted only when the eye was lined up, via the optical instrument, with the astronomical referent. Being handheld, the accuracy of such instruments depended upon, and in turn consolidated, the fixed gaze of the cartographer, so that the practices of cartography once again effected the privileging of the monocentric viewpoint. The insistent invocation by Shakespearean figures of these astronomical bodies attests to the construction of a subject position guaranteed—by means of the infallibility of its optical geometry, its cartographic methods and its instruments—in diametric opposition to the constancy of the sun and the Pole Star. Richard II offers only one example of the many Shakespearean rulers who repeatedly designate their sovereignty through reference to the sun (Richard II 3.2.32–49, 3.3.61–66), while Julius Caesar famously defines himself as being

as constant as the Northern Star,
Of whose true fixed and resting quality
There is no fellow in the firmament.
The skies are painted with unnumbered sparks;
They are all fire, and every one doth shine;
But there's but one in all doth hold his place.
So in the world; 'tis furnished well with men,
And men are flesh and blood, and apprehensive;
Yet in the number I do know but one
That unassailable holds on his rank,
Unshaked of motion . . .

(Julius Caesar 3.1.60–70)

"I am he," Caesar concludes, exemplifying an emergent subjectivity, almost invariably associated in Shakespearean drama with the "great man," whose reference to the field of geometrical optical space both guarantees and represents his preeminent position in the symbolic realm, the world of politics, society, and knowledge.

This speech, of course, proves to be Caesar's last. It directly precedes and even provokes his assassination. Richard II, similarly, is deposed, melting away before "the sun of Bolingbroke" (4.1.251). In fact, wherever it appears in Shakespearean drama, this guaranteed stability granted by the privileged central viewing position in the scopic economy will prove to be both illusory and liable to dissolution.

3. "Melted from the Smallness of a Gnat to Air"

Jacques Lacan has emphasised precisely this instability of the centralized mastery of the post-Renaissance subject in his discussion of the gaze. "I see only from one point, but in my existence I am looked at from all sides" he remarks. The gaze "is presented to us only in the form of a strange contingency, symbolic of what we find on the horizon."[18] What the Elizabethan subject of cartography finds on the horizon, at the edges and the limits of its maps, threatens the organization of that subject's own position. The distortion of the margins of what we might call this Elizabethan "world picture" reveals the means of its construction and, implicitly, the "strange contingency" of the centralized viewing position upon which it depends. This skewed perspective from the frame of the map thereby operates in the same way as Lacan's description of the anamorphosis in Holbein's *Ambassadors*, which decomposes the site of privileged vision by demanding from the spectator an eccentric viewing position:

> All this shows that at the very heart of the period in which the subject emerged and geometral optics was an object of research, Holbein makes visible for us here something that is simply the subject as annihilated . . .
> For us, the geometral dimension enables us to glimpse how the subject who concerns us is caught, manipulated, captured, in the field of vision.[19]

Lacan identifies the emergence of anamorphoses in the development of the geometrical optical principles that produce both Albertian perspective painting and those maps based on Mercator's projection. These anamorphoses appear in pictorial art as grotesquely elongated shapes which only become legible from an oblique perspective, an alternative viewing position to that of the centralized spectator. They are thereby symptomatic of the limits of the optical economy being instituted, and of the inherent failure of that system to guarantee the place of the subject within it. Within the "systematic establishment of the geometrical laws of perspective formulated at the end of the fifteenth and the beginning of the sixteenth centuries," Lacan remarks, the appearance of anamorphosis represents "a sensitive spot, a lesion, a locus of pain, a point of reversal of the whole of history."[20]

Elsewhere I have discussed the manifestation of this "locus of pain" in the Dover Cliff scene from *King Lear* (F, 4.5).[21] In that scene, the displacement of the central viewing position emerges by means of the reversed line of sight which Edgar directs upwards from the foot of the cliff, once Gloucester has (supposedly) fallen through the vanishing point of the linear perspective Edgar had previously described from above. The imaginary Dover Cliff offers (as elsewhere in Shakespearean drama) a symbolic location to mark the farthest limit, the end of Lear's Britain. This representative function again links this scene to the role played by the distorted edges of the Elizabethan map, in which the enlargement of the northern and southern landmasses betrays the means employed in the construction of the map, and the political and commercial interests invested in it. In both cases, from the symbolic limits of a geographic entity (Lear's Britain, Wright's world), an anamorphic perspective returns to displace the pictorial or cartographic economy and the viewing subject's secure place within it. In various forms, this disarming gaze will return again and again throughout Shakespearean drama.

For now, however, we should note one other moment in which Shakespeare's later plays describe the reverse of this perspective with the same acuity, and according to the same precise geometry of linear perspective, as Edgar's representation of Dover Cliff. In *Cymbeline*, Innogen discusses with Pisanio the departure of Posthumus. The verbal picture they create situates the mariner on his ship at the vanishing point of this perfectly modulated perspective, the inverse position of that occupied by the navigator or cartographer when reading the map or plotting the ship's location according to the sun and Pole Star:

Pisanio.   For so long
As he could make me with this eye or ear
Distinguish him from others he did keep
The deck, with glove or hat or handkerchief
Still waving, as the fits and stirs of's mind
Could best express how slow his soul sailed on,
How swift his ship.
Innogen.   Thou shouldst have made him

> As little as a crow, or less, ere left
> To after-eye him.
> *Pisanio.*   Madam, so I did.
> *Innogen.* I would have broke mine eye-strings, cracked them, but
> To look upon him till the diminution
> Of space had pointed him sharp as my needle;
> Nay, followed him till he had melted from
> The smallness of a gnat to air, and then
> Have turned mine eye and wept
>
>   (1.3.8–22)

The mathematical diminution of space here operates in an identical fashion to that of Edgar's speech on Dover Cliff. In both, the illusion of distance depends upon a series of metonymic reductions, decreasing the proportions of the visual plane step by step until it reaches vanishing point. In the *Lear* passage, crows and choughs appear the size of beetles, a man no bigger than his head, fishermen like mice, a ship "diminished to her cock, her cock a buoy / Almost too small for sight" (F, 4.5.13–20).[22] In *Cymbeline*, as the Arden editor observes, "this diminution is suggested by several subtle devices. Sail contrasts with handkerchief: eye and ear are resolved into eye alone, and they to eyestrings, and the eye image may be implicit in 'needle': similarly the life-size figure of Posthumus yields to crow, crow to gnat, and gnat to thin air".[23] As well as indicating the muscles or tendons of the eye, which were thought to crack at death or loss of sight, "eye-strings" might refer to the line of vision stretched between Innogen's "eye" and the vanishing point, threaded through the "eye" of the needle. The point of this needle, at which Posthumus vanishes into the distance, provides a punctilious correlative for what Lacan above calls the "locus of pain" from which an alternative perspective emerges to reduce the stable place of the subject to nothing.

Innogen, in short, positions herself at the origin of what Ptolemy (and Alberti after him) called the "centric ray" between the cartographer and the prime meridian, or the spectator and the vanishing point of the painting. According to the cartographic and navigational economies discussed so far, however, that locus of mastery really ought to be occupied by the male adventurer, the mariner on his ship. The text emphasizes Posthumus's suitability to occupy this position in its insistence on the power and fixity of his eye, which could "behold the sun with . . . firm eyes" (1.4.11), recalling the means by which the eye of the navigator or surveyor plotted a position on the map according to the sun through an astrolabe.

This position, however, in the passage quoted, is "usurped" by a woman, so that Posthumus finds himself caught in the diminishing field of the picture's vanishing point, struggling in vain to remain discernible, trying to "make" the viewer "with this eye or ear / Distinguish him from others." The Folio version of the play actually reads "*his* eye" at this point, which could only mean Posthumus's own eye, so that the text and its editors replay this struggle between the viewer and the viewed to attain the position of visual dominance, to be the maker of the picture rather than to be made by it.

Through Innogen's insistent imagination of the scene, however, the text ultimately installs hers as the central viewpoint from which this perspective picture appears. She composes the picture and Posthumus's place in it, telling Pisanio "Thou shouldst have made him / As little as a crow, or less." In fact, her dilemma in the play is precisely that she attempts to position herself too actively, too masterfully, marrying whom she pleases against the will of her parents. In this play, feminine disobedience constitutes the reversed perspective which disrupts the centrality of the viewing subject. Like Posthumus in the passage just quoted, Innogen's father Cymbeline also suffers displacement from the site of the sovereign eye, for although he is king, he proves to be subject to domination by his queen (1.1.104–107). Just as anamorphosis features as an enigmatic stain on the perspective painting, and the exaggeration of the polar regions renders the representation of those areas on Mercator's map wildly unreliable, the woman's perspective appears as an illegible distortion in the masculine optical economy of a play such as this. Tellingly, Cymbeline's discovery at the end of the play of his queen's designs prompts the remark "Who is't can read a woman?" (5.6.48).

4. "We the Globe Can Compass Soon"

Two-dimensional maps were not the only product of the new cartography. The sixteenth and seventeenth centuries also saw modifications, and a widespread proliferation, in the creation and sale of spherical models of the earth, so that Hakluyt could draw a distinction in 1589 between "the olde imperfectly composed, and the new lately reformed Mappes, Globes, Spheares, and other instruments of this Art...."[24]

Model globes, unlike two-dimensional maps, were of little practical use for the charting of exploratory or colonial ventures. Even more than the flat maps, however, they did possess a particular iconographic potency, as witnessed by the ubiquity of globes or orbs in contemporary royal portraiture. The "Armada" portrait of Elizabeth I offers one famous example among many, in which "a globe is tipped at an angle towards the viewer, and its meaning is derived from the central figure of the queen, whose imperial hand extends to grasp the whole world".[25] Not only monarchs, but politicians of all ranks and nationalities invested in the visual capital of the globe. Returning to Holbein's *Ambassadors*, painted in London in 1533, we might note that both terrestrial and celestial globes lie among the range of objects, symbolic of the Renaissance sciences and arts, furnishing the background to the figures of Jean de Dinteville and Georges de Selve. More specifically, the globes denote geometrical knowledge, for between the two figures Holbein displays also sundials, a quadrant, a set square, a German book on arithmetic, and a lute: these details, according to Stephen Greenblatt, "virtually constitute a series of textbook illustrations for a manual on the art of perspective."[26] As an instrument of geometrical practice, therefore, the globe plainly contributes to and participates in the valorization of the scopic position of the emergent Renaissance subject. This recalls the way in which Ptolemy's methods of flat cartographic projection—which offered a basis for both Mercator-style maps and Albertian pictorial perspective—also began by envisaging the spectator placed before a globe.

However, the augmented emblematic power of the model globe contributes to the iconography of this incipient subjectivity in other ways as well. If the two-dimensional map—along with the astronomical, navigational, and geometrical techniques required to produce and use it—situates its viewer in a centralized and exalted locus of optical mastery, a comparable metaphorical effect results from the visual contrast in any picture of the world reduced to the dimensions of a model glcbe alongside an enlarged human figure. The erect and frozen figures of Elizabeth or the Ambassadors ("stiffened in their showy adornments," as Lacan describes them) are granted, by these portraits, a representational and spatial dominance inversely proportional to their relationship with a shrunken world.[27] The globe thereby appears manipulable, within the reach and grasp of the human subject, reduced to the status of an object of learning, a commodity for possession, or a territory inviting political rule.

Shakespeare's Julius Caesar has already provided one instance of the exaltation of the subject within a geometrical and cartographic economy. He also exemplifies the appearance, in the metaphorical vocabulary of the plays, of this emblematic contrast between a diminished globe and an augmented human figure. Cassius, complaining to Brutus of the emergence of a new, imperial political idiom represented by the rise of Caesar, remarks,

> Why, man, he doth destride the narrow world
> Like a Colossus, and we petty men
> Walk under his huge legs, and peep about
> To find ourselves dishonourable graves
>
> (1.2.136–139)

The attenuated gaze of the "petty men" who "peep about" also offers a contrast with the heightened omnivoyance of the giant, surveying a world contracted into a map or globe beneath his feet.[28] This shortsightedness, of course, will indeed bring Cassius to his "dishonourable grave," for he kills himself after mistaking Titinius's victory for defeat. The text explicitly attributes this error to Cassius's myopia ("my sight was ever thick"), which he fails to redress by urging Pindarus to "get higher on that hill," a vain attempt to approach the panoramic visual mastery of the colossus (5.3.20–21). Increased stature, implementing a perspective from above, brings its own optical advantages, which—as Cassius's death proves—could prove strategically critical. We might recall in this connection Richard III before the Battle of Bosworth field, calling for "some men of sound direction" to "survey the vantage of the ground" (*Richard III* 5.2.15–16), or else the assault on Orleans in *1 Henry VI*, which begins with the same kind of cartographic reconnaissance: the English, from "yonder tower" in the suburbs, ". . . overpeer the city, / And thence discover how with most advantage / They may vex us with shot or with assault" (1.5.8–13).

The heightened gaze associated with the gigantic figure, capable of casting the net of an all-encompassing vision over the diminutive globe, bears obvious similarities not only to the reader poring over the map, but to the view of the surveyor who drafts it. During his surveys of England and Wales, the cartographer Christopher Saxton was granted by the Privy Council special privileges requiring Mayors, Justices of the Peace and other officials "to see him conducted unto any towre, castle, high place or hill, to view that country."[29] Similarly, in *Cymbeline*, when both Innogen and Cloten follow Pisanio's map to Milford Haven, Cloten expresses the hope that "Pisanio have mapped it truly" (4.1.2), while Innogen's remark suggests that he has at least followed the surveyor's practice of taking his bearings from the highest available point: "Milford, / When from the mountain-top Pisanio showed thee, / Thou wast within a ken" (3.6.4–6). The visual advantages of such altitudes were attested by another contemporary surveyor, John Norden. Referring to a particularly lofty point, "whereon standeth the principall beacon in Cornwall as in a place beste deseruing it," Norden wrote that

> vpon that hill a man bendinge his eye to whatsoeuer parte, shall obserue that all the Countrye rounde about it as it were falleth at the feete of this. And from this hill may be seene a parte of *Deuonshire* eastwarde aboue 30 myles, and almoste to the landes ende westewarde aboue 40 myles: The seas north and south, with there dispersed Iles, are likewise playnlye discouered.[30]

Norden envisages the landscape he surveys as if it were already mapped, inscribed with a set of compass directions, reduced to a configuration of perspectival distances, framed by preexistent geographical limits: Land's End, the north and south coasts, a border between Cornwall and Devon. The countryside falls prostrate "at the feet" of the surveyor, offering itself up for dissection by a heightened, omnivoyant gaze representative of the new confidence and prestige which accrued to the cartographic arts at this time. This attitude also infiltrates many of Shakespeare's plays. In *A Midsummer Night's Dream*, Puck can "put a girdle round about the earth / In forty minutes" (2.1.175–176), while Oberon makes the cartographic tenor of this metaphor even more explicit: "We the globe can compass soon, / Swifter than the wand'ring moon" (4.1.96–97). Another practitioner of magic, Prospero—identified by one critic with the geometer John Dee[31]—can envisage with apparent ease the dissolution of "the great globe itself" (*The Tempest* 4.1.153).

The contrast between a shrunken or "narrow" world and the figure of the colossus astride it recurs throughout another of the Roman plays. *Antony and Cleopatra* repeatedly figures Caesar's protege according to an identical conceit. At the beginning of the play Antony shares this exalted position with Octavius and Lepidus, as "triple pillar of the world" (1.1.12). His first speech makes explicit the contrast between "the dungy earth," in which "kingdoms are clay," and the dimensions of his own body or ego: "Here is my space." His self-aggrandizement, according to which he will "stand up peerless," corresponds with his contraction of the world to a fragile construct: "Let Rome in Tiber melt, and the wide arch / Of the ranged empire fall" (1.1.35–42). The gradual diminution of the status of Lepidus will reduce the triumvirate to a rivalry between the remaining two, so that a few scenes later Antony can be considered "the demi-Atlas of this earth" (1.5.23).

This word "Atlas" was, in Shakespeare's time, increasingly becoming associated with the cartographic representation of the earth. According to Lloyd Brown, the first widely distributed map collection to use the word in its title was Mercator's *Atlas sive Cosmographicae meditationes* . . . , of which the first part was published in 1595.

> A genealogical tree in the introductory text gave the ancestry of Atlas, the mythological character who led the Titans in their war against the god Jupiter, and was therefore condemned to support the heavens on his shoulders.[32]

José Rabasa, however, offers an alternative explanation for the use of the name in connection with cartography, claiming that "Mercator first coined the name Atlas after the mythical King of Libya 'who was supposed to have made the first celestial sphere'".[33] Both suggestions are consistent with our discussion so far of the Shakespearean (and more widespread Renaissance) employment of the emblematic relation between world and subject: that of a titan whose vast dimensions enable him to hold the weight of the celestial dome, and that of a king who reduces the cosmos to a model.

Ultimately, Antony stands alone as a figure of colossal proportions, independent of his rival, in a metaphor which echoes and develops that used in the earlier play to describe his patron Julius Caesar. Cleopatra describes her dream of "an Emperor Antony":

> His face was as the heav'ns, and therein stuck
> A sun and moon, which kept their course and lighted
> The little O o'th'earth . . .
> His legs bestrid the ocean; his reared arm
> Crested the world. His voice was propertied
> As all the tuned spheres, and that to friends;
> But when he meant to quail and shake the orb,
> He was as rattling thunder. For his bounty,
> There was no winter in't; an autumn 'twas,
> That grew the more by reaping. His delights
> Were dolphin-like; they showed his back above
> The element they lived in. In his livery
> Walked crowns and crownets. Realms and islands were
> As plates dropped from his pocket
>
> (5.2.78–91)

This passage combines in one extended conceit the metaphorical usages of all the cartographic optical structures discussed so far. The world is reduced to a representation, either an orb which shakes at the mere sound of Antony's voice, or the two-dimensional map of a "little O" drawn on paper. Antony, in contrast, has attained the stature of a giant, straddling the ocean, with his acquisitive grasp on the world signified by the reduction of its component "realms and islands" to "plates," a word denoting both appetite and silver coin. His gaze, like that of the cartographer and the navigator, is fixed in reference to the celestial bodies, "a sun and moon" shining in the "heavens" of his face. At such moments, along with the cartographical shrinking and mastering of the world, there emerges a corresponding increase in the stature of "man": the beginning, according to Lacan, of the ego's era, which will facilitate and collude with the acceleration of imperialism and capitalism.[34]

In the English history plays, various kings claim the same titanic status as Shakespeare's Roman protagonists. Richard II, as mentioned earlier, portrays himself as a sun god, whose sovereign gaze radiates from above, reducing the globe to a "terrestrial ball" (*Richard II* 3.2.33–49). In the sequel to this play, Prince Hal attributes an equivalent stature to Hotspur—whose assumption of a commanding and dissecting gaze over the map of Britain has already been noted—when he remarks, "When that this body did contain a spirit / A kingdom for it was too small a bound" (*1 Henry IV* 5.4.88–89). Having defeated his rival and taken the throne, "King Harry" now describes his own determination to retain the crown in terms of gargantuan struggle: "put the world's whole strength / Into one giant arm, it shall not force / This lineal honour from me" (*2 Henry IV* 4.3.175–77).

These plays, however, also produce another figure of planetary proportions, a "globe of sinful continents" (*2 Henry IV* 2.4.288). Falstaff, as the incarnation of a world of misrule that Hal must renounce in order to achieve political maturity, appears to repeat the transcription of the earth into a model or map, albeit one in the shape of a man: "Banish plump Jack, and banish all the world" (*1 Henry IV* 2.5.485). However, in his exorbitant dimensions and the flamboyance of his character, Falstaff instead comes to signify what escapes the clinical and calculating gaze of geometry as represented by Prince Hal's telling eye for political expediency. "Why, you are so fat, Sir John, that you must needs be out of all compass, out of all reasonable compass, Sir John", remarks Bardolph (1

Henry IV 3.3.20–22). To be "out of all compass" is to be beyond the reach of cartographic representation, for "compass" could refer to two different instruments familiar in Shakespeare's time: the magnetic device to locate direction, and the geometrical implement for drawing circles. Falstaff, as the representative of a world Hal distances himself from in his ascent to the throne, also embodies what cannot be mastered in the illusory relation between gigantic ego and diminished world.

Indeed, each of the plays mentioned so far provides, along with the metaphors which elevate its protagonist to the stature of a colossus, accompanying images of that figure's deflation. Richard II, for instance, exchanges his "large kingdom for a little grave" (*Richard II* 3.3.152), and Hal remarks of Hotspur's death, "ill-weaved ambition, how much art thou shrunk!," adding that "two paces of the vilest earth / Is room enough" to contain the body of his defeated rival (*1 Henry IV* 5.4.87–91). Antony repeats this reaction as he stands over Julius Caesar's corpse:

> O mighty Caesar! Dost thou lie so low?
> Are all thy conquests, glories, triumphs, spoils,
> Shrunk to this little measure?
> (*Julius Caesar* 3.1.149–151)

Antony's own fall from the political summit figures in more elaborate terms. His status, as "The triple pillar of the world transformed / Into a strumpet's fool," appears ambiguous from first few lines of the play (*Antony and Cleopatra* (1.1.12–13). Not long after the scene related by Octavius, in which Antony and Cleopatra publicly map their empire by listing its dominions (3.6.3–16), Antony's defeats, rather than his achievements, begin to figure in colossal terms:

> The greater cantle of the world is lost
> With very ignorance; we have kissed away
> Kingdoms and provinces
> (3.10.6–8)

At this point, his mastery of a submissive globe seems so uncertain that "the land bids me tread no more upon't, / It is ashamed to bear me" (3.11.1–2).

However, Antony expresses the evanescence of this egomorphic gigantism most explicitly in his dialogue with Eros after the next battle against Octavius, describing his dissolution into nothing from a figure of gigantic visibility, a cynosure. Like a cloud in the shape of "A towered citadel, ... or blue promontory," Antony's imperial image, which had seemed to loom over the earth, has evaporated, becoming "indistinct / As water is in water" (4.15.2–14). He declines from an Atlas figure with the entire world in his grasp to one who cannot even contain his own body: "Here I am Antony, / Yet cannot hold this visible shape" (ll. 13–14). As he makes this speech, in the BBC version of the play, Antony discards his armor, displaying to the audience the dramatic equivalent of a decomposing body, shedding its aspect of armed and statuesque potency.

The same contrast between the contained or self-sufficient ego, and its dissolution, structures the dominant idiom of another Roman play, *Coriolanus*. Caius Martius's political preeminence depends upon his capacity to integrate the civic collectivity into his own colossal stature, but his contempt for the public works against this process, nearly provoking the citizens into a dangerous realisation of their individuality, figured once more in explicitly cartographic terms:

> *Third Citizen* .... truly I think if all our wits were to issue out of one skull, they would fly east, west, north, south, and their consent of one direct way should be all at once to all the points o'th' compass
> (2.3.21–24)

Incapable of contracting this "many-headed multitude" into a single frame, Coriolanus becomes the last of the figures from the Roman plays to attempt the assumption of colossal stature, and to suffer its subsequent disintegration. In his arrogance, he offers a particularly characteristic figure of one elevated (in his own eyes as well as others') to an exaggerated and tenuous mastery over a diminished world—"The man is noble, and his fame folds in / This orb o'th' earth" (5.6.124–125)—claiming the right to assert his supremacy over the people, even if they threaten to execute him:

> pile ten hills on the Tarpeian rock,
> That the precipitation might down stretch
> Below the beam of sight, yet will I still
> Be thus to them
> (3.2.3–6)

This passage participates in the same Albertian pictorial principles as Edgar's Dover Cliff speech in *Lear*, and the description of Posthumus's departure in *Cymbeline:* a vertiginous perspectivism that once again proves liable to decomposition. Looking down upon the citizenry from his position of self-assured superiority, Coriolanus, like the other figures discussed so far, embodies the exorbitant stature and panoramic vision of the colossus. Here, the prospect of Coriolanus's fall from the extravagantly multiplied altitude of the Tarpeian Rock into a vanishing point "below the beam of sight" represents the threat of collapse implicit within this structure.

5. "Bid Kings Come Bow"

The anthropomorphic projections of the "ego's era," therefore, result in what Lacan describes as the "hominisation of the world, its perception in terms of images linked to the structuration of the body."[35] Teresa Brennan points out that this perceptual and representational transaction takes as its ideal, specifically, the male body and its conventional association with activity. This ego produces, as its object, an inert, submissive body. In one sense, psychoanalysis can be read as the exploration of this dialectic, whereby masculinity and femininity respectively affiliate with one of the two poles of this activity-passivity opposition. Cartography collaborates in this version of gender insofar as it subjugates the geographical contours of the land under the rubrics of a two-dimensional projection or a spherical model, "passifying" the world beneath the geometrical net cast from an erect and masterful gaze.[36] Lacan, moreover, describes this "symbolic system" as a "conquest, rape of nature, transformation of nature, hominisation of the planet," again implying the forcing of a passive femininity by an active masculinity.[37] We have observed already that Elizabethan surveyors like John Norden imagined the countryside offering itself submissively to their view in precisely this way, and recent critics have begun to discuss the feminization of both Britain and the New World through the mapping of the terrain by a specifically male gaze.[38]

Shakespearean chorography involves the same subjection of both land and female body to a masculine gaze, for example, when conflating the siege of a city, or the invasion of a territory, with the pursuit and rape of a woman. So, in *Henry V*, the king graphically evokes, in a single threat, the imminent "hot and forcing violation" of both the walls of Harfleur and of its maidens (3.3.90–126). By the end of that play, Princess Catherine embodies the land of

France, forced to submit to Henry's mastery. This metaphorical correlation proves indissociable from the royal and imperialist gaze, for the superimposition of Catherine's body over the French cities can only be perceived from Henry's standpoint and according to his perspective:

> King Henry. . . . you may, some of you, thank love for my blindness, who cannot see many a fair French city for one fair French maid that stands in my way.
> King Charles. Yes, my lord, you see them perspectively, the cities turned into a maid—for they are all girdled with maiden walls that war hath never entered
>
> (5.2.313–319)

The Oxford editor points out the reference here to the popular Elizabethan perspective toy "which showed different images when viewed from different angles."[39] Like the kind of anamorphic painting exemplified by Holbein's *Ambassadors*, such a device betrays an inconsistency in the masterful viewing position of the subject, a contradiction which can be traced in Shakespeare's metaphor. King Henry, emphasising the stability of his viewpoint and the fixity of his gaze, imagines Catherine blocking his line of sight, which would otherwise reach out to encompass the wider territory of France. When King Charles suggests that Henry can see both woman and cities "perspectively," what seems to be the evocation of an omnivoyant gaze actually undermines the centralized visual location Henry had claimed for himself, for the perception of two different aspects, in either the device referred to by Shakespeare or the anamorphic painting, requires a change of viewpoint, a new perspective, displacing the fixed eye of the subject. In this passage, therefore, the feminization of the land, or conversely the mapping of the female body, simultaneously solicits and disrupts the mastery of the male gaze.

In *King John*, the city of Angiers represents another female body to be anatomized, undressed and penetrated. John, in a conceit progressing from the town's "eyes," which are "winking," to its "waist," from which the belt of stones will be "dishabited," equates the threat posed by the French forces with the ravishment of a female body (2.1.208–234). The subsequent transactions of the play—conducted through a repetitive enumeration of the territories under debate—almost reach resolution in the betrothal of Blanche and Lewis, which again occurs in consistently cartographic mode. Blanche—whose name designates her as a blank space, available for inscription—provides the parchment upon which a map may be drawn that redefines the boundaries between France and England. Blanche is a "treaty," a "book of beauty," a list of territories ("Anjou and fair Touraine, Maine, Poitou..."), a white page onto which princes copy, narcissistically, their own images, or an empty mirror in which they see their own masterful reflections, just as Lewis sees himself "Drawn in the flattering table of her eye" (2.1.481–503). However, just as "commodity" makes maps, it also revises them when they are out of date, and in the accelerating cartographic politics out of which the text is written, the lifespan of a particular strategic alignment, as expressed in a given map, can prove brief. When Pandulph appears and demands France's allegiance to Rome against England, the alliance forged by the marriage becomes invalid. Blanche, the map on which the compromise borders were drawn, simply rips apart like a parchment:

> Which is the side that I must go withal?
> I am with both, each army hath a hand,
> And in their rage, I having hold of both,
> They whirl asunder and dismember me
> (3.1.253–56)

Through the power of representation, the female body is transmuted into a chart, a political carte blanche or blank cheque, to be torn up when no longer of use.

After the conclusion of peace between France and England, as ratified by the redrafted map of Blanche's betrothal to Lewis, Constance establishes her own protest against this cartographic structure. She does so by means of a gesture that refuses to participate in the competition to occupy the spectatorial mastery of the male gaze cast over a passive terrain:

> [*She sits upon the ground*]
> To me and to the state of my great grief
> Let kings assemble, for my grief's so great
> That no supporter but the huge firm earth
> Can hold it up. Here I and sorrows sit,
> Here is my throne, bid kings come bow to it
> (2.2.70–74)

The new "state" founded by Constance establishes a conflicting subject position, an alternative play of gazes, and a different relationship with the earth from that of the two kings. She abolishes the elevated stature from which the land may be cartographically surveyed, and replaces it with a spectatorial position—a "throne"—closer to the "huge firm earth," as that which resists diminution to the proportions of a model globe. Her own gaze, from this level, once again offers a reverse perspective that subverts the view from above. Yet it is not submissive, for kings have to "bow to it," to look down in order to engage with it, thereby becoming implicated in that debased and lowering gaze which displaces their visual dominance.

Constance's posture at this moment, however, provides a critique of the male scopic economy rather than a viable political alternative to it. For, like John's mother Eleanor in the same play, she must rely for the exercise of any practical power on her capacity to infiltrate the privileged position of her son. Once she loses Arthur, the tactical advantage he represents for her is replaced by "grief," which "Stuffs out his vacant garments with his form; / Then have I reason to be fond of grief" (3.4.97–98). While this state of grief may delineate the limits and repressions of the masculist cartographic gaze, it ultimately derives its only potency from the dominant scopic structure, which the text does not permit it to replace or permanently disable.

6. "Acts Commenced on this Ball of Earth"

In another manifestation of this masculine gaze, *Antony and Cleopatra* provides, before the audience sees her for itself, a description of the heroine that superimposes her figure over the contours of the Egypt she rules, translating both into a text or a panorama, supine beneath the traversing eye of the male reader. "Would I had never seen her!," remarks Antony, to which Enobarbus replies, "O, sir, you had then left unseen a wonderful piece of work, which not to have been blessed withal would have discredited your travel" (1.2.144–147).

The mention of "travel" serves to contextualize the surveying gaze under discussion within a contemporary culture of sightseeing. References to Elizabethan and Jacobean travelers provide evidence that the emergence of the cartographic economy, and the subjectivity it heralds, although modeled upon the privileged view of the sovereign and the explorer, was not confined only to the monarchy and its immediate circle, as the Bastard's satire in *King*

John suggests. Having achieved a sudden elevation in social status, Faulconbridge parodies the dinner conversation of the well-traveled Elizabethan gentleman, the "picked man of countries," displaying his familiarity with foreign places, sights, and names:

> talking of the Alps and Apennines
> The Pyrenean and the River Po,
> It draws toward supper in conclusion so.
> But this is worshipful society,
> And fits the mounting spirit like myself;
> For he is but a bastard to the time
> That doth not smack of observation
>
> (1.1.193–208)

Yet in a wider context, this passage also suggests that to "smack of observation" was not even exclusively the prerogative of those who actually ventured beyond England's shores. For Faulconbridge gives his travelogue in the form of the questions and answers of "an Absey book" (ll. 195–200), a primer or introductory language manual, in which such chorographic lists were common.[40] These connections demonstrate the popularity, not so much of actual experience in other countries, or even of travel within Britain, but of what might be called "closet travel," in reference to the words of Gerard Mercator in the Preface to his *Atlas* of 1595, who suggests that the reader of his maps "by speculation in his closset, may travell through every province of the world."[41] Many contemporary writers confirm the existence of this evidently substantial readership, consisting of those "mounting spirits" who enjoyed easy access to maps as stimulants to their imagination of, or their learning, reading, hearing, and talking about, foreign lands. R. A. Skelton quotes the editor of a town-atlas published in 1581:

> What could be more agreeable than, in one's home far from danger, to gaze in these books at the universal form of the earth [and] ... to acquire knowledge which could scarcely be had but by long and difficult journeys?[42]

The existence of this market for maps suggests the increasing potency of both cartographic representation and its textual equivalent in prose, poetry, and drama, to establish and disseminate its characteristic scopic economy across a wide range of readers.

Unless Faulconbridge's "bastards to the time" made up the entire theatergoing public, therefore, a considerable number of Shakespeare's audience must have had some experience, if not of actual touring, then of maps or traveler's descriptions representing various parts of the known world. Shakespearean drama, with its ubiquity of geographical references, confirms its spectators in the positions prescribed for them by the cartographic economy: not only through the rhetorical and theatrical representation of the spatial developments involved, but in the actual encounter that takes place between audience and stage. It does so, however, in a thoroughly conflicted way.

In the first place, the theater itself offers a manifestation of the reduction of the world to a model for consumption by the spectator. The emblematic figure of Rumour invokes this role of the stage in the prologue to *2 Henry IV*: "I from the orient to the drooping west, / . . . still unfold / The acts commenced on this ball of earth" (Induction 3–5). The world and its histories can be folded and unfolded like a map, diminished to the size of a ball, the object of (a) play, while "acts" of global significance become equivalent in scope of those performed on the stage. It is hardly necessary, in this connection, to recall the name of the theater built by Shakespeare's company in 1599. The titles of a number of contemporary atlases and map collections may offer a less familiar correlation between stage and cartography, from the *Theatrum Orbis Terrarum* of Abraham Ortelius (1570 and later editions), to Speed's *Theatre of the Empire of Great Britain* (1611).

However, the prologues of the plays often seem less than confident in their ability to contain the world within the frame of the stage. In the Prologue to *Henry V*, the Chorus expresses more obvious reservations about the translation of world into theater when it wishes for

> A kingdom for a stage, princes to act,
> And monarchs to behold the swelling scene.
> . . . But pardon, gentles all,
> The flat unraised spirits that hath dared
> On this unworthy scaffold to bring forth
> So great an object. Can this cock-pit hold
> The vasty fields of France? Or may we cram
> Within this wooden O the very casques
> That did affright the air at Agincourt?
> O pardon: since a crooked figure may
> Attest in little place a million,
> So let us, ciphers to this great account,
> On your imaginary forces work.
> Suppose within the girdle of these walls

> Are now confined two mighty monarchies,
> Whose high upreared and abutting fronts
> The perilous narrow ocean parts asunder
>
> (ll. 13–22)

This passage opens the play with an overt delineation of the geographical relationship between England and France, reliant—like the other Shakespearean charts of the nation discussed so far—on a correlation between the land and a "girdled" female body, protected by inviolable boundaries, as exemplified by the habitual references to precipitous coastlines and an encircling sea. We can also recognize the precariousness of the demarcation between the nation and its others, sundered by an ocean both "perilous" and "narrow."

The evocation of this familiar chorography, and its theatrical efficacy, depend upon the same "imaginary forces" operating among the audience that contemporary writers describe at work in the "closet travel" or vicarious sightseeing of Elizabethan readers poring over maps in their studies. But in drama, by contrast, the surveying eye produced by such a cartographic imagination operates communally, not in isolation. For the institution of a single spectatorial eye plainly conflicts with the actual conditions of Elizabethan and Jacobean public theater, in which the relationship between audience and stage was dispersed, interactive, dialogic, and communal.[43] The "wooden O" of the Shakespearean theater could not actually play to a single, fixed or privileged spectatorial position. On the contrary, the round auditorium instituted a circular array of viewpoints which crossed and recrossed the stage, according to the conflicting perspectives elicited by the play. The Prologue hints at this conflict between a single privileged gaze and the multiple eyes of the public theater when it expresses the desire for "monarchs to behold the swelling scene." In order to achieve the perfect illusion of three-dimensional cartographic perspective, so that a "kingdom" may be equated with a "stage" and "princes" with actors, the drama needs to play to the monocentric viewpoint of the sovereign eye, as typified by the seat of the monarch watching a court masque.[44] In its failure to isolate in the audience such a privileged gaze, the stage degenerates into what the Prologue calls a "flat unraised" representation, with the same two-dimensional limits and anamorphic distortions as a map or painting.

What, then, would the successful establishment of this singular viewing position involve? For one thing, the repression of the vestigial medieval theatrical relationship between audience and stage, and the historical foreclosure of the gaze, insofar as it constitutes a multiplicity of perspectives, or a return of the line of sight upon the spectator from the stage. And how would the resulting theater look? Precisely, I would say, like the "realist" Shakespeare productions which dominated the nineteenth century stage, in which a visually "convincing" illusion could be produced on a vast stage behind the frame of the proscenium arch.[45] At that time, furthermore, cartography was completing its long project of subjugating the entire British Empire beneath a single mapping gaze, culminating in the Ordnance Survey of Ireland, and the triangulation of the Indian subcontinent under the direction of sir George Everest, after whom the highest point on the globe was subsequently named in implicit acknowledgement of the colonising role of the surveyor's omnivoyance.[46] That these two movements coincided should not be surprising if, as my reading suggests, the space of the stage and that of cartography are conterminous, so that identical strategies and perceptual systems play from one to the other. It is the singular eye/I, as representative of an ascendent subjectivity instituted by this reconfigured space, which will find itself increasingly central to the theater, the painting, the map, and the political sphere of post-sixteenth-century Europe.

Notes

1. See Jacques Lacan, *Écrits: A Selection*, trans. Alan Sheridan (London: Tavistock, 1977), p. 71; *The Four Fundamental Concepts of Psychoanalysis*, trans. Alan Sheridan (London: Penguin, 1979), pp. 79–119; *The Seminar of Jacques Lacan Book I: Freud's Papers on Technique 1953–1954*, trans. John Forrester (Cambridge: Cambridge University Press, 1988), pp. 74, 76. My interpretation of the historical context of Lacan's theory of the ego and the gaze owes much to Teresa Brennan's convincing refutation of the common objection to Lacan's "ahistoricity": see Teresa Brennan, *History After Lacan* (London: Routledge, 1993), pp. 7–8, 39–40 and *passim*.

2. Lacan, *The Four Fundamental Concepts*, p. 86.

3. All Shakespeare quotes, unless otherwise stated, are from the *Complete Works*, ed. Stanley Wells, Gary Taylor et al. (Oxford: Clarendon, 1988). In the case of *King Lear*, quotes are from the Folio text (F) as given in that edition.

4. Terence Hawkes discusses Lear's division in terms of cartographic "reduction" in *Meaning by Shakespeare* (London: Routledge, 1992), pp. 121–140.

5. Samuel Edgerton, "From Mental Matrix to Mappamundi to Christian Empire: The Heritage of Ptolemaic Cartography in the Renaissance", in *Art and Cartography*, ed. David Woodward (Chicago: University of Chicago Press, 1987), pp. 10–50, 46.

6. As I have discussed at length elsewhere: see Philip Armstrong, "Uncanny

Spectacles: Psychoanalysis and the Texts of *King Lear*", in *Textual Practice* 8.3 (Winter 1994), pp. 414–434.

7. Christopher Marlowe, *Tamburlaine the Great*, ed. J. S. Cunningham (Manchester: Manchester University Press, 1981).

8. Ethel Seaton, "Marlowe's Map", in *Marlowe: A Collection of Critical Essays*, ed. Clifford Leech (Englewood Cliffs, N.J.: Prentice-Hall, 1964), pp. 36–56.

9. Richard Hakluyt, *The Principal Navigations, Voyages, Traffiques and Discoveries of the English Nation*, Vol. 1 (London: Macmillan, 1903), p. 356.

10. Hakluyt, *Principal Navigations*, vol. 2, p. 161.

11. J. D. Rogers, Voyages and Exploration: Geography: Maps", in *Shakespeare's England: An Account of the Life and Manners of his Age*, Vol. 1, ed. C. T. Onions and Sidney Lee (Oxford: Clarendon, 1916), pp. 170–197, 179–181.

12. Peter Barber, "Monarchs, Ministers and Maps, 1550–1625", in *Monarchs, Ministers and Maps: The Emergence of Cartography as a Tool of Government in Early Modern Europe*, ed. David Buisseret (London: University of Chicago Press, 1992), pp. 57–98, 44.

13. Samuel Edgerton, *The Renaissance Rediscovery of Linear Perspective* (New York: Basic Books, 1975).

14. John Dee, *The Mathematicall Preface to the Elements of Geometrie of Euclid of Megara, 1570* (New York: Science History Publications, 1975), sig. B1v–B2r.

15. John Dee, *Essential Readings*, ed. Gerald Suster (Great Britain: Crucible, 1986), pp. 47–53.

16. E. B. Knobel, "The Sciences: Astronomy and Astrology", in *Shakespeare's England* ed. Onions and Lee, pp. 444–461, 453.

17. Lloyd A. Brown, *The Story of Maps* (London: Cresset, 1951), pp. 180–185.

18. Lacan, *The Four Fundamental Concepts*, p. 72.

19. Ibid., pp. 88–92.

20. Jacques Lacan, *The Seminar of Jacques Lacan, Book VII: The Ethics of Psychoanalysis 1959–1960*, trans. Dennis Porter (London and New York: Routledge, 1992), p. 140.

21. Armstrong, "Uncanny Spectacles," pp. 429–432.

22. For a discussion of this Albertian pictorial space in *Lear* see Jonathan Goldberg, "Perspectives: Dover Cliff and the Conditions of Representation", in *Shakespeare and Deconstruction*, ed. G. Douglas Atkins and David M. Bergeron (New York: Peter Lang, 1988), pp. 245–65.

23. J. M. Nosworthy (ed), *The Arden Shakespeare: Cymbeline* (London: Routledge, 1969), p. 16.

24. Hakluyt, *Principal Navigations*, vol. 1, p. xviii.

25. J. B. Harley, "Meaning and Ambiguity in Tudor Cartography", in *English Map-Making 1500–1650*, ed. Sarah Tyacke (London: British Library, 1983), pp. 22–45, 33.

26. Stephen J. Greenblatt, *Renaissance Self-Fashioning: from More to Shakespeare* (Chicago: University of Chicago Press, 1980), p. 17.

27. Lacan, *The Four Fundamental Concepts*, p. 88.

28. Again, a famous portrait of Elizabeth offers a pictorial comparison: in this case, the "Ditchley" portrait, in which the Queen "towers over an England drawn after the Saxton model" (Richard Helgerson, *Forms of Nationhood: The Elizabethan Writing of England* (Chicago: University of Chicago Press, 1992), p. 112).

29. Brown, *The Story of Maps*, p. 167.

30. William Ravenhill, "Christopher Saxton's Surveying: An Enigma", in *English Map-Making*, ed. Tyacke, pp. 112–119, 117–118.

31. Francis Yates, *The Occult Philosophy in the Elizabethan Age* (London: Routledge, 1979), p. 77.
32. Brown, *The Story of Maps*, p. 165.
33. José Rabasa, "Allegories of the *Atlas*", in *Europe and Its Others: Proceedings of the Essex Conference on the Sociology of Literature July 1984*, Vol. 2, ed. Francis Barker et al (Colchester: University of Essex, 1985), pp. 1–15, 1.
34. See Lacan, *Écrits*, p. 71; and Brennan, pp. 39f.
35. Lacan, *Seminar I*, p. 141.
36. The pun is Lacan's, from *Écrits*, p. 42.
37. Lacan, *Seminar I*, p. 265.
38. Helgerson discusses at length the institution of a "cult of Britain," producing the nation as a female figure to be anatomized, for example, in Drayton's *Poly-Olbion* (Helgerson, pp. 118–120). Similarly, Peter Hulme conducts a compelling analysis of the feminization of the Americas in early colonial encounters, in his article "Polytropic Man: Tropes of Sexuality and Mobility in Early Colonial Discourse", in *Europe and Its Others*, Barker et al., pp. 17–32.
39. Gary Taylor, ed., *The Oxford Shakespeare: Henry V* (Oxford: Clarendon, 1982), p. 279.
40. A. J. Honigmann, ed., *The Arden Shakespeare: King John* (London: Routledge, 1954), p. xlvii.
41. Quoted in Rabasa, "Allegories of the *Atlas*," p. 7.
42. Quoted in R. A. Skelton, "Maps of a Tudor Statesman", in *A Description of Maps and Architectural Drawings in the Collection Made by William Cecil . . .*, ed. R. A. Skelton and John Summerson (Oxford: Printed for Presentation to Members of the Roxburghe Club, 1971), pp. 3–35, p. 3.
43. See Robert Weimann's *Shakespeare and the Popular Tradition in the Theatre: Studies in the Social Dimension of Dramatic Form and Function* (Baltimore: John Hopkins, 1978) for an unsurpassed discussion of the communal and dialogic nature of Shakespearean drama. Weimann does emphasise, however, that this medieval tradition of interactive theater inherited by the Elizabethans was in transition. My discussion here might suggest some of the perceptual paradigms that influenced this evolution.
44. Stephen Orgel describes how, in the Jacobean masque, "Through the use of perspective the monarch, always the ethical centre of court productions, became in a physical and emblematic way the centre as well . . . only the King's seat was perfect." Stephen Orgel and Roy Strong, *Inigo Jones: The Theatre of the Stuart Court* (Berkeley: University of California Press, 1973), Vol. 1, p. 7.
45. For example, *King John*, one of the most cartographically-inclined of the plays discussed in this essay, was a favorite subject for the extravagantly "realistic" and historically authentic performances of the nineteenth century, best exemplified by Planché's "antiquarian" production at Covent Garden in 1823–1824, and Kean's 1852 version which, according to the Arden editor, "brought theatrical pedantry to its high point" (Honigmann, p. lxxv).
46. See Mary Hamer's "Putting Ireland on the Map" (in *Textual Practice* 3.2 (Summer 1989, pp. 184–201) for a discussion of the political and representational stakes in the Ordnance Survey of Ireland, which took place between 1824 and 1846. Sir George Everest joined the Trigonometrical Survey of India in 1818, becoming Surveyor-General in 1830, and retired in 1843, shortly after completing the survey of the Himalayas.

Androgynous "Union" and the Woman in *Hamlet*

JAMES W. STONE

> Some wish to see in Hamlet a womanish, hesitating, flighty mind. To me he seems a manly, resolute, but thoughtful being.

> I cannot see Hamlet as a man. The things he says, his impulses, his actions entirely indicate to me that he was a woman.
> —Sarah Bernhardt

H*AMLET* HAS PROVEN to be an interpretive mystery for critics interested in gender, a play whose proverbial excess of meaning has led some critics to gender the excess and the mystery of the text itself as feminine. Since the problem of this problem play is femininity as such, Ernest Jones was prompted to call *Hamlet* the Sphinx of modern literature, and Jacqueline Rose, following T. S. Eliot, calls it the Mona Lisa.[1] In what follows I will explore the various ways androgyny, the collapse of sexual difference, is represented, whether in figuring Hamlet as a feminized, impotent man, or Gertrude as a masculinized, castrating woman. The penetration or invagination of one sex by the other leads, I argue, to the collapse of moral difference and of meaning, an undoing of boundaries described in terms of "incest," "jointure," "union," and making opposites "common." I aim to show how even the foundational distinctions between soul and body, and love and death, implode, since they depend upon a gendered hierarchy whose implicitly exclusionist assumptions the play disjoints.

Many gender critics of the 1970s, including some Shakespeareans, advanced the term "androgyny" to designate the harmonious reconciliation of sexual difference and friction.[2] Theirs is an essentially comic notion deriving from the *discordia concors* or coinci-

dentia oppositorum of Renaissance Neoplatonism as repopularized in Jungian psychology. This view of androgyny is imbued with the pious and nostalgic aim of recapturing the paradisiacal union of male and female components before the fall into separate and divisive sexes. Tragedy, according to this account, results from the impossibility of maintaining androgynous balance between man and woman. I believe instead that in *Hamlet* Shakespeare represents the way that androgynous union engenders dissolution and death, both of which the play typecasts as feminine. The thesis that Hamlet's tragedy lies in his having to expel the woman in himself in order to take manly action and to re-establish sexual difference is belied by the catastrophic "union"—a word whose importance I will explore below—that concludes the tragic action.[3] The union that erases the ambiguously gendered divisions between mind and body, deeds and words, duty and affect, gives rise to a catastrophic crisis of nondifference. This tragic endpoint reiterates precisely the quandary which diseases Denmark at the opening of the play, when the absence of difference signifies that nothing is taboo, including incest, adultery and murder.

The woman in Hamlet is as much a threat to him as the invaginating "mother"—"*hysterica passio*" (2.4.57)—is to Lear, the inextricable "woman's part" (2.5.20) is to Posthumus, and the (s)mothering Volumnia is to Coriolanus. Hamlet's inaction, which he and others characterize as feminine, stems from the fact that he is "as patient as the female dove" (5.1.273) and prone to "such a kind of gaingiving as would perhaps trouble a woman" (5.2.205).[4] A defining axiom of the misogyny that pervades *Hamlet* is that the baser matter that contaminates male spirit is woman, in whose folds man is sexually implicated. Man's figuring of himself as spirit is ultimately literalized (fatally—"the letter killeth") as matter because man is born of woman. Shakespeare may intend a pun upon the Latin *mater* to suggest a resonant conflation of "mother" and "matter." Hamlet makes a pointed juxtaposition of these two words when Rosencrantz and Guildenstern relate that Gertrude wants to meet him in her closet: "But sir, such answer as I can make, you shall command—or rather, as you say, my mother. Therefore no more, but to the matter. My mother, you say—" (3.2.314–16). In the closet scene itself, Hamlet's opening remark is "Now, mother, what's the matter?" (3.4.7). The punning association of matter with *mater*, body with woman, points to the woman's part—her "country matters" (3.2.115)—that constitutes every man (as divided-invaginated).[5]

The maternal inheritance or matter from which Hamlet struggles to disburden himself is oddly associated with his loquaciousness. In his third soliloquy he curses his propensity for words and feelings rather than deeds, for which Claudius has accused him of being "unmanly" (1.2.94):

> Why, what an ass am I! This is most brave,
> That I, the son of a dear father murthered,
> Prompted to my revenge by heaven and hell,
> Must like a whore unpack my heart with words
> And fall a-cursing like a very drab,
> A stallion!⁶
>
> (2.2.568–73)

The play associates the dilatory circumlocution of "words, words, words" (2.2.192) with the unchaste female who makes of man the necessarily debased image of herself—"whore," "drab," "stallion."⁷ Hamlet contrasts his purity of devotion to his ghostly father's memory with the contaminating adulteration that results from material embodiment: "And thy commandment all alone shall live / Within the book and volume of my brain, / Unmix'd with baser matter" (1.5.102–04). But just what distinction obtains between the father's spoken commandment and the feminizing words that Hamlet so outspokenly inveighs against for coming between himself and his filial duty? The mediation point between male and female speech is the body that both sexes share, that "mixture"⁸ of brain, book and matter that no verbal legerdemain can slight, no rationalization gloss over.

Hamlet's moment of resolute clarity unwittingly betrays his most persistent blind spot. For all his verbal facility, the speaking subject fails to note one of the basic tenets of his education in rhetoric and philosophy: the *res* or substance of an idea is its matter, whereas the word that gropes to express it concretely is the *verbum*. By the logic of this standard rhetorical distinction, the matter or substance of Hamlet's thoughts is feminine, while the words of the paternal commandment are masculine. Precisely when Hamlet insists upon his unmixed indebtedness and loyalty to paternal spirit (*verbum*) he betrays the maternal origin without which his and his father's words would be groundless because immaterial. If one hierarchy posits male spirit as that which inseminates, informs or animates female matter, a subversive and opposite conception insists on the ideational matter that gives birth to words, words that express at best imperfectly their material / maternal original.⁹

Hamlet feels that his inheritance from suckling Gertrude's maternal matter is moral because corporal contamination: "I am myself indifferent honest, but yet I could accuse me of such things that it were better my mother had not borne me" (3.1.122–24).[10] The original malaise of origin is exacerbated in the next developmental stage of incorporating the drab-whore-stallion's language—another kind of matter—whose sole profit, Hamlet suspects, is the ability to articulate his malaise, curse it and thereby suffer it the worse. Hamlet's apostrophe to Gertrude—"Frailty, thy name is woman" (1.2.146)—applies as well to (the woman in) himself. He is a subject divided by the loss (of purity, of self-presence, of the father)[11] that subjectivity presupposes, since the speaking subject attempts to recoup via language a loss that language itself has occasioned. Although words render Hamlet too effeminate to perform male deeds, the law of the father that enjoins the son to take dutiful action in the father's name expresses itself by means of the same linguistic mechanism that makes its fulfillment, in the third soliloquy quoted above, seem impossible. Words are indifferently the vehicle of both paternal law—Hamlet's pledge of filial allegiance to "thy commandment" (1.5.102) and the "ghost's word" (3.2.280); "Now to my word" (1.5.110), he says as he screws up his courage—and of its breach and adulteration. The recognition of this nondifference between male and female speech, between performative and expressive utterance, is what undoes Hamlet's best intentions to act (1.5.29–31), leaving him prisoner to his ineffectual self-reproaches, which are the melancholic introjection of his misogynistic reaction to the women in whose folds he senses himself helplessly implicated.[12]

Since woman is the Other who symbolizes self-loss for the man, it is no surprise that Hamlet's soliloquies are touched with a misogynistic animus and a melancholic infatuation with suicide as release from feminine and feminizing loss. The violence that Hamlet is called upon to effect in the father's name is what spells the sacrifice of those feminine qualities of loquacious inaction that some critics have regarded as Hamlet's most ingratiating characteristic. It is these same feminine qualities, however, that excite in Hamlet the urge to violence in the first place, a violence that aims to expel the feminine from within him. This violence is turned suicidally inwards; "manly" action gives way to melancholic enervation. Hamlet's initial resolve to remain faithful to his father's memory dissolves into suicidal self-disgust:

Androgynous "Union" and the Woman in Hamlet 75

> O that this too too sullied flesh would melt,
> Thaw and resolve itself into a dew,
> Or that the Everlasting had not fix'd
> His canon 'gainst self-slaughter. O God! O God!
> (1.2.129–32)

Dissolution of the sullied because "solid" (Folio) flesh motivates the suicidal urge, whose promise is the body's liquefaction. Ophelia, whom many critics have regarded as Hamlet's estranged feminine self,[13] will seek the same watery solace, the dissolution of resolution, in her suicide. In Hamlet's case suicide is figured in terms of orgasmic melting and post-coital flaccidity, the relieving of a tension.[14] The impulse for such release through sexual climax is paradoxically Hamlet's sense of disgust at being indissolubly imbedded in his sexual body. Insofar as his body is sullied by sexuality, it is regarded as feminine. The law of the father forbids trying to escape the feminine by means of masturbatory self-slaughter: seeking to kill desire by extinguishing the demands localized in the phallus. But man's imperative goal of self-identity is fractured under what it type-genders paranoiacally as the subversive influence of feminine difference and dissolution. Male "resolve" to do the father's bidding suddenly means quite the opposite, "resolve" as suicidal dissolve, which frees one from paternal obligation. This contradictory use of the same word instances what Freud calls the antithetical meaning of primal words.[15] What Freud sees as a difference of meaning that divides the putatively self-identical can be subsumed as well under the rubric of difference of gender. Antithetical gender confusion is implicit in the liquid imagery of the passage, which may be interpreted as male sexual discharge or the symbol of dearly besought female dissolution of the father's law.

In this first soliloquy Hamlet curses the lust that hastens Gertrude to an incestuous remarriage, a lust that patently belies her masking self-representation as "Niobe, all tears" (1.2.149).[16] Here unfolds a curious paradox: To forgo the whoring maternal flesh Hamlet contemplates resolving himself into a watery dew, but this water gets refigured as the salt water of woman's tears, which represent the hypocritical disguise of a body more compact with lust than mourning. If being embodied taints Hamlet with the legacy of woman, his proposed escape from the maternal body by dissolving it is no less implicated in the language of female lust and hypocritical masquerade. The extinction that death promises as end point is but the return to an inescapable origin—what Hamlet will designate in his most famous soliloquy as the "undiscover'd country" (3.1.79)—a maternal presence that dissolves duty and the father's law, such as the everlasting father's "canon 'gainst self-slaughter." Suicide is an escape from the maternal yet also the temptation *of* the maternal as that which licenses a return to (intra-uterine?) deliquescence.[17]

Laertes serves as Hamlet's mimetic double with respect to the imagery of water. He is the rival who swears to take action immediately upon hearing of Ophelia's death by drowning, rather than avoid the responsibility for vengeance by dwelling upon thoughts of watery dissolution or the expense of melancholy tears:

> Too much of water hast thou, poor Ophelia,
> And therefore I forbid my tears. But yet
> It is our trick; nature her custom holds,
> Let shame say what it will. *[Weeps.]* When these are gone,
> The woman will be out.
>
> (4.7.184–88)

Laertes expels womanly tears as the only means of preserving his manly vigor intact. The same dewy tears that Laertes seeks to purge are the responsibility-dissolving liquefaction, the sweet consummation of death, that Hamlet dreams of merging with by melting into. But in the closet scene Hamlet adopts a more "masculine" position, asking his father not to look upon him with pity lest he "convert / My stern effects. Then what I have to do / Will want true colour—tears perchance for blood" (3.4.128–30). Hamlet's forswearing of tears for the rhetoric of blood vengeance will make him indistinguishable from Laertes by the time that they square off together in the graveyard scene.[18]

Whether tears in Hamlet's first soliloquy represent Niobe's sincere expression of grief or Gertrude's masquerade of seeming, they serve variously to define the bifurcated feminine. In his initial appearance in the play, Hamlet in black dress takes pains to distance himself from ornamental or seeming mourning, dismissing tears as so many feigned motions of actors:

> Seems, madam? Nay, it is. I know not "seems."
> 'Tis not alone my inky cloak, good mother,
> Nor customary suits of solemn black,
> Nor windy suspiration of forc'd breath,
> No, nor the fruitful river in the eye,
> Nor the dejected haviour of the visage,

> Together with all forms, moods, shapes of grief,
> That can denote me truly. These indeed seem,
> For they are actions that a man might play;
> But I have that within which passes show,
> These but the trappings and the suits of woe.
>
> (1.2.76–86)

His scorn for seeming notwithstanding, soon enough Hamlet will act if not feign the madman's part. In this passage and what follows I am concerned with the feminine associations of neither feigning nor madness, but rather with the inconsistent disavowal of tears and of playing.

In his third soliloquy the fickle prince admires the Player, the man who plays the woman's part, for his convincing simulation of tears. By the time that the players arrive in Elsinore, Hamlet has come to believe that public show is the sole means to plumb private conscience and that the only sincere expression of inner grief is paradoxically its impersonation on a public stage, completely reversing his earlier contempt for the actor's "fruitful river in the eye." Initially Hamlet envies the woman's role portrayed by the Player because it differs so markedly from the female roles that he characterizes himself as having played up to this point, the roles of antic fool and madman. Hecuba's "bisson rheum" (2.2.502) in response to the slaying of her husband "would have made milch the burning eyes of heaven / And passion in the gods" (2.2.513–14). This conflation of weeping and lactary nurturing, as if the slain husband is his wife's child (Niobe, all tears), serves to foil Gertrude's tearful posturing, but ultimately Hamlet comes to recognize Hecuba's reality as that of an impersonated representation, a "fiction" evacuated of real motive, as yet another masquerading "nothing":

> O what a rogue and peasant slave am I!
> Is it not monstrous that the player here,
> But in a fiction, in a dream of passion,
> Could force his soul so to his own conceit
> That from her working all his visage wann'd,
> Tears in his eyes, distraction in his aspect,
> A broken voice, and his whole function suiting
> With forms to his conceit? And all for nothing!
> For Hecuba!
> What's Hecuba to him, or he to her,
> That he should weep for her? What would he do
> Had he the motive and the cue for passion

> That I have? He would drown the stage with tears,
> And cleave the general ear with horrid speech,
> Make mad the guilty and appal the free,
> Confound the ignorant, and amaze indeed
> The very faculties of eyes and ears.
>
> (2.2.544–60)

If Hecuba were not a representational fiction, one would conclude from this passage that emotion secures action: Feminine tears are not opposed to masculine revenge but are instead the motivating guarantee of its success. However, it is precisely the feminine side of his nature that Hamlet scapegoats for his "pigeon-liver'd" (2.2.573) cowardliness, castigating himself in this same soliloquy, as we have seen, for being a wordy drab-whore-stallion. The very words by which Hamlet bolsters his courage to act are the vehicle for dilation[19] since they defer action by substituting for it. The various distinctions that Hamlet mediates between sincere and feigned tears, acting and playacting, deeds and words[20] can all be subsumed under the general rubric of male and female. But such easy dichotomies do not hold, for the play insists on the antithetical collapse of primal antinomies.

Hamlet charts clear-cut distinction between himself and the Player's fictional Hecuba, the good woman, but he is able to locate scant difference between himself and the real bad woman whose flesh and word are indistinct from his. Difference obtains between men until they are linked sexually by the bond of a common woman. Hamlet remarks the difference between his father and Claudius—"So excellent a king, that was to this / Hyperion to a satyr" (1.2.139–40); and he interjects the difference between his cowardly self and the archetypal hero into the triangle formed by his rival father figures—"My father's brother—but no more like my father / Than I to Hercules" (1.2.152–53). Because the bad woman makes of Hyperion (Hamlet's father) a satyr (Claudius), of Hercules a Hamlet, then by the chiastic terms of the analogy she makes of Hamlet a lascivious satyr like Claudius. Of a self-possessed man she makes the effeminate coward that is Hamlet's consistent self-identification when taking stock of himself in the first four soliloquies.

Hamlet blames the bad woman with whom he is inextricably intertwined for his vacillation between virile resolve and conscientious scrupling. That man and woman are interconnected—that man is dependent, not author of himself—gives rise to his misogyny. The origin of his disgust *for* woman is man's origin and telos in woman, in what he metaphorizes as her "undiscover'd country." The darkness of this region of sex and death is what Hamlet points to as the cause of his effeminizing cowardice:

> Thus conscience does make cowards of us all,
> And thus the native hue of resolution
> Is sicklied o'er with the pale cast of thought,
> And enterprises of great pitch and moment
> With this regard their currents turn awry
> And lose the name of action.
> (3.1.83–85)

Conscience is masculine "resolution" to do one's duty. In antithetical fashion it also acts to resolve (dissolve) obligation, in the feminizing sense advanced in my reading of the liquid images above. The decline of "pitch" may suggest fears of post-coital flaccidity and the loss of manliness. But the resolution assured by conscience is "native," a gift from the mother. How can conscience impel one forward to take manly action, on the one hand, yet transform one into an irresolute coward, on the other? As the swelling of thought and of conscientiousness that forecloses action, religious conscience prohibits murder and leaves vengeance to God alone. A very different conscience is expressed by the Ghost, the unwelcome paternal superego that exacts the killing of Claudius even as it forbids Hamlet to kill himself. Conscience makes contradictory demands because it fails to reconcile the masculine and feminine elements that it comprises. It epitomizes the gendered ambivalence (androgyny) between male and female, spirit and body, action and cowardice: binarisms that don't align themselves in any consistent parallelism, but rather criss-cross androgynously.[21]

Hamlet's melancholy and madness are, like conscience, represented in terms of the feminine that both fractures and empowers him.[22] Although Hamlet castigates himself for being "unpregnant of my cause" (2.2.563) due to cowardice, Claudius sees in his nephew's psyche a woman whose plotting he likens to an oedipally menacing parturition:

> There's something in his soul
> O'er which his melancholy sits on brood,
> And I do doubt the hatch and the disclose
> Will be some danger.
> (3.1.166–69)

Here for a change feminine melancholy is thought to give rise to consequential activity. Like Richard II's self-reflexive "My brain I'll prove the female to my soul, / My soul the father, and these two beget / A generation of still-breeding thoughts" (5.5.6–8), Hamlet's broodings are his parthenogenic progeny (brood); they disclose the only (living) kin he is willing to acknowledge. Gertrude characterizes Hamlet's madness as his brooding and breeding internal female:

> This is mere madness,
> And thus awhile the fit will work on him.
> Anon, as patient as the female dove
> When her golden couplets are disclos'd,
> His silence will sit drooping.
>
> (5.1.279–83)

The oscillation from the fit of "mere" (French "mother") madness to patient silence, both characterized as feminine extremes, traces Hamlet's manic depression in terms of feminine fickleness.[23] Hamlet is capable of both destructive violence and peaceable generativity, the feminine double bind that constitutes him.[24]

Once the feminine is abstracted from the physical body and becomes a disembodied metaphor, it ceases to be threatening. Following literary and philosophical convention, Hamlet refers to the soul that informs his body as the feminine anima. This feminine in himself bonds homosocially with the same element in Horatio, Hamlet's soulmate: "Since my dear soul was mistress of her choice, / And could of men distinguish her election, / Sh'ath seal'd thee for herself" (3.2.63–65). Horatio displaces Ophelia as Hamlet's bosom bondman because he is safely desexualized. He is feminine insofar as he represents the allegorized rational soul, but he has excised the (feminizing) madness and passion of sexual desire, whose deleterious world-historical influence is personified in the play as the fickle whore Fortune. Hamlet admires in Horatio that he has been

> As one, in suff'ring all, that suffers nothing,
> A man that Fortune's buffets and rewards
> Hast ta'en with equal thanks; and blest are those
> Whose blood and judgement are so well commeddled
> That they are not a pipe for Fortune's finger
> To sound what stop she please. Give me that man
> That is not passion's slave, and I will wear him

In my heart's core, ay, in my heart of heart,
As I do thee.
(3.2.66–74)

We have seen that Hamlet contrasts "the motive and the cue for passion" that should inspire him to act with the Player's imaginarily motivated passions. Since the prince is "patient" like a female dove and "patient" and "passion" are etymologically equivalent in designating passive suffering, then what Hamlet envies in Horatio is his freedom from female melancholy, the manic depressive roller coaster sometimes figured as Fortune's wheel.[25]

Female Fortune is also identified with the type of wheeling and extravagant opportunism that Hamlet so despises in Rosencrantz and Guildenstern: male varlets whose "privates" are collusively cross-coupled with the "secret parts of Fortune" (2.2.234–35) to form an illicit because hermaphroditic union. Like the whore Fortune they try to manipulate Hamlet's pipe: "You would play upon me, you would seem to know my stops, you would pluck out the heart of my mystery, you would sound me from my lowest note to the top of my compass" (3.2.355–58). At this point Hamlet regards himself no longer as a male whore, a minion-slave of the strumpet Fortune, whose threat, which Rosencrantz and Guildenstern personify, has become manifestly external and therefore easier for Hamlet to confound. In act 4 Hamlet will take fatal Fortune into his own hands by disposing of his old schoolfellow conspirators and thus disburdening himself of the feminizing menace that they personify. And by the ultimate scene of the play he will be able to bolster his sense of masculine courage by heaping abuse upon the foppish courtier Osric, who represents the no longer threatening feminine that the mature Hamlet can easily dismiss.

One consequence of Hamlet's inability to isolate and then excise the woman from himself is that the distinctions he tries to draw between other people are as confused as he is self-divided sexually. In the closet scene with his mother, Hamlet protests too much in overdrawing the contrast between the "counterfeit presentment" (3.4.54) of the elder Hamlet and of Claudius. Beneath the son's defensively schematic opposition between ideal and nightmare father figures, Hyperion and satyr, lurks the doubt that they are not so different after all, since Gertrude has held both in common. Although Hamlet asserts that "sense to ecstasy were ne'er so thrall'd / But it reserv'd some quantity of choice / To serve in such a difference" (74–76), he criticizes in his mother the appropriation of sense by ecstasy and the resulting loss of difference. With the woman on top sense loses its hierarchic superiority over sensuousness, its subversive contrary, and reason becomes merely the instrument for satisfying desire: "And reason panders will" (88). That Hamlet's father represents reason and his stepfather will is only an ideal presentment shown to be "counterfeit" since reason and will are not opposed but in collusion, rendered common in Gertrude's faulted vice.[26] It is as if the elder Hamlet (reason) acts as pander-advocate for his own cuckolding, the willful coupling of Claudius and Gertrude. What belies the schematically contrasting portraits that Hamlet uses to badger his mother is his description of Claudius as "a king of shreds and patches—" (103), followed immediately by the stage direction "*Enter Ghost.*" The referent of Hamlet's interrupted word portrait is indifferently Claudius and the elder Hamlet, since invoking the one seems to call up the other. Gertrude says that Hamlet's vision of the Ghost is an hallucination induced by "ecstasy" (140), the very faculty whose improper dominance Hamlet said caused Gertrude's failure to recognize the difference between Claudius and the elder Hamlet. The ultimate failure of proper difference is that the rational faculty of differentiation in both Hamlet and Gertrude has ceded place to mother and son's common bond of ecstasy.[27]

In a way similar to his counterfeit portrayal of the collapsed rival father figures, it is impossible for Hamlet to separate Gertrude and Ophelia despite their ostensible differences. Whereas he tries but fails to keep the father figures separate, Hamlet doesn't seem to want to distinguish between the women in his life. What he calls Ophelia's "painting" (3.1.144) dovetails with his criticism of Gertrude's masquerade of mourning. The sexual contamination that Hamlet insists upon attributing to his mother is transferred to Ophelia, who is the target of her friend's obscene wit just before their joint spectatorship of *The Murder of Gonzago*. The remark that Ophelia should sequester herself in a "nunnery" (3.1.121) is famously subversive: Is a nunnery where a young woman goes to preserve her chastity, or a brothel in which she squanders it; a place of sexual renunciation, or one of carnal indulgence? Does this once fundamental distinction still make any difference? Gertrude's position as whore (in her son's eyes) crosses over indifferently onto Ophelia's chaste body, making of apparently antithetical contraries an indistinguishable conjunctive union.

It is against this union of what should be opposites—ideal and debased fathers, chaste and unchaste women, spirit and body—

that Hamlet inveighs when he attacks the conjunction of sexual opposites: "I say we will have no mo marriage" (3.1.149). Precisely this copular mixing of the sexes has informed Hamlet since birth, and we have seen that it is this contamination of origins that engenders mature thoughts of suicide. Hamlet can no more escape the fallen transformation of chastity (the "honesty" of mind) into heterosexual coupling (the telos of bodily "beauty") than he can avoid his own originary embodiment: "The power of beauty will sooner transform honesty from what it is to a bawd than the force of honesty can translate beauty into his likeness" (3.1.111–14). Beauty belies honesty because honesty itself is not honest; honesty panders beauty. Hamlet thematizes the way that corporal beauty gives the lie to honesty when he plays upon the possibility of lying in the sexual sense with the nunnery-destined because dishonest Ophelia: "Lady, shall I lie in your lap? . . . That's a fair thought to lie between maids' legs." The provocative allusions to "country matters" and to Ophelia's reductive, genital "nothing" (3.2.110–20) imply that Hamlet's lying in her beautified lap is the cause of dishonest moral lapse in herself and others. Revulsion is Hamlet's response to the genital materiality of woman, which makes of her chastity a nothing, of her honesty a lie.

Hamlet's misogynistic banter early in 3.2 is a prelude to the staging of *The Murder of Gonzago*, a play within the play that thematizes the origin of man's disgust for woman, whose effects have already evidenced themselves preposterously in Hamlet's prescriptive fore-play with Ophelia. In recounting the scene of his death, the Ghost tells Hamlet that "the serpent that did sting thy father's life / Now wears his crown" (1.5.39–40), the crown symbolizing both his kingship and his wife's genitalia.[28] The liquid poured in the ear is a deathly bane that undoes the vital liquid that King Hamlet once disseminated in a homologous orifice. The contrary valences of the liquid image—semen = life versus semen = poison—instance Shakespeare's antithetical *pharmakon*. King Hamlet is represented as emasculated. Coppélia Kahn notes the sexual confusion that the Ghost engenders in Hamlet in asking the son to identify with the feminized father: "The elder Hamlet is in the feminine position of being penetrated by the man who has already penetrated his wife."[29] The play within the play that Hamlet stages is an attempt to recall, replay and thereby undo the scene of the elder Hamlet's death.[30] If Hamlet sees a mimetic representation of his father penetrated and the reaction to it of the guilty spectators, he reasons that this will provide him sufficient motive for taking manly revenge, which entails the reassertion of the law of the father that the murder (and Gertrude's adultery) breached.

Manly revenge may be all the easier if Hamlet can demonstrate that his adversary, who wears the sexually ambiguous crown, is only a castrated, petticoat king, a replicated reflection of the turn that he effected upon his brother king. Perhaps Hamlet identifies the feminine in his own conscience with something similar in his stepfather, which will make the latter vulnerable to being caught by the play within the play: "The play's the thing / Wherein I'll catch the conscience of the King" (2.2.600–01). The Mousetrap conflates Claudius's captured conscience with Gertrude's, whose pet name, "Mouse," is echoed in the closet scene. After the play within the play Hamlet uses the same "king"/"thing" rhyme and another double entendre with vaginal referent to express his confidence that Claudius has been hollowed into an empty shell: "The King is a thing . . . / Of nothing" (4.2.27–29).[31] If both Claudius and King Hamlet are reduced to a feminized nothing, the distinction between them must have collapsed in Hamlet's mind.

Stanley Cavell advances the provocative thesis that Claudius is both father and mother in Hamlet's dumb-show, because it substitutes Claudius as a veil for Hamlet's mother, the murderer behind the murderer. ("None wed the second but who kill'd the first" [3.2.175].)[32] The dumb-show is a re-visioning of the unseen original murder, which it reenacts with the mother-father (Claudius covering for, and acting at the behest of, Gertrude) taking the masculine position by pouring poison into the man's ear, reversing the scenario in the primal scene (of intercourse), where the woman is the passive receptacle of what the man pours.[33] My quarrel with Cavell is his assumption that Gertrude was passive in the primal scene, whereas in the murder scene she turns around suddenly and assumes the aggressor's stance. We may suspect that Hamlet has entertained the deep fantasy of a "masculine" Gertrude all along: In the primal scene that continues to haunt his unconscious, Hamlet is traumatized by the vision of his father castrated (feminized) in the act of intercourse.[34] Gertrude is imagined as the masculine aggressor in the two original scenes of sex and murder, of Death (Hamlet's "consummation / Devoutly to be wish'd" [3.1.63–64]) as the punning conflation (climactic-extinctive) of these two senses, which are but different manifestations of the same horror in the male imagination. In appropriating the masculine powers of her husband, Gertrude renders him impotent, the ghostly hollow of his former self, and so she must proceed adulterously to some other man to satisfy her swelling urge for sexual jointure. Hamlet describes the fierceness of Gertrude's desire for his father in terms that ominously suggest a voraciousness that, like a parasite's, devours its object to the bone and so must prey elsewhere: "She would hang on him / As if increase of appetite had grown / By what it fed on" (1.2.143–45). Gertrude's devouring orality knows no bounds, for every taboo which poses a resistance only serves the more to excite her transgressive desire.

The confusion of man and woman explicitly reaches the collapsing point of nondifference when Hamlet takes his leave of Claudius in order to begin his journey for England. He propounds a syllogism which intertwines the sexes incestuously and androgynously:

Ham. Farewell, dear mother.
King. Thy loving father, Hamlet.
Ham. My mother. Father and mother is man and wife, man and wife is one flesh; so my mother.

(4.3.52–55)

Hamlet's ostensibly innocent allusion to the biblical idealization of sexual union in marriage points instead of a nonideal, incestuous materialization. The prince is revolted by the interchangeability of parts (partners) in the sexual act, whose locus Sonnet 137 suggestively designates as the genital "common place" (1.10),[35] the place where man and woman (as well as the elder Hamlet and Claudius, the ideal and degraded father images) become indistinguishable in the chiastic coupling of mother-father. Ernest Jones explains the mother-father confusion in terms of the psychoanalytic "combined parent concept" (113), in which the child imagines its parents as one flesh in coitus. Hamlet's chop-logic employs the rhetorical commonplace of chiasmus to signify and to predicate the reduction of sexual difference to the common genital site where the sexes are indifferently one (androgynous).

It is the misogynistic representation of woman as duplicitous masquerader that marks the focal point of *Hamlet* as a tragedy; the play passes beyond the ideal specularity of comedy to a specifically linguistic duplicity and subjectifying self-division, the principle of difference which patriarchal, misogynistic discourse takes woman to be.[36] Gertrude's crossing of sexual boundaries and collapsing of difference informs the androgyny that so conspicuously marks Hamlet's character. Whereas female unfaithfulness suggests a complication that comic transvestism turns into a joke, insofar as the transvestic disguise miraculously defuses the charge of cuckoldry, the perception of woman's adultery in the tragedies incites a catastrophe of nondifference. Gertrude's incestuous duplicity sloughs off external disguises that are merely specular and therefore comic in favor of a masculinely aggressive jointure, effected via duplicitous language, of things that are normally and normatively contrary. Her violation of the incest taboo, which insists on keeping one's husband and brother-in-law distinct, leads to a collapse of difference in general. It is on account of Gertrude, the "imperial jointress" (1.2.9), i.e., the one who undoes difference by effecting jointure, that "the time is out of joint" (1.5.196). She is responsible for making "the night joint-labourer with the day" (1.1.81) and for the undoing of propriety (proper difference) that results when "the funeral baked meats . . . coldly furnish forth the marriage tables" (1.2.180–81)

Woman is the principle of difference that paradoxically collapses difference, reducing Claudius, Hamlet, and Hamlet's father to the commonly denominated nexus of Gertrude's shared body. The word "common" occurs several times to designate the universal reductionism of death: "Thou know'st 'tis common: all that lives must die" (1.2.72); "[Reason's] common theme / Is death of fathers" (1.2.103–4). Death is the common lot of everyone born of woman's "common place," the uncanny home (*unheimlich heim*) that makes of woman man's genesis (womb) and his destined end (tomb). In the "To be, or not to be" soliloquy, Hamlet's fears of death situate their imaginary locus in "the undiscover'd country, from whose bourn / No traveller returns" (3.1.79–80). The latent pun on the genital sense of "country" equates death with woman's hell, her not so Elysian Fields.[37] The nether country is where man and woman are at one in the three developmental stages of birth, copulation, and death.[38]

The sexes are made common in the primal scene of copulation and of death. Often in Shakespeare's plays "death" puns upon the chiastic indistinction (or so the man imagines) of the sexes in orgasm. Death as the climactic collapse of male potency also points to castration anxiety. Although these senses of "dying" are not foregrounded in *Hamlet* at the level of local wordplay, they are a motivating thematic concern overall. Love is literalized (materialized) as death in the figure of Lamord, the Norman knight who rides "incorps'd" (4.7.86) upon the back of his horse, whose punning name collapses death (*la mort*) and love (*l'amour*, or the Latin *amor*). The erotic instincts aim towards the same release of tension that death grants, and life and death are tellingly juxtaposed ("incorps'd") in Laertes's exclamatory pseudo-recognition, "Upon my life, Lamord" (4.7.91). Lamord is like Hamlet a death messenger who adorns himself in the gallant's fashionable jewels: "the brooch indeed / And gem of all the nation" (4.7.92–93). In mimetically similar terms Ophelia describes Hamlet as formerly "Th' expectancy and rose of the fair state, / The glass of fashion and the mould of form" (3.1.154–55), though of course he subsequently drapes himself in deathly black, as if to say that love and mourning describe the singular and identical trajectory of every embodied consciousness. The love gem as poisoned death trafficer comes to a head in the "union" jewel of the final scene of the play.[39]

Life and death are conjoined in a cyclical and interanimating feeding process:

> *Ham.* For if the sun breed maggots in a dead dog, being a good kissing carrion—Have you a daughter?
> *Pol.* I have, my lord.
> *Ham.* Let her not walk i' th' sun. Conception is a blessing, but as your daughter may conceive—friend, look to't.
> (2.2.181–86)

Conception is corruption, and conversely; life generates spontaneously from death, only to provide more grist for death's maw. Hamlet himself is the maggot son bred from the conjunction of living sun (Hamlet as father) and dead matter *(mater)*: "I am too much in the sun" (1.2.67), he laments, as if to suggest that his exalted origins have overripened and putrefied. The necrophilic self-identification as cadaver-bred maggot suggests at once a sperm breeding and a parasite feeding. Love reduced to deathly parasitism is an analogue for the way that the liquid poured in King Hamlet's ear and the union wine consumed in the final scene are both conjunctive-inseminating and poisonous, with the latter sense parodic of and parasitic upon the former, taking precedence. The chaliced union wine is a parasitic parody of the Communion wine of the Last Supper, the drinking and eating of a dead body in order to gain life thereby.

Whether sex is poisonous or generative is also at the heart of the characterization of Ophelia, who is regarded with extreme ambivalence as an exemplar of unchaste beauty in life and chaste idealization in death.[40] In terms of the analogy by which she is fixed in the passage quoted above from act 2, scene 2, Ophelia is like rotting flesh which breeds, only to have her brood turn around and devour its life source incestuously. Flesh as food for maggots—"We fat all creatures else to fat us, and we fat ourselves for maggots" (4.3.21–23)—contrasts with Laertes' remark at Ophelia's funeral about the regenerative powers of her virgin body to conceive immaculately: "Lay her i'th' earth, / And from her fair and unpolluted flesh/ May violets spring" (5.1.231–33).[41] Maggots or violets; dishonest or virginal woman; conception as curse or as blessing? To these confused binarisms Gertrude adds the "Lamord" question: epithalamion or funeral?

> [scattering flowers] Sweets to the sweet. Farewell.
> I hop'd thou shouldst have been my Hamlet's wife:
> I thought thy bride-bed to have deck'd, sweet maid,
> And not have strew'd thy grave.
>
> (5.1.236–39)

Dead flowers substitute for marital defloration and "dying." Gertrude the jointress again does what Hamlet reproached her for in act 1 when he complained that "the funeral bak'd meats / Did coldly furnish forth the marriage tables" (1.2.180–81). Elegy is but a cover for matrimonial lust in Hamlet's deflating satire.[42]

The collapse of love and death reaches its hyperbolic climax when Hamlet and Laertes, the rival lovers, leap into (penetrate) the open grave for one last necrophilic embrace (with Ophelia, with / against each other). Hamlet can achieve his devoutly wished love consummation only with a corpse, and in the next scene he will consummate his death wish by becoming incorpsed in himself. Hamlet points to the paradox of Laertes's being "buried quick" (5.1.274) with Ophelia, an act of hyperbolic excess that he vows to imitate mimetically:

> And if thou prate of mountains, let them throw
> Millions of acres on us, till our ground,
> Singeing his pate against the burning zone,
> Make Ossa like a wart. Nay, and thou'lt mouth,
> I'll rant as well as thou.
>
> (5.1.275–79)

Hamlet and Laertes become indistinguishable in their rhetorical overreaching, as well as in their ostentatious sacrifice of the quick for the dead. Earlier in this scene, before he knows that the grave is destined for Ophelia, Hamlet feels confident that he can distinguish between the living and the dead in much the same way as he can differentiate between truth and lying. He says that the

Gravedigger "lies" in the grave in both senses of the word. "Thou dost lie in't, to be in't, and say 'tis thine. 'Tis for the dead, not for the quick: therefore thou liest" (122–24). When Hamlet jumps into the grave, he literalizes his earlier wordplay (3.2) about how much he would like to lie with Ophelia's nothing, her death(nothing)-breeding genitals (nothing).

The state of the union (political, matrimonial) that words like "Lamord" symbolize is epitomized not only in the incestuous union of Gertrude and Claudius—their love is the elder Hamlet's death—but also in the pearled "union" (5.2.269) that joins and unjoins the lovers. "Union" is both union (marriage jewel) and disunion (poison), a *liebestod* that reengages the paradoxically inseminating poison of the primal scene/murder scene. "Union" is one of Freud's uncanny "un" words whose primal sense is antithetical, both itself and not itself.[43] This doubling dissolution is gendered (by men) as feminine, as that which introduces difference into male notions of self-identity predicated on self-sameness. As the union pearl is dissolved in the cup of wine, so too the royal place in the hierarchy which the union symbolizes—"the term is normally reserved for pearls of finest quality, such as might be in a royal crown" is the Arden editor's footnote (410)—is dissolved in death, reminding us of Hamlet's malcontent satire on the power of death to undo social as well as sexual distinction by making common the king and the commoner:[44] "a king may go a progress through the guts of a beggar" (4.3.30–31)[45] thanks to the anal reductionism of "impolitic worms," for which "your fat king and your lean beggar is but variable service, two dishes, but to one table" (4.3.23–24).[46] Since Hamlet has referred to himself as a beggar (2.2.272), in death he and Claudius will be indistinguishably incorpsed. The androgynous "Lady Worm" (5.1.87) is the phallic penetrator and oral, feminine devourer that reduces the courtier, lawyer, and jester, the mother and her son, to the same level as the commoner in the grave. As high is reduced to low on the axis of social status, so sexual distinctions are likewise undone in death, as in birth and intercourse. Their collapse is what sets off the chain of deaths in the play, which in turn viciously reestablishes the cycle of sexual nondifference (a corpse of whichever sex is still a just a corpse).

Critics have frequently remarked upon Hamlet's shift in character upon his return from England, usually describing it in terms of a new resolution and stoicism. I prefer instead to see in the later Hamlet someone who is far less anxious about the collapse of boundaries, to the point that he decides that there is but one way to resolve his formerly unresolved anxiety about nondifference: destroy difference via the massive implosion that death effects. The death that Hamlet once feared so obsessively ultimately becomes the lover he embraces (graphically symbolized when he enters Ophelia's grave). When Hamlet assumes the manly role of avenger in the final scene and realizes the fantasy playacting of Lucianus, he penetrates the feminized Claudius with his poisoned phallic sword. Revenge seeks by repetition of the primal scene to undo the original crime. But the compulsion to repeat engages as well the drive towards death, fulfilling Hamlet's prophetic sense that his realization of manhood was fated to achieve but a reductive quintessence of dust, a return to residual matter (*mater*). Hamlet's consummating manly gesture is vitiated in that the hero collapses again into his mother: like hers, his affiliation (union) with the husband-father, whom he has addressed as "mother," is fatally poisonous, a suicidal resolution figured as liquifying dissolve.[47] The androgynous sexual mixture[48] that consummately joins male and female, I have argued, is the indistinction of death. Death returns man to the undiscovered country whence he originated, the place where he and woman are joined (*foutre*) in a common fault or fold, cross-coupled in nondifference. It is through metaphors of "mixture," "jointure," and "union"—rendering the sexes "common"—that Shakespeare plays out the poisonous consequences of androgyny.

Notes

My epigraphs from this ambivalently androgynous actress are gleaned respectively from M. Maurice Shudofsky, "Sarah Bernhardt on *Hamlet*," *College English* 3 (1941): 293–95, and Marjorie Garber, *Vested Interests: Cross-Dressing and Cultural Anxiety* (New York: Routledge, 1992), 38. In *The Masks of Hamlet* (Newark: University of Delaware Press, 1992), 105–6, Marvin Rosenberg offers a cento of original reviews of Bernhardt's 1899 performance, from which it appears that the ambivalent critics were roughly evenly divided on the issue of whether her Hamlet tended more (or too much) towards the masculine or the feminine. Marcel Pagnol suggested that since Hamlet "does not have the reflexes of a man," perhaps his theatrical role better suits a woman: "Hamlet is for me, without any doubt, a *philosophe d'un sexe douteux* whose role could be perfectly played by a great *comedienne*." (Quoted in Norman Holland, *Psychoanalysis and Shakespeare* [New York: Farrar, Strauss and Giroux, 1979], 183.)

1. Ernest Jones, *Hamlet and Oedipus* (Garden City: Doubleday, 1949), 25–26. Jacqueline Rose, "Hamlet—the *Mona Lisa* of Literature," *Critical Quarterly* 28 (1986): 35–49.

Androgynous "Union" and the Woman in Hamlet   91

2. See Mircea Eliade, *The Two and the One*, trans. J. M. Cohen (Chicago: University of Chicago, 1965); June Singer, *Androgyny: Towards a New Theory of Sexuality* (Garden City, N.Y.: Anchor, 1976); Carolyn Heilbrun, *Toward a Recognition of Androgyny* (New York: Knopf, 1973). Heilbrun defines androgyny as "a movement away from sexual polarization and the prison of gender toward a world in which individual roles and the modes of personal behavior can be freely chosen" (ix). This early champion of androgyny believes that Hamlet's tragedy consists in having to eschew androgyny and destroy Ophelia, his saving feminine self, in order to accomplish the manly task of vengeance. See also Heilbrun's more recent discussion in *Hamlet's Mother* (New York: Columbia University Press, 1990).

3. David Leverenz makes the most persuasive case for the beneficent value of Hamlet's feminine side in his influential essay, "The Woman in Hamlet: An Interpersonal View," in *Representing Shakespeare*, eds. Murray Schwartz and Coppélia Kahn (Baltimore: Johns Hopkins University Press, 1980). "Hamlet is part hysteric, as Freud said, and part Puritan in his disgust at contamination and his idealization of his absent father. But he is also, as Goethe was the first to say, part woman. And Goethe was wrong, as Freud was wrong, to assume that 'woman' means weakness. To equate women with weak and tainted bodies, words, and feelings while men possess noble reason and ambitious purpose is to participate in Denmark's disease that divides mind from body, act from feeling, man from woman" (111). In *Shakespeare's Division of Experience* (New York: Summit Books, 1981), Marilyn French concurs with Carolyn Heilbrun that action is the province of the man, whereas Hamlet's "primary response to experience is to 'feel' it—through sensation, emotion, or reflective thought. Hamlet's response to life, then, is 'feminine'" (147). In *The Mystery of Hamlet* (Philadelphia: J.B. Lippincott, 1881), the Victorian scholar Edward P. Vining made the first detailed argument for Hamlet as a woman, locating Hamlet's femininity in such features as his melancholy, playacting (masquerade), hysteria, faintness, mysteriousness, gentleness, wordy poetizing, (feigned) madness, lack of strength or courage to act—features "that are far more in keeping with a feminine than with a masculine nature" (48). Vining thought that Hamlet was in fact a woman disguised at birth as a man, like Ovid's Iphis, because Gertrude knew that her husband wanted a boy. From his mother's disguise of him as a girl, Hamlet learned "dissimulation" (82). The following toss-off is typical of Vining's tendentiousness: "Hamlet has a woman's daintiness and sensitiveness to perfumes" (77).

4. Unless otherwise noted, all quotations from *Hamlet* are from the Arden edition of the play, ed. Harold Jenkins (New York: Routledge, 1982).

5. Margaret Ferguson discusses the conflation of mother and matter in "*Hamlet*: Letters and Spirits," in *Shakespeare and the Question of Theory*, eds. Patricia Parker and Geoffrey Hartman (New York: Methuen, 1985). Ferguson argues that the hysteria that Freud diagnosed in Hamlet results from the hero's maternal/material legacy: "As we hear or see in the word 'matter' the Latin term for mother, we may surmise that the common Renaissance association between female nature in general and the 'lower' realm of matter is here being deployed in the service of Hamlet's complex oedipal struggle. The mother is the matter that comes between the father and the son—and it is no accident that in this closet scene Hamlet's sexual hysteria rises to its highest pitch" (295). See also Patricia Parker, "*Othello* and *Hamlet*: Dilation, Spying, and the 'Secret Place' of Woman," *Representations* 44 (Fall 1993): 60–95.

6. In lieu of the Folio's *scullion*, the reading printed in the Arden edition, I opt tendentiously for the Second Quarto's *stallion* = "male whore," a choice of

words that better fits Hamlet's sense of compromised masculinity. The animal virility suggested by *stallion* is undercut by the reference to prostitution which Hamlet and *Hamlet* associate with women.

7. In his commentary on the function of language in Lacan, Mikkel Borch-Jacobsen points to the way speech disengages the speaker from the present immediacy of intuition, absenting the object that speech intends to capture by naming it, and thereby opening up a loss within the speaker himself that makes of him a subject. "The subject speak[s] in order to say nothing: 'Words, words, words. . . .' Speech, instead of saying something, now speaks itself and thus speaks the truth, which is precisely that speech says nothing—nothing other than the 'hole in the real' that is the subject at the moment when he speaks" (139). Naming the object leaves in its wake "nothing but words, words, words—*that is, a subject*" (193). *Lacan: The Absolute Master*, trans. Douglas Brick (Stanford, Calif.: Stanford University Press, 1991). The "nothing" that the subject speaks is gendered feminine in Hamlet's bawdy remarks to Ophelia during the play within the play. For the male, to become a subject is to fall under the sign of woman.

At a spring 1994 symposium at Berkeley on "Rhetorics of Early Modern Masculinity," Patricia Parker spoke about the efforts of Renaissance authors to achieve stylistic *virilitas*. Their goal was a sinewy (*nervosus*) style, which these anti-Ciceronian rhetoricians attempted to ground in the male body (*nervus* = "penis"). But no male could express a virile style in words whose *lingua*-derived *copia* was gendered feminine. In the epistle dedicatory to his *A Worlde of Wordes* (1598), John Florio commented anxiously on the emblematic proverb, "*Le parole sono feminine, & i fatti sono maschii*, Wordes they are women, and deeds they are men." Like Hamlet, Florio sensed his project for a virile style hopelessly compromised by its imbrication and entrapment in woman's textual web. See Parker's essay, "On the Tongue: Cross Gendering, Effeminacy, and the Art of Words," *Style* 23.3 (1989): 445–65. Here Parker demonstrates how Erasmus' *Lingua* treatise (1525) associates the loquacious male with the "loud and babbling harlot" of Proverbs 7, a passage relevant to Hamlet's self-characterization as a wordy whore. Parker discusses the way that Erasmus prefers manly *brevitas* to excessive verbal *copia*: "The arts of rhetoric as devices for amplifying a theme ('*amplificandi rationes*') are not only contrasted with deeds but linked to a loquacity gendered as 'foolish and womanish' ('*stultam ac muliebrem loquacitatem*')" (449).

8. My contention that the male fears being compromised and contaminated by his dependency upon the mother's body is deeply indebted to Janet Adelman's *Suffocating Mothers: Fantasies of Maternal Origin in Shakespeare's Plays*, Hamlet to The Tempest (New York: Routledge, 1992). Adelman argues that the feminine presence that divides Hamlet's male identity is the mother regarded as whore: "He himself is subject to his birth: he would imagine himself the unmixed son of an unmixed father, but the whore-mother in him betrays him, returning him to his own mixed [*mixture* = "sexual intercourse" (OED 1e)] origin, his contamination by the sexual female within" (30).

9. I owe to Joel Altman the tenor of my remarks about the way that *res* and *verbum* reverse the gender hierarchy of spirit over matter.

10. Erasmus' *Lingua* begins with a proverb that suggests that the verbose male is he who has sucked too long at the mother's breast: "*Ubi uber, ibi tuber; fatti maschii, parole femine*" ("Where there is a breast, there is a swelling; facts are masculine, words are feminine") (460; quoted in Parker).

11. The son's loss of the father results in the impossible duty to restore him, to avenge the dead by undoing the adulterous usurpation of Claudius and Gertrude.

12. In the closing chapter of *The Gendering of Melancholia* (Ithaca: Cornell

University Press, 1992), Juliana Schiesari analyzes the male's scapegoating of woman in *Hamlet*, Burton's *The Anatomy of Melancholy*, and Freud's works. "The melancholic's desire for the father's gaze is concomitant to and inseparable from a profound denigration of women, who are typically accused of all the horrible things the melancholic can also accuse himself of: duplicity, inconstancy, inhumanity, animality, and base materiality. Obviously, the melancholic projects on women the lack that he would deny in himself, except of course when he addresses himself in the voice of his own superego" (239). This observation leads to a reading of Burton that is relevant as well to my dissection of Hamlet: "In diagnosing, as Freud too would, the female melancholic as phallicly needy, Burton blushingly foregrounds his own sexual deprivation, his own 'unmanliness.' Much later, in discussing love melancholia, Burton does not mince words when he says outright that melancholia 'turns a man into a woman' (3: 142)" (252). Hamlet suffers from an inversion of love melancholy since the woman in him makes him too disillusioned to love any woman. In "Mourning and Melancholia" (*Standard Edition of the Complete Psychological Works of Sigmund Freud*, trans. and ed. James Strachey [London: Hogarth Press, 1955–74], 14: 239–58), Freud instances Hamlet's melancholia, his self-reproaches and suicidal impulses, as the turning against his own ego of a repressed hostility towards a once loved object. The ambivalently cathected object is introjected, i.e., internalized as the ego's own object, as opposed to the release of the object that occurs in mourning. Julia Reinhard Lupton and Kenneth Lupton invoke Lacan's reading of Freud in arguing that whereas *Oedipus Rex* ends with the recognition of castration, *Hamlet* begins with it. Hamlet is like a little girl, they assert, in recognizing castration immediately: "Since the little girl is mourning something that was never there in the first place, we would argue that her relation to the phallus is melancholic rather than mournful. We could say that she *mourns mourning*—that is, that she mourns the lack of any real object that could be mourned, or, more precisely, that she mourns the lack of a lack that could be restored." *After Oedipus: Shakespeare in Psychoanalysis* (Ithaca: Cornell University Press, 1993), 56. Janet Adelman takes issue with "critics who use the model of Freud's 'Mourning and Melancholia' [who] generally assume that the lost object is Hamlet's father; but Hamlet's discovery of the whore inside himself suggests that the lost, introjected, and then berated object is his mother" (256–57). See also Ranjini Philip, "The Shattered Glass: The Story of (O)phelia," *Hamlet Studies* 13 (1991): 73–84.

13. In "Creativity and its Origins," D. W. Winnicott anticipates Carolyn Heilbrun (see n.3 above) in arguing that the male and female elements in Hamlet are in harmony until his father dies. Thereafter he rejects the female and projects it onto Ophelia, whom he then maligns for her femininity. *Playing and Reality* (New York: Routledge, 1971).

14. Avi Erlich regards the "flesh" in this speech as a representation of the "solid" penis, which Hamlet wishes poured out orgasmically "into a dew." *Hamlet's Absent Father* (Princeton: Princeton University Press, 1977), 65. Erlich's analysis is at times stretched and tendentious, but his book remains probably the most detailed compendium of psychoanalytic readings of the play.

15. See the essay by this name, S. E. II: 155–61.

16. Julia Reinhard Lupton and Kenneth Lupton comment on the identification of Hamlet with Niobe: "Niobe, becoming her tears, is a favored Renaissance figure of narcissistic identification with loss; she thus becomes an image of the melancholic petrification to which Hamlet and *Hamlet* are subject. Niobe's metamorphosis materializes the watery fate imagined in the soliloquy's opening line" (115).

17. At several points in *The Interpretation of Dreams* (S. E. 4 & 5), Freud discusses water as a dream element that symbolizes woman, especially with regard to male fantasies of birth and of returning to the womb.

18. Laertes appeals to the blood/tears opposition in defending the incorruptibility of his descent and the chastity of his mother:

> That drop of blood that's calm proclaims me bastard,
> Cries cuckold to my father, brands me harlot
> Even here between the chaste unsmirched brow
> Of my true mother.
>
> (4.5.116–20)

This confidence about origins contrasts with Hamlet's nagging fear that Gertrude may have cuckolded King Hamlet and so have branded her son a bastard and a harlot.

19. In a series of articles Patricia Parker has argued the centrality for Shakespearean tragedy of "dilation" in the rhetorical and temporal senses, as well as in the sense of delation or accusation. I use the word to describe how Hamlet's delay in the midst of resolution leads to self-accusation; dilation engenders delation. See especially Parker's "Shakespeare and Rhetoric: 'Dilation' and 'Delation' in *Othello*," in *Shakespeare and the Question of Theory*, eds. Patricia Parker and Geoffrey Hartman (London: Methuen, 1985): 54–74.

20. Again the relevant foil for Hamlet is Laertes, whose deeds in defense of his slain father contrast with Hamlet's soliloquizing. Claudius rouses Laertes to action by appealing to the bad example of Hamlet: "But to the quick of th'ulcer: / Hamlet comes back; what would you undertake / To show yourself in deed your father's son / More than in words?" (4.7.122–24). The wordy son is the mother's son who can only rail ineffectually against bastardy, whereas the father's son is a man who vindicates his legitimacy in deed.

21. Even at the zero degree of etymology, some critics have construed the word "conscience" to express an irreconcilable sexual divide, since it may allude in its first syllable to the female genitalia, while its independent root designates disembodied mind. In his edition of Shakespeare's sonnets (New Haven: Yale University Press, 1977), Stephen Booth glosses "conscience" in Sonnet 151 as "cunt knowledge." "Any word with *con* in it appears to have invited Shakespeare and his contemporaries (see Congreve, *con* and *noc*) to play on the commonest name for the female sex organ" (526). Other critics who comment on the sexual sense of "conscience" are Erlich, *Hamlet's Absent Father* 188, 229–30, and Parker, "*Othello* and *Hamlet*: Dilation, Spying, and the 'Secret Place' of Woman," 83.

22. In her Foucault-inspired account of madness as that which opposes rational closure, Karin S. Coddon anatomizes the "feminization of madness" (392) in the play. "Suche Strange Desyngns': Madness, Subjectivity, and Treason in *Hamlet* and Elizabethan Culture," in the edition of Hamlet edited by Susanne L. Wofford (Boston: Bedford Books, 1994): 380–402. For a critical history of madness, love melancholy, and hysteria in connection with Ophelia, see Elaine Showalter, "Representing Ophelia: Women, Madness, and the Responsibilities of Feminist Criticism," in *Shakespeare and the Question of Theory*, eds. Patricia Parker and Geoffrey Hartman (New York: Methuen, 1985): 77–94.

23. Juliana Schiesari surveys the way that melancholy from Aristotle to Freud has been associated with male genius, whereas women have been relegated to the realm of unproductive mourning. (See especially the introductory chapter of *The Gendering of Melancholia*.) I argue, however, that Hamlet's melancholy is at times figured as feminine and productive, not exclusively as feminine and debilitating.

24. Erlich is perhaps not at his credible best when he offers an analysis of the sexual oscillation in this passage in terms of erection and detumescence: "'His golden couplets disclosed' strikes me as a possible though disguised reference to ejaculation, with 'couplets' referring to Hamlet's testicles and 'disclosed' to an orgasmic bursting out. Similarly, 'His silence will sit drooping' seems a description of a post-coital penis" (*Hamlet's Absent Father* 176). Erlich calls ejaculation what I describe as parturition.

25. Peter Erickson contrasts the feminine side of Hamlet manifested in his soliloquies with the male element foregrounded in Hamlet's relationship with Horatio. By the end of the play it is Horatio whom Hamlet asks to perpetuate his memory, as opposed to the usual means of passing on one's legacy by linking with a woman who in turn gives birth to a male heir. Since Gertrude's conduct corrupts the ideal of motherhood, Erickson argues, Hamlet turns to the chaste, passionless Horatio instead. "In a world where love between men and women has become irrevocably duplicitous, sexuality can be avoided by turning to male ties to fashion a dependable bond." *Patriarchal Structures in Shakespeare's Drama* (Berkeley: University of California Press, 1985), 77. If Hamlet and Horatio are soulmates and the anima is gendered feminine, however, this would indicate that the male-male bond does not so much escape the feminine as sublimate it by abstracting it from the body.

26. See Adelman, *Suffocating Mothers* (252–53) for the way that the play inscribes woman's responsibility for moral fault in her material body. "Fault" was a slang term for the female genitals, and the French *foutre* = "sexual intercourse" was pronounced the same way.

27. Ophelia remarked earlier upon Hamlet's "unmatch'd form and feature of blown youth / Blasted with ecstasy" (3.1.161–62). Ex-stasis defines madness as eccentricity, the alienation of the self from its rational center.

28. For the double valence of "crown," see Valerie Traub, *Desire and Anxiety: Circulations of Sexuality in Shakespearean Drama* (New York: Routledge, 1992), 30.

29. Coppélia Kahn, *Man's Estate: Masculine Identity in Shakespeare* (Berkeley, University of California Press, 1981), 135. In opposition to Kahn's view of the ear as a vaginal analogue, it is also possible to regard the murder as an act motivated by homosexual jealousy ("the primal eldest curse . . . A brother's murder" [3.3.37–38]) with the ear as locus of anal penetration. Jonathan Goldberg critiques what he regards as Kahn's compulsory heterosexism in "*Romeo and Juliet's* Open Rs," in *Queering the Renaissance*, ed. Jonathan Goldberg (Durham, N.C.: Duke University Press, 1994). In the same anthology, Richard Rambuss' "Pleasure and Devotion: The Body of Jesus and Seventeenth-Century Religious Lyric" cautions against the uncritical assumption, popular among heterosexist critics, that any penetrated body must be a female one, and that the site of entry is necessarily vaginal. Richard Crashaw, for example, imagines the wounds that penetrate Christ's body on the cross in homoerotic terms. In "The Death of Hamlet's Father" (*Essays in Applied Psychoanalysis* [London: Hogarth, 1951], I, 323–28), Ernest Jones argues that the poison is semen, the ear a displaced anus, so a homosexual rape is at issue. Norman Holland sums up the debate as follows: "One need not choose between heterosexual or homosexual insemination for, in the unconscious, there is no negation. Rather, both apply; and the fact that the symbol is ambiguous suggests an ambiguity in the play's presentation, one that reaches to an early level of infantile confusions" (194). Context must determine symbolic usage, so it may be plausible to see the ear of the original murder as a homoerotic locus, while its replay in *The Murder of Gonzago* foregrounds the hetero sex act as murderous-castrating.

The critics' lack of consensus over anal versus vaginal interpretations may reflect the ambiguously oscillating, androgynous orientation of the text itself.

30. See Alexander Grinstein, "The Dramatic Device: A Play Within a Play," in *The Design Within: Psychoanalytic Approaches to Shakespeare*, ed. M. D. Faber (New York: Science House, 1970), 147–53. Grinstein believes that the play within the play follows the same laws as Freud's analysis of the dream within a dream: it is an attempt to undo a past event.

31. In "*Othello* and *Hamlet*: Dilation, Spying, and the 'Secret Place' of Woman," Patricia Parker comments on these two references—"conscience" and "nothing"—to the woman in Claudius. Of the first she says that catching the King's conscience "elicits the 'con- ,' count, or euphemistic 'country matter' lurking within this monarchical 'con-science' and its closeted secrets" (83).

32. Central to Janet Adelman's argument is Hamlet's fantasy of Gertrude as the phantom murderer of Claudius: "The playlet is in fact designed to catch the conscience of the queen" (31).

33. This is Cavell's summary comment in *Disowning Knowledge* (Cambridge: Cambridge University Press, 1987): "One's belief in Gertrude's power is surely not lessened if in constructing the primal scene from the fantasy/dumb-show one finds a man collapsing not upon her pouring something into him but upon her having something poured into her (the reversal of passive into active)" (185).

34. Avi Erlich is the critic who writes most extensively about the castration of King Hamlet in the primal scene. See especially chapter four of *Hamlet's Absent Father*. For textual evidence of castration, one may point to King Hamlet's lament that he was "cut off even in the blossoms of my sin" (1.5.76) and his injunction to Hamlet to "Remember me" (1.5.91), which suggests that the son is called upon to restore (re-member) the father's missing phallus.

35. The "common place" is what in *King Lear* Edgar calls the "indistinguish'd space of woman's will" (4.6.273), where "will" refers both to volition and to the genitalia. Desdemona's fetishistic handkerchief, associated metonymically with her private parts, is said to be a "common thing" (3.3.302), and in the brothel scene Othello addresses his wife as a "public commoner" (4.2.73). Troilus's misogyny similarly points to the way that his Cressida is common to everyone because she makes her "thing" public, open to all comers.

> This is, and is not, Cressid.
> Within my soul there doth conduce a fight
> Of this strange nature that a thing inseparate
> Divides more wider than the sky and earth.
>
> (5.2.143–46)

Lars Eagle suggests (*Shakespearean Pragmatism: Market of his Time* [Chicago: University of Chicago Press, 1993], 238n.) that Ophelia regards Hamlet in much the way that Troilus sees himself divided when he regards himself reflected in Cressida. Ophelia's "O woe is me / T' have seen what I have seen, see what I see" (3.1.152) might be paraphrased as "This is and is not Hamlet." In Hamlet's eyes, he is divided because he sees Ophelia as double (duplicitous), chaste and not chaste. In *A Theater of Envy* (Oxford University Press, 1991), René Girard asserts that Ophelia is "contaminated with the erotic strategy of a Cressida and the other least savory Shakespearean heroines. What Hamlet resents in Ophelia is what any human being always resents in another human being, the visible signs of his own sickness" (285). Cressida and Ophelia are both objects of a misogynistic gaze that sees double when it sees woman, because it sees woman as common and therefore duplicitous. See also the discussion of "common" in Parker's *Representations* article.

36. To anyone familiar with his work, Joel Fineman's influence on my reading of duplicitous desire will be apparent. Fineman contrasts the giddy and playful androgyny of Shakespeare's transvestite heroines to the untransvested, unveiled duplicity of Gertrude: "Symmetrical desire, a structure of homosexual jealousy that is resolved in the comedies by apportioning out to each pair of rivals a matching pair of beloveds, is precisely what we have unresolved in *Hamlet*, where, correspondingly, we might say woman herself, as woman, because her name is 'frailty'—is the image of androgyny." "Fratricide and Cuckoldry: Shakespeare's Doubles," in *Representing Shakespeare*, 82. Fineman argues that woman's androgyny becomes the mirror for man's difference from himself: "The dialectic of Difference and No Difference contained by the original fratricide structure is transferred by Shakespeare to another formula of mirroring reciprocity, to themes of women and their 'frailty,' to a kind of masculine misogyny that finds in the ambiguity of woman its own self-divided self-consciousness, its own vulnerability, its mortality" (89). In *Shakespeare's Perjured Eye: The Invention of Poetic Subjectivity in the Sonnets* (Berkeley, University of California Press, 1986), Fineman accounts for the difference between genders as originating in the feminine: "In a formula whose lusty misogyny is recognizably Shakespearean, we can say that in Shakespeare's sonnets the difference between man and woman is woman herself" (17). In a typical Neoplatonic schema, man is figured as the sun, woman as the moon, in service of an "orthodox erotics for which woman is the Other to man, the *hetero* to *homo*, precisely because her essence is *to be* this lunatic difference between sameness and difference" (120).

37. *King Lear* makes explicit the way that sex and death coalesce in woman's vaginal hell: "But to the girdle do the gods inherit, / Beneath is all the fiend's. / There's hell, there's darkness, there is the sulphurous pit; burning, scalding, stench, consumption" (4.6.125–28).

38. For woman's antithetical symbolization of both life and death, see Freud's essays, "The Theme of the Three Caskets" and "The Uncanny," in *On Creativity and the Unconscious*, ed. Benjamin Nelson (New York: Harper & Row, 1958).

39. Much of my meditation on Lamord is indebted to Ferguson, "Hamlet: Letters and Spirits," 298–304. As an especially apt instance of the "Lamord" wordplay, Ferguson quotes the epigraph to chapter 15 of Stendhal's *Le Rouge et le Noir*:

> Amour en latin faict amor;
> Or donc provient d'amour la mort,
> Et par avant, soulcy qui mord,
> Deuils, plours, pieges, forfaitz, remords.

40. Valerie Traub argues that the only certifiably chaste woman is a dead woman. In life Ophelia is suspect because she is mobile and open, whereas in death her closure and immobility secure her chastity, thus making her available for the first time as an object worthy of Hamlet's romantic love (25–33). This conception of a safely enclosed because dead Ophelia is at odds with Patricia Parker's analysis in her *Representations* article. "In contrast to the 'natural modesty' of women reported in Pliny and repeated in Crooke, Ophelia, in the 'melodious lay' (4.7.182–83) of her drowning, floats more openly, face up, 'her clothes spread wide' (175) in lines the ear may hear, given other such Shakespearean instances, as the spreading 'wide' of her '*close*'" (75). Parker glosses "spread" as "open for copulation." Traub completely ignores the pronounced sexual innuendo of Ophelia's death song: maids who open their "chamber doors" in losing their

virginity (4.5.53), and the many phallic references to young men who "do't if they come to't— / By Cock, they are to blame" (60–61), to "sweet Robin" (4.5.184), and to the death garlands of "long purples" or "dead men's fingers" (4.7.168–71). In dying Ophelia is foul (phallic)-mouthed, thus anything but closed-mouthed. For the chaste as dead woman, see also Carol Thomas Neely, *Broken Nuptials in Shakespeare's Plays* (New Haven: Yale University Press, 1985). Peter Stallybrass gives a brilliant reading of open versus closed women's bodies in "Patriarchal Territories: The Body Enclosed," in *Rewriting the Renaissance*, eds. Margaret Ferguson, Maureen Quilligan, and Nancy Vickers (Chicago: University of Chicago Press, 1986): 123–42.

41. It is a measure of Laertes's ingenuous fatuity that he forgets his two earlier conversations in which violets are associated with the fading of love and death (1.3.5–10, 4.5.180–83). In this quotation from act 5 as well as in Shakespeare's Ovidian poetry, the purpled violet may suggest graphically and etymologically love's wound as consequence of phallic violation (violets/violence).

42. Rhetorically, the elegiac cast that Gertrude gives to the shadowing of love by death corresponds to the isocolonic and oxymoronic formalism of Claudius, which also yokes contraries together in order to repress their contariety:

> Therefore our sometime sister, now our queen,
> Th'imperial jointress to this warlike state,
> Have we, as 'twere with a defeated joy,
> With an auspicious and a dropping eye,
> With mirth in funeral and with dirge in marriage,
> In equal scale weighing delight and dole,
> Taken to wife.
>
> (1.2.8–14)

This facile reconciliation of opposites via juxtaposition, this specious balancing of equal and homologous units (isocolon), is the object of Hamlet's critique, whose preferred rhetorical mode employs paronomasia to subvert and satirize isocolon. Of course Hamlet wants his own set of tidy moral contraries, provided that they not be reconciled. For discussion of Claudius's use of isocolon, see Stephen Booth, "On the Value of *Hamlet*," in *Reinterpretations of Elizabethan Drama*, ed. Norman Rabkin (New York: Columbia University Press, 1969), esp. 148–149, and Ferguson, 292–93.

43. James Calderwood discusses "union" in terms of the frequent "hyphenisation of relations that leads to the total undifferentiation" in phrases like "uncle-father" and "aunt-mother" (2.2.372), and in Hamlet's confusing address of his (step)father as his "mother." "All such repellent, hyphenised 'unions' flow poisonously into the cup from which Gertrude drinks in the final scene and which Hamlet forces upon the already dying Claudius with the words, 'Drink off this poison. Is thy union here?' (5.2.331). Hamlet's killing of Claudius is, in this context, an act of restorative destruction, an undoing of unions that came into existence not through the linking of like to like but through the disintegration of proper differences." *To Be and Not To Be: Negation and Metadrama in "Hamlet"* (New York: Columbia University Press, 1983), 63. This returns me to my earlier invocation of René Girard's notion that the only way Hamlet can establish his difference from the feminine (the hymenated hyphenization) is by means of effecting masculine violence.

44. Steven Mullaney argues that because the playhouses were set in the marginal Liberties of London, the drama was able to arrogate to itself the license of having common men impersonate kings. Defenses of hierarchical degree, like

Ulysses's famous speech in *Troilus and Cressida*, were evacuated by virtue of their parodic-representational frame; hence, difference was made common. *The Place of the Stage: License, Play, and Power in Renaissance England* (Chicago: University of Chicago Press, 1988), esp. 51–52.

45. Francis Barker comments that this line "is extraordinary (if it is so at all) for its insistence on the democracy of mortality in contrast with the hierarchized body politic of the living world, not for the corporeal expression in which the idea emerges." *The Tremulous Private Body* (London: Methuen, 1984), 23.

46. Lalita Pandit points out that in the *Saxo Grammaticus* tale, when Amleth is questioned regarding the whereabouts of the eavesdropper (the unnamed Polonius figure) whom he has killed, he replies that "the man had gone to the sewer, but had fallen through its bottom and been stifled by the floods of filth, and that he had been devoured by the swine that came up all about the place." In Shakespeare's play Hamlet responds to Claudius's inquiry about where Polonius is by saying, "At supper. . . . Not where he eats, but where a is eaten" (4.3.17, 19). The homology of "supper" and "sewer," of eating and defecating, suggests a cannibalistic relationship between master and source texts as well as between living and dead bodies. "Language and the Textual Unconscious: Shakespeare, Ovid, and Saxo Grammaticus," in *Criticism and Lacan*, eds. Patrick Colm Hogan and Lalita Pandit (Athens: University of Georgia Press, 1990): 248–67 (264). The corpse of Alexander may be food for worms but also fecal dust used to stop a "bung-hole" (=anus, *OED* 6) (4.1.198).

47. In *Psychoanalysis and Shakespeare*, Norman Holland writes: "The finale, in which Hamlet and his mother die together, projects the wish to 'die' with the mother, to return to her womb in a sexual way" (167). A counterpoint to the union of mother and son that death effects results when Gertrude drinks the poisoned union wine: she gives the lie to the union that her imperial jointure posited, since her death uncovers the differential severing that any jointure presupposes, the separation by death (of/from one's betrayed spouse) that jointure aims to repress.

48. In *Suffocating Mothers*, Janet Adelman points out that union is just another version of Hecate's "mixture rank" (3.2.251), the poison that kills Hamlet's father: "Each is the poisonous epitome of sexual mixture itself and hence of boundary danger, the terrifying adulteration of male by female that does away with the boundaries between them" (28).

Interlinear Trysting and "household stuff": The Latin Lesson and the Domestication of Learning in *The Taming of the Shrew*

Thomas Moisan

Sly.   Is not
a comonty a Christmas gambold, or a tumbling-trick?
Page. No, my good lord, it is more pleasing stuff.
Sly. What, household stuff?
Page. It is a kind of history.
Sly.   Well, we'll see't.
                    (*Taming of the Shrew*, Induction 2.137–42)[1]

. . . .
Titus. Soft, so busily she turns the leaves! Help her.
What would she find? Lavinia, shall I read?
This is the tragic tale of Philomel,
And treats of Tereus' treason and his rape—
And rape, I fear, was root of thy annoy.
. . . .
Demetrius. What's here? a scroll, and written round about.
Let's see:
[Reads] "Integer vitae, scelerisque purus,
         Non eget Mauri jaculis, nec arcu."
Chiron. O, 'tis a verse in Horace, I know it well,
I read it in the grammar long ago.
                    (*Titus Andronicus*, 4.1.45–49, 4.2.18–23)

T HAT THERE ARE ADVANTAGES to knowing one's Ovid, and that there are, conversely, considerable disadvantages in having forgotten one's Horace, and that there is dramatic capital to be made out of both facts are all truths Shakespeare put to use in *Titus Andronicus*, and from which in contexts and with consequences less grim, he derives profit in other plays, where characters operating from positions of linguistic inequality negotiate unevenly with each other along the linguistic and cultural frontier of translation. We have a celebrated example of the political uses of such inequality and translation in Henry's courtship of Katherine in *Henry V* (5.2.98–280), a memorably comic Latin grammar-cum-Welsh pronunciation lesson in *The Merry Wives of Windsor* (4.1.7–85), and a less celebrated but no less interesting tutorial in the scene that provides the locus of this paper, the Latin lesson of 3.1 in *The Taming of the Shrew*, the exchange between Lucentio and Bianca in which Lucentio, scion of the conventional "devious lover" figure Shakespeare inherited from his putative source Gascoigne and through him Italian and Roman comedy,[2] is disguised as a Latin tutor and seeks to court Bianca both under the increasingly anxious surveillance of his disguised rival and pseudomusic tutor Hortensio and, literally, "between the lines" of the Ovidian text he pretends to be teaching her. It is a scene less notable for what happens than for what does *not* happen: for the language instruction not given, for the translation of Ovid not made, and for the seduction of Bianca that gets at least partially deflected and deferred; and it derives a good measure of its humor from our sense of it as an exercise in pedagogical harassment and manipulation thwarted, manipulation of a literal sort if, following the suggestion of at least one editor, we include Hortensio's overly zealous fingering exercises as part of what gets thwarted,[3] manipulation of a more subtle and intellectual kind in the form of Lucentio's attempt to exploit his position as tutor, not only to gain access to Bianca, but to use the very foreignness of the Latin text, and the powerful license of the translator both to disregard what the text says and make it say what he wants it to say, as a mask and vehicle for his overture to Bianca, interpolating seduction both between *and* in place of the lines.

In what is to follow I would suggest that precisely for all that does not happen in it, the "translation" scene offers an illumination of the play of which it would seem but a marginal moment and of the social issues and tensions that traverse that play. When read against the backdrop of contemporary concerns over the uses and abuses of learning, particularly classical learning, and especially when applied to the education of women, the scene presents a travesty of what happens when learning and what Sly calls "household stuff" collide,[4] when Latin becomes a part of Baptista's domestic decor and an extension of his attempt to keep his daughters a part of that decor. At the same time, in a play set so self-consciously in a "foreign" land, the Latin lesson exemplifies the uses of things foreign, and in particular the domestication of foreign language, throughout the play, offering a comic peek at the acculturating power of translation, and a comic rehearsal of that process of cultural expropriation in which Nietzsche would assign translation a central part, whereby a culture "*vergangene Zeiten und Bucher sich einzuverleiben sucht,*" "seeks to embody past epochs and books into its own being."[5]

Above all, however, in the degree to which it could be argued that the translation scene contributes to Bianca's social development, it evokes contemporary critics' worst fears about the corruptive potential of learning in general and theater in particular, and recalls other moments in the *Shrew* in which the play seems at once to embrace a didactic function only to allegorize its own didactic insufficiency and insincerity,[6] its very indebtedness to the conventions of Roman comedy a cheerful affiliation with a form cited by detractors and apologists of the stage alike in debating the role of plays, and plays in translation, in propagating "family values." So it is, for example, that in the Prologue to his "prodigal son" play, *The Glasse of Gouernement (1575)*, George Gascoigne, whose *Supposes* is commonly taken as one of the sources of Shakespeare's *Shrew*, simultaneously proclaims his play a morally instructive "tragicall Comedie" and renounces the very tradition by which a play like *Supposes* had been nourished:

> A comedie, I meane for to present,
> No *Terence* phrase: his tyme and mine are twaine:
> The verse that pleasde a *Romaine* rashe intente,
> Might well offend the godly Preachers vayne.[7]

On the other hand, in the Dedication of the 1598 printing by John Legate of Terence's translated plays, Terence, presented as "a Latin author taught to speake English," is alliteratively hailed as "a comicall Poet pithie, pleasant, and very profitable," whose "fraudulent flatterer," "grimme and greedie old Sire," "roysting ruffian," "minsing mynion," and "beastly bawd" were all intended by their creator, and translated into English, to show us how "to avoid such vices, and learne to practise vertue," so that the readers of these plays may safely "vse them, & not as most doe such autors, abuse them."[8]

Indeed, purveying seduction under the cloak of learning, the translation scene might be taken to epitomize what Philip Stubbes saw as the peculiarly pedagogical mendacity of theater, which Stubbes derides with incantatory vehemence, not simply for its failure to inculcate the good it pretends to teach, but for its success in teaching "al kinde of sinne and mischeef": "if you will learne cosenage: if you will learne to deceiue: if you will learne to play the Hipocrit: to cogge, lye and falsuffie: if you will learne ... to sing and talke of bawdie loue and venery ... you neede to goe to no other schoole, for all these good Examples, may you see painted before your eyes in enterludes and playes."[9] In short, in a play the central fable of which concerns and celebrates the "taming of a shrew," the domestication of learning in the translation lesson might well be "constered" as a practicum and frame for the training of a shrew.

And, to be sure, read simply as a piece of dramatic action, the scene stands as a "defining moment" in the relationship of Lucentio and Bianca and in the representation of Bianca's character, with the dynamics of the exchange an adumbration of what Lucentio will and, more significantly, will *not* gain by the end of the play, and with Bianca's behavior the first clear indication that she is not the passive "blank" her name suggests and everyone, or, rather, every male, seems to suppose. In turn, the scene has invited interpretive comment as but exhibit "A" in a reading of the play that would take the relationship of Lucentio and Bianca as but a transparent foil for and vindication of the relationship of Petruchio and Katherina, and, *pace* Stubbes, would "conster" Bianca's education as mis-education and license for connubial corruption, her classroom a school for the wrong kind of wife.[10]

Nor, though, does the significance of the scene end there. For in a play that, as Marianne L. Novy has put it, "gives lip service to patriarchy and victory to youth,"[11] the genuinely undercover advances of Lucentio, bearing a text intoning the ruination *Priami regia celsa senis* (3.1.29), of "the lofty palace of Priam the *ancient*" [italics mine],[12] "beguile" and subvert the intentions of two representatives of the older set: the patriarch Baptista, whose professed and self-congratulatory desire to be "liberal" in his daughters' upbringing leads him to bring "[s]choolmasters" into his house in the first place (1.1.91–99); and the "old pantaloon" Gremio, who funds his own amatory undoing by providing his rival Lucentio with both the access and the erotic instructional materials through which to court Bianca in his employer's stead (1.2.144–47). So too, in its use of a Latin lesson as camouflage for Lucentio's pursuit of Bianca, the translation scene epitomizes the uses, or misuses, to which education and formal "learning" are put throughout the play, with educational projects and the value of learning invoked only to be genially disregarded, subordinated to other plans, or simply, and just as genially, trashed, the ridicule to which they are subjected personified in the stock figure of the hapless, and perhaps spurious "Pedant" who fecklessly wanders into the play just in time to provide fodder for one of the "wily servant" Tranio's schemes.[13] "O this learning, what a thing it is," the deluded Gremio exclaims as the disguised and newly hired Lucentio promises to use all of the "words" at his scholarly disposal, and in the books Gremio has provided, to "plead" love to Bianca; "O this woodcock," notes Grumio in editorial aside, "what an ass it is" (1.2.159–60). Let's not be "so devote to Aristotle's checks / As Ovid be an outcast quite abjured" (1.1.32–33), the canny Tranio admonishes his master, Lucentio, upon their arrival in Padua at the outset of Act 1, as the latter declares his commitment to study with a becoming junior-year-abroad zeal and comparable credibility:[14] "In brief, sir, study what you most affect" (40), and Bianca's Latin lesson, with Ovid as primer, is the result.

Indeed, and much to our purpose here, in the degree to which the translation scene brings briefly to the foreground the treatment of education and formal learning in the Shrew, it reminds us of the prominence in the play of more practical educational projects and brings into metonymic focus the curiously synergetic, and ultimately, I would argue, parasitic relationship in the play of the educational and domestic. Now, at a glance, the vectors in this relationship seem to go decidedly in one direction, with much of the "bounded" or domestic space we encounter in the play employed as classrooms of one sort or another, and with many of the "things" we encounter, the semiology of which Lena Cowen Orlin has exhaustively parsed,[15] from books and musical instruments, to clothing and even quasi-, or not so quasi-, pornographic paintings, deployed as materials in broadly defined exercises in pedagogical outreach, in teaching lessons and—with a nod to the humanist elision of intellectual and moral formation—inculcating and modifying certain behaviors.[16] One obvious effect of this association in the play is, of course, the conversion of the domestic, and particularly its localization as domicile, into an arena for the care, feeding, and augmentation of masculine and patriarchalist control. Hence, Petruchio's house becomes the location of his "taming-school," to which Kate is taken, most unwillingly, to matriculate and, as Petruchio had threatened earlier, to domesticate her, "to bring her from a wild Kate to a Kate / Conformable as other household Kates" (2.1.277–78); and it is Petruchio's house to which Hortensio, a failed suitor and soon-to-be failed tamer, resorts as a not terribly apt auditor and would-be "patriculator" (4.2.50–58), while the banquet over which Lucentio presides at the end of the play reconstitutes itself as a public *examen* for the three new wives, the ultimate pass-fail, no-partial-credit test in which the only lesson for which the wives are responsible is that of obedience. In contrast to Gaston Bachelard's "topophiliac" reading of bounded space as "protective" and intimate,[17] the Shrew comically dramatizes the domestic as a site for contestation and an apparatus for indoctrination, a decidedly unprotective and vulnerable space, its atmosphere embodied in the cryogenic cold which Grumio brings into Petruchio's house from outside, but which the interior of Petruchio's house neither repels nor soon, or soon enough for Grumio, at least, dispels (4.1.1–45).

At the same time, though educational projects of a practical and social nature have a way of encroaching upon domestic space in the Shrew, it is also true that what the play, or what Sly calls in that interesting elision, the "comonty," transacts is the domestication, not only of Kate as one more, as Petruchio punningly classifies her, "household Kate,"[18] but of learning itself, with the simultaneous commodification and transformation of the objectives and processes of education into "things," and "things" for the home. We get a socially satiric hint of this "reifying" commodification—and its corruptive potential—in the Induction, when the meddling Lord, having ordered his men to carry the inert Sly to his "fairest chamber," instructs them to deck out the room with "all my wanton pictures," the better to persuade Sly that he really is a lord (Induction 1.46–47). And the hint is amplified in the play proper when Gremio, who seems to hope that Bianca will prove the sort of bibliophile who does, indeed, judge a book by its cover, insists that the books—"[a]ll books of love"—which he is going to have the disguised Lucentio use as his texts be "very fairly bound" and "very well perfum'd" (1.2.144–45, 151–52). "O this learning, what a *thing* [italics mine] it is!"

No less a "thing" is language instruction, and in representing Baptista's attempt to include it among his "household stuff," the play could be said simply to reflect what R. C. Simonini, Jr. described some time ago as the "vogue of foreign language study" cultivated in aristocratic *and* middle-class households from the middle of the sixteenth century[19]—though with a distinctly satiric lens. For, to extrapolate from the evidence of the translation scene, Latin instruction domesticated is traditional Latin instruction traduced, and offers little to allay the misgivings of the age about the wisdom of educating women—Roger Ascham's paean to the scholastic virtues of his star pupil Elizabeth notwithstanding[20]—and much to underscore the truth in the contemporary William Vaughan's truism that "A tutor should not be overfriendly with his student."[21] "Proposterous ass," Lucentio, the fake classics tutor, chides Hortensio, the fake music tutor, at the outset of the scene, in an attempt to browbeat his rival into letting him deliver his Latin "lecture" to Bianca before her music lesson (3.1.9–14), and in doing so strikes the keynote for the genuinely "preposterous"[22] inversions of decorum that mark the ensuing "lesson." "I am no breeching scholar in the schools," Bianca declares, arrogating to herself the authority to dictate the order and schedule of her lessons, and dropping a hint, in the process, of the terms to which she would expect any subsequent, nonacademic relationship to adhere. "I'll not be tied to hours nor 'pointed times, / But learn my lessons as I please myself" (3.1.18–20), an echo, we will recall, of the hedonistic notion of curriculum Tranio had recommended to Lucentio, but also a fundamental contravention of the role of the student and of the conditions by which students were expected to abide, the severity and regimentation of which have been amply documented by T. W. Baldwin and, quite recently, by J. W. Binns.[23] Moreover, in pointedly reminding her pseudotutors of what, in the dramatic context, one would imagine should have been quite obvious, namely that she is "no breeching scholar," which most editors have glossed as meaning "a schoolboy liable to be flogged,"[24] Bianca exempts herself from the culture of violence which, as Roger Ascham's pleas in *The Schoolmaster* for more gentle tactics only confirm,[25] was integral to Latin instruction and, of course, to the upbringing of children in general. "[I]f you forget your *qui's*, your *quae's*, and your *quod's*," Sir Hugh Evans admonishes his student William in *The Merry Wives of Windsor*, "you must be preeches" (4.1.77–78); or, as Vaughan much more menacingly declares, "[R]ods are expedient for the chastisement of the corruptions of the soul."[26] Dictating the conditions of her tutelage, Bianca simultaneously prescribes its form and adopts a rhetorical posture far more like that of the pedagogue than pupil, as she interrogates Lucentio as to the place in the text where they left off and commands him to "conster" it (3.1.26–30).

And if, as Walter J. Ong has argued, the normative conventions for the inculcation of Latin functioned as a masculine puberty rite, reinscribing masculine dominance in the authority and exclusionary eloquence of Latin discourse,[27] then Bianca's inversion of the roles of teacher and student has inevitable gender implications as well, and alerts us to the hints of gender inversion that inflect the characterizations of Lucentio and Bianca at various moments in the play, hints lodged inconspicuously and untranslated in various bits and pieces of classical reference with which the verbal surface of the *Shrew* is laden. One instance, and, perhaps, a comic warning of the power of classical learning to inculcate incorrect, or culturally inappropriate lessons, especially in weak minds, comes very early in the play when Lucentio tries his hand at classical analogy by way of Vergil to demonstrate the extremity of his immediate infatuation with Bianca, "confessing" to Tranio,

> That art to me as secret and as dear
> As Anna to the Queen of Carthage was,
> Tranio, I burn, I pine, I perish, Tranio,
> If I achieve not this young modest girl.
>
> (1.1.150–53)

Moreover, Lucentio's association of himself with one of Renaissance authors' favorite classical avatars of female victimization is interestingly underscored in the First Folio text of the play when, quoting, or misquoting, a theatrical progenitor in Terence, Tranio invokes the reassuring tag, "*Redime te captam quam queas minimo*" (1.1.159), with the feminine form "*captam*," which in the dramatic context modifies Lucentio, appearing in place of the masculine accusative form, "*captum*"—though most modern editors "correct" the Folio and restore the masculine form.[28] And if classical analogy has provided Lucentio with a feminine association, symmetry demands reciprocity for Bianca, which is what she may receive at the end of the translation scene, when the spurned Hortensio, sensing that he has been bested by his Latin teacher rival, follows misogynist tradition in directing his deepest resentment at the woman, vowing renunciation if Bianca has "cast thy wandering eyes on every stale" (3.1.88); though generally taken as a hawking reference in which Bianca plays the hawk to Lucentio's decoy pigeon, the image, particularly with its epithet "wandering," also evokes the figure of the peregrine hero of classical lore, Dido's "pious" victimizer, Aeneas, for example, or, more likely, in the context of this scene, the wandering worthy who figures so prominently in the text Lucentio has not been translating, Ulysses, a reading that brings the slighting reference to Lucentio as a "stale" into proximity with another "common" contemporary valence of the word, that of "prostitute."[29]

At the same time, to give ear to such possibilities in the classical periphery is to find more equivocal and ludic the representation of gender at the heart of the translation scene. For even as the *Shrew*, as a number of critics in recent years have compellingly argued, calls attention to its own theatricality,[30] so does it make it more difficult for its audience to differentiate the female character Bianca from the boy actor and theatrical apprentice playing her, and, thus, a more complex matter to accept unblinkingly Bianca's assertion that she is "no breeching scholar." Heard in this way, Bianca's remark bears a double resonance and two-fold blatancy: a blatant defiance of the prevailing rules for young scholars, and a blatant lie, since it is clear to everyone that the actor uttering this line has, in fact, much more in common with the "breeching scholar" than with the young woman Bianca. The hint that Bianca is not precisely what she seems only echoes, of course, the duplicity in which Lucentio and Hortensio are engaged in the scene and infuses it with the sort of liberating, transgressive energy which one associates with a *fabliau*, and that percolates throughout the *Shrew*, providing an insurgent counternote to the socially prescriptive and patriarchalist fantasy that is its central fable. In a play which, we have become accustomed to acknowledging, absorbs as a central motif the image of "supposing" from its source in Gascoigne's play, *Supposes*,[31] the intramural contention of the Latin lesson reminds us of the recurrence in the play of a more transgressive variation on "supposing" in the image of "facing," assuming a mask or pose *and* defiantly maintaining a lie, "braving," or "facing the matter out," as Katherina accuses Petruchio of doing in the previous scene when he insists to Baptista and all of the assembled suitors that Katherina has given her consent to have him as a husband (2.1.289). "Where is that damned villain, Tranio, / That fac'd and braved me in this matter so" (5.1.108–9), demands Lucentio's father, Vincentio, after Tranio had, to his master's face, clung to his assumed identity as Lucentio, thus denying his own servitude and his master's mastery (5.1.63–111). "Sirrah, I will not bear these braves of thine," the out-faced Hortensio tells his rival tutor at the outset of the Latin scene, momentarily dropping his own mask as just another hired music tutor to assume the posture of social superiority scorned (3.1.15). In the "in-your-face" domestic anomie of the Latin lesson scene, where the exercise of translation becomes a vehicle for misrepresentation, Bianca's interlinear skepticism, "I trust you not" (3.1.43), affords the aptest rendering of and gloss upon the text Lucentio is purveying.

And, of course, Bianca's distrust might be affected by her familiarity with the language that is not being taught her. To be sure, part of the comically transgressive energy released in this scene arises both from our sense that we cannot be certain who knows more, or less, about Latin here, the tutor or the "tutee," or whether, to paraphrase Casca, the Latin in question is equally Greek to both, and also from the possibility that we as audience, and as critics, are being teased and "braved" as much as the characters onstage. In, for example, his compendious assault upon the questions of how much Latin Shakespeare could have known and how and when he was likely to have learned it, T. W. Baldwin speculates in passing that the selection of the first epistle in Ovid's *Heroides* as Lucentio's text would imply that in her Latin competence Bianca was at the level of a fifth or sixth former,[32] a plausible surmise *if* we assume that finding a text appropriate to Bianca's grade level was important either to Lucentio or to his employer Gremio, whose mix of priorities seems to comprise "small Latine," more *eros*. Still, even if Bianca can translate little or nothing of her Latin text, and is impervious both to the possible corruptions, textual, that is, which editors have noted in the Ovidian text Lucentio is using and to possible lapses in Lucentio's erudition,[33] it is clear that she does at least know enough about the rhetoric of learned disputation to be a credit to Baptista's humanist educational pretensions and to be able to translate her own suspicions and resistance into the patter of academic discourse. Seizing upon what may in fact be a questionable piece of commentary by Lucentio in identifying the grandson of Aeacus as Ajax rather than Achilles,[34] Bianca employs the rhetoric of academic quibbling to express her emotional suspicions:

> I must believe my master; else, I promise you,
> I should be arguing still upon that doubt.
>
> (3.1.54–55)

Evincing no hard evidence that either mentor or pupil knows much about the language, or text, in question, the Latin lesson may offer the most immaculate demonstration of the license of translation, translation so unfettered as to owe nothing to its original at all!

In this respect, however, the translation exercise stands as but the most sustained example in the *Shrew* of the role and treatment generally accorded the various snippets of foreign language that dot especially the early portions of the play. If, as Benjamin observes, "translation is only a somewhat provisional way of coming to terms with the foreignness of languages."[35] the nontranslation and not infrequently incorrect transcriptions in the *Shrew* of foreign language have the effect of italicizing that foreignness, of rendering the language quoted less important for what it communicates than for the use to which its "foreignness" and failure to communicate can be put. In part, the invocation of foreign expressions provides a conventionally comic instrument of social intimidation and one-upmanship, a means of asserting an otherwise inconspicuous or nonexistent superiority, and as such plays its part in detonating the class and generational rivalries that define the subtext of the *Shrew*. "Therefore *paucas pallabris*" (Induction.1.5), commands the debt-evading Sly in "facing" down his creditor, the Hostess, underscoring his bogus claim to nobility and descent from "Richard Conqueror" (sic) with an equally bogus command of Spanish,[36] while the rich "pantaloon" Gremio, certifying his kinship with stock *senex* figures, summons a stock piece of comically pretentious faux latinity in a futile attempt to assert the dignity of his age and wealth against the importunate advances of Petruchio, who has jumped the courtship queue in his haste to claim Katherina: "Backare! you are marvellous forward" (2.1.73).[37] On the other hand, we have those gratuitous interjections in Italian which seem so much a sort of linguistic "dress-ups," and which in calling attention to themselves as interjections make their grammatical imperfections seem all the more evident, as in Tranio's First Folio remark, "*Me pardonato*," which a number of editors sedulously correct and print as "*Mi perdonato*" (1.1.25). Now, one editor, H. J. Oliver, in allowing the First Folio readings of this and other pieces of incorrect Italian to stand, notes that such interventions, errors notwithstanding, are still "good enough to give the illusion that the speakers are Italian";[38] I would suggest, however, that, quite to the contrary, they serve to show that the speakers are *not* Italian, and that their linguistic forays only accentuate their English-ness and the robustly domestic agenda of this play, which acknowledges its "foreign" setting and theatrical pedigree only to distance itself from them, even as the discourse of classical learning and allusion is at once translated into and domesticated by the "household stuff" of the abortive Latin lesson.

Still, notable as the translation scene may be for what does not occur and what does not get translated, the text it leaves largely ignored and encased within its un-or mistranslated Latin looms nonetheless large over it, complicating our sense of what the scene does transact, and, indeed, becoming more conspicuous in it the more it is "effaced" by Lucentio's interlinear glosses and Bianca's deflections of them. What significance that text has is open, of course, to some question. For though in bringing Ovid into Baptista's home, Lucentio would seem to be satisfying both his own amorous designs and his employer's specifications concerning the content of Bianca's instructional materials, yet the particular text Lucentio selects here, the First Epistle of the *Heroides,* is probably not the sort of Ovid which Gremio had in mind, or from which sprang Ovid's lurid reputation among sundry Renaissance commentators, such as Vives, who warns women in particular to shun the corruptions, nontextual, of Ovid's more licentious books "like as of serpents or snakes."[39] Instead, for Erasmus, at least—whose colloquy, *A Mery Dialogue, Declaringe the Propertyes of Shrowde Shrewes, and Honest Wyves,* has been cited as "either a source or an analogue" for the *Shrew*—[40] "the *Heroides* are more chaste," and offer matter more suitable for "callow youth" than Ovid's "*amatoriae,*" and Erasmus even singles out "the epistle of Penelope to Ulysses," the very one Lucentio pretends to translate, as "wholly chaste."[41] In fact, at a glance, a text centered on the proverbially patient and faithful Penelope might seem intended simply to provide an ironic counterpoint to the rather less patient and coolly uncommitted Bianca.

Yet behind such incongruities lie interesting congruencies between the Latin lesson and the text it does not teach, and with them a demonstration of some interesting uses of literary domestication. To have occasion to juxtapose Penelope and Bianca is, of course, to recognize an obvious if comic parallel between their dramatic situations, and in the degree to which Bianca's deft negotiation of the "lessons" of her imported and self-appointed tutors evokes Penelope's deft deflection of the advances of her self-invited suitors, it also permits us to recall the genuine interweaving of art and domesticity that forms the "fabric" of Penelope's delaying strategy, with Penelope's daily weaving followed by nightly unweaving a paradigmatic example of the commodification of art and of the uses to which one can put even a text that isn't there. Indeed, in the only lines from Ovid's text that actually surface in the Latin lesson scene, art and the domestic literally commingle, with the recollected description of Troy and Priam's ruined palace the effluence of dinner-table conversation, and a picture outlined with a little wine:

> atque aliquis posita monstrat fera proelia mensa,
>   pingit et exiquo Pergama tota mero:
> 'hac ibat Simois; haec est Sigeia tellus;
>   hic steterat Priami regia celsa senis.'
>
> (31–34)

["And someone about the board shows thereon the fierce combat, and with scant tracing of wine pictures forth all Pergamum: 'Here flowed the Simois; this is the Sigeian land; here stood the lofty palace of Priam the ancient."]

Still, what this detail only serves to underscore and metonymize is the larger act of literary domestication that turns the heroic into the *Heroides*, distilling and framing the epic narrative of *The Odyssey* within the rhetorical agenda of Epistle I and Penelope's writing chamber, and ostensibly giving voice to Penelope's point of view. Yet domestication can be an instrument of manipulation, and, to recall an earlier speculation, did Bianca actually know Latin and the *Heroides*, all the more might she be inclined to say, "I trust you not," in part, perhaps, because of Lucentio's handling of the Ovidian text, but in part because of the text itself. For one thing, though Ovid's poem enables Penelope to tell Ulysses what life has been like in Ithaca without him, the only part of her epistle that Lucentio chooses for translation is, as we have seen, a mere piece of scenery, a part of Penelope's account of an account of the ruined Troy, significant in its new context at most, as we have noted, as a humorous hint of the subversion of the patriarch's best laid plans. Decontextualized, the excerpt helps to deconstruct its original. For in a play that culminates in Katerina's bet-winning celebration of a domestic order that envisions the husband committing "his body / To painful labour both by sea and land," while his wife lies "warm at home, secure and safe (5.2.149–51), Lucentio's selection has the effect of silencing and suppressing a radically different and far unhappier perspective on the domestic arrangement Katherina's exposition dutifully idealizes.

On the other hand, the decontextualization produced by Lucentio's excerpt is but an extension of the decontextualization and deconstruction that mark Ovid's expropriation of epic history, and reminds us that Troy domesticated is Troy miniaturized and trivialized, with all of Pergamum inscribed on a table with, and within, a little wine, the circumscription of its boundaries mirrored by the linguistic framing of Ovid's word order: "*exiquo Pergama tota mero*" (32). With the field of epic exploits reduced, the focus on Penelope's domestic sufferings is intensified, though it is surely debatable whether Penelope profits from the scrutiny and from having her sufferings and endurance translated into a one hundred and sixteen line letter of concentrated complaint. Given a voice, Penelope is also given all of the rhetorical dexterity at Ovid's disposal with which to be made to appear to "lay a guilt trip" on her errant husband, as when she poses a rhetorical question laced with praeterition to give an ironic pointedness to her enumeration of some of the most oppressive results of Ulysses' being "shamefully absent," "*turpiter absens*":

> quid tibi Pisandrum Polybumque Medontaque dirum
>   Eurymachique avidas Antinoique manus
> atque alios referam, quos omnis turpiter absens
>   ipse tuo partis sanguine rebus alis?
>
> (91–94)

["Why tell you of Pisander, and of Polybus, and of Medon the cruel, and of the grasping hands of Eurymachus and Antinous, and of others, all of whom through shameful absence you yourself are feeding fat with store that was won at cost of your blood?"]

In the process of Ovid's "translation," that is, the patient, prudent Penelope of Homer emerges as someone distinctly more petulant, and in the degree to which she is both possessed of considerable rhetorical sophistication and an inclination to use it to upbraid her husband, she is invested with a kinship with a character-type who for Elizabethan readers would have been a most recognizable domestic literary commodity, the querulous wife.

And, indeed, that kinship is amplified in the translation of the *Heroides* with which it is generally agreed that Shakespeare would have been familiar, George Turbervile's, first published in 1567, and republished several times before the period most often assigned to the composition of the *Shrew*.[42] In part, that amplification could be attributed to the sheer amplitude and, as Frederick Boas notes in his edition of Turbervile's translation, the characteristically Elizabethan taste for pleonasm that mark Turbervile's style, doubling the one hundred and sixteen lines of complaint Penelope recites in Ovid, and turning the rhetorical question cited above (91–94) into two sentences and twice the number of lines.[43]

More important, while staying close to Ovid's language, with "renderings" that are, as Boas expresses it, "comparatively seldom wrong,"[44] Turbervile nonetheless exploits the license of the translator to editorialize, and nudges his readers towards seeing the story of the epistle as one of wifely jealousy. As Deborah Greenhut has contended,[45] such are the thrust, and almost literally, the "bottom line" of the "Argument" Turbervile appends to his translation (2), and he reinforces the point in translating the pseudo-Ovidian "Replie" by Ulysses, noting in the "Argument" of that piece the judgment that in the "Replie" Ulysses "quittes himselfe of all such blame / As by his wife imputed was," and that "[w]hat so she did object to him, / The Greeke reanswered very trim" (310.5–8). And if, again, Turbervile augments the suggestion of complaint in Penelope's rhetorical question simply by lengthening it, he simultaneously leaves untranslated the participial phrase in Ovid that gives Penelope's lament its bite, namely, "*turpiter absens*" (93), thus suppressing any reminder that the "absent" Ulysses may by being absent have done something, not only to occasion Penelope's distress, but to warrant her censure, while excising from Penelope's conjugal grief its implicit appeal to conjugal justice.

"Familiarizing" Penelope, Turbervile, in turn, conceives of the process of translation in the language of domestic consumption, repeatedly invoking the conventional rhetoric of self-effacement, with the odd effect, on the one hand, of accentuating the distance between the Ovidian original and his own rendering of it, while, at the same time, making his own product seem more modest, more familiar, more accessible, more, again, in Petruchio's punning words, "[c]onformable as other household Kates" (2.1.278). So it is that, in a fit of literary anorexia, Turbervile hopes that his patron, Sir Thomas Howard, will prove the sort of lord who is willing to accept "slender gyfts," seeks Howard's protection for "my slender Muse" (v–vi), concedes in defending his translation against "the Captious Sort of Sycophantes" that his translation is a "thing but slender (342), and invites his "Reader" to join him in a "slender" and "base banquet" (ix).

As an example, then, of the ways in which literary translation interacts with the pressure of cultural domestication, Penelope's Epistle hovers conspicuously about the translation scene of the *Shrew* as its unvoiced lesson, as one more intrusive, albeit invisible, tutor. And though in leaving this text untranslated and its lesson unvoiced, the scene would seem to resist the pressure of domestication, in fact, it could be argued that that pressure is simply deflected and comically displaced onto the very next scene, the wedding scene, where Petruchio mockingly dons the "face" of heroic rescuer in order to justify his determination to yank the unwilling Katherina peremptorily away from Baptista's wedding banquet:

> Grumio,
> Draw forth thy weapon, we are beset with thieves,
> Rescue thy mistress if thou be a man.
> —Fear not, sweet wench, they shall not touch thee, Kate;
> I'll buckler thee against a million.
> (3.2.235–39)

Here, of course, in one of the moments that illuminate the antipaternalist subtext of the play, Petruchio disrupts the domestic rites of the father in order to assert his own rights as husband, though in doing so he parodically supplies the ending Penelope's Epistle in the *Heroides* lacks, in effect restoring the epic version of the ending, with its classically violent restoration of domestic tranquility through the thieving-guest-slaughtering return of Odysseus.

Indeed, far from resisting the pressure of domestication, the translation scene could be said to signal a total capitulation to it, with the lessons it teaches having nothing to do with "learning" as such and everything to do with the configurations of behavior that define the relations and circumscriptions of the sexes—and, more precisely, the circumscription of the female sex—in this insistently domestic play. And if, as we have seen, the scene travesties some of the norms of instruction and seems to invert the roles of student and teacher, in doing so it also translates the student into the studied, leaving us on our own to speculate on what Bianca may have learned from the behavior of Lucentio, while italicizing, rather as a piece of *ekphrasis*, what Hortensio, at least, as we have noted above, has learned from his observation of Bianca.

> Yet if thy thoughts, Bianca, be so humble
> To cast thy wandering eyes on every stale,
> Seize thee that list; if once I find thee ranging,
> Hortensio will be quit with thee by changing.
> (3.1.89–92)

Not for Hortensio is it to think with detachment about the parallels between Bianca and the classical personage whose letter does not get translated, any more, of course, than it would have been for Medon, Eurymachus, Antinous, and their *confrères* to compliment

Penelope on her pluck and inventiveness, so that Hortensio's inability to read the analogue this scene at once evokes and evades ironically brings the analogue closer. In fact, if he were inclined at this point to cast his disillusionment and growing misogyny into a position on educational policy, Hortensio might well count himself among those "manye" critics of women Vives invokes, "who sayth, the subtiltie of learning should bee a nourishment for the maliciousnesse of nature."[46] As it is, however, for Hortensio, Bianca's domestic education has utility, not for what Bianca may learn but for what may be learned about her.

In this way, and in its harnessing of learning to a domestic agenda, the translation scene lesson merely illuminates the permeable boundary shared by learning and domestication throughout the play, where, from the moment of Bianca and Kate's first appearance (1.1.48 ff.) and culminating in their last (5.2.65 ff.), women's behavior and potential as domestic partners become the stuff of male speculation, in both the ordinary and root meanings of the word, and public examination. Still, in turning Bianca's lessons into tableaux in which Hortensio observes her and grades her on criteria decidedly nonintellectual, the translation scene reminds us, not only of the way in which the definition of female character in the play is very much a male construction, but of how restrictive the males' choice of building materials is, with women construed in dichotomous terms and with a precariously fine line dividing the two, and separating "sweet Bianca" from Bianca the potential shrew. At the same time, in a play that ostensibly—even ostentatiously—concerns itself with domestic management, the translation scene offers a subversive interlude that suggests that a play may be especially instructive in dramatizing its own instructional limitations, and, above all, reminds its audience of what a malleable, and manipulable, a thing learning, for all of its patriarchalist prescriptions, is.

Notes

1. Unless otherwise stated, citations of Shakespeare's plays are taken from *The Riverside Shakespeare*, ed. G. Blakemore Evans (Boston: Houghton Mifflin, 1974).

2. See Geoffrey Bullough, *Narrative and Dramatic Sources of Shakespeare*, (London: Routledge and Kegan Paul, 1957), vol. I.; also, *The New Cambridge Taming of the Shrew*, Ann Thompson, ed. (Cambridge: Cambridge University Press, 1984), 9–17.

3. See the note on 3.1.s.d, by Brian Morris, ed., *The Taming of the Shrew, The Arden Shakespeare* (London: Routledge, 1989), 218.

4. In its note on Sly's comment, The Riverside text, 113, warily glosses "household stuff" as "house furnishings" or "domestic goings-on"; see also Lena Cowen Orlin's comment that "[t]hrough the term 'household stuff', the performances of things, of persons, and of plays are suggestively analogized," in "The Performance of Things in *The Taming of the Shrew*," *The Yearbook of English Studies* 23 (1993): 183.

5. Friederich Nietzsche, *The Joyful Wisdom*, II, trans. Thomas Common, *The Complete Works of Friedrich Nietzsche*, ed. Oscar Levy, 18 vols (New York: Russell & Russell, 1909–11; rpt. 1964), 10, 115.

6. Though one senses, for example, that the audience is being teased, the players in the Induction of the Quarto *Shrew* claim, at least, to see the play they are about to perform as exemplary, "a good leson for us my Lord, for us that are married men" (Induction 1.64), in *A Pleasant Conceited Historie, called The Taming of a Shrew As it hath beene sundry times acted by the right Honourable the earle of Pembrooke his seruants* (London: Nicholas Ling, 1607), STC 23669. This claim does not surface in the Folio *Shrew*, where the players place emphasis on the therapeutic value of a "pleasant comedy," with its "mirth and merriment" (Induction 2.129–36).

7. George Gascoigne, *The Glasse of Gouernement* (London: 1575).

8. Publius Terentius Afer, *Fabulae Comici Facetissimi et Elegantissimai Poetae* (Cambridge: 1598), STC 23890.

9. Philip Stubbes, *The Anatomie of Abuses: Contayning A Discouerie, or Breife Summarie of such Notable Vices and Imperfections, as now raigne in many Christian Countreyes of the Worlde: but (especiallie) in a verie famous Iland called AILGNA of late, as in other places, elsewhere* (London: 1583), STC 23376, f. L5, L8–M1.

10. In such homologous terms, for example, has the scene been scanned quite recently by Dennis S. Brooks, who in "'To show scorn her own image': The Varieties of Education in *The Taming of the Shrew*," *Rocky Mountain Review of Literature* 48 (1994): 18, declares that "the pupil's mastery of the tutor . . . foreshadows the wife's mastery of the husband."

11. Marianne L. Novy, "Patriarchy and Play in *The Taming of the Shrew*." *English Literary Renaissance* 9 (1979): 279; see also Jeanne Addison Roberts, *Shakespeare's English Comedy: The Merry Wives of Windsor in Context* (Lincoln: University of Nebraska Press, 1979), 122.

12. Citations of the *Heroides* will be inserted in parentheses and are, until otherwise stated, from Publius Ovidius Naso, *Heroides and Amores*, trans. Grant Showerman (1914; rev. Cambridge: Harvard University Press, 1986). In George Turbervile's translation, with which it is not unlikely that Shakespeare was familiar, the reference to Priam's age is rendered no less forcibly: "aged Priam's Hall / and Princely house"; see Turbervile, trans., *The Heroycall Epistles of the learned Poet Publius Ovidius Naso* (1567), ed. Frederick Boas (London: Cresset Press, 1928), 5.

13. In his note on 4.2.63, Morris, Arden *Shrew*, 255, offers instances of the comic uses to which schoolmasters are put in Shakespeare's early plays.

14. In "The Lord-Treasurer's Advice to his Son," Sir William Cecil, Lord Burghley, exhorts his son to "suffer not thy Sons to pass the *Alpes*, for they shall learn nothing there but Pride, Blasphemy and Atheism; and if by Travelling they get a few broken Languages, that will profit them no more, than to haue the same Meat served in divers Dishes," in *Instructions for Youth, Gentlemen and Noblemen by Sir Walter Raleigh, Lord Treasurer Burleigh, Cardinal Sermonetta, and Mr. Walsingham* (London: Randall Minshull, 1722), 50.

15. Orlin, "The Performance of Things," esp. pp.171 ff.
16. See Morris, Arden *Shrew*, 133; Thompson, Cambridge *Shrew*, 34–35; and Brooks, "To Show Scorn," passim.
17. Gaston Bachelard, *The Poetics of Space*, trans. Maria Jolas (Boston: Beacon Press, 1969), xxxi–ii, 149–50.
18. That the "taming" of Katherina needs to be read in financial terms and as a financial investment is central to the thesis of a paper by Donald Hedrick, "Commodity Kate: Shakespeare's Shrew and the Domestication of Money," delivered at the meeting of the Shakespeare Association in Atlanta in April, 1993.
19. R. C. Simonini, Jr, "Language Lesson Dialogues in Shakespeare," *Shakespeare Quarterly* 2 (1951): 319. Indeed, in a paper written for the meeting of the Shakespeare Association of America, in Albuquerque, April, 1994, "'Loytering in Love': Ovid's *Heroides*, Pleasure, and Household Stuff in *The Taming of the Shrew*," 21, and n. 38, Patricia Phillippy cites the pretensions exemplified by Baptista's educational plans for his daughters as the very sort of "parental mismanagement" of female children castigated by contemporary continental and English educators and conduct book writers.
20. Roger Ascham, *The Schoolmaster* (1570), ed. Lawrence V. Ryan (Charlottesville: University Press of Virginia, 1967), 56, 87.
21. William Vaughan, *The Golden-grove, moralized in three books A worke very necessary for all such as would know how to governe themselues, their houses, or their countrey* (London: Simon Stafford, 1600), STC 24610, f. X2v. In addition to being far too friendly with his student, Bianca, Lucentio might also qualify simply as bad company, or the sort of temptation Richard Pace feels students should abstemiously avoid; see Richard Pace, *De Fructu Qui Ex Doctrina Percipitur* (1517), ed. and trans. Frank Manley and Richard Sylvester (New York: Frederick Ungar Publishing Company, 1967), 114–15.
22. In "Preposterous Events," *Shakespeare Quarterly* 43 (1992): 198–99, Patricia Parker argues that the epithet "preposterous" here serves to link the action of this scene with a long list and significant subtext of "preposterous events," inversions of what should come first with what should follow, that create a pattern of upheavals throughout Shakespeare's plays.
23. T. W. Baldwin, *William Shakespeare's Small Latine, Lesse Greeke*, 2 vols. (Urbana: University of Illinois Press, 1944), 1 passim; J. W. Binns, *Intellectual Culture in Elizabethan and Jacobean England: The Latin Writings of the Age* (Leeds: Francis Cairns, 1990), 292.
24. Riverside, 124; Morris, Arden *Shrew*, 219; see also the glosses on this word by Barbara Mowatt and Paul Werstine, ed., *The Taming of the Shrew*, The New Folger Library Shakespeare (New York: Washington Square Press, 1992), 108, and H. J. Oliver, ed., *The Taming of the Shrew*, The Oxford Shakespeare (Oxford: Oxford University Press, 1984), 158.
25. Ascham, 37–38, 60.
26. Vaughan, *The Golden-grove*, f. X5v; on the culture of violence in which boys studied Latin, see Walter J. Ong, S. J., *Fighting for Life: Context, Sexuality, and Consciousness* (Amherst: University of Massachusetts Press, 1989), 131–4.
27. Ong, "Latin Language Study as a Renaissance Puberty Rite," *Rhetoric, Romance, and Technology* (Ithaca: Cornell University Press, 1971), 113–41; see also Ong, *Fighting for Life*, 129–39; and Parker, "Preposterous Events," p. 199.
28. Allowing the reading of "*captam*" from the First Folio to stand, "uncorrected," H. J. Oliver in the Oxford *Shrew*, 114, accepts the inappropriate feminine form as but one of a number of mistakes in transcriptions of foreign words and expressions that punctuate the early parts of the play.

29. Noting the possibility that the reference is to hawking, Oliver, Oxford Shrew, 162, comments, "Perhaps that is the sense here, but the word came also to mean anyone who allures to deceive (and so particularly a prostitute, especially one serving as a decoy)."

30. See Karen Newman, "Renaissance Family Politics and Shakespeare's The Taming of the Shrew," in Fashioning Femininity and English Renaissance Drama (Chicago: University of Chicago Press, 1991), 35–50, an earlier version of the article, with the same title, appearing in English Literary Renaissance 16 (1986): 86–100; Juliet Dusinberre, "The Taming of the Shrew: Women, Acting, and Power," Studies in the Literary Imagination 26 (1993): 67–84; Michael Shapiro, "Framing the Taming: Metatheatrical Awareness of Female Impersonation in The Taming of the Shrew," Shakespeare Yearbook 23 (1993): 143–66.

31. See Cecil C. Seronsy, "'Supposes' as the Unifying Theme in The Taming of the Shrew," Shakespeare Quarterly 14 (1963): 15–30; and Thompson pp. 31–32.

32. Baldwin, William Shakespeare's Small Latine, 1.589.

33. See Oliver's speculation on the possibly intended corruptions and questionable commentary, Oxford Shrew, 158–159.

34. See Oliver's note on 3.1.50, Ibid., 159

35. Walter Benjamin, "The Task of the Translator: An Introduction to the Translation of Baudelaire's Tableaux Parisiens," Illuminations: Essays and Reflections, trans. Harry Zohn (New York: Schocken Books, 1969), 75.

36. See Morris, Arden Shrew, 153; Oliver, Oxford Shrew, 89.

37. See Morris's note on 2.1.73, Arden Shrew, 200, on the comic pedigree of backare; see also Morris's reference in the same note to John Lyly's Midas (1592), 1.2, for a very comparable use of backare as a comically maladroit gesture of social pretense.

38. Oliver, note on 1.1.25, Oxford Shrew 107. Simonini, "Language Lesson Dialogues," 323–24, argues that such expressions typify the "kind of polite conversation that was taught in the dialogue manuals for learning Italian, such as Florio's First Fruites and Second Frutes (1591)."

39. Juan Vives, A Very Fruitfull and pleasant booke, called the instruction of a Christian woman, trans. Richard Hyrde (London: 1585), STC 24862, 37–39; see also Thomas Lodge, The Complete Works of Thomas Lodge (Glasgow, Scotland: 1883), 1:19; and William Prynne, Histriomastix (1633), ed. Arthur Freeman (New York: Garland Press, 1974), 912.

40. Richard Hosley, "Sources and Analogues of The Taming of the Shrew," The Huntington Library Quarterly 27 (1963–4): 298–9.

41. Cited in Baldwin, William Shakespeare's Small Latine, 1.239.

42. Frederick Boas, Introduction to Turbervile's Heroycall Epistles of the learned Poet Publius Ovidius Naso, xv–xvi.

43. Ibid., xvii.

44. Ibid., xviii.

45. Deborah S. Greenhut, Feminine Rhetorical Culture: Tudor Adaptations of Ovid's Heroides (New York: Peter Lang, 1984), 81–2.

46. Vives, A Very Fruitfull and pleasant booke, 18.

"Are We Being Historical Yet?": Colonialist Interpretations of Shakespeare's *Tempest*

BEN ROSS SCHNEIDER, JR.

Not long ago, Carolyn Porter, in the article "Are We Being Historical Yet?," assessed the achievements of the "new historicists." Agreeing with Louis Montrose that new historicism was "on its way to becoming the newest academic orthodoxy," especially in Renaissance studies, she concluded, that although new historicism had provided a much-needed corrective to traditionally ahistorical literary study, the answer to the question raised in her title was "No."[1] In what follows I shall extend her critique to recent work on *The Tempest*, a play that has attracted widespread attention among new historicists as a paradigm of early modern colonialism.[2] My findings corroborate Professor Porter's conclusion: we still have a long way to go before we can feel even somewhat confident that we are historicizing, if we ever can.

According to Professor Porter, it is their fixation on Foucault's conceptualization of power that stands between the new historicists and effective historicization.[3]

> Foucault's perspective on the discursive field apparently fosters [a tendency in new historicist practice] to exclude, which is a necessary precondition for addressing a particular cultural discourse, but then to repress the fact of that exclusion, so that a particular discourse, or set of discourses, comes to stand for the horizonless field of Discourse.[4]

Thus she watches Stephen Greenblatt and Steven Mullaney marginalize the very others (Algonkians, Welsh) whose othering they so clearly deplore, erasing their history, in the process of showing how power on the Foucauldian model, "absolutized as a transhistorical force, . . . relentlessly produces and recontains subversion."[5] As a result, we are

> limited to one set of discourses—those which form the site of a dominant ideology—and then reifying that limit as if it were coterminous with the limits of discourse in general. It is this issue of framing the discursive field which new historicists most urgently need to address.[6]

It is "this issue of framing" that I shall address again in a study of eight recent analyses of *The Tempest*. By choosing colonialism as a frame, and then "reifying" it as if it were "coterminus with the limits of discourse in general," I find that the new historicists do indeed marginalize not only a large field of pertinent contemporary discourse, but also *The Tempest* itself. For as we are constantly reminded, we must explore, "both the social presence *to* the world of the literary text and the social presence *of* the world in the literary text."[7] To carry out this project, we must answer the question, "What difference did *The Tempest* make to which fields of discourse?" By too assiduously implementing the colonialist frame, the eight critics I study here effectively forestall any attempt to answer the question in terms of a full range of possibilities, despite the ostensible variety of approaches they take to the play.

Thomas Cartelli (1987)[8], basing his account on the work of African and Caribbean writers, takes the stance that Shakespeare is to blame for the way in which British imperialists have justified colonial oppression on the model of Caliban's apparent ineducability. Curt Breight (1990)[9] holds that the play is innocent of this charge, and is instead an exposé of James I's rule, in which Prospero's disciplinary measures caricature the crown's terror tactics in such broad strokes that a Jacobean audience could not miss them. Exactly reversing this position, Lori Leininger (1980)[10] perceives that far from exposing the injustices of the society in which it is embedded, the play is guilty of trying to cover them up, although it fails to handle all sorts of exasperating anomalies. Expressing the same dissatisfaction in more theoretical terms, Paul Brown (1985)[11] maintains that *The Tempest* actually "intervened" in "an ambivalent and even contradictory contemporary discourse" of colonialism:

> This intervention takes the form of a powerful and pleasurable narrative which seeks at once to harmonize disjunction, to transcend irreconcilable contradictions and to mystify the political conditions which demand colonialist discourse. Yet the narrative ultimately fails to deliver

that containment and instead may be seen to foreground precisely those problems which it works to efface or overcome.[12]

The team of Francis Barker and Peter Hulme[13] is more interested in the contradictions in our own society: "The onus on new readings, especially radical readings aware of their own theoretical and political positioning, should be to proceed by means of a critique of the dominant readings of a text."[14] Stephen Orgel (1987)[15], in the exhaustive Introduction to his splendid Oxford edition, avoids theoretical terminology, but his treatment is patently a deconstruction of the traditional idealist reading. Eric Cheyfetz,[16] who approaches colonialism and The Tempest via the metaphor of translation finds interesting parallels between Prospero as dictator of an official language and the way in which official languages are used in the conquest of native peoples. Finally, Stephen Greenblatt (1988) in his "Martial Law in the Land of Cokaigne"[17] frames his critique with his own theory of "salutary anxiety," derived from an anecdote of Bishop Latimer, and showing that governors, Prospero being a case in point, may raise the threat of imminent calamity in order to win credit for averting it.

For some reason the great variety of theoretical underpinning in this set of essays does not produce a corresponding variety of interpretation. All critiques proceed in much the same fashion to dismantle a presumed "authorized version" of the play that idealizes and romanticizes Prospero as a noble regenerator of fallen humanity.[18] Or to put it in the words of Barker and Hulme, "athwart its alleged unity, the text is in fact marked and fissured by the interplay of the discourses that constitute it."[19] When we have deconstructed the play, we find ourselves standing in the presence of naked power. It becomes evident, as one surveys these new historicist interpretations, that the "fissures" most commonly detected tend to be the same ones:

The storm:
All but one of these critics pick, as the opening fissure in the romantic surface of the play the "refreshingly subversive"[20] storm scene that begins the play in which helpless, hapless nobles must endure the insults of desperate mariners trying to save the ship.[21] Immediately power reveals itself in subversion. The nearly unanimous choice of this scene is symptomatic of the whole critical approach. By framing the scene as colonial discourse, these critics foreclose the possibility that the storm (in nature and society) rep-

resents and dramatizes, as in *Lear*, the social disorder that ensues when a state is irresponsibly governed. What does the title signify? It seems more likely that *The Tempest* is participating here in contemporary discourse on government, about which I shall have more to say later.

Prospero's self-contradictory and contradicted prologue (1.2) [22]

In his long exposition to Miranda, telling her who they are, how they got here, and what they are doing now, Prospero, according to these critics, is at cross-purposes with himself. While his anger at the usurpers of his dukedom seems to know no bounds, he at the same time blames his overthrow on his inattention to duty, his having retired from public affairs to study "liberal arts."[23] Here we see power at work, disguising its own motives and intentions, even from itself. Here contemporary discourse on anger could be relevant, but the critical approach closes the door in advance on any nonpolitical explanation.

Further, by giving credit to "Providence Divine" (1.1.159) for casting them upon the island, Prospero implies that he legitimately rules the island by some sort of manifest destiny.[24] But the ensuing scenes with Ariel and Caliban make it clear that Caliban's mother once owned the island and that Caliban inherits it from her.[25] In short, the official version, for Miranda's ears only, is wrong: Prospero rules not by manifest destiny but by force.[26] Again the frame marginalizes other options, for it is not a forgone conclusion that Prospero's primary reason for taking charge of the island is to make it his colony.

However, it turns out that Caliban has attempted to rape Miranda. Is he an innocent victim of colonial exploitation or a criminal deservedly punished for a crime? The question could be left open in the name of that plurality on which Orgel insists in his introduction. But the frame does not allow plurality, and the critics here surveyed do their best to weaken the force of the rape. First, say they, Prospero brings up the matter of the rape to divert attention from Caliban's rightful claim to the island; and second, colonialists always excuse their barbarity by attributing sub-human characteristics to the native population. Read properly, this business about rape is just another colonialist tactic, a tired excuse for repressive violence.[27]

This rationalization is not very convincing in terms of the text that it effaces, but which is nevertheless still there. To establish the rape = excuse theory, one must overturn three witnesses, including the would-be rapist himself still lusting after the victim. And if Caliban and Ariel are opposites, as we are certainly invited to suppose, the colonialist frame marginalizes this way of looking at the play as well.

Prospero's outbursts:
Barker and Hulme speak of "Prospero's well-known irascibility."[28] Chiefly noted are

—his impatient asides to Miranda during his introductory speech;[29]
—his annoyance at Ariel's plea for freedom;[30]
—his "hysterical" response to Caliban's claim of prior ownership;[31]
—his irate chastisement of Ferdinand, his own choice for his daughter's hand, on a trumped-up charge;[32]
—his obvious joy at the suffering of his enemies;[33]
—and certainly his exasperated realization, in the midst of the masque celebrating the betrothal of Ferdinand and Miranda, that if he doesn't act fast he may soon be murdered by Caliban's junta.[34]

Prospero's frequent and "puzzling" losses of temper do indeed mar the beautiful surface of a romantic *Tempest*. But are they really leaks in the play's romantic envelope which reveal the ugly colonialism within, or do they better fit another paradigm? Again the frame cuts off speculation.

However, close on the point where Prospero's rage peaks (4.1.145) comes Prospero's renunciation of vengeance and his abjuration of magic, acts which introduce real problems for the colonialist hypothesis, for, if we accept this reversal at face value, he repudiates his whole career as a despot. Again, instead of leaving us in a state of negative capability, the frame requires an elaborate exercise in looking the other way. In so doing the colonialist critics simply erase the climax of the play.

For Paul Brown, after the masque, after the trivialization by ridicule of Caliban's rebellion, after the celebration of upper-class solidarity in the wedding of Ferdinand and Miranda, Prospero's project is finished; he has "euphemized" his own power politics so well that he has virtually nullified himself, and now has nothing to do but go home and wait for death. "The completion of the colonialist project signals the banishment of its supreme exponent even as his triumph is declared."[35] Curt Breight, using the analogy of Prospero's scare tactics to James I's technique of death sentences and reprieves, sees Prospero's reformation in almost exactly the same way, as a further exercise of power.[36] Stephen Orgel argues that the ending in reconciliation and renunciation is a total sham. The evil brother has not repented; Prospero may not ultimately keep his promise to break his wand; he has not given up a daughter, but won a throne: in returning to Milan he will reach all the goals that his magic was meant to achieve. In the end we witness, not the renunciation of magic, but magic's "triumph."[37] Nor are Thomas Cartelli and Lori Leininger fooled by the ending, a vain attempt to hide an outrage that refuses to be hidden.[38] Francis Barker and Peter Hulme allow some ambivalence, but "the lengths [they say] to which the play has to go to achieve a legitimate ending may ... be read as the quelling of a fundamental disquiet concerning its own functions within the projects of colonialist discourse.[39] It's just a cover-up after all, and the play is an egregious hypocrite. Here the application of the colonialist frame requires the "refutation of the ending."[40]

It is not just the climax that has been effaced,[41] but with it an extensive field of early modern European discourse on which it draws and to which it reports. Prospero's change of heart occurs just after Caliban and his fellow-mutineers have been punished for their assault on his life. Ariel is reporting the status of his chastening of the upper-class conspirators.

>   Your charm so strongly works 'em
> That if you now beheld them, your affections
> Would become tender.
> Pros.   Dost thou think so, spirit?
> Ari. Mine would, sir, were I human.
> Pros.   And mine shall.
> Hast thou, which art but air, a touch, a feeling,
> Of their afflictions, and shall not myself
> One of their kind, that relish all as sharply
> Passion as they, be kindlier mov'd than thou art?
> Though with their high wrongs I am strook to th'quick,
> Yet, with my nobler *reason*, 'gainst my *fury*
> Do I take part. The *rarer* action is
> In *virtue* than in *vengeance*.
>
>   (5.1.17–28)

Some years ago Eleanor Prosser[42] traced this passage to John Florio's translation of Montaigne's essay *On Cruelty.* Florio's language is indeed close (I have emphasized the words that both he and Shakespeare use):

> He that through a naturall facilitie and genuine mildnesse should neglect or contemne injuries received, should no doubt performs a *rare action*, and worthy commendation: but he who being toucht and stung to the quicke with any wrong or offence received, should arme himselfe with *reason* against this *furiously* blind desire of *revenge*, and in the end after a great conflict yeeld himselfe master over it, should doubtlesse doe much more. The first should doe well, the other *vertuously*: the one action might be termed Goodnesse, the other Vertue. For it seemeth that the very name of Vertue presupposeth difficultie, and inferreth resistance, and cannot well exercise itselfe without an enemy.[43]

Long before Florio had translated these words (1603), Thomas Elyot had expressed very much the same sentiment in his handbook for gentlemen, named *The Governour* (1531), under the heading "Of Pacience in sustayninge wronges and rebukes:"

> Unto hym that is valyaunt of courage, it is a great payne and difficultie to sustayne Iniurie, and nat to be forthwith reuenged. And yet often tymes is accounted more valyauntnesse in the sufferaunce than in hasty reuengynge.[44]

In awarding points for degree of difficulty, Elyot manages to anticipate Montaigne. King James I, in his letter of advice to his son (1603)—citing Cicero's advice to *his* son (*De Officiis*), Seneca's essay on clemency, the *Aeneid*, and Aristotle's *Ethics*—counsels the apparent future king to

> Embrace trew magnanimitie, not in beeing vindictiue, which the corrupted Judgements of the world thinke to be trew Magnanimitie, but by the contrarie, in thinking your offendour not worthie of your wrath, empyring ouer your owne passion, and triumphing in the commaunding your selfe to forgiue.[45]

In his *Characters of the Virtues and Vices* (1608), Joseph Hall, later Bishop, counsels likewise:

> The Patient Man finds that victory consists in yielding. He is above nature, while he seems below himself. The vilest creature knows how to turn again, but to command himself not to resist, being urged, is more than heroical.[46]

These echoes suggest a common origin, and, of course, they have one: in the writings of the Roman moralists:

> [Do not] listen to those who think that one should indulge in violent anger against one's political enemies and imagine that such is the attitude of a great-spirited, brave man. For nothing is more commendable, nothing more becoming in a preeminently great man than courtesy and forbearance. (Cicero, *De Officiis*)[47]

> Revenge is the confession of a hurt; no mind is truly great that bends before injury.... There is no surer proof of greatness than to be in a state where nothing can possibly happen to disturb you.... The lofty mind is always calm, at rest in a quiet haven; crushing down all that engenders anger, it is restrained, commands respect, and is properly ordered. (Seneca, *Moral Essays*)[48]

Editors of *The Tempest* are puzzled by the fact that "virtue" and "vengeance" don't seem to be correlatives.[49] In Roman discourse of morality they are.

The idea that Shakespeare is the universal man, tied to no time or place, dies very hard, so hard that even the scholars most dedicated to rehistoricizing him cannot seem to break themselves of the habit of thinking of him as one of us, seeing his times through our eyes. Between us and Shakespeare lie the development of capitalist society, and the French, romantic, and industrial revolutions. But we read Shakespeare almost as if nothing had happened. Should we not, in order to understand him, his audience, and, by virtue of the uncompromising law of believability, his characters, become familiar with the "ethic" that preceded The Protestant Ethic and The Spirit of Capitalism? What notions of good and bad governed early modern decision-making? Social historians generally agree that they were quite different from ours. According to Karl Marx,

> The Bourgeoisie, wherever it has got the upper hand, has put an end to all feudal, patriarchal, idyllic relations. It has pitilessly torn asunder the motley feudal ties that bound man to his 'natural superiors,' and left remaining no other nexus between man and man than naked self-interest, than callous cash payment. It has drowned the most heavenly ecstacies of religious fervor, of chivalrous enthusiasm, of philistine sentimentalism, in the icy water of egotistical calculation. It has resolved personal worth into exchange value, and in place of the numberless indefeasible chartered freedoms, it has set up that single unconscionable freedom—Free Trade. (*Communist Manifesto*)[50]

In his fact-filled study, *The World We Have Lost* (1965), Peter Laslett quotes this passage as the "words [of] the most penetrating of all observers of the world we have lost."[51]

The great Max Weber expands on Marx's "icy water of egotistical calculation" in his *Protestant Ethic and the Spirit of Capitalism*, but has more to say about the ethic that comes before in his *Essays in Sociology:*

> The ancient economic ethic of neighborliness [was fostered] by the guild, or the partners in seafaring, hunting and warring expeditions. These communities have known two elemental principles: first, the dualism of in-group and out-group morality; second, for in-group morality, simple reciprocity: 'As you do unto me I shall do unto you.' From these principles the following [consequences] have resulted for economic life: for in-group morality the principled obligation to give brotherly support in distress has existed. The wealthy and the noble were obliged to loan, free of charge, goods for the use of the propertyless, to give credit free of interest, and to extend liberal hospitality and support. Men were obliged to render services upon request of their neighbors, and likewise, on the lord's estate, without compensation other than mere sustenance. All this followed the principle: your want of today may be mine tomorrow. This principle was not, of course, rationally weighed, but it played its part in sentiment. Accordingly, higgling in exchange and loan situations, as well as permanent enslavement resulting, for instance, from debts, were confined to outgroup morality and applied only to outsiders.[52]

For Jurgen Habermas, Marx's "egotistical calculation," stripped of its emotive ramifications, becomes the "purposive-rational" behavior of modern western man, in which right action is whatever makes sense given the goal, as opposed to "symbolic interaction," in which right action is that which coincides with mutually-understood social norms, in default of any ultimate goal.[53] Today a "rational choice model" governs the research of most political scientists, though it is now strenuously challenged (see, for instance, Sven Longstreth, Frank Steinmo and Kathleen Thelen, *Structuring Politics: Historical Institutionalism in Comparative Analysis*, ch. 1).[54] For Shakespeare's society, if we are to take the advice of the social historians, a "symbolic interaction model" would produce a better fit.

Karl Polanyi, in *The Great Transformation*, holds that although "purposive-rational" ethics go hand in hand with industrialization, no truly purposive-rational society has ever existed, except, perhaps for a short time in the "satanic mills" of Dickens's England, when some level starvation was rationalized as necessary for labor to become a commodity in fact. Before and since, though they have tolerated a high degree of rationality in human relations, "free market" societies have simply refused to tolerate starvation. In 1944 Polanyi wrote

> The outstanding discovery of recent historical and anthropological research is that man's economy, as a rule, is submerged in his social relationships. He does not act so as to safeguard his individual interest in the possession of material goods; he acts so as to safeguard his social standing, his social claims, his social assets. He values material goods only in so far as they serve this end.[55]

Or, as Shakespeare put the case, out of the mouth of Iago into the ear of Othello:

> Who steals my purse steals trash; 'tis something, nothing;
> 'Twas mine, 'tis his, and has been slave to thousands;
> But he that filches from me my good name
> Robs me of that which not enriches him,
> And makes me poor indeed.
>
> (3.3.155–61)

Or again, from the mouth of Cassio: "O, I have lost my reputation! I have lost the immortal part of myself, and what remains is bestial" (2.3.262–65).

The "norms" of which these social scientists speak are, of course, a prominent feature of those "primitive" societies that captivate the anthropologists: for example, Marcel Mauss in his classic *The Gift: Forms and Functions of Exchange in Archaic Societies*, introduced by E. E. Evans-Pritchard (1954)[56] and Marshall Sahlins in *Stone Age Economics*, his amazing account of the idyllic life of actual hunters and gatherers.[57] In *The Gift: Imagination and the Erotic Life of Property*, Lewis Hyde explored the function of these same Stone Age economics in the production of art.[58] The Romans apparently remembered or observed or retained vestiges of this pre-agricultural age, and admired it, as Seneca testifies in quoting Virgil's *Georgics*:

> No ploughman tilled the soil, nor was it right
> To portion off or bound one's property.
> Men shared their gains, and earth more freely gave
> Her riches to her sons who sought them not.

What race of men [comments Seneca] was ever more blest than that race? They enjoyed all nature in partnership. Nature sufficed for them . . . and this her gift consisted of the assured possession by each man of the common resources.[59]

When we study Kwakiutl society, we try to find out what the *Kwakiutls* think they are doing before we decide what *we* think they are doing. If it were known that every Kwakiutl had access to a book of rules for righteous living, we would certainly consult this book before presuming to explain Kwakiutl behavior. Closer to home, before we declare the Jacobean position on colonialism, shouldn't we know what ethical tools the Jacobeans brought to the task of judging it? For Shakespeare's society hundreds of moral rule books are available, but they are almost never consulted. The result, to use Habermas's terms, is that we're trying to impose a "purposive-rational" model on a society controlled by "symbolic interaction," about as sensible a procedure as using the Boy Scout's Law to explain the Kwakiutls.

Considering our manifest need for cultural material pertaining to Shakespeare's work, it is difficult to imagine how we can have overlooked the ocean of early modern ethical discourse opened to us in Ruth Kelso's monumental bibliography of Renaissance books pertaining to the *Doctrine of the English Gentleman* (1929) and *The Doctrine for the Lady* (1956).[60] These works comprise almost 1500 titles, about one-third in English. And Professor Kelso does not include classical moralists in their own or modern languages, which would more than double that number. In her second book she summarizes her findings as follows: "the bulk of all that these treatises contain is made up of commonplaces, culled mostly from the ancients, whose names besprinkle the pages of all writers. . . . There is plenty of evidence that these same commonplaces were not of mere academic interest, for the letters, speeches, and fiction of the time are full of the same ideas and rules for conduct."[61] The famous "humanists" who populated Renaissance universities made their livings by teaching grammar, rhetoric, poetry, history and moral philosophy.[62] Since both rhetoric and history were given strong moral emphasis, it may be said that the universities were to a great extent schools of virtue. At Oxford and Cambridge, undergraduates may still "read" moral philosophy for the B.A. degree.

Perhaps we have slighted Renaissance morality because we're following a false scent. Although a great many classical writers were re-discovered and re-born during the Renaissance, there was no re-naissance of moral philosophers, because they never died, and couldn't be reborn. They simply weren't what happened, and therefore they do not figure in our history of the Renaissance.[63] So, for example, Kerrigan and Braden's *Idea of the Renaissance* (1989) abandons the period's enormous investment in morality in order to pursue a vision of personal, political, and philosophical development leading to democratic (bourgeois) individualism and Kantian idealism.[64] Similarly, in a chapter of his book on the Senecan tradition actually entitled "Stoicism in the Renaissance," Braden omits any mention of Stoicism's domination of school and college education and the self-improvement market.[65] In such ways the vast ocean of moral discourse on which Shakespeare's plays float has been drained out of the past by the Whig view of history and the idea of progress.

We may also be victims of a misdefinition of Stoicism leading to the mistaken notion that Shakespeare rejected the whole system. If Stoicism is defined simply as lack of feeling, as we tend to do,[66] then Shakespeare is obviously not a Stoic. But Stoics have lots to say about responsibility, reciprocity, courage, integrity, reputation, fortune, love, duty, death, education, government, and many other categories of life. They cannot be reduced to their position on passion. And because Stoic discourse only makes explicit for Shakespeare's generation a precapitalist ethical scheme whose origins are the tribal experience, antiquity, Christianity, chivalry, the Roman occupation itself, and school and university education, it only reinforces habits that already make up the fabric of society. Although his status as an intellectual requires him to show familiarity with their discourses, the Stoics do not really "influence" Shakespeare. They are already an integral part of his reality and of the test of probability that his characters must pass.

Fortunately for us Professor Kelso's list of those ancients most commonly cited in conduct books is very short, consisting solely of Plato, Aristotle, Cicero, and Seneca.[67] Since only scholars commonly read Greek, that leaves Cicero and Seneca in command of the greater part of the reading public. Apparently the principal conduits of classical moral thought in Shakespeare's time were Cicero's *De Officiis* and Seneca's *Essays* and *Epistles*, in particular his *De Beneficiis*, a comprehensive philosophical investigation of every possible ramification of gift exchange (translated into English in 1578).

De Officiis was the first classical text ever printed. (1465)[68] The *British Museum Catalogue* lists 11 printed editions of it before 1600—eight interlinear trots, one English without Latin, and two in Latin. Eighteen more editions were published before 1700. For comparison, the *BMC* lists no edition of any dialogue of Plato in any language printed in England before 1600, and only one edition of Aristotle's *Ethics*, a translation into English of Brunetto Latini's compendium of its "preceptes of good behauour and perfighte honestie." Sir Thomas Elyot, in his famous *Governour* (1531), a standard work on the training of gentlemen, lists three essential texts: Plato's works, Aristotle's *Ethics*, and *De Officiis*. "Those three bokes," Elyot says, "be almost sufficient to make a perfecte and excellent governour".[69] In *The Complete Gentleman* (1622), Henry Peacham implies that *De Officiis* is a standard beginning Latin text, along with Aesop's Fables for beginning Greek.[70] In the preface to his translation of 1681, Sir Roger L'Estrange calls *De Officiis* "the commonest school book that we have," and goes on to observe, "as it is the best of books, so it is applied to the best of purposes, that is to say, to training up of youth in the study and exercise of virtue." King James I's own *de officiis*, *Basilikon Doron*, in which he tells his son Prince Henry his duties as man and ruler, refers him to Cicero fifty-five times, sixteen of them to *De Officiis*.

"In the Renaissance no Latin author was more highly esteemed than Seneca," said T. S. Eliot.[71] Montaigne confesses that his oeuvre is totally dependent on Seneca and Plutarch.[72] Erasmus, Justus Lipsius, and J. F. Gronovius published "famous editions" of Seneca's *Essays* in the sixteenth and seventeenth centuries.[73] The British Museum Catalogue shows that in 1547 the first Senecan epistle was translated into English by R. Whyttynton, Poet Laureate. Arthur Golding translated his *De Beneficiis* in 1578, quite soon enough for Shakespeare to have read it before writing *The Merchant*, and in 1614 Thomas Lodge translated the complete moral works. Something called *Seneca's Morals*, probably a compendium of excerpts, was published in English in 1607. Then, in 1678, Sir Roger L'Estrange published *Seneca's Morals by Way of Abstract*. By 1793 it had gone into seventeen editions. I found a copy (Cleveland: 1856) in my mother-in-law's Illinois farmhouse.

If Ann Jennalie Cook is right, the field of discourse I have been describing would have been a major means of communication between Shakespeare and his audience, for her copious evidence shows that the best educated and most well-read segment of society, and therefore the most steeped in classical morality, composed the main body of his audience.[74] Some discourses dominate the way other discourses are understood, as for instance, nowadays, feminist discourse. Was not Stoicism, in the comprehensive sense I argue for here, such a discourse during the Renaissance?

Discourse of Anger

If what I am proposing is true, it is no surprise that Montaigne's essay on Cruelty, where Professor Prosser found the passage on virtue and vengeance, is a remake of Seneca's treatise on Anger.[75] For Seneca, this passion is one of the two most destructive that plague mankind. (The other is Lust.)

> Anger [he says] is temporary madness. For it is equally devoid of self-control, forgetful of decency, unmindful of ties, persistent and diligent in whatever it begins, closed to reason and counsel, excited by trifling causes, unfit to discern the right and true.[76]

If we identify Prospero as an exemplar of the Senecan angry man, his behavior is easier to explain. He joins a sizable list of Shakespeare's angry madmen, whose fury drives them down an irreversible course to certain disaster, notably Lear, Hotspur, Coriolanus, Macbeth, Othello, and Timon. Anger interrupts the tale of Prospero's deposition—that he had himself to blame only adds fuel to the flame. Anger bridles at Ariel's recalcitrance. Anger punishes Caliban's insubordination with extreme cruelty.[77] Anger makes him unable to contain his hatred of Ferdinand, his chosen heir, because he is the son of his mortal enemy. And anger produces his evident glee at the success of his punishments of the conspirators.

It is only an illusion of romantic critics that Prospero is in control of his domain. (In their adaptation of *The Tempest* for Restoration audiences, Dryden and Davenant emphasize his bungling incompetence.[78]) "A man cannot be called powerful—no, not even free if he is the captive of his anger," says Seneca.[79] Anger is in charge, and Prospero dances to its tune. No wonder he explodes into the most remarkable rage in his daughter's memory when he remembers, during the masque, that he is about to be murdered by Caliban and his drunken crew. We have been watching a slow burn. When will he have peace? Seneca speaks to his predicament:

> Rage will sweep you hither and yon, this way and that, and your madness will be prolonged by new provocations that constantly arise. Tell me, unhappy man, will you ever find time to love? What precious time you are wasting upon an evil thing! How much better would it be at this present moment to be gaining friends, reconciling enemies, serving the state, devoting effort to private affairs, than to be casting about to see what evil you can do to some man, what wound you may deal to his position, his estate, or his person . . .[80]

When, prompted by his "nobler reason" (5.1.26), he admits his common humanity—admits "feeling [the same] passion as they" (5.1.24)—the play is again speaking the language of Stoicism, for following reason to such a conclusion is Seneca's recommended therapy for anger.

> No man of sense will hate the erring; otherwise he will hate himself. Let him reflect how many times he offends against morality, how many of his acts stand in need of pardon; then he will be angry with himself also.[81]

Whereas Seneca gloomily insists that we are all as bad as the worst, Elyot trusts that we are all as good as the best:

> Of no better claye (as I mought frankely saye) is a gentilman made than a carter, and of libertie of wille as moche is gyuen of god to the poore herdeman, as to the great and might emperour.[82]

But perhaps equating up is no different from equating down.

Observing that we do not get revenge on dumb animals who injure us, Seneca wonders why we are so hard on our own species:

> For what difference does it make that [a man's] other qualities are unlike that of dumb animals if he resembles them in the one quality that excuses dumb animals for every misdeed—a mind that is all darkness?[83]

That "darkness[84] that fills the mind" torments Seneca—

> not so much the necessity of going astray, as the love of straying. That you may not be angry with individuals, you must forgive mankind at large, you must grant indulgence to the human race.[85]

From here it is an easy step to Prospero's final position with respect to the "beast Caliban" (4.1.141), "This thing of darkness I acknowledge mine" (5.1.275),[86] not so puzzling a remark in its moral context as it is in the strictly-framed view of colonialist critics.[87]

Discourse of Freedom

At the climax of the play, then, Prospero wins freedom from the darkness that fills his mind. "Freedom" is another of *The Tempest*'s power words, so important that Shakespeare uses his dramatic medium's points of strongest emphasis to call it to our attention. Three acts close on freedom, and the play ends with the word "free." At the end of act 1, Ariel asks for his freedom. At the end of act 2, Caliban runs offstage shouting "Freedom, high-day!" Act 4 ends with Prospero promising Ariel his freedom after one more task.

If freedom is mastery, act 3 also ends on freedom, when Prospero has his enemies where he wants them. This is the same kind of freedom that Caliban crowed about at the end of act 2. But the only true freedom in all these act endings is the one that the audience may or may not give the actor of Prospero by applauding his last line: "As you from crimes would pardoned be / Let your indulgence set me free."

Much of *The Tempest* is devoted the pursuit of freedom as power. At the end of act 2, this kind of freedom comes into vivid contrast with an entirely different kind. As act 2 closes, Caliban goes offstage singing that he will no more "fetch in firing / At requiring. . . . Freedom, high-day! high-day, freedom! freedom, high-day, freedom!" (2.2.184–187). The very next scene opens, "*Enter Ferdinand bearing a log,*" introducing an entirely different attitude toward fetching firing at requiring. This juxtaposition highlights a dialog between two senses of freedom that drives the play as a whole. Let's call them freedom of the soul and freedom of the body.

Before the play starts, before Antonio usurped his dukedom, Prospero sought freedom of the body from the cares of office and retired to his chamber to study the "liberal arts" (1.2.73). Again, the context is Stoic. Seneca opposed the study of "liberal arts," because their aim was to make money. The one exception was philosophy, which Prospero obviously *hadn't* studied.[88] Cicero takes a very dim view of reluctant administrators like Prospero, declaring flatly: "to be drawn by study away from active life is contrary to moral duty."[89] Following this emphasis on doing one's job, James I warns his son and heir not to seek

> for knowledge nakedly, but that your principall ende be, to make you able thereby to vse your office; . . . not like these vaine Astrologians, that studie night and day on the course of the starres, onely that they may, for satisfying their curiositie, know their course."[90]

Prospero's magic, be it black or white, is analogous to Gyges's ring, but as Plato wrote his whole *Republic* to prove, Gyges's ring is a snare and a delusion: absolute power over one's fellow men is not the route to freedom. Cicero tells the whole story of Gyges in *De Officiis*.[91]

Seneca thought that a man who avoided public service had "died even before he was dead."[92] The ancients and their Renaissance popularizers agree that rulers have an especially strong obligation to serve the public. "The citizen who is patriotic, brave, and worthy of a leading place in the state . . . will dedicate himself unreservedly to his country, without aiming at influence or power for himself," says Cicero.[93] In fact, Seneca agrees, "ruling [is] a service, not an exercise of royalty."[94] And moreover, "Instead of sacrificing the state to themselves, [rulers] have sacrificed themselves to the state."[95] Elyot echoes these sentiments, saying "that auctorite, beinge well and diligently used, is but a token of superioritie, but in very dede it is a burden and losse of libertie."[96] On this note James I begins his advice to his son, reminding him "that being borne to be a king, ye are rather borne to *onus,* th[a]n *honos.*"[97]

As defined in Stoic discourse, freedom is a state of mind, not of body. As Ferdinand very significantly says, provided that we are tuned in to this dialog, he is as happy to be a slave for Miranda's sake "as bondage e'er of freedom" (3.1.89) If it is the way to win her, he accepts bondage to labor as eagerly as Prospero, Ariel, and Caliban seek freedom from it. Love, as defined so beautifully in this scene, is mutual voluntary servitude, and voluntary servitude is the only freedom *The Tempest* offers. When Alonso and Prospero give each other their children in the denouement, this ancient ritual of gift-exchange signifies peace between them. There are two ways of establishing cooperation in society: enslavement (either to a master or to the law, as in modern democratic societies); and reciprocal exchange of benefits (gifts or services).

Starting from the Aristotelian premise that man is a social animal, Cicero finds that the social bond is established by means of a system of "mutual interchange of kind services; . . . [for] those between whom they are interchanged are united by the ties of an enduring intimacy."[98] Hence

> we ought to follow Nature as our guide, to contribute to the general good by an interchange of acts of kindness, by giving and receiving, and thus by our skill, our industry, and our talents to cement human society more closely together, man to man.[99]

Seneca allegorizes the social cement in the process of answering some questions about the Three Graces (*Gratiae,* as in "gratitude," "congratulate," "gratuity," "gracias," etc.). First, why are there three of them?

> Some would have it appear that there is one for bestowing a benefit, another for receiving it, and a third for returning it. . . . Why do the sisters hand in hand dance in a ring which returns upon itself? For the reason that a benefit passing in its course from hand to hand returns nevertheless to the giver; the beauty of the whole is destroyed if the

course is anywhere broken, and it has most beauty if it is continuous and maintains an uninterrupted succession. In the dance, nevertheless, an older sister has especial honor, as do those who earn benefits. Their faces are cheerful, as are ordinarily the faces of those who bestow or receive benefits. They are young because the memory of benefits ought not to grow old. They are maidens because benefits are pure and undefiled and holy in the eyes of all; and it is fitting that there should be nothing to bind or restrict them, and so the maidens wear flowing robes, and these, too, are transparent because benefits desire to be seen.[100]

For Elyot the virtue that cements us all together

is called humanitie whiche is a generall name to those vertues in whome seme to be a mutuall concorde and loue in the nature of man. And all thoughe there be many of the said vertues, yet be there thre principall by whome humanitie is chiefly compact; beneuolence, benificence ["goode tournes"], and liberalitie.

By virtue of this instinct human beings, while still inferior to God, are superior to beasts.[101]

Essentially what happens in *The Tempest* is that Prospero tries to gain freedom by maximizing his power—the Gyges ring method—but eventually, perhaps prompted by Ferdinand and Miranda, he melts into a generous paradigm. He learns that a cruel master cannot ever have the joy of a willing servant. That discovery, I believe, induces Prospero's change of heart, and that is what his epilogue is about: Prospero (duke/actor), having used magic/stagecraft to coerce his subjects (audience/islanders/citizens of Milan) into obedience, now breaks his magic wand/theatrical spell and frees his erstwhile slaves (audience/islanders/citizens). Essentially, he commits unilateral disarmament. Of such grand gestures, Seneca says, "To help, to be of service . . . [to give] benefits, imitates the gods; he who seeks a return [imitates] money-lenders."[102] The antisocial duke has come a long way.

A typical actor/audience relationship differs radically from the duke/citizen relationship that has prevailed up to this point, for it is a form of the reciprocal benefit system we have been discussing, in which the actor gives entertainment and the audience returns applause. It is love, it is mutual satisfaction: gratitude warms both sides of the footlights. Perhaps, if Prospero now alters radically his tactics of rule and becomes a magnanimous and just ruler concerned only with the welfare of the city entrusted to him, the people will be grateful, and will serve him with all their hearts. The moralists believe so. Tyranny never works, says Elyot, brandishing potent authorities

> For the beneuolente mynde of a gouernour nat onely byndeth the hartes of the people unto hym with the chayne of loue, more stronger than any materiall bondes, but also gardeth more saulfely his persone than any toure or garison. The eloquent Tulli, saithe in his officis, A liberall harte is cause of beneuolence, although perchance that power some tyme lackethe. Contrary wise he saith, They that desire to be feared, nedes must they drede them, of whom they be feared. Also Plini the yonger saith, He that is nat enuironed with charite, in vaine is he garded with terrour; sens armure with armure is stered. Whiche is ratified by the mooste graue philosopher Seneke, in his boke of mercye that he wrate to Nero, where he saith, He is moche deceiued that thinketh a man to be suer, where nothynge from hym can be saulfe. For [only] with mutuall assurance suertie is optained.[103]

But the final effect of a good deed cannot be assumed in advance, for if it is calculated, then it isn't a good deed: it's a deal. It's entirely up to the citizens of Milan, as it is to an audience at the end of a play, whether to catcall/kill the actor/duke or applaud/serve him and "with [their] indulgence [to] set [him] free"—by gratefully applauding his willing service.

The colonialist approach perceives that Prospero's final gambit fails. After all, Antonio and Sebastian do not burst into tears and fall on their knees.[104] But read in terms of the relevant field of discourse, their inaction signifies no failure. In Stoic terms, Prospero is concerned with getting control over himself, not over his enemies. Stoicism also puts a different spin on the situation: what we have here is clemency, not forgiveness, and the point is to deprive the injuror of any enjoyment from watching the injured one's anger and chagrin. On this point Elyot says

> The best waye to be aduenged is so to contemne Iniurie and rebuke, and lyue with suche honestie, that the doer shall at the laste be therof a shamed, or at the leste, lese [lose] the frute of his malyce, that is to say, shall nat reioyce and haue glorie of thy hyndraunce or domage [damage].[105]

Hall's *Characters* (1608) focuses on the glory of imperturbability, rather than on the repentance of the perturber:

> The Valiant Man['s] power is limited by his will, and he holds it the noblest revenge, that he might hurt and doth not.[106]

Furthermore, when we reach the end of a Shakespearean comedy things seldom are settled. There is never any guarantee that the remedies discovered in the green world will serve when the persons of the play return to the real world. The poet says good-bye and good luck. He has shown the audience what they are capable of (both good and evil). Now they're on their own. Will gratitude for Prospero's new start overcome the years of his neglect? The sulking characters remain to keep this question on the table.

But wait: there's still that final note of despair. When Prospero tells us, in his epilogue that after his return to Milan his "every third thought will be [his] grave." Can we call this a happy ending? Their vision still hampered by their frame, the colonialist critics who pick up on this talk of the grave think not.[107] Again Stoic discourse sheds a better light on the passage. Cicero said "to think as a philosopher is to learn to die." Montaigne used this sentence as the title of a long essay on death.[108] Epictetus exhorts, "Let death . . . be daily before your eyes . . . and you will never think of anything mean."[109] Montaigne would have us

> combat [death] with a resolute minde. And being to take the greatest advantage she hath upon us from her, let us take a cleane contrary way from the common, let us remove her strangenesse from her, let us converse, frequent, and acquaint our selves with her, let us have nothing so much in minde as death, let us at all times and seasons, and in the ugliest manner that may be, yea with all faces shapen and represent the same unto our imagination. At the stumbling of a horse, at the fall of a stone, at the least prick with a pinne, let us presently ruminate and say with our selves, what if it were death it selfe? and thereupon let us take heart of grace, and call our wits together to confront her. . . . The premeditation of death is a fore-thinking of libertie.[110]

Again Montaigne sounds like Seneca, who is always advising that "the soul must be hardened by long practice, so that it may learn to endure the sight and the approach of death."[111] Indeed Seneca is antiquity's expert on death, and one gathers that he conceives of a man's life as a tale that has no meaning until it's over. For a duke, one assumes, dying well would mean dying well-beloved. Furthermore, since death is one of those common denominators that level out the distinction between the angry man and his victim, thinking on death will ease Prospero's fury.[112] "Nothing will give you so much help toward moderation as the frequent thought that life is short and uncertain here below; whatever you are doing, have regard to death."[113] Finally, one must come to terms with death in order to achieve that precious freedom of the soul, because fear of death is certainly the ultimate slavery. "To think on death," counsels Seneca, is to "think on freedom. He who has learned to die has unlearned slavery; he is above any eternal power, or, at any rate, he is beyond it."[114]

These sentiments and those I have already quoted, I argue, tether *The Tempest* to the discursive field of early modern ethical discourse, to which the play reports back, in terms defined by that field, a vivid illustration of what it means to be free.

* * * * *

The colonialist critics have laid to rest forever the idealist interpretation of Prospero, and definitively located the mythos of colonialism in his treatment of Caliban. But it appears that we do find, upon extending Professor Porter's critique of new historicism to *The Tempest*, that the oversights she describes in the work of Greenblatt and Mullaney do also occur in new historicist work on *The Tempest*. The play is too large to look at through the knothole of colonialist discourse. In so doing these critics unconsciously silence other kinds of discourse that the play could clearly hear, and overlook the rhetorical strategy by which the play talks back to the "horizonless field." Certainly *The Tempest* hears and contributes to many other fields of discourse: Arthurian legend, Jungian archetypes, Freudian psychoses, regeneration rituals, vegetation cults, Plato's three parts of the soul, good angels/bad angels, chess, Italy, drama theory, Shakespeare's life, magic, the ethics of magic, and who knows what else? And discourse of colonialism does of course participate. But if we open the window far enough to include Stoicism, Prospero's conquistadorial activities become a product of his anger, and his colonizing becomes a category of tyranny, which by definition governs by enslavement. Since both anger and tyranny are bad, and their consequences are bad, the play deplores colonization. But *The Tempest*'s relation to colonialism is more complex than the view from the colonialist critics' window.

Notes

1. Carolyn Porter, "Are We Being Historical Yet?" *South Atlantic Quarterly* 87 (1988): 743–86, especially 750, 782.

2. In "Discourse and the Individual: The Case of Colonialism in *The Tempest*," Meredith Anne Skura tests the claims of colonialist critics against an exhaustive reconstitution of contemporary English discourse on the new world. She

finds that records of British colonization were not available to Shakespeare when he wrote *The Tempest*, at which time colonialist discourse in England was still in its romantic phase. She also contributes a most useful comprehensive survey of extant literature on *The Tempest* (*Shakespeare Quarterly* 40 [Spring 1989]:42–69]. However, the ugly practices of other nations had been published abroad long before the writing of *The Tempest*, and Montaigne protests against them in the very essay "Of Canniballes" to which Shakespeare clearly refers in Gonzalo's speech at 2.1.143–60. (*The essays of Michael lord of Montaigne*, trans. John Florio, World's classics [London: Frowde, 1904], vol. 1, chap. 30.

3. Similar doubts about Foucaldian methods have recently been voiced in other quarters. See essays in *The New Historicists*, ed. H. Aram Veeser (New York: Routledge, 1989) by Frank Lentricchia: "Foucault's Legacy: a New Historicism?" 231–42; by Gerald Graff: "Co-Optation," 168–81, esp. 172; and by Brook Thomas: "New Historicism and Other Old-Fashioned Topics," 182–203, esp. 202.

4. Porter, "Are We Being Historical Yet?" 771.

5. Ibid., 767.

6. Ibid., 770–71.

7. Ibid., 747, Porter quoting Greenblatt.

8. Thomas Cartelli, "Prospero in Africa: The Tempest as Colonialist Text and Pretext," in *Shakespeare Reproduced: The Text in History and Ideology*, ed. Jean E. Howard and Marion F. O'Connor (New York & London: Methuen, 1987), 95–115.

9. Curt Breight, "'Treason doth never Prosper': The Tempest and the Discourse of Treason," *Shakespeare Quarterly* 41 (1990): 1–28.

10. Lori Leininger, "Cracking the Code of The Tempest," *Shakespeare: Contemporary Critical Approaches*, ed. Harry Garvin (Lewisburg, Pa.: Bucknell University Press, 1980), 121–131.

11. Paul Brown, "'This thing of darkness I acknowledge mine': The Tempest and the Discourse of Colonialism," *Political Shakespeare: New Essays in Cultural Materialism*, ed. Jonathan Dollimore and Alan Sinfield (Manchester: Manchester University Press, 1985) 48–71.

12. Ibid., 46.

13. Francis Barker and Peter Hulme, "Nymphs and Reapers Heavily Vanish: The Discursive Con-texts of *The Tempest*," *Alternative Shakespeare*, ed. John Drakakis (London: Methuen, 1985).

14. Ibid., 195.

15. Stephen Orgel, "Introduction,' *The Tempest*, The Oxford Shakespeare (Oxford: Oxford University Press, 1987), 1–87.

16. Eric Cheyfetz, *The Poetics of Imperialism: Translation and Colonization from The Tempest to Tarzan* (New York: Oxford University Press, 1991).

17. Stephen Greenblatt, "Martial Law in the Land of Cokaigne," *Shakespearean Negotiations: The Circulation of Social Energy in Renaissance England* (Berkeley: University of California Press, 1988), 129–98.

18. They have been anticipated by at least two critics of the play who reject the "authorized version" without the aid of theory. As early as 1906, Lytton Strachey objected to the received opinion that Prospero portrays a "spirit of wise benevolence," perceiving instead

> an unpleasantly crusty personage, in whom a twelve years' monopoly of the conversation had developed an inordinate propensity for talking. These may have been the sentiments of Ariel, safe at the Bermoothes; but to state them is to risk at least ten years in the knotty entrails of an oak, and it is sufficient to point out that if Prospero is wise, he is also self-opinionated and sour, that his gravity is often another name for pedantic severity, and that there is no character in the play to whom, during some part of it, he is not studiously

disagreeable. (*Books and Characters, English and French* [New York: Harcourt Brace, 1922], 68)

Sixty-two years later John P. Cutts read Prospero as another Faustus, manipulating people for his own enjoyment, an almost certain candidate for damnation whose repentance likewise comes too late. (*Rich and Strange: A Study of Shakespeare's Last Plays* [Pullman: Washington State University Press, 1968]).

19. Barker and Hulme, "Nymphs and Reapers Heavily Vanish," 197.
20. Breight, "Treason doth never Prosper," 10.
21. Breight, "'Treason doth never Prosper,'" 10, 18; Brown, "'This thing of darkness I acknowledge mine,'" 53; Barker and Hulme "Nymphs and Reapers Heavily Vanish," 198; Cheyfetz, *The Poetics of Imperialism*, 156; Leininger, "Cracking the Code of The Tempest," 122; Orgel, "Introduction," 4, 13.
22. All citations of Shakespeare's plays are taken from the Riverside Shakespeare, edited by G. Blakemore Evans, 1974.
23. Brown, "The thing of darkness I acknowledge mine," 59–60; Cheyfetz, *The Poetics of Imperialism*, 76; Orgel, "Introduction," 8, 14, 15–16, 21, 52; Breight, "'Treason doth never Prosper,'" 10, 14; Greenblatt, "Martial Law in the Land of Cokaigne," 46, 142–43, 156, 160.
24. Orgel, "Introduction," 36, 47, 52; Brown, "'This thing of darkness I acknowledge mine,'" 59; Greenblatt, "Martial Law in the Land of Cokaigne," 147, 154; Breight, "'Treason doth never Prosper,'" 10, 17, 23.
25. Cartelli, "Prospero in Africa," 105; Barker and Hulme, "Nymphs and Reapers Heavily Vanish," 195, 198–200, 202; Brown, "'The thing of Darkness I acknowledge mine,'" 65; Cheyfetz, *The Poetics of Imperialism*, 161; Leininger, "Cracking the Code of The Tempest," 125; Orgel, "Introduction," 41, 49.
26. Brown, "'This thing of darkness I acknowledge mine,'" 109.
27. Cartelli, "Prospero in Africa," 106, 107, 110; Brown, "'This thing of darkness I acknowledge mine,'" 58, 61–62; Breight, "'Treason doth never Prosper,'" 10; Barker and Hulme, "Nymphs and Reapers Heavily Vanish," 199; Cheyfetz, *The Poetics of Imperialism*, 161; Orgel, "Introduction," 41, 49.
28. Barker and Hulme, "Nymphs and Reapers Heavily Vanish," 196.
29. Breight, "'Treason doth never Prosper,'" 24; Brown, "'This thing of darkness I acknowledge mine,'" 60.
30. Brown, "'This thing of darkness I acknowledge mine,'" 60; Barker and Hulme, "Nymphs and Reapers Heavily Vanish," 199; Greenblatt, "Martial Law in the Land of Cokaigne," 160; Orgel, "Introduction," 15, 22; Cheyfetz, *The Poetics of Imperialism*, 159.
31. Barker and Hulme, "Nymphs and Reapers Heavily Vanish," 199; Cartelli, "Prospero in Africa," 106–7; Greenblatt, "Martial Law in the Land of Cokaigne," 157; Orgel, "Introduction," 23, 28.
32. Breight, "'Treason doth never Prosper,'" 11; Greenblatt, "Martial Law in the Land of Cokaigne," 143, 144; Orgel, "Introduction," 28–29.
33. Breight, "'Treason doth never Prosper,'" 18; Greenblatt, "Martial Law in the Land of Cokaigne," 143.
34. Breight, "'Treason doth never Prosper,'" 11; Brown, "'This thing of darkness I acknowledge mine,'" 196; Barker and Hulme, "Nymphs and Reapers Heavily Vanish," 202; Cheyfetz, *The Poetics of Imperialism*, 77; Greenblatt, "Martial Law in the Land of Cokaigne," 144; Orgel, "Introduction," 50.
35. Brown, "'This thing of darkness I acknowledge mine,'" 67.
36. Breight, "'Treason doth never Prosper,'" 22–23.
37. Orgel, "Introduction," 54.

38. Cartelli, "Prospero in Africa," 116; Leininger, "Cracking the Code of The Tempest," 127–130.
39. Barker and Hulme, "Nymphs and Reapers Heavily Vanish," 202.
40. The critical malpractice of "refuting the ending" was first identified by Richard Levin in *New Readings vs. Old Plays* (Chicago: University of Chicago Press, 1979). Edward Pechter finds the practice still prevalent in his "New Historicism and Its Discontents," *PMLA* 102 (1987): 292–303, esp. 299.
41. The advocates of a benevolent magus also ignored Prospero's change of heart, because it contradicted their hypothesis as well. In their interpretations, D'Orsay Pearson ("'Unless I Be Reliev'd by Prayer': The Tempest in Perspective," *Shakespeare Studies* 7 [1974]: 253–82, esp. 273) and Joseph Summers ("The Anger of Prospero," *Dreams of Love and Power: On Shakespeare's Plays* [Oxford: Clarendon, 1984]) restore the climax, Pearson having Prospero recover from the sin of magic, and Summers, relying on intra-textual evidence, having him recover from a seizure of anger, thus anticipating what follows here.
42. Eleanor Prosser, "Shakespeare, Montaigne, and the Rarer Action," *Shakespeare Studies* 1 (1965): 261–64.
43. Montaigne, *The essays of Michael lord of Montaigne*, 2:11.
44. Thomas Elyot, *The Governour*, Everyman edn. (London: Dent, 1907), 235.
45. James I, "Basilikon Doron," *Political Works of James I*, ed. C. E. McIlwain (Cambridge: Harvard University Press, 1918), 3–52, esp. 41.
46. Joseph Hall, "Characters of Virtues and Vices," *Works*, ed. Philip Wynter (New York: AMS Press, 1969), vi:89–125, esp. 97.
47. Cicero, *De Officiis*, trans. Walter Miller, Loeb edn. (Cambridge: Harvard University Press, 1968) 89.
48. Seneca, *Moral Essays*, trans. John W. Basore, The Loeb Classical Library (London: W. Heinemann, 1928–1935), 1:268–9.
49. In their glosses on the line both Frank Kermode (Arden edn. [London: Methuen, 1958]) and Stephen Orgel (Oxford edn, [Oxford: Oxford University Press, 1987]) feel the need to explain (unconvincingly) why "vengeance" (5.1.28) is not balanced by "forgiveness" or "pardon." See also Prosser, "Shakespeare, Montaigne, and the Rarer Action," 262.
50. Karl Marx, *Communist Manifesto* (Chicago: Regnery, 1954), 12–13.
51. Peter Laslett, *The World We Have Lost* (New York: Scribner, 1965), 17.
52. Max Weber, *Essays in Sociology*, ed. Hans Gerth and C. Wright Mills (New York: Oxford University Press, 1946), 329.
53. Jürgen Habermas, *Toward a Rational Society: Student Protest, Science, and Politics* (Boston: Beacon Press, 1970), 91–93.
54. Sven Longstreth, Frank Steinmo and Katherine Thelen, *Structuring Politics: Historical Institutionalism in Comparative Analysis* (Cambridge: Cambridge University Press, 1992) chap. 1.
55. Karl Polyanyi, *The Great Transformation [1944]* (Boston: Beacon Press, 1957), 46.
56. Marcel Mauss, *The Gift: Forms and Functions of Exchange in Archaic Societies*, trans. Ian Cunnison (New York: Norton, 1954).
57. Marshall Sahlins, *Stone Age Economics* (Chicago and New York: Aldine-Atherton, 1972), 2–14.
58. Lewis Hyde, *The Gift: Imagination and the Erotic Life of Property* (New York: Vintage Books, 1979).
59. Seneca, *Moral Epistles*, trans., Richard M. Gummere, The Loeb classical library (Cambridge, Mass.: Harvard, 1917–25), 2:423–24.
60. Ruth Kelso, *The Doctrine of the English Gentleman in the Sixteenth Cen-

tury (Gloucester, MA: Peter Smith, 1964); *Doctrine for the lady of the Renaissance* (Urbana: University of Illinois Press, 1956).

61. Kelso, *Doctrine for the Lady of the Renaissance*, 322.

62. Paul Oskar Kristeller, *Renaissance Thought and Its Sources*, ed. Michael Mooney (New York: Columbia University Press, 1979), 22.

63. Ibid., 25, 36–37, 128.

64. William Kerrigan and Gordon Braden, *The Idea of the Renaissance* (Baltimore: Johns Hopkins University Press, 1989).

65. Gordon Braden, *Renaissance Tragedy and the Senecan Tradition: Anger's Privilege* (New Haven: Yale University Press, 1985).

66. For a random example, consider Marvin Vawter, "'Division 'tween Our Souls.': Shakespeare's Stoic Brutus," *Shakespeare Studies* (Columbia: University of South Carolina Press, 1974), 173–95, esp. 173–79. Or consider William R. Elton's *magnum opus*, *King Lear and the Gods* (San Marino, Calif.: Huntington Library, 1966), a book heavily documented by primary sources, in which Stoicism stands for little else than hardness of heart. Though Elton calls upon Cicero many times, he pays no attention to *De Officiis*, his most important (and most pragmatic) book.

67. Kelso, *Doctrine for the Lady of the Renaissance*, 311.

68. Cicero, *De Officiis*, xvii.

69. Elyot, *The Governour*, 47–48.

70. Henry Peacham, *The Complete Gentleman, The Truth of Our Times and The Art of Living in London*, ed. Virgil B. Heltzel (Ithaca: Cornell University Press, 1962), 29.

71. T. S. Eliot, "Shakespeare and the Stoicism of Seneca," *Selected Essays* (New York: Harcourt, Brace, 1950), 107–120, esp. 52.

72. Montaigne, *The essays of Michael lord of Montaigne*, 1:161.

73. Seneca, *Moral Essays*, 1:xv.

74. Ann Jennalie Cook, *The Privileged Playgoers of Shakespeare's London 1576–1642* (Princeton: Princeton University Press, 1981).

75. Seneca, "De Ira," *Moral Essays*, 1:107–355.

76. Ibid., 1:107.

77. Cf. Breight, "'Treason doth never Prosper,'" 20–21, 24–26.

78. Cf. Matthew M. Wikander, "'The Duke My Father's Wrack': The Innocence of the Restoration *Tempest*," *Shakespeare Survey*, ed. Stanley Wells (Cambridge: Cambridge University Press, 1991), 91–98, esp. 91, 93, 95, 97.

79. Seneca, *Moral Essays*, 1:263.

80. Ibid., 1:325.

81. Ibid., 1:143.

82. Elyot, *The Governour*, 202.

83. Seneca, *Moral Essays*, 1:323.

84. The Latin word is "caligo," one meaning of which, according to the *Oxford Latin Dictionary* is "moral and intellectual darkness."

85. Seneca, *Moral Essays*, 1:185.

86. Lear's anger similarly subsides when he learns "to feel what wretches feel" (3.4.34) and recognizes in Poor Tom a fellow human being.

87. Brown, "The thing of darkness I acknowledge mine," 64; Cartelli, "Prospero in Africa," 111; Greenblatt, "Martial Law in the Land of Cokaigne," 157; Orgel, "Introduction," 23; Leininger, "Cracking the Code of The Tempest," 127.

88. Seneca, *Moral Epistles*, 2:349.

89. Cicero, *De Officiis*, 6.

90. James I, "Basilikon Doron," 38–39.

91. Cicero, *De Officiis*, 305.
92. Seneca, *Moral Epistles*, 3:5.
93. Cicero, *De Officiis*, 89.
94. Seneca, *Moral Epistles*, 2:399.
95. Seneca, *Moral Epistles*, 3:271.
96. Elyot, *The Governour*, 140.
97. James I, "Basilikon Doron," 3.
98. Cicero, *De Officiis*, 59.
99. Ibid., 25.
100. Seneca, *Moral Essays*, 3:13.
101. Elyot, *The Governour*, 147.
102. Seneca, *Moral Essays*, 3:155.
103. Elyot, *The Governour*, 155.
104. Greenblatt, "Martial Law in the Land of Cokaigne," 46; Breight, "'Treason doth never Prosper,'" 13; Orgel, "Introduction," 23; Cheyfetz, *The Poetics of Imperialism*, 158.
105. Elyot, *The Governour*, 236.
106. Hall, "Characters of Virtues and Vices," 96.
107. Breight, "'Treason doth never Prosper,'" 20; Barker and Hulme, "Nymphs and Reapers Heavily Vanish," 67; Brown, "The thing of darkness I acknowledge mine," 68; Cheyfetz, *The Poetics of Imperialism*, 176; Orgel, "Introduction," 29.
108. Montaigne, *The essays of Michael lord of Montaigne*, 1:xix.
109. Epictetus, *Discourses of Epictetus with the Encheiridion and Fragments*, trans. George Long (London: George Bell, 1877), 387.
110. Montaigne, *The essays of Michael lord of Montaigne*, 1:80–81.
111. Seneca, *Moral Epistles*, 2:251.
112. Cf. Seneca, *Moral Essays*, 1:353.
113. Seneca, *Moral Epistles*, 3:319.
114. Seneca, *Moral Epistles*, 1:191. Montaigne thinks of the day of death as the only day in our lives when "whatever the pot containeth must be shown" (1:71).

"The name and all th' addition": King *Lear*'s Opening Scene and the Common-Law Use

CHARLES SPINOSA

1. Introduction

NOT LONG AGO literary thinking about *King Lear* could be roughly divided among four perspectives. First, there was the Christian and humanist view.[1] It generally followed a purgatorial line of reasoning in claiming that, while Lear started off as a petty-minded autocrat, in his downfall he discovered how to feel and express basic human warmth.[2] Lear then went on to follow this learning with such energetic moral and intellectual forthrightness that his personal intensity transcended the misery of his actual sublunary death.[3] Second, in response to this Christian/humanist reading, arose the counterproposal, frequently based on historical or imagistic studies, that claimed that Lear remained an unregenerate pagan whose great strength of mind and character focused solely on the present and the sensuous and in doing so showed two things: (1) Human beings learn by suffering alone, and (2) since suffering results in neither transcendence nor profound meanings, what suffering teaches is not worth learning.[4] Third, while these two views worked with and through broad theological and philosophical propositions about the nature of the world and of the gods, another more psychologistic approach thought about Lear as a father and developed a picture of the Shakespearean family romance. Here Lear turns out to be variously a sponge for love, a senile or puerile father who finds all the various sides of his character reflected in his children, or a man who feels shame at his incapacity to love and who then avoids opening himself to others by theatricalizing them.[5] Fourth, essays of a political cast covered such issues as how the play reflects the change from an aristocratic to a bourgeois state, how political language is related to authority, and finally how the play develops the meaning of abdication.[6] This taxonomy should not be taken to imply that up until a certain recent moment in *Lear* criticism, essays remained confined to one or another of these categories. The richest essays clearly crossed categories. Nevertheless, until recently, essays drew most heavily on one or another of these approaches.

Today's richest essays, however, focus on issues that explicitly cross and contest the convenient categories of the past. So, for instance, Jonathan Dollimore, writing as a cultural materialist, reads *King Lear* as criticizing, on the one hand, the fixed psychological subject of the family romancers and the humanists and, on the other hand, the politics of property that was simply taken for granted by previous political critics. According to Dollimore, the play shows that power and property relations are prior to any law of human kindness or indeed any feeling of human warmth whatsoever,[7] and that the then current distribution of power and property produced both war and incomplete lives. In her feminist reading, Marianne Novy argues, similarly, that patriarchal structures of power and property deny a mutuality in feeling between men and women. This absence created, in Jacobean England, a peculiar theatrical distance between people that generated anger, political upheaval, and finally depended on female forgiveness (a tortured form of human warmth) for any stability at all.[8] As in Dollimore's essay, Novy's blends issues of family romance and politics. Lastly, Stephen Greenblatt, in his recent new historicist reading, sees *King Lear* as both subverting and promoting the central established institutions in a rather complicated way. *Lear* shows on the one hand that those institutions subversive of the central state apparatus are theatrical through and through (he has in mind nonconforming religious institutions) and on the other hand that the state's means of exposing this theatricality are themselves theatrical. According to Greenblatt, the post-*Lear*, as opposed to Barber's post-Christian, world turns out to contain only theatrical representations representing nothing more than other representations, and all these representations are sustained by the memory, perpetuated in the theater, of the now-falsified belief in some always already meaningful ground of representation. Consequently, the notions of the cosmos, the established state, and the autonomous individual become understood—though not necessarily felt—as evacuated and emptied of redemptive or pathetic meaning.[9] Hence Greenblatt's reading crosses through and contests all the various types of earlier readings.

These new readings (to which could be added those that claim *Lear* gives us a new nonauthoritarian language[10]) depend both in their broad approach and in their close readings on the proposition that property, patriarchal identity, and the established law and religion of the state maintained themselves with high enough degrees of effectiveness and consistency to make sense of the intense critical examination under which the play placed these institutions. It is on these grounds of stability that the older Christian/humanist, anti-humanist, psychologistic, and political readings are like the contestational cultural materialist, feminist, and new historicist readings. The Christian/humanist and anti-humanist readings had a stable cosmos; the psychoanalytic had a stable family-romance story (that produced instabilities); the political had stable state forms (even if there was instability in going from one form to another). Likewise, the cultural materialist has stable forms of landed power; the feminist, stable forms of patriarchal power; and the new historicist, stable forms of theatricalizing power. Perhaps, it is impossible to help ourselves from reading certain stable cultural configurations that we know emerged from the early modern period back into that period. Nevertheless, this essay will attempt to read against the grain of these stabilities imported into the early modern period and attempt to recognize the extent to which from the last decade of the sixteenth century through the Civil War, the English failed to find an inner thread of consistency among the various forms that property, personal identity,[11] and law could take.

This ambition will be aided by a curious fact about the early modern social configuration. In contrast to today's vague crises such as citizen apathy and crime which have no central *focusing* context but do share a stable background set of cultural disciplinary and technological practices,[12] this early modern crisis in property-holding, personal identity, and law received focused shape and definition primarily in the context of landholding. Yet, the general background cultural practices behind landholding were not stable. They were brought into turmoil by the same practices that were bringing turmoil to the land law. For, in trying to bring order to the institution of the use (an early form of the trust), the common law drew into itself a pre-legal practice—trusting promises of friends—whose effects were so contrary to its basic notions of land as public and alienable, landholding as subject to mortality, and the law as primarily a matter of custom that none of these, neither publicity, alienability, mortality, nor a customary law could be taken for granted as foundational anymore. Indeed, from 1536 when the Statute of Uses interdicted the use as a way of holding land in the present—but not as a way of holding a future right to land—the common law so turned against itself that it found nothing but confusion and congestion at the heart of English social practice. At its most fantastic, as Chief Justice Popham suggested in his argument in *Chudleigh's Case* (1595), this statute enabled settlements of land to be made to a man and his heirs so that title would shift from one possible heir to another whenever any law suit was initiated against the one of them who held title.[13] Such a settlement made the family's holding immune to the workings of the common, customary law.

Under such circumstances, where even *Chudleigh's Case* failed to settle once and for all the confusions of landholding, law, and personal identity, a play such as the one described by Dollimore, Novy, and Greenblatt, that revealed stresses in property, identity, and law would amount to the simplest form of mimetic reporting. *King Lear* goes a good deal further than this by attempting to develop a sharp understanding of the nature of the problems in personal identity, property, and law associated with the proliferation of the use. It shows what would come of property, identity, and law by employing a prototypical use to organize an entire political society. It directly examines two matters that the common lawyers did not know how to approach. First, it seeks to understand the necessity of the use to the English way of being. So, in part, this essay sees *King Lear* as the English myth of the first use. Second, since Shakespeare is primarily concerned with the sort of personal identities dealing with uses establishes, he goes beyond the legal pro-use arguments, which focused on the tranquility uses promised the English nation,[14] to see how heroically passionate personal identities would replace dutiful, traditional identities. Consequently, this essay will try to shift the grounds in the debate over whether modern forms of personal identity arose and were playing a dominant part in Shakespeare's day. This essay will suggest that the late-sixteenth and early-seventeenth centuries had as many well-developed forms of personal identity competing for dominance as it had competing ways of holding land.[15]

In this essay, however, Shakespeare's exploration of property, law, and personal identity will be limited to the notoriously difficult first scene in order to show how the play establishes its use and how two structurally different forms of the early modern identity (self-constituting supervisorial identity revealed in Lear, on the one hand, and deep psychological identity hearkened to by Kent and Cordelia, on the other) organize themselves around the use, each in conflict with the other. In contrast to these early modern selves, Goneril and Regan stand out as representatives of a feudal, calculative organization of identity, and consequently they, as we shall see, fail fully to grasp the point of the proto-use Lear establishes.

Hence, this essay investigates how Shakespeare shows that certain kinds of modern identity are at stake in establishing and accepting the proliferation of uses. There are three other lesser consequences to these claims. It should become clear in this essay that certain presuppositions regarding early modern social stability in essays like Dollimore's, Novy's, and Greenblatt's should be revised. Also, we should learn why the first scene of the play does not show us a puerile,[16] senile,[17] or nursery-tale[18] Lear. And we should see why, in lacking an understanding of the use, many commentators have, against their better judgments, been forced to follow Regan's analysis in interpreting Lear's actions in the first scene. "'Tis the infirmity of his age," she says, and "he hath ever but / slenderly known himself."[19]

2. Personal Identity and Property

In order to see that *King Lear* begins with Lear putting his kingdom in a proto-use and to see the legal, political, personal, and ontological consequences of such an act, we shall have to understand the relation between landholding and personal identity in the early seventeenth century and what a use was as well as what a proto-use could be. J. G. A. Pocock has familiarized us with the now common constructivist account of the general relation between landholding and personal identity.[20] According to this account, the late sixteenth and early seventeenth centuries see the fading of the civic-virtue model of landholding where landed estates are understood as producing the wealth necessary for having the leisure to conduct public business, including warfare. On the civic-virtue model, the amount and productivity of the land one held determined one's suitability for public service from yeomen suitable for juries, to gentry suitable for service as justices of the peace and as members of the House of Commons, to the lesser nobility suitable for lord lieutenancies and other sorts of royal service. (Most successful merchants purchased landed estates in order to attain a clearly recognizable status identity appropriate to their wealth.) But regardless of one's *status identity* in this hierarchy, if one was landed, one's *personal identity* was based on one's nonmanual (i.e., leisured) practices for governing those who engaged in the manual labor on one's private estate. So, the move from the private governing of an estate to public governing functions was small.

In contrast to this notion of an estate that was governed and personal identity that was governing rose, according to Pocock, the mercantile understanding of wealth, where goods and money and, most important, credit became the paradigm property in terms of which one could come to understand oneself. Goods, money, and credit were not used to beget the leisure for public governing but rather to increase investing and acquisitive behavior. While landed estates were supposed to produce people who governed, estates of credit produced people who burnished images of creditworthiness. One can read the shift as going from a world where difficult civic virtues were cultivated to one where people were cowed by worries over how the market regarded them. Or one can read the shift as from a world of barbaric leisure to a world steeped in the cultivation of the refined sentiments and lifestyles that produce social trust.[21] Pocock's account, which is too thick-grained for this essay, depends on the same constructivist understanding of the relation of personal identity to property as is employed in this essay. Consequently, this essay's claims will come out more clearly if this common constructivist understanding of the relation of possession to personal identity is articulated.

To begin with, this picture of the relation of personal identity to property starts with the Heideggerian/Bourdieuvian claim that, put in legal terms, possession precedes and determines personal identity. To make sense of this claim we have to begin by wondering how people come to have intentions about things to begin with. People (babies) only come to a consistent way of dealing with their own actions within an environment that includes the body, conventional uses of the body, interrelated equipment, and conventional purposes for the equipment. We suppose that a baby can only have determinate, nonreflexive comportments toward things once it comes to have a consistent coordinated use of its limbs, its posture, its eyes, its ears, its fingers, and so on.[22] For only on the basis of such a bodily environment, which infant development researchers disaggregate into "invariants,"[23] could anything perceived or manipulated appear to have the necessary consistency to be a thing.

If we wonder how the uncoordinated baby with wants comes to be coordinated enough to have consistent, intentionalistic comportments towards things, we should imagine various caregivers handling it in such ways as to encourage certain consistent coordinated muscular usages for dealing with itself and things. Gradually enough consistency develops in these usages so that individual things and people can appear in their appropriate interrelations.[24] Moreover, since the human being is always already doing something within this environment, its encounter with its own self will be understood in terms of the things and purposes involved in the activity. The baby or person encounters a self as the one who does some particular thing and as possessed by the environment (in which it has been socialized) for doing it.[25]

This account, as developed so far, sets out the Heideggerian/Bourdieuvian constructivist picture of how selves depend on bodies being socialized into certain conventional and equipmental environments. But how do we move from here to the claim that possession in an ordinary sense and not just a social environment determines the structures of personal identity? We should see that as the equipmental environments that we are involved with develop, so do our ways of dealing with ourselves and the environment, and eventually we come to take those environments with which we are most familiar as possessed by us.[26] That is, instead of feeling that something is always coming up that draws us into an unexpected set of tasks (which is how we experience being possessed by an environment), we come to find that, after long habituation, we can easily cope with most of what happens in certain environments. We then do not experience ourselves in the grip of the situation so much as experience the situation in our own grip. We have, at that point, a skillful mastery over it. We can perpetuate the environment and innovate in it within its terms. The environment, then, is possessed as much as it is possessing. And our personal identities are defined in terms of this basic possession. This basic sense of possession as mastery over an environment is, also the early modern common-law sense of possession. Hence there is a close connection between the constructivist philosophers of social practice, especially Heidegger and Bourdieu, and the common-law thinking about landholding practice.

But naturally the understandings of self develop beyond mastered environments. Common-law thinking about practice is a useful guide here. For, in a complicated environment, different aspects may be possessed or owned in different ways in which the law acknowledges as different kinds of expectations or possessory rights and duties. Moreover, the law distinguishes, on the basis of this sense of possession deriving from mastery, occasions where obligations cross mastered environments. So, clearly, the obligations between a feudal lord and his free landholder would be, in large part, possessory, and even more so would be the obligations between a feudal lord and his villein. But, at the other end of the spectrum from lord and villein, the obligations between one feudal lord and another when they both were equally tenants of the king would not be possessory. Also, a lord meeting his free tenant on the highway would have many obligations toward him even though the relevant mastered environment would be no more than his body and his horse. These obligations would be, again, cross-contextual, because they obtain between one relevant mastered environment (body and horse) and another. On the king's highway, for instance, one could not take the other's property; one could not damage the other's person; one had to perform one's undertakings. These obligations fell under the headings of trespass and covenant. Generally, in common-law societies, one has contractual (cross-contextual) obligations with people like oneself (and their servants) and has possessory relations with things, animals, and people that directly serve what one has mastery over.

Growing up with different primarily important equipmental environments will produce within broad limits[27] different understandings of who the one who acts is. And whether and which people are dealt with as mastered and on what terms they can be mastered will be determined by the contingencies of the projects undertaken in the context, and the consequent determination of the limits of mastery will determine how the line is drawn between what is inside a context and what involves crossing contexts. It almost goes without saying that different kinds of personal identities can be created and destroyed by changing the line between the contractual and the possessory. Slaves and villeins are persons with few contractual rights and obligations. And because of our experience with slavery, we tend to esteem contractual relations over possessory ones. The sixteenth- and seventeenth-century common lawyers worried precisely about the reverse valuation. With the use, the contractual was trivializing the possessory. That is why we must focus clearly on how the possessory relation produces different kinds of selves. So, recurring to Pocock's general constructivist account, if one primarily deals with landed estates and the attendant servants and community of laborers that one governs, one will see oneself as governing. If one deals primarily with manipulations of a credit market, one will encounter oneself as one who manages the feelings of trust.

If this theoretical account is persuasive, it is so for two reasons. First, it draws on and orders into a picture general constructivist observations and intuitions that are now widely shared. Second, this account links the common constructivist picture to our intuitions about a customary law. This account shows what sense it makes to think of possession as part of any customary life. It also accounts for why different social customs in different environments will make widely different determinations about which obligations are possessory (because they deal with mastery) and which are contractual (because they deal with crossings between mastered contexts). *Different environments will describe the nature and the limits of mastery differently* both on account of the nature of mastery in different environments—mastering different kinds of land, animals, and people all amount to different kinds of activity—and on account of various historical contingencies. To see, though, the different kinds of possessory personal identity developed in the late-sixteenth and early-seventeenth centuries, we must turn discussion to the use.

3. The Use

A use is a simple form of trust. A man who for one reason or another does not want to hold his land by law might grant his land to a friend with the private and, perhaps, unenforceable agreement that his friend will do as the grantor wishes with the land. Such a transaction establishes a use, since the friend would hold the land to the use of the grantor who would either take the profits of the land himself or determine who else should have them. After the grant of the land, the former landholder would be called the beneficial owner or *cestui que use*. Such a transaction may seem to us like nothing more than a desperate strategem to avoid a bank foreclosure or an IRS action. But thinking about landholding on this, our, scale misses the point. Our identities and means of productivity do not depend, by and large, on our landholdings. So imagine, first, that the profits of our land were our primary means of productivity and that landed estates were the ultimate source of productivity for almost all members of our nation. Imagine, second, that a separate court, a court of conscience, might enforce the basic parts of the above private agreement. Imagine, third, that we may not devise our land by will, as this possibility was not available in the common law until 1540. Lastly, imagine, in this context, what sort of new powers a use would provide. Suppose we have dynastic ambitions and want the land to remain within our family for so long as we should have heirs. Then we simply communicate this desire, as informally as we please, to a friendly group of *legal* landholders (the feoffees to uses), and they will maintain our wishes and communicate them to their successors forever. For, as legal landholders, they could legally remove anyone from the land and thus always hold it open for the appropriate one of our stipulated heirs. In this way, the land would become virtually perpetually inalienable. No one could ever sell it or grant it again, for so long as we have heirs. Ultimately, this restraint on alienability could mean that almost all sources of productivity would be held in the hands of the same families no matter how unresourceful the offspring were. Just as bad as inalienability for common-law notions of landholding, the estate in land could spring from one beneficial to another owner across an expanse of time without any beneficial owner holding it in between. This could happen if, for instance, we told our feoffees that the land was to go to our male heirs. If during a particular generation, no male heirs were produced, the feoffees to uses could simply hold the land as placeholders. More to the point, suppose we wanted to leave complicated conditions on particular future beneficial owners. We could instruct our feoffees that the use of the land should go to X unless Y returns from Rome and eschews the Romanish faith, in which case the land goes to Y. Then the beneficial estate could shift from X to Y on grounds that may have nothing to do with X's life or estate governance. Such a stipulation also went against the heart of common-law thinking.

Now, if we take the common-law way of life as Edward Coke, the premier common-law thinker of the age, took it, then we would hold that *owning* land included three basic practices that we still more or less take for granted. (1) The owner ought to be able to dispose of the land as he or she wants; selling or granting the land, therefore, meant that the purchaser or grantee was to get all, or virtually all, of the rights the previous owner had, with only certain well-understood and traditional exceptions. (2) No tricky grant could ever defeat the *continuous* progress of ownership in time. Since land could not be ownerless, a grant failed when it did not stipulate a capable owner when the land fell vacant. (3) Even such conditions as could be imposed on a landholder's holding had, in general, to be up to the landholder to fulfill or to fail to fulfill. So, following point one, no one ought to be able to sell or grant an estate while withholding from the grant or sale the right to alienate the land at will for longer than one generation. Following point two, if one granted land to one's male heirs, and a generation failed to produce such an heir, then the grant was defeated. And following point three, no third party returning from Rome and Romanish ways could defeat one's estate in land.

On these three practices hung the common-law notion of landholding and having an identity as a landholder. The basic notion behind these practices was that the success of any landholder's estate was to depend on that landholder's success in governing his own family, in cultivating his land, in marketing the land's products, in dealing wisely with the community of husbandmen and craftsmen that supported the productivity of the estate, and in maintaining a trustworthy reputation in the wider community. The use could destroy all these legal and landholding practices. Indeed, in a world of uses, individuals, whose hold over their land was inalienable, subject to temporal discontinuities, and subject to the inscrutable whims of others, would tend to find themselves engaged in the practice of dealing with the stipulations of the past and of being more fearful of their fellows' acts than concerned with the consequences of their own. Hence, the structure of personal identity would change. In such a world, common-law notions of property as the basis for exploring one's productive capacity within a community would become meaningless as people concerned themselves with the manipulations of various disaggregated conditional rights. So, landholding also would change. And the customary law would, in the end, be superseded by procedures for determining how to interpret the idiosyncratic whims of original beneficial owners. Thus, the nature of the law itself would change.

A quick survey of the four stages in the development of the use shows the use's subversive tendencies in each stage. Scholars suppose that the use got its start informally. A landholder who agreed to grant away a certain parcel of land on a certain date but who was called out of the county might well have decided to grant the land to a friend with the informal condition that the friend make the promised grant good. The Franciscans, however, discovered the long-term potential of such an informal arrangement. Since their oaths of poverty prevented them from holding property either individually or corporately, they essentially gave their wealth to the aldermen of Canterbury who held it to the exclusive use of the Franciscans. This arrangement allowed them to become the beneficial owners of land, buildings, and chattels. Since such long-term uses provided landholders with flexible ways of settling land, with the means to avoid paying feudal incidents (essentially death taxes), and with a means of devising land by will (which treated the use as a chattel), long-term uses rapidly caught on. Yet, until the mid-fifteenth century, the feoffees to uses had no legal duty to do as the beneficial owner wished. Until then the use really existed as a concrete expression of informal trust.

But, starting in 1446 with *Mirfyn v. Fallen*,[28] the Chancellor began to enforce, under what came to be called his equitable jurisdiction, the terms of the use as matters of conscience that could be adjudicated, and the second stage of the history of the use began. Instead of judging each case as it presented itself, the Chancellor's court developed principles of consideration and notice to determine if a use had been raised, if a beneficial grant could be revoked, if an alienation of a beneficial interest was good, and so on.[29] Naturally, as uses became more formal, they became more popular. According to Chief Justice Frowike in the period after the Chancery started supervising uses, most of the land in England came under the use.[30] Without even describing the use in *King Lear*, it ought to be easy to see that the play ignores the defining characteristic of this stage in the history of the use. The possibility that matters of conscience could be formally enforced plays no part in the drama. This stage in the history of the use ended with the passage of the Statute of Uses in 1536.

The Statute attempted to bring uses into conformity with the accepted landholding practices of the common law by adjudging the legal interest held by the feoffees to uses to be in the beneficial owners. The Statute also says that the resulting common-law legal interests were supposed to be like the beneficial interests. But the Statute did not spell out what was to be done with the future legal interests that would go to beneficial owners not yet in being. Under the old law of uses, these interests were preserved for as long as necessary by the feoffees to uses. Under the common law, such a future interest, if good at all, was a contingent interest, and the recipient of such an interest had to be capable of taking the land when the contingency occurred. (The common law had no placeholders.) Also, in the common law, the current possessor of land could usually defeat a contingent interest. By the 1570s, the courts were interpreting the Statute liberally to permit common-law protection of the bizarre estates that could be created with uses. In *Brent's Case*, Chief Justice Dyer even coined the term *scintilla juris* to describe the title the old feoffees retained to protect these uncommon-law interests.[31] By the 1590s the consequences of the rulings in the 1570s were beginning to be seen. Grand original beneficial owners had encumbered their heirs with conditions and inalienable land. At this point, the fourth stage in the history of the use began.

In this stage, the courts endeavored to cut back on what settlements involving uses could do, and *Chudleigh's Case* is regarded as having made the most significant retrenchment. In it, all the justices guided by Edward Coke and Francis Bacon were understood as having decided that estates created by uses had to conform to all the common-law rules. The reasoning, however, so far as it retained a scaled-back *scintilla juris*, not only remained confusing but also left a peculiar and strictly placeholding title in the common law. A placeholding title was nothing more than a scaled-back trusteeship, imagined along the lines of the title someone has to a place on line when one is holding it for someone else.[32] So the decision potentially undermined the common-law order, and remained unsatisfying. Cases like *Fitzwilliam's Case* (1604)[33] and *Mildmay's Case* (1605)[34] returned to the thinking in *Chudleigh's Case* in the surcharged manner that seeks to emphasize the truth of the case while ignoring the reasoning that reached it. In *Stanhope's Case* (probably argued in or shortly after 1604 and therefore when Shakespeare was writing *King Lear*), Bacon shows his queasiness about the earlier judgment by introducing a new distinction that would later serve as the ground for undoing *Chudleigh's Case*.[35] By 1609 in *Manning's Case*, the justices reopened the thinking that led to the curiosity of the placeholder. In this case, they determined that the law would give full protection to a future estate that did not yet have an estateholder and the law would give this protection without the invention of a placeholder in being. But, with this decision, the justices reopened the possibility of perpetually inalienable land.

None of these claims about the law, legal history, or about *Chudleigh's Case* should be taken to suggest that Shakespeare had legal training or was a court watcher. Shakespeare, as we shall see, was interested primarily in the way the use affected personal identity. In this, his interest was like that of the deepest of common-law thinkers between 1595 and 1609 and beyond. And like the common lawyers, Shakespeare sought to determine if the English customary practices (the common-law practices[36]) could tolerate the incorporation of those practices of human warmth and trust that support the use. After all, the use is no more than an arrangement founded on trust between friends. Banning the use would amount to banning concrete expressions of such trust.[37] But, unlike the common lawyers, Shakespeare could ask more plainly whether personal identities built solely on human love could mix with or displace personal identities built out of customary duty.[38] Shakespeare, then, asked this question by imagining a king who established a personal identity based on a personal rule twenty-four years before Charles I's fact.

4. *King Lear* and the Prototype of the Use

The first scene of the play opens with a mood of uneasy formality. Kent and Gloucester, two of the king's counselors, are acting like men who have found themselves in agreement at a meeting but who do not know how to get on informally once they are away from the Council table. Kent speaks first. "I thought the King had more affected the Duke of Albany than Cornwall," (1.1.1–2) Kent says, showing, as we see retrospectively, that Lear did have an apt understanding of the characters of his daughters' husbands. Gloucester answers with diplomatic agility. His answer is simply a description, but it implies, although the implication could be denied, a reason why Lear chose not to divide his kingdom according to the deserts of the husbands. Gloucester says, "[I]n the division of the kingdom ... equalities are so weigh'd that curiosity in neither can make choice of either's moiety" (1.1.3–6). In other words, Lear decided to give Albany and Cornwall exactly equal portions to forestall them from finding in the division the sort of slights to their honor that could lead to hostilities. But then, Kent asks, "Is this not your son, my Lord?" (1.1.7), and with this question Gloucester begins to let the social formalities drop. In the blink of a line or two Gloucester is speaking to Kent with an overly-familiar crudeness, born perhaps in nervousness, but betraying—as most critics have pointed out—a morally indelicate sensibility.

Yet Gloucester ought not to be measured only by his crude jokes about Edmund's conception. His extra-customary (i.e., extra-legal) recognition of and affection for Edmund ought to be taken into account. For whoresons, contrary to what Gloucester says, need not be acknowledged. They need not be introduced to royal counselors. And they need not be provided with study on the continent like that which Hamlet's, Horatio's, and Laertes's fathers had provided for their sons.[39] Gloucester makes this provision. But he does not do it in the mode of high courtliness—he can not speak *to* or *of* Edmund in his counselor's tones. So we witness something slightly bizarre: Edmund's identity as the Earl of Gloucester's acknowledged bastard son depends solely on the Earl of Gloucester's excessive and coarse affections. The claims of human warmth and the duties of custom and law do not run together. A personal identity can be built on a warmth that ignores the mundane constraints of the customary law. Gloucester enacts, then, what Lear seeks to explore, as we shall see in the rest of the scene. The point here, to underline it, is that the duties of law and of normal dutiful affection are limited by past habit and current custom, but the claims of passion are defined by excessive feeling (feeling that exceeds dutiful affection), and, as such, these claims are untempered by the stability of social forms. Yet these passionate claims may be the foundation of a personal identity.

As we approach the heart of the scene, suddenly Lear, his daughters, and other counselors march on stage with great courtly fanfare. Lear announces to the public that he is about to reveal his darker purpose, which is, the division of his kingdom that has already been decided on in Council. Two curious points ought to be remarked upon. First, by dividing his kingdom into three, Lear is following not royal custom,[40] but simple common-law custom. Under the scheme of primogeniture as practiced in England, when a man's heirs were solely daughters, they took equal portions of his estate as co-parcenors. This common-law scheme sways the thinking of everyone in the play since no character doubts that this tripartite division (as opposed to the actual one enacted) makes sense. Lear has decided, though, to make some adjustments to the common-law custom by giving Cordelia a greater share than her sisters, and for that reason, in addition to other reasons of policy, he must grant his land away before he dies. (Land could not be willed under the amended common law.)

Second, the ceremonial actions on stage constitute an enactment. For us in the days of writing and mass communication, an enactment is nothing more than a signing ceremony. But for Lear and men through the Middle Ages (with the practice continuing through the early seventeenth century), the enactment ceremony held as much importance as the thinking that led to the enactment. For in a pre-literate culture (or a semi-literate one still abiding by the forms of its pre-literate past), any enactment had to make a grand appeal to the memories of men so that they could be expected to recall both the reasons given for the enactment and the precise terms of the enactment. Under the common law, the good, honest, and substantial men *(probi homines)* of any county were expected to know the terms by which their neighbors held their land, since these men could be impaneled to give that information. Consequently, a good landholder had to be able to manage a memorable public ceremony for alienating his land. Lear could be no exception. This historical reflection goes part way towards explaining the love test.

Lear rigs up the love test in order to show his subjects why the land is being divided as it is. We know that it is largely a matter of public display and not a matter of love, because, as Gloucester has already indicated, the division of land between Goneril and Regan has had more to do with Lear's understanding of the honor code and bellicosity of their husbands than of these daughters' love.[41] But the love test is not all that is rigged up. In light of Lear's actual enactment, we may see that his explanation for the division, that is, that he seeks to "shake all business and care" (1.1.38) from his age and "[u]nburthen'd crawl toward death" (1.1.40) turns out to be, like so many preambles to so many statutes, only a half-truth. It is a reason easy to remember, created for the public's consumption. In fact, Lear does expect to maintain certain authorities.

The final part of his enactment turns out to have detailed reservations, which might be likened to savings at the end of a statute. So, to speak contrary to the near consensus, whatever Lear is doing in this enactment, he is not simply abdicating. Here is Lear's actual enfeoffment to Albany and Cornwall:

> I do invest you jointly with my power,
> Pre-eminence, and all the large effects
> That troop with majesty. Ourself, by monthly course,
> With reservation of an hundred knights
> By you to be sustain'd, shall our abode
> Make with you by due turn. Only we shall retain
> The name and all th'addition to a king; the sway,
> Revenue, execution of the rest,
> Beloved sons, be yours.
>   (1.1.129–37)

Generally, there are two ways to make legal sense of this grant. We could say that Lear has made a formal, common-law, conditional grant of his kingdom, and in such a grant he would have a right of reentry if any of the conditions were broken. We would then see his reservation of the one hundred knights and the rest as though he had reserved a rent of £100 per annum. But interpreting his grant this way leaves two problems. If Lear's intention was simply to make a common-law grant and reservation, we must wonder why he did not simply claim his common-law right of reentry as soon as Goneril refused to entertain his one hundred knights (1.4.292). And we must wonder what he could mean by retaining, in addition to the rights of lodging and the one hundred knights, the name and all the addition of a king. Presumably, this means that he retains more than the way he will sign his name.[42] Later, Gloucester cryptically indicates that this phrase might have been meant to stand in the place—though it does so inadequately—of a whole series of more specific reservations developed in the Council meeting that took place before the enactment (1.2.23–25). But whatever Lear means by "addition" here, it most likely goes beyond any technical common-law thinking. For, under common-law thinking, one cannot both give up an office with authorities and responsibilities, Lear's "all" as he emphatically puts it later in the play (2.4.248), and nevertheless hold on to the office.

On the whole, Lear's grant makes best sense if it is understood to get around the technical common law by establishing a prototype of the use. He establishes his daughters as the feoffees to the use and retains a beneficial interest as *cestui que use*.[43] In other words, he indeed grants his daughters everything under common-law rules, but while giving them all the common-law duties of kingship, he expects still to retain everything pertaining to the name and the perquisites of the king; in short, he intends to maintain the special authority of a king that goes beyond the particular authorities involved in performing each of his customary, common-law duties.[44]

What kind of consistency, integrity, and effectiveness could Lear's non-customary authority have? We may say that it is the authority that binds people in trust, the authority of human warmth that makes the prototypical use work. But Shakespeare's point is to explore the nature of this authority. Indeed, by the time Lear invests his sons-in-law, Shakespeare has already begun this exploration. For, the authority of the use, the authority implicit in trust, is also precisely the authority that a memorable ceremony has over people. An enactment is memorable *in its details* because it harmonizes with our general way of doing things. And this authority that comes from hearkening to our general way of doing things is superior to the authority of the customary common-law practices. It lends them their particular authority. What makes customary duties or practices *particularly* binding, as they are felt to be, is not just the *habit* of performing them but rather is the way these duties or practices *harmonize* with the rest of one's duties and practices. They *feel right* when taken together. And this same rightness or harmony is also what gives any simple not-legally-binding act of trust among friends its authority. For we trust our friends and endow them with authority over our affairs because we recognize that they are in tune with our way of doing things. This authority in excess of habit is what Lear retains and is Shakespeare's theatrically glamorized version of the particular authority of the protouse. In Lear's case, the harmonic authority is the particularly charismatic, regal authority[45] that derives from manifesting that and how all of a nation's disparate customs and practices fit together to give a coherent, shared way of doing things. Lear's excessive authority is especially powerful, then, because it does not simply rely on the sense of rightness or of fitting-together-ness of a small set of practices such as the practices that constitute a friendship. So far as his new authority succeeds, it must draw on the rightness or harmony of his kingdom's practices taken as a whole. We may say that his authority is that of a culture figure.

Lear seeks, then, to become king in right of the authority of the excessive (beyond habitual) feelings of warmth that reside in the hearts of his subjects for him. Such warmth is magnified in Lear's case because, beyond handling the habitual functions of kingship, Lear as king is already the one who shows his people that they have a recognizable, coherent national life. By giving up the common-law authorities of kingship—such as negotiating treaties, entertaining ambassadors, collecting revenue, running a council that legislates, establishing law courts, and the rest—but still retaining title to these duties, Lear signals that he is identifying himself with his special non-customary authority. He retains title to the common-law duties and rights, that is, by retaining the authority that authorizes them. But to identify himself with this superior authority so entirely means that Lear is also attempting to make himself into the primary figure of English authority that, as such figures do, has the job of gathering together the excessive sentiments and feelings of the kingdom and showing the appropriateness and worthiness of such feelings.[46] And the main requirement for maintaining this kind of authority, this addition of a king, amounts, as we see very concretely in Lear's enactment scene, to managing the story people tell of their king.[47] Lear, as an authority figure, is identifying himself with the authority of stories people tell about such figures. Indeed, the authority he is establishing for himself is also precisely that of the stories we tell ourselves about who we are. Those stories clearly have authority over us, can force us to screw up our courage or to respond with shame, yet these stories owe us no service with any cash value. They are prior to anything pragmatic. Yet they establish our personal, political, and national identities so far as we have them.[48]

How, in a world that common sense could comprehend, could Lear *become* such a pure figure of authority without doing the sorts of things required by someone in that role? Simple, he gives over all the mundane common-law duties to his daughters and continues to collect the esteem for carrying out these duties. He, in other words, sets up a proto-use in order to become a beneficial king, not a king in law.[49] But for such a use to work he must have absolute confidence in his feoffees to the use. Lear, in this case, must be the cynosure of his feoffees' adoration. For how else could he be assured of their continued faithfulness to his royal wishes? We may now see too why, in principle, Shakespeare could not have Lear describe what he is doing very clearly, why, for instance, he could not forthrightly say that he wanted to become an authority figure or a ceremonial king instead of saying that he wanted to retire (1.1.38–40). Virtually anything he said during the enactment would be understood according to the average intelligibility of the common customs. So if he said that he wanted to be a ceremonial king, this would indicate that he wanted to retain the strictly common-law right to preside over ceremonies whenever they occur. If, alternatively, he had tried to break out of average, everyday meanings and said that he wanted to rule in right of adulation or love, this would sound as though he already knew about uses and sought to overturn the common customs of the realm, which was precisely not the case. One should not, however, assume that Shakespeare thought in this in-principle fashion. Rather, it is enough for Shakespeare to sense that Lear was in the sort of position where he could not spell out his wishes without having them misinterpreted. The love test enables Lear and Shakespeare to make the extra-legal point of establishing a proto-use by means of the drama of the ceremony.

Lear obviously sought a memorable dramatic display that would justify the appropriateness of his division of the kingdom. That the display was no real love test may be seen, as has been noted, in that he has already worked through the division in Council, which probably included Albany and Cornwall, and in that he assigns Goneril her section before even hearing Regan's or Cordelia's speech. But why would Lear choose a love test at all?[50] Presumably he could have chosen any number of public displays to justify his division. The love test, which as commentators have pointed out is more of a flattery test than a love test, tests precisely whether his daughters are willing to treat him *not as the man he is but as the father-figure, the authority figure, he aspires to become.* He seeks for them to relate themselves to him more as to a cultural figure that gives meaning to their lives than as a man, an actual father, or an actual king. Goneril and Regan understand this desire, at least halfway, and flatter him as though he were their ultimate meaning-giving being. Cordelia, though, finds every aspect of this enactment repulsive.

Stanley Cavell has argued in defense of Cordelia against Coleridge's charge that she displays a sullen pride.[51] Cavell says that Cordelia cannot speak warmly because she is in a paradoxical position. She is being asked to *flatter* Lear with adoration when in fact she truly adores him.[52] No one, Cavell argues, can flatter truly. Common life, though, shows Cavell's position must be wrong. We can state many true things with inflections that are insincere. We may joke about an insult received that truly cuts us. We may tell glossy stories about our work that are true in content, though we may feel that the glossiness is a deceptive register in which to discuss our work's truth. Could Cordelia somehow lack this ability, the ability in speaking, to open up one or another kind of expressive space in which others would hear her claims? No. She may disdain such talking, especially since her sisters live and die by it, but she can inflect the tone of her words as well as anyone else in the play. Listen to the peculiarly humble indignation with which she addresses Lear later in the scene.

> I yet beseech your Majesty,
> (If for I want that glib and oily art
> To speak and purpose not, since what I well intend,
> I'll do't before I speak), that you make known
> It is no vicious blot, murther or foulness,
> No unchaste action, or dishonour'd step
> That hath depriv'd me of your grace and favour,
> But even for want of that for which I am richer
> A still-soliciting eye, and such a tongue

> That I am glad I have not, though not to have it
> Hath lost me in your liking.
>
> (1.1.222–32)[53]

How could anyone answer this? Should Lear speak to her inflection or address her point? In general, Cordelia's speeches are brilliantly and variously unanswerable. Her speeches from her famous and severe "Nothing, my lord" (1.1.86) in answer to Lear's initial request all the way to her equally famous and generous "No cause, no cause" (4.7.75) are absolutes that block further engagement. Cordelia is not, however, cryptic or taciturn. What she thinks comes across very clearly as in her farewell to Burgundy, which so refuses a response from him that it is spoken in the third person: "Peace be with Burgundy!" she says, "Since that respect and fortunes are his love, / I shall not be his wife" (1.1.246–48). Even late in the play when Cordelia speaks to Kent, her fellow traveler in the plain-speech party, she forecloses any easy response. Her tenderness has about it a frozen marble absoluteness: "O thou good Kent!" she says, starting warmly and familiarly enough, "how shall I live and work / To match thy goodness? My life will be too short, / And every measure fail me" (4.7.1–3). By the end of this little speech, Kent has become a bloodless example that she must strive to match.

In listening to Cordelia, we hear an inverse of Lear. She treats her identity as more than an embodiment of her kingdom's customs for a princess and as more than a role among other roles, even a role from which she has a modicum of distance. For Cordelia's claim that she loves Lear only according to general customarily established bonds is a notorious lie (1.1.94–96). She has an affection for Lear that exceeds all duty. And her sense of herself, as does Lear's sense of himself, depends on such affection. Lear employs the excessive affection he believes his daughters (and subjects) have for him in order to set up a proto-use that enables him to constitute himself by means of the harmonic authority kingship and fatherhood bear. Thus he becomes an authority figure with no pragmatic, customary duties. He shows us a personal identity that has been self-constituted on the basis of the public affections of others. Conversely, in order to identify herself wholly with the wonderful excess of love she feels, Cordelia cuts herself off from the intermingling of words and intentions. She will not constitute herself in words that may be bandied about. She does not want to become any part of the shared, memorial stories of the kingdom.

Her social bonds and her heart remain unentwined as we all infer from her fullest answer to Lear's request for a statement of her love:

> Good my Lord,
> You have begot me, bred me, lov'd me: I
> Return those duties back as are right fit,
> Obey you, love you, and most honour you.
>
> (1.1.94–97)

To repeat, by its palpable falsehood this response calls attention to what Lear and Cordelia share and to how they are different. Both Lear and Cordelia are concerned with having an identity that goes beyond that defined by the duties of custom. Lear publicly speaks and acts in order to manipulate the surplus of good feeling people develop for their customs *as a whole*. As such, he endeavors to become a proto-Kantian, self-constituting, transcendental subject.[54] He seeks to determine the nature of the domain in which normal thinking and action take place. Cordelia also defines herself in terms of the surplus of feeling people develop for their customary way of life. But Cordelia does not identify herself with the harmony or interrelatedness of the customs, which are the source of the feeling; rather she identifies herself with the excessive feeling itself. And, since in her case her customary way of life is centered on honoring her king and father, the excessive feeling that she identifies as constituting her self is her own extra-ordinary love for Lear. She understands herself in terms of her inner feeling of love and hence becomes a psychological subject that acts to preserve its *private*, unique inner sense.

Lear's request, therefore, looks to Cordelia like an attempt to deny her precisely what is most important, the private purity of her inner, defining passion. For if she were to heave her heart into her mouth and specify her inner feeling in words, these words would be matter for report, recitation, and inflection for so long as people remembered the enactment. Against the generalized public interpretation of her words, Cordelia could not preserve her peculiar and personal inner sense of her feeling. For as people reinflected and reinterpreted the meaning of her words, her sense of her inner meaning would itself become infected by her own registration of the general interpretation given her words. Her inner feeling would be robbed of its purity.[55] That is why she cannot speak and why she finds her sisters' speeches so fulsome.

Likewise, for Lear, Cordelia's refusal denies him precisely the possibility that his constitution of his personal identity as the figure of authority depends on. Lear requires that his daughters and subjects will explicitly relate themselves to him not as the man Lear who has his ground in customary law but as the figure of authority that embodies the abiding harmony and coherence of the practices according to which and in which they live. How Lear does this may be made clear by recurring to the structure of activity in the enactment. In this enactment, Lear takes on the role of the king as authority figure. He invests himself in the glamour of that position for the sake of providing a richly memorable occasion. Once in that role—like an actor on a stage—how he behaves determines how the role of king is to be understood. And once in the business of presenting the authoritative royal figure, Lear must see it through to the end. When Cordelia refuses to play along, he must follow the course that the logic of authoritative royal absoluteness dictates. If he were to portray anything short of that, he would tarnish the symbol he seeks to become. Lear knows that when an authoritative king is questioned in public, as when, for us, reason as a whole is questioned in public (think of terrorism[56]), no one may come between the dragon and his wrath (1.1.121).

This brings us to Kent, Cordelia's spokesman. Although Kent is of the plainly speaking, deeply psychological party with Cordelia, Kent seems to understand an important feature of what Lear is up to better than Cordelia. Kent understands the nature of Lear's grant, that it is a proto-use and therefore that its terms and existence depend on Lear's will. "Reserve thy state" (1.1.148) he admonishes, and "Revoke thy gift" (1.1.163), he says a few lines later.[57] But if Kent understands this feature of Lear's new identity best, why does he fight with him during the public ceremony? Can he fail to know that Lear must follow the contours and directives of public display once he set out on that path? Does Kent fail to understand that flattery is essential to the kind of being into which Lear hopes to transform himself?

In order to answer these questions, we must determine what Kent thinks goes wrong in the enactment. That answer comes readily to hand. He thinks that Lear has forgotten himself and genuinely believes that Cordelia does not love him in the excessive way he requires. "Thy youngest daughter does not love thee least," Kent argues, "Nor are those empty-hearted whose low sounds / Reverb no hollowness" (1.1.151–53). Kent believes that Lear had better terminate this enactment until he can get it better scripted. Or he had better find a way to give Cordelia her "more opulent" third. Lear could, for instance, use Kent's metaphor of a hollow bell ring-ing more clearly to belittle Goneril and Regan's flattering protestations and reward Cordelia. But to follow Kent's advice here, Lear would have to shunt aside his absolute glamorized figure and commit himself to precisely the kind of thoughtful give and take he has abjured in favor of playing the part of the pure authority figure.

Although Kent recognizes these two sides of kingship, he does not see clearly that Lear is attempting to institutionalize one at the *absolute* expense of the other. Kent's own excessive love and respect for Lear, man and king, is so intertwined with his sense of customary and legal obligation to Lear, man and king, that he cannot conceive of Lear as truly breaking them apart. And the plan as initially conceived need not have forced Kent to this realization. For, so long as Lear could rely on Cordelia to enforce his will and the compliance of her sisters,[58] Lear's division of his roles would remain no more than a switch in the mode in which the public was to regard him. Where before he principally received the respect due a king, henceforth he would principally receive the adulation due to a culture's figure of authority. The difference would have appeared to Kent as one of inflection. Kingship and the charismatic influence of an authority figure went together for Kent. This we can hear in his first extended address to Lear:

> Royal Lear,
> Whom I have ever honour'd as my King,
> Lov'd as my father, as my master follow'd,
> As my great patron thought on in my prayers,—
> (1.1.138–41)

Kent mixes the honor due a king with the love due a father, the imitation due a master, and the obligation due a patron. He can address Lear as "Royal Lear" or "Good my Liege" (1.1.119), but he may also say with the familiarity of his "thou": "What would'st thou do, old man?" (1.1.145). For Kent, Lear was already the beneficial king as well as the legal king.[59] Acting as beneficial king, he could call back grants; as legal king, he could not, but, for Kent, the two went together. Kent fears, and becomes incensed over, the possibility that Lear truly intends to leave all calculating intelligence and statecraft behind without the protection afforded by all the previous requisite precautions of his calculating and magisterial statecraft. Kent's plain thinking rebels against this possibility because Lear defies precisely that darker inner purpose Lear had proposed and worked out in Council. Kent calls it "folly" (1.1.148) and "hideous rashness" (1.1.151) and, in perhaps his most apt metaphor (since he casts the problem as something inner), a "foul disease" (1.1.163) to follow the directives of Cordelia's obstinacy. As Kent sees things, the situation has taken off on its own without the control of the inner sense, the good planning and policy that made sense of the enactment ceremony to begin with. For Kent, the advocate of plainness, what counts are those darker, inner senses. When Lear disinherits Cordelia, he is taking the point out of the enactment. To go on to enact his wrath is, to Kent's mind, to be guided by the general structuring principles and style of authority, not the specific intention that shows up within that general style. Thus, for Kent, Lear's actions abuse the particular inner sense behind the particular enactment.

Now we have before us two interpretations of Lear's proto-use, Lear's—that he could construct an identity as royal authority figure that would be based solely on the extra-legal, unifying sentiments of his subjects—and Kent's—that Lear had always already had an extra-legal ownership of royal rights and authority based on the love of his subjects for Lear. What then shall we say was Shakespeare's understanding of the use?

Shakespeare begins his questioning of the use by developing terms the common lawyers would not quite have known how to handle. By focusing on a ceremonial enactment scene that defines the new Lear, Shakespeare implicitly claims that the proper register for understanding the beneficial owner is that of a culture figure which, like a national legend or national work of art, makes a people more sensitive to the general unity in their practices that harmonizes their daily activities. This figure then, gathers a people to recognize and cultivate its identity. (In regard to the average use, we might speak, instead, of a family dynasty's founding figure setting the style for the family's particular practices. His heirs and successors are expected to hold to the terms of the settlement out of love for their founder and sympathy with his way of life.) Lear seeks to figure forth *his* understanding of royal authority—that the king is most king by supervising the way people feel about their customs—in such a way that his supervision of himself as an authority figure draws his kingdom together and gives it a unity deeper than the simple lawful one it would otherwise have.[60] This is what it means to say that his understanding of his use is that it makes him self-constituting. But this self-constitution must take into account the sentiments of others. So to remain self-constituting, he must supervise how others see him. He must supervise what is in the hearts and on the lips of his subjects. But he does not want to do this on the basis of what today looks like propaganda where he would hearken back to a generally accepted legend and manipulate it to his own purposes. He wants his country's practices to reverberate with the being of King Lear and constitute his personal style as the style with which these practices make best sense. That is what the use is supposed to enable him to do, to act at being himself, and that is why the adulation of those closest to his way of acting, those who most share his own style, *his own daughters*[61] is so essential. Why not, otherwise, put the legal care of his kingdom in his Council as a whole, while he becomes king in name and perquisites? This focus on the personal identity of Lear himself, man and king, is what Shakespeare sees and what is held in common between Lear's and Kent's understanding of the use. Shakespeare transforms questions about the use, and the affection that the use depends on, into questions about the personal identity of a self (Lear's) constituted as the general unifying style in which common practices and particular actions make sense. So it is not really important whether Lear was already a beneficial owner of his kingship before the enactment as Kent thinks. What is important is that Lear is willfully constituting a complete and deeply personal identity that will be solely that of a beneficial owner who depends on the publicly expressed love and trust of those nearest him and who attempts to hold that love in place by expressing how the practices of those nearest to him hang together. This kind of personal identity is modern but not in virtue of its inwardness or its concern for the average everyday details of life but in virtue of its self-constituting independence. And the questions that Shakespeare asks are whether such a self may exist and whether common customs might still have some hold over such a seemingly independent identity. But with just this much analysis, we can see why Lear has appeared as many commentators have seen him.

As Lear establishes himself, his life is both his individually and reflective of the general unifying style that harmonizes his nation's practices, so those critics who, following Coleridge, sense in the opening scene of *King Lear*, the resonances of a fairy tale are genuinely responding to Lear's attempt to become a culture figure. A fairy-tale figure and an authority figure are not all that different after all. Followers of Maynard Mack, who see *King Lear* as exhibiting characters with intense psychological realism and who are also archetypal patterns, are responding, in part, to Lear's attempt to make his particular individuality into a figure of authority.[62]

We have now seen how Shakespeare's examination of the authority by which a proto-use works shows that the use implies the establishment (at least inchoately) of a new modern kind of self-constituting personal identity, one that devotes itself to intensifying the practices of love or friendship that support uses. Lear tries to become such a figure on a national scale. Understanding Lear this way allows us to sense the grandeur of his ambition and also his lack of selfishness. For the point of establishing the proto-use may not be so much to aggrandize himself personally as it may be to bring additional unity to his kingdom. Yet we may also account for and sympathize with the grounds of the more traditional understandings of Lear as a sponge for love or senile or puerile or consumed with shame, though the basis of these interpretations is more complicated. To see it, we must start by examining Cordelia and Kent.

Cordelia and Kent, as should be obvious, exhibit the inwardness that is more usually identified as the main characteristic of the modern personal identity. We see this respect for their own inwardness and that of others exhibited in their plain speaking. Are the practices brought into focus by the use responsible for this inward form of identity too? For Shakespeare the answer is, at least in part, yes. But it may be objected that Cordelia and Kent's devotion to plain speaking, along with France's, are not a response to Lear's ambitions to reshape the nature of rule but are rather a simple reaction against the spin doctoring of Goneril and Regan. These sisters do speak out of the practice of glamorizing elaboration when they describe their love for Lear. It is indeed this practice that enables Goneril, in particular, to make Lear's indignation look like wildness and senility later in the play when she exaggerates his childishness (1.4.218–20, 234–35, 325–26).[63] And Cordelia clearly hates such speech acts. Yet, although Cordelia's and Kent's plainness may be understood as a tactical response to spin doctoring, Lear's attempts, both in the enactment scene and in his new way of being, to bring out and publicly focus the deepest matters of heart turns Kent's and Cordelia's tactical practice into one that determines their identities. For however Kent and Cordelia's tactic of plain speaking originated, Lear's actions which appeal to their inner love as a fundamental support of the new state, make their inward love their determining characteristics in Lear's world. But, unfortunately, the more Lear's world requires their inner love as its support the more Kent and Cordelia dare not express their strong, passionate, excessive love of Lear. And the reasons why they dare not express this love of an authority figure does, as critics have found, yield to the resonances of the Freudian family romance.[64] But the vibrations given out by Cordelia in particular are more Lacanian than Freudian. In the first scene, for instance, we see that Cordelia is particularly sensitive to the sentiments Lear tries to have her express—love of Lear himself—because these are the ones she nurses and shelters. The problem with expressing these sentiments is that putting them into shared and public words—and all words are shared and public—means acknowledging that others may have a share in these sentiments. Worse, once these sentiments are honestly expressed, others may repeat, report, inflect, and register them. And Cordelia's own understanding of her inner senses would then be shaped by the meanings these words came to have.[65] So in order to protect the purity of her inner sense, Cordelia resists speaking like her sisters. Indeed, both Kent and Cordelia adopt the *tactic* of plain speaking, which amounts to speaking only according to duty or custom, because it keeps them from endangering the integrity of their inner senses. For Shakespeare, then, the practices of the use that come to dominate landholding include not only the production of the self-constituting self trying to organize a public space but also the response to this of certain selves as vexed inward selves.

So far everything that has been written in this section is in direct contradiction to Goneril and Regan's analysis of Lear's actions in the first scene. And, traditionally, they are judged to understand Lear best in this scene. Therefore something should be said about Goneril and Regan and their evaluations. Goneril and Regan are wonderful in their innocence. They are both innocent of having any abiding relation to their nation's style, which Lear seeks to embody, and any single passionately felt sentiment that organizes all their excessive desires such as Cordelia's love for Lear. They are, in the terms of this play, characters innocent of character, if by character we mean the self-constituting harmonizing or the deep-psychological characters of Lear, Cordelia, and Kent. They have their social roles and ample portions of animal cunning, and in this we may roughly characterize their identities as conventionally feudal. For with impeccable animal cunning and clever calculativeness, they develop stories of Lear's rashness and senility that appeal to convention in order to satisfy their own momentary desires. Consider what they later make through their spin doctoring of Lear's attempts to maintain his royal demeanor. But without organizing stories or passions of their own, their excessive desires simply do not have anything to control them. This is why their desires lack any deep meaning and rich consistency. We are later shocked, for instance, to hear Goneril say, just before developing a military strategy, that she would rather lose the coming battle than lose Edmund to Regan (5.1.18–19). By this time, she has been so exquisitely calculating and generally so much in control that we tend to pass over our momentary response. But, as we soon see, with the poisoning, Goneril shows herself to be consumed with Edmund, and England has become her secondary concern. Goneril's motivations do not issue from the ideas and plans of an organized, unified character so much as from the instinctive promptings for satisfaction. Regan's motivations have the same nature. For what reasons do she and Goneril desire to reduce their father in authority and esteem? Are they seeking a particular kind of rule as Shakespeare's Henry IV was? Do they smell vice in England? Do they feel slighted of the royal revenues needed for provisioning Lear and his entourage? After discussing what they take to be Lear's fault—that he has cast off Cordelia too rashly—here is Goneril's explanation of why they must reduce their father:

> [I]f our father carry authority with such disposition as he bears, this last surrender of his will but offend us.
> (1.1.303–5)

That is all they understand of their motivation. The authority that Lear still bears—and even Goneril recognizes that he still bears authority—is an unjustifiable annoyance that one day may truly offend. Goneril's whole thought amounts to clearing an obstacle, like a misplaced chair, out of the way so that it will not, at some future point, impede her way.

But if Goneril and Regan are figures of calculative intelligence, should we not treat their observations of others as having a sort of judicial fairness? Their coldly reasonable explanation of the opening ceremony has caught the eye of many a commentator:

> Gon. You see how full of changes his age is; the observation we have made of it hath not been little: he always lov'd our sister most; and with what poor judgment he hath now cast her off appears too grossly.
> Reg. 'Tis the infirmity of his age; yet he hath ever but slenderly known himself.
> (1.1.287–93)

Lear has always been rash, inclined to action rather than self-knowledge, and now in his waning years has even lost what little self-restraint and thoughtfulness he had had before, they suggest. Under Goneril and Regan's gaze, Lear's story is that of the real life Ralph Hansby or Brian Annesley or Sir William Allen, all men who in the late-sixteenth century gave their estates to their daughters with Lear-like results.[66] I suspect that though Regan's words have comforted many by their complacency—they are on a par with explaining a religious experience as the effect of a spicy dinner—none has accepted the wisdom of these words without lingering heartburn. An analogy shows easily enough both what is compelling and what is wrong with Regan's view. In managing a business, the owner must, like Lear, always keep an eye to the atmosphere inside his company and the image it has among customers and vendors. The owner, as the focus and embodiment of the business, may have to make changes to improve that image or adjust that atmosphere. If compliance with company policies has been lax, dismissing a seemingly invulnerable officer might very well induce employees to greater punctiliousness. But a resistant core of employees might be depended on to find and disseminate the *real* reason for the termination, the hushed-up embezzlement, the affair, the festering resentment. It is all political machinations, they will say knowingly. Everything derives from the whim of the boss; the whole organization is based on *the infirmity of his age*. Regan speaks for all who reason only with animal cunning and therefore know themselves but slenderly.[67]

But even if Goneril and Regan are calculative malcontents who eye the world with animal cunning, does not Lear himself affirm their view of him? Does he not admit that in a fit of anger he mistreated Cordelia and that he rashly forgot himself? Here are his words:

> O most small fault,
> How ugly didst thou in Cordelia show!
> Which, like an engine, wrench'd my frame of nature
> From the fix'd place, drew from my heart all love,
> And added to the gall. O Lear, Lear, Lear!
> Beat at this gate, that let thy folly in,
> And thy dear judgment out!
>
> (1.4.264–70)

How is Lear thinking? Though it is easy for commentators to see Lear as recognizing here the truth Cordelia stood for, Lear does not say that Cordelia was faultless. He speaks as one who over-reacted to a *small* fault. But this is not quite Lear's point either. Rather he speaks as one who was taken over by Cordelia's small fault, as though by a demonic possession, for the fault acted on him as a machine of siege acts. To capture Lear's sense, we might say that Lear regrets that he did not know how to be Lear better. "O Lear, Lear, Lear!" he says. He has put himself in the position where he expects to affect the world by supervising the role of Lear through various inflections of that role's style, and in the ceremony scene he got carried away; he felt solicited to vent spleen when he should have done something else. But he does not adduce from this that he should stop acting the part, theatrically glamorizing himself as an authority figure. He does not think now that he ought to revoke his gift and employ his one hundred knights to ensure he gets the gift back. He goes on playing his role. This means that, while he speaks these words, he must beat his head to make his dramatic point which is about the size of Goneril's wrong in contrast to Cordelia's and his. The judgment Lear regrets the loss of is a culture figure's judgment of how to inflect the temper of those whom he believes admire him. And Lear does not get control of this skill until he learns that, in the world where he rules by inflecting the feeling of rightness that people have toward the organization of their everyday practices, the old conventional pragmatic ethos of fair play and justice has no place. But this wisdom arrives, for us if not Lear, much later in the play.

Notes

I would like to thank Joel Altman, Steve Knapp, Thomas Barnes, Hubert Dreyfus, Cheryl Johnson, Martha Bohrer, and Andrew Cole who commented on earlier versions of this essay.

1. Although Christian and humanist views differ on the meaning of redemption and of purgatorial suffering, their similarity in evaluating the effect of redemption and purgatorial suffering in *King Lear* is close enough to treat the two views as one, at least for the purposes of this essay.

2. Speaking as a humanist, A. C. Bradley remarks: "There is nothing more noble and beautiful in literature than Shakespeare's exposition of the effect of suffering in reviving the greatness and eliciting the sweetness of Lear's nature." See A. C. Bradley, *Shakespearean Tragedy* (1904; Greenwich, Conn.: Fawcett, n.d.), 234.

3. Many Shakespeareans rally under this banner. Here is a list of a few: A. C. Bradley, *Shakespearean Tragedy*, 269; Charles Jasper Sisson, *Shakespeare's Tragic Justice* (London: Methuen & Co. Ltd., 1963), 75–78; Rosalie L. Colie, *Paradoxia Epidemica* (1966; Hamden, Conn.: Archon/The Shoe String Press, 1976), 472–73, 478–79; William Empson, *The Structure of Complex Words* (1951; Cambridge: Harvard University Press, 1989), 156–57; Hugh L. Hennedy, "King Lear: Recognizing the Ending," *Studies in Philology* 71 (1974): 383–84; Northrop Frye, "King

Lear," *Northrop Frye on Shakespeare*, ed. Robert Sandler (New Haven: Yale University Press, 1986), 119–21; Harold C. Goddard, "King Lear," *William Shakespeare's King Lear*, ed. Harold Bloom (New York: Chelsea House Publishers, 1987), 9–43; and Maynard Mack, *King Lear In Our Time* (Berkeley: University of California Press, 1965), 114–117. William C. Carroll makes a similar argument for Edgar who, as Poor Tom, learns how to feel and also how to rule, in his "'The Base Shall Top Th'Legitimate': The Bedlam Beggar and the Role of Edgar in *King Lear*," *Shakespeare Quarterly* 38 (1987): 426–41.

4. Again, I will just list a handful of Shakespeareans who hold this view: Ruth Nevo, "King Lear," *Tragic Form in Shakespeare* (Princeton: Princeton University Press, 1972), 259–305, esp. 303–5; William R. Elton, *King Lear and the Gods* (1966; Lexington: The University Press of Kentucky, 1988), 171–263; Thomas P. Roche, Jr. "'Nothing Almost Sees Miracles': Tragic Knowledge in *King Lear*," *On King Lear*, ed. Lawrence Danson (Princeton: Princeton University Press, 1981), 136–62, esp. 161–62; Barbara Everett, "The New *King Lear*," *Shakespeare: King Lear*, ed. Frank Kermode (New York: Macmillan, 1969), 184–202; Stephen Booth, *King Lear, Macbeth, Indefinition and Tragedy* (New Haven: Yale University Press, 1983), 5–57; Derek Peat, "'And That's True Too': 'King Lear' and the Tension of Uncertainty." *Shakespeare Survey*, ed. Kenneth Muir, 33 (1980): 43–53. Paul Alpers draws on this perspective in his argument that Lear reveals to us the incoherence of thinking in terms of autonomous individuals having complete perspectives for understanding. See his "*King Lear* and the Theory of the 'Sight Pattern,'" *In Defense of Reading*, eds. Reuben A Brower and Richard Poirier (New York: E. P. Dutton, 1962), 133–52.

5. Representatives of the "family romance" approach are: C. L. Barber, "Inextricable Ruthlessness and Ruth: *King Lear*," *The Whole Journey* (Berkeley: University of California Press, 1986), 282–97, esp. 292; Harry Berger, Jr., "*King Lear*: The Lear Family Romance," *The Centennial Review* 23 (1979): 348–79; Stanley Cavell, "The Avoidance of Love: A Reading of *King Lear*," *Must We Mean What We Say* (Cambridge: Cambridge University Press, 1976) 267–353; Thomas McFarland, "The Images of the Family in *King Lear*," *On King Lear*, 91–118; Robert B. Heilman, "The Unity of *King Lear*," *Shakespeare: King Lear*, 169–178; Janet Adelman, intro., *Twentieth Century Interpretations of King Lear* (Englewood Cliffs, N.J.: Prentice-Hall, 1978), 1–21; Janet Adelman, "Suffocating Mothers in *King Lear*," *Suffocating Mothers* (New York: Routledge, 1992), 103–29; Stephen Greenblatt in his early essay, "The Cultivation of Anxiety: King Lear and his Heirs," *Raritan* 2.1 (1982): 92–116; Coppélia Kahn, "The Absent Mother in *King Lear*," *Rewriting the Renaissance*, eds. Margaret W. Ferguson, Maureen Quilligan, and Nancy J. Vickers (Chicago: University of Chicago Press, 1986), 33–49; and Jeffrey Stern, "*King Lear*: The Transference of the Kingdom," *Shakespeare Quarterly* 41 (1990): 299–308. Stern is particularly interesting because he sees that Lear does not intend to give up his power with his supposed abdication but rather to continue in power by relying on Cordelia—as is roughly the thesis here. Stern, however, has Lear rely on Cordelia as surrogate wife and mother.

6. A sampling of the political essays includes: George Orwell, "Lear, Tolstoy and the Fool," *Shooting an Elephant and other Essays* (New York: Harcourt, Brace, 1945), 32–52; Kenneth Burke, "*King Lear*: Its Form and Psychosis," *Shenandoah* 21.1 (1969): 3–18; Alvin B. Kernan, "*King Lear* and the Shakespearean Pageant of History," *On King Lear*, 7–24, L. C. Knights, "Shakespeare's Politics: With Some Reflections on the Nature of Tradition," *Interpretations of Shakespeare*, ed. Kenneth Muir (Oxford: Clarendon Press, 1985), 85–104; Sidney Shanker, "*King Lear*, 'Ideology' as Structure, *Shakespeare and the Uses of Ideology* (The Hague: Mou-

ton, 1975), 137–177; Paul Delany, "King Lear and the Decline of Feudalism," PMLA 92 (1977): 429–440; Jonas A. Barish and Marshall Waingrow, "'Service' in King Lear," Shakespeare Quarterly 9 (1958): 347–355; Sigurd Burckhardt, "The King's Language," Shakespearean Meanings (Princeton, N.J.: Princeton University Press, 1968), 260–284; and Harry V. Jaffa, "The Limits of Politics: King Lear, Act I, Scene I," Shakespeare's Politics, ed. Allan Bloom and Harry V. Jaffa (New York: Basic Books, 1964), 113–145.

7. Jonathan Dollimore, "King Lear (c. 1605–6) and Essentialist Humanism," Radical Tragedy (London: Harvester Wheatsleaf, 1984), 189–203, esp. 197–198.

8. Marianne Novy, "Patriarchy, Mutuality, and Forgiveness in King Lear," Love's Argument: Gender Relations in Shakespeare (Chapel Hill: University of North Carolina Press, 1984), 150–163.

9. Stephen Greenblatt, "Shakespeare and the Exorcists," Shakespearean Negotiations (Berkeley, Calif.: University of California Press, 1988), 94–128.

10. Lawrence Danson, Tragic Alphabet (New Haven: Yale University Press, 1974), 163–197 and James L. Calderwood, "Creative Uncreation In King Lear, Shakespeare Quarterly 37 (1986): 5–19. Kenneth J. E. Graham's essay "'Without the form of justice': Plainness and the Performance of Love in King Lear, Shakespeare Quarterly 42 (1991): 438–461, argues along these lines but does not claim so much that a new nonauthoritarian language is invented as that a transformed plainness provides for the preservation (not the triumph) of justice.

11. The term "personal identity" has developed a large degree of ambiguity from the variety of questions philosophers and other scholars in the humanities have put to this commonsensical term. Of its four principal uses, this study focuses on one. Nevertheless, to avoid confusion, it is worthwhile to say which uses of the term this study eschews as well as which one it embraces. When "personal identity" is used, it is not meant to get either (1) what distinguishes human persons from robots, apes, angels, corporations, or anything else that may seem to qualify as a person or (2) how we distinguish different token instances of persons who have the same type descriptions or (3) how we reidentify a human person as he or she changes contexts. When "personal identity" is used here, it is intended to refer to the cluster of meaningful ways of acting and believing which, if changed, would lead a person to say that he or she was a different person. Note that someone who has reordered his or her life might claim to be a different person even though the standard criteria of reidentification (e.g., continuity of memory, identical DNA structure) may show the person to be the same. This set of distinctions is heavily indebted to Amélie Oksenberg Rorty's Introduction to The Identity of Persons (Berkeley, Calif.: University of California Press, 1976), 1–2.

12. I accept in general terms the diagnosis of our current cultural situation set out by Martin Heidegger in "The Question Concerning Technology," The Question Concerning Technology and Other Essays, trans. William Lovitt (New York: Harper & Row, 1977), 3–35 and Michel Foucault's similar view in Discipline and Punish, trans. Alan Sheridan (New York: Random House, 1977). For Foucault's account of his relation to Heidegger, see Michel Foucault, "The Return of Morality," Politics Philosophy Culture, ed. Lawrence D. Kritzman (New York: Routledge, 1988), 250.

13. Chudleigh's Case is the most important case for understanding the Elizabethan-Jacobean use. (Indeed, what Roe v. Wade is for privacy and court power today, Chudleigh's Case was for the use, law, and personal identity then.) The argument just mentioned in the text is taken from Popham's printed report of the case: Sir John Popham, Reports and Cases, vol. 79 of The English Reports, ed. Max A. Robertson and Geoffrey Ellis (London: Stevens and Sons, Ltd., 1907), 1193. The report of the Chief Justice of the Common Pleas Court, Sir Edmund

Anderson, is also important. See Sir Edmund Anderson's *Les Reports du Treserudite Edmund Anderson, Chivalier, Nadgairs, Seigniour Chief Justice del Common Bank*, vols. 1 & 2, vol. 123 of *The English Reports*, ed. Max A. Robertson and Geoffrey Ellis (London: Stevens & Stevens, Ltd., 1912), 310–344. The best, printed report of the case is Edward Coke's *The Reports of Sir Edward Coke*, vol. 76 of *The English Reports*, ed. Max A. Robertson and Geoffrey Ellis (London: Stevens & Sons, 1907), 1:113b–140b, normally designated 1 Co. Rep. 113b–140b. Coke seems to present all the arguments. But he makes it look as though his argument clinched the case when it is more likely that the very similar arguments of Bacon, Popham, and Anderson drew majority support. Francis Bacon's argument in *Chudleigh's Case* may be found in *The Works of Francis Bacon*, ed. James Spedding, Robert Leslie Ellis, and Douglas Denon Heath, 14 vols. (London: Longman, Green, and Co., 1859) 7:617–636. After the case, Bacon gave up his conventional antiuse view and set out his more developed view of the use in his 1600 "Reading on the Statute of Uses" before Grey's Inn. This may also be found in his *Works*, 7:395–445. Close analysis of the arguments in *Chudleigh's Case* and in Bacon's Reading has been rare, and this absence has led to confusions. For the few close analyses, see the following. Percy Bordwell, "The Conversion of the Use into a Legal Interest," *Iowa Law Review*, 21 (1935): 1–49. Percy Bordwell, "Alienability and Perpetuities IV," *Iowa Law Review*, 24 (1939): 649–657. William Henry Rowe, *Scintilla Juris* (London: W. Stratford, 1808), 1–60. William Henry Rowe, notes, *The Reading Upon the Statute of Uses* by Francis Bacon (London: W. Stratford, 1804), 71–246. Charles Spinosa, "Shakespeare and Common-Law Understanding," diss., University of California, Berkeley, California, 1992, 102–150. Edward Burtenshaw Sugden, Notes, *The Law of Uses and Trusts* by Lord Chief Baron Gilbert, 3rd ed. (London: W. Reed, 1811), 527, n. 4. A good general account of the history of the use appears in A. W. B. Simpson, *A History of the Land Law* (Oxford: Clarendon Press, 1986), 173–241 and in Simpson's *A History of the Common Law of Contract* (Oxford: Clarendon Press, 1975), 316–374.

14. 1 Co. Rep., 132b–134b.

15. Those who argue for the significant presence of modern inward selves with unique fates run from Burckhardt to Maus. A short list includes Jacob Burckhardt, *The Civilization of the Renaissance in Italy*, trans. S. G. C. Middlemane (London: George G. Harrap & Co. Ltd., 1929), 303–333; Erich Auerbach, "Farinata and Cavalcante" and "The Weary Prince," *Mimesis* (Princeton: Princeton University Press, 1953), 174–202, 312–333; Joel Fineman, *Shakespeare's Perjured Eye* (Berkeley: University of California Press, 1986); Elizabeth Hanson, "Torture and Truth in Renaissance England," *Representations* 34 (1991): 53–84; and Katharine Eisaman Maus, "Proof and Consequences: Inwardness and Its Exposure in the English Renaissance," *Representations* 34 (1991): 29–52. Those who argue against a significant presence of modern forms of personal identity in Shakespeare's day are: Francis Barker, *The Tremulous Private Body* (London: Methuen, 1984); Catherine Belsey, *The Subject of Tragedy: Identity and Difference in Renaissance Drama* (London: Methuen, 1985); Jonathan Goldberg, *James I and the Politics of Literature* (Baltimore: Johns Hopkins University Press, 1983); Ann Rosalind Jones and Peter Stallybrass, "The Politics of *Astrophil and Stella*," *Studies in English Literature* 24 (1984): 53–68; and Patricia Fumerton, "'Secret' Arts: Elizabethan Miniatures and Sonnets," *Representations* 15 (1986): 57–97.

16. A. C. Bradley, *Shakespearean Tragedy*, 205, Maynard Mack, *King Lear in Our Time*, 94.

17. A. C. Bradley, *Shakespearean Tragedy*, 232.

18. Samuel Taylor Coleridge, *Shakespearean Criticism*, ed. Thomas Middleton Raysor (London: J. M. Dent, 1960) 1: 50, n. 1.

19. William Shakespeare, *King Lear*, ed. Kenneth Muir, Arden edition (London: Routledge, 1986) 1.1.292–93. Subsequent references to this edition of *King Lear* will appear in the text. The reasons for using this traditional edition rather than a quarto or folio text will not be developed here. However, selecting one or the other of these texts would not require significant alterations in the arguments here.

20. A distinction needs to be made between the *ideological* understanding of personal identity based on speculations concerning property and the *practical production* of personal identity based on the practices that constituted landholding. Speculative accounts of the nature of property during the early seventeenth century were mostly proto-Lockean and assumed personal identities strikingly like those of the atomic Lockean subject. See J. P. Sommerville, *Politics and Ideology in England 1603–1640* (London: Longman, 1986), 145–188. The legal cases that dealt with more technical questions concerning the practices of landholding reveal that the common lawyers in practice understood that estates determined the nature of the estateholder, and they generally dreaded the absolute willful control of land the use provided and much proto-Lockean theory imagined. In understanding légal practice and social practice in general, this essay shall concern itself with case law rather than ideology.

21. J. G. A. Pocock, "The Mobility of Property and the Rise of Eighteenth-Century Sociology," *Theories of Property*, ed. Anthony Parel and Thomas Flanagan (Waterloo, Ontario: Wilfrid Laurier University Press, 1979), 147–155.

22. This is not to say that the visual world has to be completely consistent with the auditory world and so on with the tactile world and motile world. Indeed, the inconsistencies are the ground of our experience of things as having a depth that includes their many various aspects. The point here is that the inconsistencies and consistencies are coordinated. For more on this matter see Maurice Merleau-Ponty, "The Intertwining—The Chiasm," *The Visible and the Invisible*, trans. Alphonso Lingis (Evanston, Ill.: Northwestern University Press, 1968), 130–155.

23. See Daniel N. Stern, *The Interpersonal World of the Infant* (New York: Basic Books-HarperCollins, 1985), 69–99.

24. This explanation is meant to be an unpacking of Wittgenstein's famous claim that we cannot come first to believe some one thing and build from there but rather must, first, believe in a whole system of claims to believe in any one claim. As to how we come to believe in a sophisticated system of claims at once, Wittgenstein says, "Light dawns gradually over the whole." Ludwig Wittgenstein, *On Certainty*, trans. Denis Paul and G. E. M. Anscombe (New York: Harper & Row, 1972), §141, p. 21.

25. Martin Heidegger gives his account of this in *Being and Time*, trans. John Macquarrie and Edward Robinson (New York: Harper & Row, 1962), 149–168, especially 153–155. Pierre Bourdieu in *The Logic of Practice*, trans. Richard Nice (Stanford, Calif.: Stanford University Press, 1990) speaks even more directly to this point when he talks of the durable system of dispositions (the *habitus*) inculcated from birth as what incarnates and perpetuates institutions such as landholding.

> Produced by the work of inculcation and appropriation that is needed in order for objective structures, the products of collective history, to be reproduced in the form of the durable, adjusted dispositions that are the condition of their functioning, the *habitus*, which is constituted in the course of an individual history, imposing its particular logic on incorporation, and through which agents partake of the history objectified in institutions, is what makes it possible to inhabit institutions, to appropriate them practically,

and so to keep them in activity, continuously pulling them from the state of dead letters, reviving the sense deposited in them, but at the same time imposing the revisions and transformations that reactivation entails. (57)

26. While Heidegger's account of "ownness" or possession is more complicated than is required for this essay, Bourdieu's account of possession is right on point.

Property appropriates its owner, embodying itself in the form of a structure generating practices perfectly conforming with its logic and its demands. If one is justified in saying, with Marx, that "the lord of an entailed estate, the first-born son, belongs to the land," that "it inherits him," or that the "persons" of capitalists are the personification of capital, this is because the purely social and quasi-magical process of socialization which is inaugurated by the act of marking that institutes an individual as an eldest son, an heir, a successor, a Christian, or simply as a man (as opposed to a woman), with all the corresponding privileges and obligations, and which is prolonged, strengthened and confirmed by social treatments that tend to transform instituted difference into natural distinction, produces quite real effects, durably inscribed in the body and in belief. (57–58)

27. What will remain constant in any environment that produces a functioning human being (as opposed to a wolf child) will be the structures of activity, contextuality, familiarity, and possession.
28. Reprinted in A. K. R. Kiralfy, *A Source Book of English Law* (London: Sweet & Maxwell, Ltd., 1957), 264–66.
29. Christopher Saint German in *St. German's Doctor and Student*, ed. T. F. T. Plucknett and J. L. Barton (London: Selden Society, 1974), 219–28 elaborates these enforceable duties of conscience at length.
30. Y. B. 15 Hen. VII, 13b (1499).
31. See *Brent's Case* (1575) in Sir James Dyer, *The Reports* vols. 1–3, vol. 77 of *The English Reports*, ed. Max A. Robertson and Geoffrey Ellis (London: Stevens & Sons, Ltd., 1907), 3:339b–341a.
32. See Sugden, Notes, 527, note 4 and Spinosa, "Shakespeare and Common-Law Understanding," 142–148.
33. 6 Co. Rep. 32a–34a.
34. 6 Co. Rep. 40a–43b.
35. Bacon, *Works* 7: 562–563.
36. J. G. A. Pocock has collected a useful series of quotations to show that common lawyers did, in fact, understand the common law to consist in the best of English customs. See his *The Ancient Constitution and the Feudal Law*, Reissue with Retrospect (Cambridge: Cambridge University Press, 1987), 30–55. His 1612 quotation from Sir John Davies is particularly compelling (32–33). Pocock does, however, overemphasize Coke's belief in the stability of custom.
37. Sgt. Yorke and Justice Mountague argued this way in the landmark *Lord Dacre's Case* (1535). See J. H. Baker and S. F. C. Milsom, *Sources of English Legal History: Private Law to 1750*, (London: Butterworths, 1986), 109.
38. Another way to put this point about the extent of Shakespeare's legal interests would be to say that Shakespeare is concerned with both the originary stage of the history of the use and the stage he was living through. Consequently, of the four main stages in the history of the use, two are mostly missing from the considerations of the play. These included and excluded stages in the history of the use are, however, worth noting.
39. If Gloucester is to send Edmund out again (1.1.31–32) and if he believes that he exhibits no less love for Edmund than Edgar, then we must assume that Edmund is receiving a training worthy of Edgar's station. Nor does Edmund deny the genuineness of his father's love (1.2.17–18). Also, we see that Edmund can formu-

late radical views in the prose of a courtier (1.2.45–52). It would also be enormously hard to believe that Kent, Cornwall, Goneril, and Regan all should admire as much as they do someone who had been ill-nurtured no matter how well-natured.

40. According to *jus coronae*, in Lear's case, the eldest daughter should take all by descent. See Sir Edward Coke, *The First Part of the Institutes of the Laws of England; or, A Commentary Upon Littleton*, 19th ed. (London: R. H. Small, 1853), 1:15b. This text is commonly referred to as Coke on Littleton.

41. This claim about the grounds for the division is based on Gloucester's early reasoning (1.1.3–6). But since any character's reasoning should be taken as normative only for that character and others like him or her and since such reasoning has the function of hearkening to particular practices outside the play and of putting those practices in a particular dramatic circumstance, one ought to be especially careful to avoid identifying oneself with Gloucester's reasoning. But Gloucester is the one character who is most concerned about the details of the original division vetted in Council (see 1.2.23–26). And nothing we subsequently discover about Gloucester would lead us to doubt his report of the original plan. Indeed, his early judgment concerning the plan—that Lear made the division on the basis of his understanding of his two sons-in-law—is supported by events. When Lear actually enacts the final part of the division, which includes the "digestion" of Cordelia's portion, he focuses on Cornwall and Albany, not his daughters or their speeches (1.1.126–38). And it surely is true that Cornwall, at least, will not tolerate slight offenses to his honor. That is one reason why he puts Kent in the stocks.

42. Kenneth Muir glosses the term "addition" here as "honours, titles, ceremonial observances" (12), but on the three other occasions where the term is used with a charged meaning, he glosses it differently. He glosses "addition" as "titles" alone at 2.2.23 (65) where the term concerns Kent's addition to Oswald's name. He glosses it as "titles and offices" at 5.3.69 (191) where the term describes the additional authority with which Regan intends to invest Edmund. And, finally, he glosses "addition" as "titles and rights" at 5.3.300 (204) where the term takes up the rewards Albany intends to dole out when he returns his royal power to Lear. The problem, as these glosses show, is that while an addition can be fanciful, as in Oswald's case, it normally refers to actual titles, offices, and rights that one holds by order of law. By glossing Lear's use of "addition" in the enactment as "honours, titles, *ceremonial observances*" (emphasis mine), Muir makes the "addition" into something centered on the ceremonial. To Muir, it is as though Lear had said that he were retaining, *for public ceremonial occasions* all of the addition he has when he formally signs his name, that is all of his titles, rights, and offices. This would be an extremely unusual grant under common law but it might be technically valid (see Coke on Littleton 4a). The grant, nevertheless, would have a severe practical defect. What would Cornwall and Albany do if each had to put on an important public ceremony at the same time in his own territory? Both would need Lear.

Harry V. Jaffa gets around this problem of the ceremonial "addition" by claiming that Lear actually retains all his royal powers, and he grants Albany and Cornwall merely ducal authorities along with the lordship of all the land. This technical legal point, Jaffa argues, is highlighted by Lear's use of the ducal coronet not the royal crown to signify delivery of the title (123).

Both of these technical common-law explanations fail to catch the passionate way in which Lear is going beyond law in both giving away all and retaining all,

"The name and all th' addition" 183

but retaining it in another register of authority. This argument will be fleshed out in the text.

43. I use the technical term *"cestui que use"* for clarity's sake only, not to imply that Shakespeare was thinking or could think in a technically correct legal fashion. Shakespeare was sensitive to a clash between the new kinds of self-constituting identities produced among beneficial owners and the older customary forms of personal identity. He saw that one identity depended on a deep trust and the other on habitual forms of behavior. He probably had some sense that, in fact, uses were most frequently developed in marriage settlements, hence he has Lear speak twice of the "dowers" he is establishing (1.1.40 and 127–128). But in common law, a dower is generally the life-interest a widow has in a third of the lands her husband held during their marriage. However, a dower could also refer to an interest a husband-to-be granted his wife-to-be at the church door before marriage. If we imagine that Shakespeare had a technical legal knowledge, then we are led to find Lear possessed with kinky imaginings of his daughters as wives-to-be. But Shakespeare does not command a technical legal understanding. He uses "dower" as "dowry," as did other nonlawyers in his day. We need only turn to *All's Well That Ends Well* to see this usage. At the end the King says to Diana that he will pay her "dower." (See *All's Well That Ends Well*, ed. G. K. Hunter [London: Methuen, 1967] 5.3.322.) So rather than think about Lear's enactment in a technical legal fashion, we would do well to imagine it as the first, prototypical use, one set up before all its implications had been worked out and set up as a nonlawyer would imagine.

We may want to note that under the law of Shakespeare's day, uses could not be established for daughters or sons-in-law in consideration of marriages already performed but could be established in consideration of natural familial love and affection. This fact suggests a source for the thinking behind the love test. This source will be developed later. One could always make a formal grant of land reserving a use for oneself; indeed, by the sixteenth century, if one made an informal grant, a bargain and sale, with insufficient consideration, the Chancery would take it a matter of conscience that a resulting use had been retained. Also, little in Lear's prototypical use suggests that he was setting up a perpetual beneficial ownership, a way of cheating death, though perpetuities were well-understood as one of the dangers of uses.

44. So far as Shakespeare's use of technical legal language is trustworthy, Lear offers confirmation for the claim that he is establishing a use when he later says that he has made his daughters his depositaries (2.4.249). Common lawyers understood the feofees to uses as "depositaries." Stephen Greenblatt in his "The Cultivation of Anxiety: King Lear and his Heirs" (112) recognized the importance of this term, but mischaracterized it as belonging to the law of bailment, which does not pertain to land.

45. Kent, obviously, is the one who draws attention to the term "authority" as capturing what Lear retains (1.4.30). Lear, however, looking from the authoritative position, might well characterize what he has retained as respect (2.4.23).

46. We would do well to understand the sort of authority figure Lear seeks to become by remembering those political leaders who drew love from their supporters more for their way of being than for their actual political accomplishments. Many praise Elizabeth I in these terms. For a more contemporary figure, John Kennedy comes to mind.

47. We know that such management is a wish that Shakespeare attributed to rulers at around this time. The duke in *Measure for Measure* expresses it plainly when he asks: "What king so strong / Can tie the gall up in the slanderous tongue?"

(*The Riverside Shakespeare*, ed. G. Blakemore Evans [Boston: Houghton Mifflin, 1974] 3.2.187–188).

48. In contrast, other accounts of this scene such as Dollimore's and Novy's assume that Lear already starts with absolute power. On those accounts, the opening scene amounts to an exercise of absolute power, not its establishment.

49. It is interesting to note that the essential argument listed against Charles I during his trial imagines a trust precisely the opposite of Lear's. While Lear sets himself up as beneficial owner who has granted his subjects (particularly his daughters) all the common-law interest in the kingdom, the Court and Cook argue that Charles I was the trustee for all the people of the kingdom (particularly the Parliament) who granted him his common-law power but who retained the beneficial interest. As in *Lear*, the technical legal nature of the trust remains in the background of the thinking about kingship in the trial. See Thomas Bayly Howell, *Cobbett's Complete Collection of State Trials*, 34 vols. (London: R. Bagshow, 1809), 4:959–1154, especially 1019, 1032, and 1009.

50. Partly, the love test may be motivated by an association with the notion that natural love and affection were good consideration for transferring uses. This became settled in law with *Sharrington v. Strotton* (1566), Edmund Plowden, *The Commentaries or Reports of Edmund Plowden*, pt. 1–2, vol. 75 of *The English Reports*, ed. Max A. Robertson and Geoffrey Ellis (London: Stevens & Sons, Ltd., 1907), 298. But technically Lear would only need this consideration if he were passing the beneficial interest he was establishing for himself to his daughters at some future time, that is, if he were passing it to them in consideration of their love and affection for him. But no one, not even Gloucester, suggests that the original plan involved anything so technical.

51. Samuel Taylor Coleridge, *Shakespearean Criticism*, 54.

52. Cavell, "The Avoidance of Love," 290.

53. Stephen Booth has shown how easy it would have been for Shakespeare to display an unequivocally simple, honest, pleasing Cordelia by removing lines 223–224 and the first half of 225 and then 229–232. See Stephen Booth, *King Lear*, 55.

54. To describe Lear as proto-Kantian in so far as Lear constitutes the space in which he will exist as an empirical agent may seen anachronistic. But Lear endeavors to do no more than what Elizabeth I achieved or liked to be understood as having achieved. See Susan Frye's *Elizabeth I* (New York: Oxford University Press, 1993).

55. Cordelia is obviously Hamlet's "heir"; she has "that within which passes show," and she protects it.

56. We will not, we say publicly, negotiate with (reason with) terrorists.

57. Lear's answer to Kent's "Revoke thy gift" justifies Kent's and our analysis of the grant as establishing a use. For a common-law grant could not be revoked. But as a matter of conscience, a beneficial owner such as Lear could always instruct his feoffees to uses to regrant him the land. Lear does not deny that he could do this. Lear says, "Thou hast sought to make us break our vow, / Which we durst never yet" (1.1.166–67). In saying this, Lear acknowledges that "revocation" is indeed a matter of will. Whether he revokes the grant or not depends on how he wants his will to be understood.

58. Crudely put, the political calculation behind giving Cornwall and Albany precisely equal portions is that the equal grants make them natural competitors. Each, or their proxies Regan and Goneril, would always be in the position of making suit to Cordelia for favors in order to obtain the upper hand against the other. For a more sophisticated—perhaps overly sophisticated—picture of the po-

litical calculations that went into the original plan for the division, see Harry V. Jaffa, "The Limits of Politics," 120–128.

59. Kent's view of the pre-use world is precisely that of St. German's student's view of the pre-Statute-of-Uses world. See Christopher St. German, *St. German's Doctor and Student*, 220.

60. Justification for this reiterated claim—that Lear intends to rule by manifesting himself as an authority figure who evokes a feeling of reverent respect from his subjects—depends mostly on how Lear does in fact act after the first scene. We see that Lear's primary way of trying to get things done after the first scene and at least until he goes mad is by calling attention to glamorized versions of himself and by transforming his desires into curses and other forms of hyperbolic expression. Lear is, in fact, famous for this. For examples, see 1.4.77, 1.4.216, 1.4.223–27, 1.4.273–87, 2.4.21–23, 2.4.274–80, 3.2.1–9, 3.2.14–24, 3.2.49–60. It is also worth pointing out that, although he may consider taking back his kingdom by force on three occasions (1.4.306–8, 1.5.37, and perhaps 3.4.16), he never takes any concrete steps to organize his thoughts or his knights for this purpose. In the first scene, then, Lear decisively puts his concern for pragmatic action aside out of a concern for image management.

61. It is worth pointing out that the common law, for technical reasons, construed a person's identity to include that of his or her heirs. "For," Coke writes, "the ancestor during his life beareth in his body (in judgment of law) all his heirs" (Coke on Littleton 22b). The technical reason for this glamorization of the relationship between ancestor and heir is that it prevents heirs apparent from thinking in any terms that would lead them to believe that they had any claim to their ancestor's fee-simple lands before he or she died.

62. Mack *King Lear in Our Time*, 45–80. Susan E. Linville tries to bring this mode of reading *King Lear* to a culmination in her "'Truth Is the Daughter of Time': Formalism and Realism in *Lear*'s Last Scene," *Shakespeare Quarterly* 41 (1990): 309–18.

63. For the effectiveness of Goneril's exaggerated descriptions of Lear, see 2.1.97–101, 2.4.140–43, 153.

64. If Cordelia's and Lear's sexes were reversed, it would be all too Freudian.

65. For instance, we see daughterly "love" receiving a rather hyperbolic sense in the first scene, but this is one small instance. Throughout the play various rumors and exaggerations color the sense of the words that recount both actions and sentiments. The way Goneril's letter to Regan colors Regan's explanation of the events at Gloucester's palace has already been referred to. There is also the repeated rumor of hostilities between Albany and Cornwall (2.1.10–11, 3.1.19–21) that makes the audience and the characters understand matters as though a battle were impending. Moreover, after seeing the events that led to Cornwall's death (3.7.65–96), we discover that a false account is in circulation (4.2.70–77, esp. 74–75). This knowledge gives us a vague anxiety about what is happening, and this anxiety is heightened when we sense that Oswald has probably lied when we took him to be reporting faithfully (compare 4.2.6–7 to 4.2.87–94). So, finally, this anxiety about reports of things said colors all events, expressions, and sentiments with a vague indeterminateness. It is, then, this expressive space of unruly anxious rumor, opened up in the scenes following the first, that explains Cordelia's reluctance to put her defining inner feelings into words. She does not want her inner feelings to circulate and come back to her in distorted form as, for instance, Edmund's claim that Edgar is one of Lear's knights comes back to vex him.

66. Charles Jasper Sisson, *Shakespeare's Tragic Justice*, 80–84; Maynard Mack, *King Lear in Our Time*, 45–46. I treat these cases rather slightingly because the

point of this essay is to suggest how Shakespeare was responding to the general changes in landholding practices that were producing changes in the way people dealt with themselves and others. Also, I claim that Shakespeare is thinking about the use in its general prototypical form not about the possible technical machinations to which uses could be put.

67. It is worth noting that Lear's use, which makes him as an authority figure, the center of interest for all rumor, gossip, and glamorizing in his kingdom, would gain for Lear a unifying control over all the spin-doctored reports that the Gonerils of Lear's world are good at disseminating. To do more than hint that Lear's world is one where reports are constantly blowing around and where "[r]eport is changeable" (4.7.92) to such an extent that it makes the kingdom changeable would require another essay.

"She is fast my wife": Sex, Marriage, and Ducal Authority in *Measure for Measure*

Alberto Cacicedo

> Children who stand in little awe of their parents, and have even less fear of the wrath of God, readily set at defiance the authority of magistrates.... It is therefore impossible that a commonwealth should prosper while the families which are its foundations are ill-regulated.
> —Jean Bodin, *Six Books of the Commonwealth*

> Feminist thought regards the sexual/familial organization of society as integral to any conception of social structure or social change. And conversely, it sees the relation of the sexes as formed by both socioeconomic and sexual-familial structures *in their systematic connectedness.*
> —Joan Kelly, "The Doubled Vision of Feminist Theory"

I

IN HER INTRODUCTION to Edmund Tilney's *Flower of Friendship*, Valerie Wayne argues that in early modern England female subjectivity is licensed only to the extent that it mirrors the male, who then acts to erase the female.[1] *Measure for Measure* has been treated as an instance. Kathleen Macluskie, for example, points out that the female characters in the play are "defined theatrically by the men around ... [them] for the men in the audience," and argues that "Feminist criticism of this play is restricted to exposing its own exclusion from the text."[2] The sexual license that *Measure for Measure* presents from the second scene, she suggests, supports the exclusion because the play makes it seem that women are centrally responsible for the decadence of Vienna and so deserve the erasure they undergo. Psychoanalytic criticism of the play addresses the same issue, focusing on what Peter Erickson calls the "avoidance of the mother."[3] From such a perspective, the sexual license of Vienna is an indication of the danger that "the mother" represents, particularly in regards to the initial dramatic complication of the play, the pregnancy of Juliet, whom we see as the hapless cause of Claudio's death sentence. That she, the visibly expectant mother, and not he is held to be the responsible party is clear in Claudio's statement that "The stealth" of his and her "most mutual entertainment / With character too gross is writ on Juliet" (1.2.154–55).[4] Were is not for such writing, one supposes, the "mutual entertainment" would have passed unremarked and Claudio would have remained free, his sexual behavior and so his masculine identity unconstrained. Juliet's pregnancy becomes a threat to Claudio's identity, metaphorically presented in the play as his prospective death.

Onto "the mother," then, is loaded the sexual guilt of Vienna, which prompts Angelo to threaten "geld[ing] and splay[ing] all the youth of the city" (2.1.230–31), as Pompey puts it. But one could argue further that the "avoidance of the mother" represents the growing conviction on Shakespeare's part that "the mother," more generally "female contamination," can in fact not be avoided by men.[5] Motherhood is "the sin you carry" (2.3.19), as the Duke tells Juliet, but it is also, as Richard Wheeler says, an "inner contamination" in Claudio himself, and by extension in all men.[6] In effect, Shakespeare is working out the implication of Benedick's offhand acknowledgment in *Much Ado* that "a woman conceiv'd me" (1.1.238). Both physiological and psychological, the "conception" of men by women marks them with "the mother." Thus, in Janet Adelman's reading of "the mother" in *Measure for Measure*, "sexuality becomes the original sin that brings death into the world," and all humans, male as well as female, are complicit in that sin.[7]

From such a perspective, *Measure for Measure* becomes part of the "reproductive anxiety" that abounds in the Renaissance.[8] In *The Arraignment of Lewd, Idle, and Unconstant Women* (1615), Joseph Swetnam puts the issue straightforwardly: "If thy head be in her lap, she will make thee believe that thou art hard by God's feet, when indeed thou art just at hell gate."[9] As Katherine Usher Henderson and Barbara F. McManus say in their summary of Swetnam's text, he "advises men to avoid marriage altogether, for it will bring nothing but misery," in large part because no woman can be controlled in her sexual and material desires, but also because women "weaken a man's strength and take away the beauty of the body," ultimately causing death.[10] In short, women are an external expression of an internal male condition, and their presence makes men externalize that condition. On the other hand, "Women are all necessary evils" for economic and for procreative reasons.[11] Claudio says about "too much liberty," that men must "ravin down their proper bane, / A thirsty evil, and when we drink we die" (1.2.125, 129–30): Swetnam implies that any contact at all with women automatically becomes "too much liberty," but that nonetheless such contact is the inevitable condition of life.[12] Thus, according to Robert Watson, although the Duke in *Measure for Measure* indulges a "fantasy of parthenogenesis" in making Angelo "at full ourself" (1.1.43), Angelo turns out to be a "bastard son": the failure of asexual reproduction is "what the Duke must . . . repair at the end by marrying Isabella."[13] Like the gentlemen in *Love's Labors Lost*, the Duke comes to recognize what all his subjects, with the exception perhaps of Angelo, seem to have acknowledged from the outset, that in regards to women, "Necessity will make us all forsworn" (*LLL* 1.1.149).

In *Measure for Measure* the consequence of forswearing, the irresistible power of "Cormorant devouring Time" (*LLL* 1.1.4), is much more insistently deadly than in that earlier comedy manqué. In *Measure for Measure*, masculine illusions of self-sufficiency built on the patriarchal denigration of women is subject to collapse *as a consequence* of the denigration itself. Claudio's death sentence presents one image of such a collapse. Ultimately, however, the play presents a less final image of the collapse, namely the state of matrimony, which constrains the female by what is, according to Lucio, "pressing to death" (5.1.521–22) the male. In what seems a typical strategy of patriarchal discourse, the play substitutes the agony of the male under the authority of the state for the erasure of the female in the relationship of marriage. As Wayne says, "reciprocal sexual control originates in and returns to the control of women's bodies, even as a means of controlling men's."[14]

And yet, in *Measure for Measure*, the destructiveness of male authority, both in its abeyance and in its assertion, precedes and defines the putative danger of "the mother." When state authority fails, rapacious men, who according to Lucio have never been "where grace was said" (1.2.18–19), make women prey to their desire. It is the Duke's failure as governor that underlies, almost as cause, Juliet's pregnancy as well as the general decadence of Vienna. Even Elbow, whose wife "was respected with him before he married her" (2.1.170–71), seems to come under the general uncontrollability of desire, doubled in his case by the confusion of his malapropisms and Pompey's wit, which cast doubt as to the paternity of Elbow's child. In the case of Elbow's wife as in Juliet's case, moreover, the fault is attributed to the woman, whose pregnancy makes her long "for stew'd pruins" (2.1.90). And yet the fact that Mistress Elbow has come into a bawdy house, where "stew'd pruins" can be human or vegetable, reflects the failure of state authority to curb male desire. To correct the failure of control, Angelo's authority is made to extend over men as well as women more costively and destructively than any corrupting force attributed to "the mother." Finally, to correct Angelo's failure and so to save Claudio—and the Duke's purposes—requires the sacrifice of Isabella, about to leave the world of men when she first appears, and of Mariana, retired from the perfidy of men behind her "moated grange," but also of Angelo's soul, Claudio's identity, and Ragozine's head. In *Measure for Measure*, then, women's bodies *are* controlled, but so are men's. If women are erased by patriarchal discourse, men too are erased, "hardly seem to fare better," as Watson says, "whether in bed or in prison."[15]

Watson argues, I think correctly, that *Measure for Measure* presents the victory of Foucault's "'bio-power': specifically, the need of the state, under the guise of personalized benevolence, simply to keep the procreative machine running."[16] But the play also shows what Freud argues about the origin of patriarchal rule, that the procreative machine requires the sacrifice of male sexual license in order to run effectively.[17] The Duke discovers that he is as subject to the imperative of that machine as are the characters whom he thinks he can shape and shift as he wills. The play presents the issue as the inevitability of marriage, from Lucio and his whore to Isabella and her bawd. But like *Troilus and Cressida* (where marriage fails to hold the wife) and *All's Well That Ends Well* (where marriage fails to hold the husband), it does so by problematizing the bond that marriage represents. Claudio's explanation to Lucio of why he is being haled off to jail does end with the "character too gross . . . writ on Juliet." But it *begins* with the assertion that he and Juliet are married:

> Thus stands it with me: upon a true contract
> I got possession of Julietta's bed.
> You know the lady; she is fast my wife,
> Save that we do the denunciation lack

> Of outward order. This we came not to,
> Only for the propagation of a dow'r
> Remaining in the coffer of her friends,
> From whom we thought it meet to hide our love
> Till time had made them for us.
>
> (1.2.145–53)

Claudio alludes to the fact that in early modern England "marriages could be made simply by the parties declaring to each other 'I ... take you ... as my wife/husband.'"[18] Fornication was not unexpected after such spousals: in a case before the Archdeaconry of Norwich in 1564, for instance, Katherine Salter asserts "that after a couple have talked of matrimony it is lawful for them to have carnal copulation."[19] Claudio's language indicates that the contract between himself and Juliet was public, "a true contract," and he seems to appeal to Lucio for confirmation of the public nature of the relationship—"You know the lady; she is fast my wife." Indeed, Claudio's assertion that he and Juliet are "fast" married by spousals and consummation is echoed in the play by the duke's scheme for uniting Angelo and Mariana.

Claudio's puzzlement, then, is not so much that "the mother" betrays their "mutual entertainment," but rather that a traditionally sanctioned form of marriage has suddenly become not only irregular, but identical with fornication in a brothel.[20] As we shall see, that had in fact happened in Catholic countries when, in 1563, the Council of Trent declared spousals entirely invalid. In an English context, what Claudio's puzzlement points to, and what Lawrence Stone underscores, is that, increasingly in the course of the sixteenth and seventeenth centuries, marriage itself—how one got married, what constituted a licit union, what steps were necessary to ensure such a union—had become a site of conflict in which subjects, the church, and the state were often at odds with each other. In early modern England, in fact, marriage was not a clearly and well defined institution.[21] There were at least three different modes of marriage, sanctioned by different legal definitions, each sometimes agreeing and sometimes disagreeing with the others. Shakespeare's plays present a brief abstract of all three. Sanctioned by canon law from the twelfth century but rejected by common law from the reign of Henry III, the most problematic of the forms of marriage was the marriage by spousals, such as Claudio asserts he has contracted with Juliet.[22] A second form of matrimony, clandestine marriages such as Romeo and Juliet contract in Friar Lawrence's cell, were accepted by common law, but invalidated in

English canon law in the revised canons of 1604.[23] And, of course, accepted by both common and canon law, public, priest-officiated, church-celebrated marriages such as that between Petruchio and Katherina became increasingly the norm, and finally were defined as the only legal form of marriage in England by the Marriage Act of 1753.[24] Not yet imposed by state authority, such "outward order," as Claudio calls it, became legally, if not popularly normative in the course of the sixteenth and seventeenth centuries. It entailed a new balance of power between couples wishing to marry and the state and its ecclesiastical and parental surrogates.

I want to argue that *Measure for Measure* traces the mutual inscription of "a sex/gender system and a system of productive relations," the "double order" in patriarchal societies that according to Joan Kelly pacifies "men oppressed by the ... maldistribution of social wealth and power" by offering all men "dominion over women."[25] My thesis is that in *Measure for Measure* the threat to male identity represented by the state's effort to limit and control sexuality is recuperated by the erasure of women in matrimony. Masculine identity is saved, just barely, in a tendentious exaltation of the common-law version of marriage over the traditional/canon law affirmation of the binding power of spousals. Furthermore, both subjections, of women in relations with men and of men in relations with the law, in turn enable an increasingly assertive, and ultimately monologic state authority.

II

If one considers the relations between husband/wife and the state, the reasons for the concern with the legality of marriage in early modern England are not far to seek. The confusion about what constitutes a licit union involves the potential wedded pair in profound doubts and complications, most of them concerning the legitimacy of their offspring. Common law, for instance, insisted so thoroughly on the public, social aspect of marriage, that it refused to consider children born before wedlock to be legitimate, even after the child's parents married. Civil law, on the other hand, made distinctions among kinds of bastard predicated in part on the intention of the copulating pair in regards matrimony and, like canon law, allowed for the post-matrimonial legitimation of hitherto illegitimate children.[26] Presumably, then, if one takes seriously Cleopatra's affirmation that the dead Antony is her "Husband"

(5.2.287), in canon as well as in civil (also called Roman or imperial) law, her children by him cease to be what Octavius calls them, "the unlawful issue that their lust / . . . hath made between them" (3.6.7–8). And, perhaps, Cleopatra's statement that Antony is her "husband" might constitute a spousal that, in canon law, establishes the two as married. In common law, a child produced as the result of the rape of an unmarried woman was always illegitimate. On the other hand, on the principle stated by John Brydall, "whose is the cow, his is the calf also," if the raped woman marries before the child is born, the child is the legitimate heir of the husband. Indeed, if a woman is married, "Albeit the wife were as common as the cartway, making open profession of her filthiness; yet her husband, if she be not altogether out of his guard, shall be adjudged the only father."[27] Canon law complicated the issue even further. According to Henry Swinburne, "a learned canon law judge" whose *A Treatise of Spousals* is the "standard handbook" on the issue,[28] since for the church the consummation of spousals by copulation turned the espoused pair into husband and wife, the rape of a woman by her espoused "friend"—what we might call date rape—converts the spousals into matrimony.[29] Of course, in common law the child of such a union, if the parents do not wed before its birth, remains a bastard. In regards to parental consent, canon, civil, and common law were in agreement: an otherwise legal marriage could not be voided by the absence of parental consent.[30]

The Marriage Act of 1753 affirms and makes rigorously standard for all people the public, church-celebrated marriage that had become normal for the propertied classes—what Stone calls the "official mode practised by the ruling elite."[31] The provisions of the law are specified by Teichman: "first than banns had to be published two weeks before the ceremony was to take place; second, that the marriage had to be solemnized in a parish church in the presence of a priest and two other witnesses; and third, that parental consent was necessary for persons under 21."[32] From the point of view of the elite families themselves, the "official mode" worked to ensure that they had some measure of control over the wedded pair and therefore over the transfer of property and influence that represented the civil aspect of the marriage contract. The problem that Claudio and Juliet have in concluding their marriage is an indication of the power that public marriages conferred on the families of the pair. But before 1753 the common law did not in fact require parental consent. Brabantio, for instance, does not argue that, absent his consent to Desdemona's marriage with Othello, the union is void. Instead, Brabantio urges the Senate and Duke of Venice to consider "That with some mixtures pow'rful o'er the blood, / Or with some dram (conjur'd to this effect) / He [Othello] wrought upon her" (1.3.104–6). Surely, says Brabantio, Desdemona's free will must have been constrained in her agreeing to so monstrous a marriage. As Stone says, in England "the powers of parents to dictate the marriage of their children was less than absolute."[33] Alan Macfarlane goes further: he argues that the absence of an explicit legal requirement for public weddings in which parental consent was presumed—in short, the English way of marriage from the twelfth century to 1753—constitutes a "subversively individualistic and contractual foundation for a marriage system."[34]

According to Stone, "What parents did have at their disposal was the power of the purse, by which they could exercise considerable economic pressure not to marry without consent." The power of the purse, and of the social conventions that underlay the purse, make Amussen caution that "The 'freedom' that historians have seen in the choice of partners by young people in early modern England was exercised within closely defined limits".[35] As Capulet says, if Juliet continues to disobey his choice of Paris as her husband, she can "hang, beg, starve, die in the streets, / For, by my soul, I'll ne'er acknowledge thee, / Nor what is mine shall never do thee good" (3.5.192–94). Similarly, the King of France in *All's Well That Ends Well* gives Bertram the choice to marry Helena or to lose his position, for the king "will throw thee from my care for ever / Into the staggers and the careless lapse / Of youth and ignorance" (2.3.162–64). These are harsh illustrations of the "power of the purse," of course, but both Capulet and the king give their dependents a choice, and a legal case could be made that Capulet and the king are not constraining marriage, but rather exercising their right, granted in English law, to favor whomever they wish. Juliet and Bertram, like Cordelia after Lear rejects her, in principle can find spouses where they will. In that fashion the letter of the law that Swinburne defines can be preserved. "The Verb *Spondeo*," says Swinburne,

> is as much as *sponte do*, that is, to give freely or without constraint, insinuating thus much, that how great soever the authority of parents is in that behalf, yet the children or parties promised or espoused, are to give their consent freely and voluntarily; or at least that they are not

to be constrained thereunto against their wills, by the rigor of covetous parents, or by any other sinister means; otherwise the contract of spousals or matrimony, made through fear, is utterly voide *ipse jure*.[36]

The mirror image of Juliet's and Bertram's "willfulness" appears in Katherina's "cursedness" in *The Taming of the Shrew*, which Petruchio must overcome so that he can eventually get "the one half of my lands, / And . . . [immediately get the] twenty thousand crowns" (2.1.121–22) that Baptista promises him. Without Katherina's consent there is, as Swinburne says, no valid contract. In *A Midsummer Night's Dream*, by contrast, the law of Athens runs exactly counter to the common and canon laws of England. If Hermia refuses to obey her father, she is given the false "choice" "Either to die the death, or to abjure / For ever the society of men" (1.1.65–66). In either case, of course, Hermia would be unable to give her free consent to marriage.

The absence of a well defined mode of marriage in early modern England, in other words, inscribes the absence of a well defined system of paternal authority. In Catholic countries, the confusion about marriage that makes English marriages "subversive" came to an end in 1563, when the Council of Trent regularized the rules of marriage along the lines of Stone's "official mode." The Tridentine law did not change the rule concerning parental authority, however. In France, therefore, beginning almost immediately after 1563 and continuing with greater and greater rigor into the seventeenth century, the lapse in the Tridentine laws was made good by secular law. Most importantly, the voluntary nature of the marriage contract was abrogated so that parents become empowered to dictate marriages to their offspring. Obviously, such parental authority presupposes that matrimony can be contracted only in the "official mode": publicity and parental control went hand in hand. From the point of view of the state, Stone indicates the general motivation of the new rules: "the monarchy felt itself to be so dependent on the patriarchal family as a model for its power, that it went to extraordinary pains to support and reinforce the latter."[37] By contrast, English law, both canon and common, retained its aspect of voluntary choice up to 1753.[38] It is therefore that Stone argues that "'Patriarchy' may . . . be too strong a word to describe a parent-child relationship" in England; and, as Macfarlane concludes, because of the inapplicability of such strong relationships, the patriarchal control of families by the state was also weaker in England than in any other European country.[39] Margaret Scott argues that in *Measure for Measure* one finds "fictional law, the like of which has never been enacted in England, nor . . . in Vienna," and makes a strong case that Shakespeare plays English laxity in marriage laws against his audience's generalized sense of post-Tridentine rigor in Catholic countries.[40] Scott concludes that therefore the particularities of English laws on marriage are not relevant to a study of *Measure for Measure*. As I see it, however, *Measure for Measure* reflects in almost every aspect the conflicted place of marriage laws and sexual and gender rules as the state affirms its interest in an ordered family life and the due succession of property rights.

III

Angelo's major concern seems to be with the application of the "official mode" of marriage to the propertied classes. He generalizes the new sexual regime of Vienna, but he has little enough interest in the case of Elbow and Froth, whom he is willing to leave to Escalus's relatively lenient judgment (2.1.135–37).[41] With Claudio, on the contrary, he cannot find any mercy that will not "make a scarecrow of the law" (2.1.1). The same distinction appears in *Cymbeline* when Cloten objects to Imogen's "contract [which] you pretend with that base wretch," and points out that

> though it be allowed in meaner parties
> . . . to knit their souls
> (On whom there is no more dependancy
> But brats and beggary) in self-figur'd knot,
> Yet you are curb'd from that enlargement by
> The consequence o' th' crown . . .
>
> (2.3.113–21)

Angelo's motivation is mystified by the sense that the duke and Lucio both express, albeit in different ways, that there is always a devil living underneath the precision of "our seemers" (1.3.54). And, of course, the play shows that sexual desire bubbles up uncontrollably in even the most precise of seemers.[42] The affective aspect of relationships, in other words, is certainly very much present in the play. But Angelo's refusal to accept the consummated spousals of Claudio and Juliet as a valid marriage is also inscribed very straightforwardly in the legal confusion about marriage of the early modern period. The Duke tells Isabella that Angelo had been "affianc'd" to Mariana "by oath, and the nuptial appointed," but that "between . . . [the] time of the contract and limit of the solemnity, her brother Frederick was wrack'd at sea, having in that perish'd vessel the dowry of his sister" (3.1.214–18). Angelo, in short, was concerned that his spousals with Mariana might be held to constitute a permanent matrimonial relationship. If so, he would be obliged to accept Mariana as his wife even though he would lose the prospect of any financial gain by the matrimony. To affirm, even by implication, the requirements of the "official mode" of marriage would make Angelo's own matrimonial state much less ambiguous.[43]

The reasons for Angelo's doubts are myriad. As we have seen, spousals had been declared invalid in common law since 1226, in the reign of Henry III. However, in canon law spousals were still held to be valid in *"foro conscientiæ,"* as the epistle "To the Reader" appended to Swinburne's *Treatise of Spousals* indicates.[44] The laws concerning the effect of spousals on the matrimonial condition of the espoused pair were especially ambiguous, however, in part because there were three versions of spousals, laboriously and subtly distinguished from each other and with very different consequences for the matrimonial state of the espoused pair. The most direct was the spousals *per verba de praesenti*, by present contract, which meant that the pair so espoused had contracted a valid marriage, even though the "outward order" required by common law had not yet been performed. Even without that "outward order," as Swinburne makes very clear, those who "have contracted spousals *de præsenti* . . . cannot by any agreement dissolve those spousals, but are reputed for very husband and wife in respect of the substance, and indissoluble knot of matrimony." Such was the case even when spousals *de praesenti* had not been consummated.[45] In other words, spousals *de praesenti* made it impossible for a pair so contracted to marry anyone else without being guilty of bigamy. A second form of spousals, *per verba de futuro*, allowed for the breaking of the contract "even if only one person renounces the contract." On the principle that the pair's voluntary agreement to marriage is absolutely essential to the validity of matrimony, the present rejection of the future contract was deemed to constitute a withdrawal of the will to marry. It is on those grounds that Angelo's spousals with Mariana seem to have been broken. The third form of spousals, conditional, makes the contracted marriage depend on the fulfillment of some matter external to the matrimony as such—for instance, the consent of parents or the settlement of dower and/or dowry. In effect, Claudio's spousals with Juliet are conditional; presumably, so are Angelo's with Mariana, although the Duke does not give enough information to determine the facts.[46] Whether the spousals were *de futuro* or conditional, however, the act of copulation converted the spousals immediately to spousals *de praesenti*[47]—hence the bed trick by which the Duke "marries" Angelo to Mariana. Furthermore, the distinction between spousals *de praesenti* and *de futuro* come down to the difference of a single word—"do" in *de praesenti* as opposed to "will" in *de futuro*. And, as Stone, quoting F. W. Maitland has it, "lovers are the least likely to distinguish precisely between the present and the future tense."[48] On so small a difference depends the matrimonial state of Angelo in canon law and therefore of his financial status in common law.[49]

But Angelo, of course, is acting on behalf of the Duke. And just as Angelo's economic interest in a narrow definition of marriage is mystified by the affective changes he undergoes in the play, so also the Duke's political motives are mystified. To be sure, we understand from what the Duke tells Friar Thomas that there are some overt political motives for the Duke's actions (1.3.35–43). Politically craven though his reasons are, one can well believe that the Duke would want to shift the blame for a rigorous enforcement of the law from himself to Angelo. The Duke's second overt reason for absconding, to test Angelo, is also credible, also seriously meant, also craven, and also partial. The play, in fact, never fully addresses the Duke's motivations, particularly for continuing in disguise even when it seems impossible for him to prevent the death of Claudio without revealing himself. Why does he affirm that "Craft against vice I must apply" (3.2.277) when a straightforward discovery of himself such as Lucio finally accomplishes for the Duke would resolve the problem immediately? The answer, it seems to me, is that without staging the discovery of Angelo, the Duke will be unable to have his political cake and eat it too—that is to say, demonstrate the need for rigorously enforcing sexual laws and at the same time be merciful in the eyes of his people. To demonstrate that not only mortality but also mercy spring from him, in other words, the Duke must continue to be "crafty." The agents of his craft at this point, moreover, are Mariana and Isabella:

> With Angelo to-night shall lie
> His old betrothed (but despised);
> So disguise [i.e., Angelo] shall by th'disguised [i.e. Mariana]

> Pay with falsehood false exacting,
> And perform an old contracting.
>
> (3.2.278–82)

By the end of the play, at any rate, Mariana's disguise has functioned as a test of Isabella's willingness to submit herself to the Duke's direction and so subordinate herself to a man. Cynthia Lewis argues that the Duke must learn the same lesson that he wishes to teach his people.[50] At this point, however, marked prosodically as it is by the passage's octosyllabic couplets, it seems that the Duke's lesson is fully articulated: women's subordination buys the miraculous political cake.

Legally speaking also, the Duke seems to want it both ways. He uses the practices of spousals encoded in English canon law when it suits him to catch Angelo; but he privileges state authority by affirming the necessity for the "official mode" of marriage encoded in common law. By the same token, as the Duke enables the canon law, he sets himself in opposition to Angelo's interest in property; but as he affirms common law, he articulates exactly Angelo's concern with "familial" property rights. How conscious the Duke is of the inconsistencies and the shifting alliances of his strategies is difficult to determine. And yet the play suggests that the Duke is encountering the "moving equilibrium" of social control that Peter Stallybrass describes as "a process in which the dominant groups have to negotiate with and respond to both each other and the subaltern classes, and in which the discourses and practices through which alliances are formed are never given in advance."[51] In *Measure for Measure* the Duke finds himself allied to Escalus, Angelo, Isabella, the Provost, Pompey, Mariana, Barnardine, Ragozine, Claudio, even Lucio in the sense that Lucio enables him to show the extent of ducal power; he also finds himself converted to friar, voyeur, pimp, stage-manager, and—absent the "accident that heaven provides" (4.3.77) in the form of Ragozine's death—executioner as well, all in order to effect the social control he seeks.

The same "moving equilibrium" is tacitly present in the Duke's description of Vienna to Friar Thomas:

> Now, as fond fathers,
> Having bound up the threat'ning twigs of birch,
> Only to stick it in their children's sight
> For terror, not to use, in time the rod
> Becomes more mock'd than fear'd; so our decrees,
> Dead to infliction, to themselves are dead,

> And liberty plucks justice by the nose;
> The baby beats the nurse, and quite athwart
> Goes all decorum.
>
> (1.3.23–31)

This is the familiar topos of "the world turn upside down."[52] Interestingly, however, the Duke's image of children out of control avoids the real issue that the play examines while at the same time giving the impression that it engages the problem directly. The Duke's language suggests that one mode of social inversion is much like another: unruly children represent the same threat to order as unruly "mothers," so that to control the child is to control "the mother." To be sure, children, albeit still in the womb, are centrally involved in Claudio and Juliet's plight. But the defining concern of the play is not the control of children, but the control of "the mother" in marriage in order to enable the control of men in the state. At the same time, while the Duke's description seems to make his own paternal authority the victim of the unruly children, it is in fact the nurse who is beaten by the baby. The reaffirmation of his authority will simply shift the site of the beating: now the Duke will be able to beat down "the mother" directly, both in anatomizing power of male desire—"the mother" as it exists in men—and in subordinating women to his own patriarchal purpose. The substitution of one inversion for another in the Duke's description acts as Stallybrass suggests: "an inversion in one sphere is legitimated as a critique of an inversion in another sphere."[53]

IV

Of course, the Duke does not legitimate the inversion of the "proper" relationship of father over children. Instead, he affirms that the carnivalesque dislocation is an unfortunate truth. The fact that the nurse ends up taking the beating, however, points to the inversion that the Duke critiques. The women in *Measure for Measure* are remarkable for the assertiveness of their subjectivity. When we first see Isabella, for instance, she is responding to the world of male power and desire by seeking to remove herself from its orbit. As with Angelo, one can focus on the affective aspect of Isabella's precision, and note that her withdrawal is as much fear of her own desires as it is rejection of male power. Rather than fornicate, she says, she would "Th' impression of keen whips . . . wear as rubies, /

And strip myself to death, as to a bed / That longing have been sick for" (2.4.101–4). Surely here the rejection of desire only discloses further desire. And that is precisely the point. Isabella *has* desires. To be sure, they have been misshapen by the form under which desire is expressed in the patriarchy, but nonetheless Isabella seeks to be her own subject. In contrast to Isabella, Juliet is an almost silent character. But she too maintains a strong subject stance. Reprehended by the Duke-as-Friar, Juliet acknowledges her fault, recognizes the mutuality of her and Claudio's culpability, and twice accepts the "shame" that has come to her (2.3.19–36). She is certainly not cast in the same mold as Hero in *Much Ado*, from whom one expects not much more than primping and swoons. There is a hint that Juliet, like the worthy ladies whom Lady Julia describes in Tilney's *The Flower of Friendship*,[54] wants to sacrifice herself because Claudio will die: "O injurious love, / That respites me a life whose very comfort / Is still a dying horror" (2.3.40–42). As I read this difficult passage, however, Juliet does not want the "respite" of her life taken away. On the contrary, she complains about the horror of the life she must lead, when every glance at her child will remind her of the horror of Claudio's death. It is an objection against the rigor of the law, not against continuing to live, that Juliet voices. Similarly, that well-to-do business woman, Mistress Overdone, objects vigorously against the new law that Angelo has imposed (1.2.104–5). Like Isabella and Juliet, Mistress Overdone is unable to intervene in the application of the law, but all three women are subjects who do not easily erase themselves. On the contrary, we come to see that their containment within patriarchal discourse is the hard-fought object of that discourse—and of the Duke's effort to impose the "official mode" of marriage.

All three women suggest a practical dislocation in the ideological place of women. The fear and control of self-assertive women in early modern England is detailed by David Underdown, who points out that "scolds" are associated not only with disobedient wives—who in the extreme version "celebrated" in the carnivalesque inversions of skimmington beat their husbands—but also with "independent" women such as accused witches and prostitutes.[55] Underdown and Amussen both indicate that the number of court cases involving scolds peaks during times of greatest social instability.[56] Amussen also points to "sketchy" evidence that during times of unrest a similar peak occurs in cases involving accusations that wives have been sexually unfaithful.[57] Amussen concludes that sexual fidelity is so closely connected to the social superordination of men, that a disobedient wife effectively gave her husband the horns of a cuckold.[58] In the case of unmarried women, sexuality was seen to be even more dangerous: "Women who bore bastards posed an implicit challenge to social and familial order by creating a 'family' without a head."[59]

What *Measure for Measure* does not, and perhaps cannot overtly acknowledge is this discourse of patriarchy, in which the Duke's political gestures are inscribed. The Duke must regularize marriage and prevent extramarital sex because his authority ultimately depends on the certainty that children are legitimate. Laws concerning bastardy in early modern England underscore the obsessive concern with the transfer of property and "honors" from generation to generation. The common law tended to leave the unmarried partners of an irregular sexual union more or less unpunished. As Macfarlane says, the only real concern of the laws was that any illegitimate offspring not be "chargeable to the parish," as a statute of 1610 stipulates; to the parents of a bastard child, the only legal "punishment" meted out was "public penance in church during a service. It is not even clear whether the father was meant to undergo the same penance as the mother."[60] The real penalties in law were reserved for the bastard child itself. Writing in 1703, John Brydall details the effects of illegitimacy: first, it "staineth the blood; for that he who is a bastard, is not permitted to challenge to himself either honour or arms from the father or mother"; second, "it renders him that is illegitimate liable to reproach"; third, it incapacitates the bastard in law, so that the bastard cannot inherit or have heirs other than "of his body"; finally, "it excludes him that is a bastard from all succession."[61] Bastard children, in effect, are so profoundly marked by "the mother" that their legal status is much the same as that of a woman unattached to a man.[62] Legally speaking, bastards were "nonpersons."[63] And yet, of the four effects of bastardy, the only one that applies to commoners with no property to leave to their offspring is the second, that "it renders him that is Illegitimate liable to reproach." Such reproach can be and actually was a very powerful tool of control, of course. Macfarlane, for instance, notes the statute of 1624 which made infanticide by mothers seeking "to avoid their shame" punishable by "death as in the case of murther."[64] But it is clear that the focus of the laws is the propertied classes, for whom, by the sixteenth century, the "official mode" of marriage would have been standard.

The method that the Duke takes to control "the mother" is, not surprisingly, exactly along the lines of the "official mode" of marriage. By the canon laws that apply to spousals, as we have seen, both the marriage of Claudio to Juliet and the marriage of Angelo to Mariana are unquestionably valid from the moment that consummation takes place: they simply lack the "outward order" that would make their offspring legitimate. And yet the Duke insists on the public, church-centered, priest officiated marriage of Angelo and Mariana, and urges Claudio to do the same by Juliet (5.1.525).[65] In effect, the Duke is imposing common law practice on the wedded pair, presumably to make absolutely unambiguous the married state of all four characters and so to certify the legitimacy of any offspring they might have. If marriage by spousals leaves unclear the matrimonial status of the contracted pair, it also leaves in legal limbo the status of offspring; the publicity required in marriages by common law, on the other hand, ensures that there is no doubt at all as to the legitimacy of offspring. As Peter Laslett makes clear, moreover, the clarity of children's legal status is, in its turn, inscribed in "the ideology of the property-owning [class] . . . [which] is bound to interpret any threat to succession as menacing its property rights, and illegitimacy is indeed a threat to the transfer of property between succeeding members of a property-owning class."[66] Ensuring that powerful families are legitimate has the effect of legitimating state authority, particularly as the state becomes more and more responsible in defining what constitutes the legal condition of matrimony. The move in France to identify parental control of marriage with royal control of the state affirms the point both as it reflects the state's power of defining a licit union and as it identifies patriarchal authority in the state with paternal authority in the household. The progressive tightening of the rules of marriage in England during the late sixteenth and early seventeenth centuries gestures towards the condition represented by France.

Mariana may well represent the ideal of womanly behavior towards which the Duke machinates all the women in the play, and by doing so reimposes his authority on the state. As Marcia Riefer says, the "moated grange" is not a wizened remainder of the "green world," but is rather a sign of Mariana's inability to contend with the ruthless social game that Angelo has played.[67] And Angelo knows as much. He is prepared to make sure that Mariana is not able to challenge his breaking of the spousals: not only have the conditions of the contract not been met, he says in public to the duke, but "her reputation was disvalued / In levity" (5.1.221–22). "At the centre of reputation," as Amussen says, "particularly for women, was sexual behavior." By contrast, Angelo's super-precise behavior ensures that his reputation will not be in question if Mariana were to bring a case against him: "Existing reputation—'common fame'—determined one's ability to contest further assaults on one's reputation."[68] But the Duke has ensured that Mariana would never come to the point of contesting openly with Angelo. The Duke-as-Friar, says Mariana, "Hath often still'd my brawling discontent" (4.1.9)—so effectively has he done so, that the brawl is never voiced. She is not, or at any rate is not allowed to be a "scold." Certainly Mariana has not seen fit to become one of the growing number of women in the seventeenth century who brought suit against their allegedly betrothed men for breach of contract.[69] In effect, between them the Duke and Angelo have put Mariana in the same position that, as it were by accident but in fact as a result of the Duke's machinations, Angelo puts Isabella when he requires her body to free Claudio. "I'll tell the world aloud / What man thou art," says Isabella, to which Angelo cold-bloodedly responds,

> Who will believe thee, Isabel?
> My unsoil'd name, th' austereness of my life,
> My vouch against you, and my place i' th' state,
> Will so your accusation overweigh,
> That you shall stifle in your own report,
> And smell of calumny.
>
> (2.4.153–59)

Indeed, if Mariana is completely docile before the Duke/Friar's compelling reasons, by the end of the play Isabella has been reduced to the same condition.[70]

The process of Isabella's silencing, her growing sense of incapacity in the face of a world controlled by men, begins in response to Angelo's proposition, but it culminates in her ambiguous final silence when the Duke offers marriage. Her silence speaks out the Duke's power in the same way that Mariana's acceptance of Angelo does. In light of what Mariana herself says about "cruel Angelo" (5.1.207 ff.), her marriage seems to be nothing short of a despairing recognition of her own irrelevancy as an unmarried woman. The Duke seems to agree: "Consenting to the safeguard of your honor, / I thought your marriage fit," he says in response to Mariana's plea that the Duke "not mock me with a husband" (5.1.418, 419–20). Her "honor," of course, is her reputation, irretrievably lost without the marriage and "saved" in only the most notional of ways by the marriage. Given what we have seen of Angelo's corruption, after all, Mariana's argument for leniency on the grounds that "best men are moulded out of faults, / And for the most, become much more the better / For being a little bad; so may my husband" (5.1.439–41) seems to lean very heavily on "a little bad" and "may." In any case, by forcing Angelo to avow his solely economic interest in Mariana, the Duke has destroyed any lingering illusion Mariana may have in the propriety of Angelo as husband.[71] She may "love" him, but as a result she is perpetually stuck with a man so blown in reputation that there can be no hope of a social recovery.

One comes to the same conclusion about all the men in the play: there is no propriety in the relationships imposed by the ending of the play except as the "little bad" in men is eked out by their social superordination. The Duke's machinations throughout the play have worked to guarantee that superordination—indeed, Mariana and Isabella cannot appear in the fifth act without acknowledging, tacitly but explicitly, their dependence on men. For Isabella the recognition is also an immediate affirmation of Vincentio's authority as duke. For the duke himself, on the other hand, Isabella is "lovely" (5.1.491) and so worthy of a proposal only after she has demonstrated that she can subordinate her cause for scolding to a mystified forbearance that just barely covers the interest of the state in marriage. If, as Amussen says, marriage in early modern England was as much a celebration of communal values as of family and personal interest, then the Duke has managed to subsume all of those elements of marriage under his own authority. In effect, from the point of view of the women, the play is a grand skimmington geared to silence them and so justify the state authority that has affected such a change. The Duke has shown that *la famille, et puis l'état, c'est moi.*

Notes

1. Valerie Wayne, introduction to Edmund Tilney's *The Flower of Friendship: A Renaissance Dialogue Contesting Marriage*, ed. Valerie Wayne (Ithaca: Cornell University Press, 1992), 61–62.

2. Kathleen Macluskie, "The Patriarchal Bard: Feminist Criticism and Shakespeare: *King Lear* and *Measure for Measure*," in *Political Shakespeare: New Essays in Cultural Materialism*, ed. Jonathan Dollimore and Alan Sinfield (Ithaca: Cornell University Press, 1985), 96 and 97 respectively.

3. Peter Erickson, *Patriarchal Structures in Shakespeare's Drama*, (Berkeley: University of California Press, 1985), 180, n. 15.

4. All quotations from Shakespeare's plays are taken from *The Riverside Shakespeare*, ed. G. B. Evans (Boston: Houghton, 1974).

5. The identification of "the mother" with the womb is standard in Renaissance physiology. Coppélia Kahn gives the phenomenon a psychological turn in "The Absent Mother in 'King Lear,'" in *Rewriting the Renaissance: The Discourses of Sexual Difference in Early Modern Europe*, ed. Margaret W. Ferguson, Maureen Quilligan, and Nancy J. Vickers (Chicago: University of Chicago Press, 1986), 36. For a physiological reading of the phenomenon, see Thomas Laqueur, *Making Sex: Body and Gender from the Greeks to Freud* (Cambridge: Harvard University Press, 1990), passim. The "mother" as disease is also commonplace. See, for instance, the account of "Margaret Fraunces, who was charged with bewitching Joanne Harvey" in 1600, but who was released when a gentleman assured the Justice of the Peace that "Harvey suffered from a disease, 'the mother', which led to fits" in Susan Dwyer Amussen, *An Ordered Society: Gender and Class in Early Modern England*, Family, Sexuality and Social Relations in Past Times (Oxford: Blackwell, 1988), 135.

6. Richard Wheeler, *Shakespeare's Development and the Problem Comedies: Turn and Counter-Turn* (Berkeley: University of California Press, 1981), 107.

7. Janet Adelman, *Suffocating Mothers: Fantasies of Maternal Origin in Shakespeare's Plays, "Hamlet" to "The Tempest"* (New York: Routledge, 1991), 87.

8. I borrow the phrase "reproductive anxiety" from Carolyn Whitney-Brown's essay, "'A Farre More Worthy Wombe': Reproductive Anxiety in Peele's *David and Bethsabe*," in *In Another Country: Feminist Perspectives on Renaissance Drama*, ed. Dorothea Kehler and Susan Baker (Metuchen: Scarecrow Press, 1991), 181–204.

9. Joseph Swetnam *The Arraignment of Lewd, Idle, and Unconstant Women or the Vanity of Them, Choose You Whether*, in *Half Humankind: Contexts and Texts of the Controversy About Women in England, 1540–1640*, ed. Katherine Usher Henderson and Barbara F. McManus (Urbana: University of Illinois Press, 1985), 202. One might hear an echo in Lear's assertion that "But to the girdle do the gods inherit, / Beneath is all the fiends'" (4.6.126–27) and in the multiple instances of "hell" as metaphor for the womb in the Sonnets, most notably Son. 144.

10. Joseph Swetnam, *The Arraignment of Lewd, Idle, and Unconstant Women*, (1615), 207 and 202, respectively.

11. Ibid., 191, 210, 212.

12. Consider Swetnam's question, "Is it not strange that men should be so foolish to dote on women, who differ so far in nature from men? For a man delights in arms and in hearing the rattling drums, but a woman loves to hear sweet music on the lute, cittern, or bandore. A man rejoiceth to march among the murdered carcasses, but a woman to dance on a silken carpet; a man loves to hear the threatenings of his Prince's enemies, but a woman weeps when she hears of wars. A man loves to lie on the cold grass, but a woman must be wrapped in warm mantles; a man triumphs at wars, but a woman rejoiceth more at peace" (ibid, 208–9).

13. Robert Watson, "False Immortality in *Measure for Measure*: Comic Means, Tragic Ends," *SQ* 41.4 (1990): 418–19.

14. Wayne, introduction to Tilney's *Flower of Friendship*, 55.

15. Watson, "False Immortality," 424.

16. Ibid., 415. I agree as well with Watson's conclusion that the play "refutes Foucault's claim that this concern was an invention of the eighteenth century" (415). To Terry Eagleton's list of Shakespeare's reading—Freud, Marx, Hegel, etc.—we must add Foucault. See Eagleton's *William Shakespeare*, Rereading Literature (Oxford: Blackwell, 1986), ix–x.

17. Sigmund Freud, *Civilization and Its Discontents*, trans. James Strachey, Standard Edition (New York: Norton, 1961), 47, 57.

18. Jenny Teichman, *Illegitimacy: An Examination of Bastardy* (Ithaca: Cornell University Press, 1982), 25.

19. Amussen, *An Ordered Society*, 110. In her note to the quotation, Amussen explains that she "has seen no evidence that it [pre-nuptial fornication] was frowned on after a public promise of marriage."

20. In England, fornication was never punishable by death. Even during the rigors of the Rump, fornication was punished by three months in jail. Incest and adultery, on the other hand, did entail the death penalty under the Rump. See Martin Ingram, *Church Courts, Sex and Marriage in England 1570–1640*, Past and Present Publications (Cambridge: Cambridge University Press, 1987), 153. Compare Ernest Schanzer's assertion that Angelo's sentence is "unquestionably legal. Claudio knows this only too well . . ." in "The Marriage Contracts in Measure for Measure," *Shakespeare Survey* 13 (1960): 83.

21. Lawrence Stone affirms that "by the sixteenth century marriage was fairly well defined," but he means that the contractual basis of marriage for "persons of property" was well defined; how one actually entered the state of matrimony was not. *The Family, Sex and Marriage in England 1500–1800*, abridged ed. (New York: Harper, 1979), 30. See also Alan Macfarlane's Review of Lawrence Stone's *Family, Sex and Marriage in England 1500–1800*, in *History and Theory* 18.1 (1979), 103–26.

22. Lawrence Stone, *Road to Divorce: England 1530–1987* (Oxford: Oxford University Press, 1990), 54.

23. Ibid., 97. In law there were no consequences for the wedded pair, but there were stiff economic penalties for the officiating priest.

24. Teichman, *Illegitimacy*, 25–26.

25. Joan Kelly, "The Doubled Vision of Feminist Theory," in *Sex and Class in Women's History*, ed. Judith L. Newton, Mary P. Ryan, and Judith R. Walkowitz, History Workshop Series (London: Routledge, 1983), 267–68.

26. John Brydall, *Lex Spuriorum: Or, The Law Relating to Bastardy. Collected from the Common, Civil and Ecclesiastical Laws*, Classics of English Legal History in the Modern Era (1703. Rpt. New York: Garland, 1978), 35–38.

27. Ibid., 84, 86.

28. Stone, *Road to Divorce*, 52. Stone indicates that the book was probably written around 1600.

29. Henry Swinburne, *A Treatise of Spousals, or Matrimonial Contracts: Wherein All the Questions Relating to That Subject Are Ingeniously Debated and Resolved* (London: S. Roycroft, 1686), 226.

30. Ibid., 4; Stone, *Road to Divorce*, 58.

31. Stone, *Road to Divorce*, 53.

32. Teichman, *Illegitimacy*, 25–26.

33. Stone, *Road to Divorce*, 58.

34. Alan Macfarlane, *Marriage and Love in England: Modes of Reproduction 1300–1840* (Oxford: Blackwell, 1986), 128–29.

35. Stone, *Road to Divorce*, 58; Amussen, *An Ordered Society*, 109. The revised canon law of 1604, which forbade clandestine marriages, tended to give parents some measure of control, at least in stopping a marriage of which they did not approve.

36. Swinburne, *A Treatise of Spousals*, 4.

37. Stone, *Road to Divorce*, 55–56.

38. By then, Stone argues, expectations concerning affective relations between

courting pairs made the provision of parental authority almost void. See Stone, *Road to Divorce*, 60–61.

39. Stone, *Road to Divorce*, 58; Macfarlane, *Marriage and Love in England*, 128.

40. Margaret Scott, "'Our City's Institutions': Some Further Reflections on the Marriage Contracts in *Measure for Measure*," *English Literary History* 49.4 (1982), 790–804.

41. A similar phenomenon seems to be at work generally in England in the last four decades of the sixteenth century. See especially David Levine and Keith Wrightson's "The Social Context of Illegitimacy in Early Modern England," in *Bastardy and Its Comparative History: Studies in the History of Illegitimacy and Marital Nonconformism in Britain, France, Germany, Sweden, North America, Jamaica, and Japan*, ed. Peter Laslett, Karla Oosterveen, and Richard M. Smith, Studies in Social and Demographic History (Cambridge: Harvard University Press, 1980), 158–75.

42. Wheeler, *Shakespeare's Development*, 93–94.

43. Jonathan Dollimore makes a similar point about the end of the play concerning Escalus' eagerness to "torture" the disguised Duke into confession: "disorder generated by misrule and unjust law ... is ideologically displaced on to the ruled." See "Transgression and Surveillance in *Measure for Measure*," in *Political Shakespeare: New Essays in Cultural Materialism*, ed. Jonathan Dollimore and Alan Sinfield (Ithaca: Cornell University Press, 1985), 78.

44. Swinburne, *A Treatise of Spousals*, sigs. A2v-A3r.

45. The summary and quotations that follow are from Swinburne, *A Treatise of Spousals*, 12–14.

46. Schanzer argues—mistakenly, I think—that Claudio's contract with Juliet is *de praesenti* (84): if it were, then there would be no condition such as the settlement of a dower to impede the matrimony. Schanzer also argues that Angelo's contract with Mariana is "*sponsalia jurata*, sworn spousals" (85). Swinburne does write about "spousals confirmed with an oath" and finds that such spousals cannot be broken except for causes that would dissolve any marriage (217–18). But that is what he says of spousals *de praesenti* as well (9). Towards the end of the book, I think, Swinburne is simply reiterating the binding nature of spousals, and so concludes that "The parties which have contracted the spousals together, are bound by the *laws ecclesiastical* of this realm, to perform their promise, and to celebrate matrimony together accordingly" (222).

47. Swinburne, *A Treatise of Spousals*, 73, 121.

48. Stone, *Road to Divorce*, 53–54.

49. Scott, who argues that no audience would have kept in mind the niceties of canon vs. common law (795–96), is surely wrong to say that ordinary people were not aware of the obligations incurred in promises made during courtship. Compare Amussen, who details instances in which women argued precisely such fine points of the law (*An Ordered Society*, 109–16).

50. Cynthia Lewis, "'Dark Deeds Darkly Answered': Duke Vincentio and Judgment in *Measure for Measure*," *SQ* 34.3 (1983): 272–73.

51. Peter Stallybrass, "The World Turned Upside Down: Inversion, Gender and the State," in *The Matter of Difference: Materialistic Feminist Criticism of Shakespeare*, ed. Valerie Wayne (Ithaca: Cornell University Press, 1991), 217.

52. For a less absolute visual image of the situation the Duke describes, see Stallybrass, *The Matter of Difference*, 203, particularly the second frame of the first line.

53. Ibid., 211.

54. Edmund Tilney, *The Flower of Friendship: A Renaissance Dialogue Con-*

testing Marriage, ed. Valerie Wayne (Ithaca: Cornell University Press, 1992), 129–32. Wayne concludes that "Their construction as subjects requires their own death, which suggests that the very best wife in this narrative is one who proves her love through her own annihilation" (64).

55. David Underdown, Revel, Riot and Rebellion: Popular Politics and Culture in England 1603–1660 (Oxford: Oxford University Press, 1985), 39–40.
56. Ibid., 29; Amussen, An Ordered Society, 121–22.
57. Amussen, An Ordered Society, 120–21.
58. Ibid., 117–18.
59. Ibid., 117.
60. Alan Macfarlane, "Illegitimacy and Illegitimates," in Bastardy and Its Comparative History: Studies in the History of Illegitimacy and Marital Nonconformism in Britain, France, Germany, Sweden, North America, Jamaica, and Japan, ed. Peter Laslett, Karla Oosterveen, and Richard M. Smith, Studies in Social and Demographic History (Cambridge: Harvard University Press, 1980), 73–74. See also James A. Brundage, Law, Sex, and Christian Society in Medieval Europe, (Chicago: University of Chicago Press, 1987), 459–63.
61. Brydall, Lex Spuriorum, 15–21.
62. In her Introduction to Tilney's The Flower of Friendship Wayne quotes The Lawes Resolution of Women's Rights, written by one T. E., and published in 1632, to the following effect: "See here [i.e., in "Eve's part in the Fall"] the reason of that which I touched before, that women have no voyce in Parliament, they make no Lawes, they consent to none, they abrogate none. All of them are understood as either married or to be married and their desires or [are] subject to their husband, I know no remedy though some women can shift it well enough" (14–15).
63. Brundage, Law, Sex, and Christian Society, 543.
64. Macfarlane, "Illegitimacy and Illegitimates," 77.
65. Despite the fact that Juliet is "groaning" and "very near her hour" (2.2.15–16), I take it that in the final scene Juliet has still not given birth—otherwise the child would remain illegitimate whether or not its parents married.
66. Peter Laslett, "Introduction: Comparing Illegitimacy over Time and Between Cultures," in Bastardy and Its Comparative History: Studies in the History of Illegitimacy and Marital Nonconformism in Britain, France, Germany, Sweden, North America, Jamaica, and Japan, ed. Peter Laslett, Karla Oosterveen, and Richard M. Smith, Studies in Social and Demographic History (Cambridge: Harvard University Press, 1980), 62.
67. Marcia Riefer, "'Instruments of Some More Mightier Member': The Constriction of Female Power in Measure for Measure," SQ 35.2 (1984): 161.
68. Amussen, An Ordered Society, 98–100.
69. Ingram, Church Courts, Sex and Marriage, 194.
70. See Riefer, "'Instruments of Some Mightier Member,'" 165. Dollimore finds a significant difference between Mariana and Isabella precisely as they are coopted by the Duke: Mariana's "exploitation [is] recast and indeed experienced by Mariana as voluntary allegiance to disinterested virtue"; Isabella, on the other hand, "conceives her weakness half in terms of women's supposed intrinsic 'frailness,' half in terms of exploitative male coercion" ("Transgression and Surveillance," 82, 83). Macluskie, on the other hand, finds both women equally contained by the "patriarchal bard" ("The Patriarchal Bard," 96–97).
71. Amussen recounts the following incident, which puts Angelo's self-interest in a highly ambiguous light: "In 1565 Margaret Underwood admitted that Thomas Deynes had talked of marriage with her, but 'he said if he might enjoy the house and land in her mother's possession that he would be content to marry with her, wherefore for that he would have had her for her land's sake as she conjectured, she made him an answer that she would no more talk with him in any matrimony [sic] matter'" (An Ordered Society, 76).

Lucrece's Gaze

STEPHEN J. CARTER

I

IN SHAKESPEARE'S *The Rape of Lucrece* Tarquin's and Lucrece's acts of seeing precede their speaking. I shall argue that a specific, constructed experience of social space *produces* their ability to speak through a sequence of narratable actions. This spatial figuration projects along gender lines. How vision is socially put together reveals the linguistic means by which Lucrece, Tarquin, 'their' narrator, and the narrative's audience come to be screens for the imaginal projection of gender.

A useful beginning may be to investigate the phenomenological acquisition of sight as documented in clinical situations. When patients who had been blind from birth first started receiving cataract operations, records of the doctors' reports on the patients' progress were collected in a study by Marius von Senden.[1] As it turned out, such "newly sighted" patients were not merely confronting a surfeit of new, different data. Their task was to learn a thoroughly new intellectual skill: how to put together the vast sensory experience contained in even the simplest, smallest movement of one's body through space. Their experience constitutes persuasive evidence that we are "taught" to posit not only an objective world outside ourselves, but also, and perhaps more importantly, a curiously objective gender inside, inseparable from our experience of being subjects. "I showed her my hand," wrote one of the doctors of a patient,

> and asked her what it was; she looked long at it, without saying a word; I then took her own hand and held it before her eyes, she said with a deep sigh: 'That's my hand.' A blind person has no exact idea even of the shape of his own body; so that I first had to hold her own hand before her in order for her to recognize mine as a hand also.[2]

The patient could be described as passing through Lacan's mirroring ego-ideal stage; she *emerges* on this side of what she sees, as a subject—opposite to and abstracted from a constructed tableau. To see, in a sense, is to be the author of oneself. Another patient described seeing

> an extensive field of light, in which everything appeared dull, confused, and in motion. He could not distinguish objects.[3]

In the course of time, however, by trial and error s/he learns to pick out such static patterns of nonmovement from the swirling of forms and colors: objects. This, as noted above, can be interpreted as the initiating, establishing event in subjectivity, setting in motion all of a life's subsequent events. Like vision, then, *being* a subject is an acquired mental process, a process of mirroring. A subject/object grid is deployed between observer and observed, such that vision does not merely interpret, but organizes, in effect produces, our social, gendered reality.

This process of linking with one's reality effects a cognitive "lack of being," the recognition that one's "realization lies in another actual or imaginary space."[4] Such a patient, like Lacan's infant,

> only sees [his] form as more or less total and unified in an external image, in a virtual, alienated ideal unity [. . .][5]

—in a mirror. The "gendered Other" gazes at his/her untouchable virtuality. Male/female as Other only knows itself by the mediating image(s) it has of the mirror-subject. It knows what it is by what it is not. This "lack of being" is initiated by, produced, and grows *with* one's capacity for sight. A patient's lack—this "rushing in" of gender—occurs in the act of making himself real in an imaginary space.

In *The Rape of Lucrece* this spatial metaphorizing of gender is apparent in the linguistically partitioned actions, and therefore the identities, of the two primary characters, Lucrece and Tarquin. I shall focus primarily, though not exclusively, on the scene of Lucrece "reading" the wall painting in which Troy's defeat is depicted. I shall argue that in her surveying of the painting—in her return from a journey into sightedness—she constructs herself as a rhetorical, gendered Other, whom she then projects back into herself as subject. As a subject she becomes a "newly sighted" space that frames what might be termed her former feminine unseen-ness. By examining the tension between the rhetorical and painterly registers in this passage (spoken by Lucrece and the narrator), in the context of its ordering of narrative voices, I shall reconstruct the means of her transformation.

II

The story of Lucrece would have been well-known to Elizabethan audiences. Its passive/active linking of her rape/suicide was left largely unquestioned. The presumed choice presented in the poem between death or shame was a foregone conclusion. The theological position counseled choosing shame, of which one could be shriven, over suicide, a mortal sin. Preferring death implied that rape was necessarily, regardless of the purity of mind, a pollution of the body's chastity, an effect which could not be undone. The Elizabethan audience could imagine, and perhaps praise, a woman's choosing a public transformation of unchastity through death, over the private shame of bodily pollution, however technically virtuous of mind she remains. A gap opens up here socially between an audience's deploying of a secular discourse within the larger theological context. The former produces a reading of female space as that which needed to be kept enclosed, unseen, pure—within a larger, allegedly protective male space. The latter, however, produces a reading that condemns Lucrece's actions as, in St. Augustine's view, a failure to see

> that while the sanctity of the soul remains even when the body is violated, the sanctity of the body is not lost; and that in like manner, the sanctity of the body is lost when the sanctity of the soul is violated, though the body itself remains intact.[6]

Shakespeare's text intriguingly anticipates and conflates these two readings. Lucrece's choice of suicide is *not* presented as the automatic secular choice it was assumed to be. The process of her reaching her decision is represented as a discursively critical task in which she challenges the casting of her rape as bodily pollution. The Elizabethan audience was potentially being made aware of its emphatically split reading: that she courageously chose and acted on a theologically incorrect reading, for which she could not be held responsible given the Roman setting of the story.

III

The activity of her "looking at" the wall painting occurs within a larger terrain of envisioning modes. These take many forms in the poem: the mutable register of Tarquin's gaze at Lucrece and Collatium's interior, and similarly of Lucrece's "regard" (for Tarquin, the Apostrophic objects, and the painting); the mind's eye of lust and shame, which as signifieds, look inward at their objects; the varied surfeit(s) of what is seen (focalized); and the presence of "painted" eyes within, and looking back from, the painting.

The narrator gradually escalates the activity of Tarquin's 'seeing' of Lucrece: from his "wanton sight,"[7] to "lustful eye" (179), to "greedy eyeballs" (368), to "willful eye" (417), to "a cockatrice' dead-killing eye" (540). Such rhetorical anaphora proliferate in tandem with the violent expansion of Tarquin's envisioning space; his license to "look," to penetrate with ever greater intensity, inscribes his movement across and into the female space of corridors, doorways, and the bedchamber of Collatium, which enclose the chaste, untrespassed inner female space of Lucrece's body. The nature of his seeing—surveying and violently reaching out—is being employed here to construct a version of incursive male space.

Female space is possessed within the envisioning male, whether Collatine or Tarquin. As the signified within Tarquin's mind's eye, she contracts.

> Within his thought her heavenly image sits,
> And in the self-same seat sits Collatine.
> That eye which looks on her confounds his wits:
> That eye which him beholds, as more divine,
> Unto a view so false will not incline [,]
>
> (288–92)

Her eye (as his signified) "which him beholds" proceeds *to, but not beyond* the boundary of his inner gaze.

> But she that never cop'd with stranger eyes,
> Could pick no meaning from their parling looks,
> Nor read the subtle shining secrecies

> Writ in the glassy margents of such books.
> She touch'd no unknown baits, nor fear'd no hooks,
>   Nor could she moralize his wanton sight,
>   More than [that] his eyes were opened to the light.
>
> (99–105)

Her enclosed passivity here seems to preclude any worldly understanding of what waits there to be read (or not) in his eyes and looks. Imposed chastity works to contain vision; it reverses the seeing/speaking progression for the female such that Lucrece literally does not see Tarquin's lust until he speaks it. Tarquin however is allowed to cross the boundary of his gaze, to pierce his own inner outrushing "look."

> Then looking scornfully, he doth despise
> His naked armor of still-slaughtered lust [,]
>
> (187–88)

An ineffectual armor against fear, his lust self-reflexively slaughters even as he inwardly gazes on its self-replenishing object.

Who does Tarquin rape? He rapes Collatium, the home and room, as female space. His vision precedes his movement through its corridors and doorways, pushing him steadily deeper into "her." He proceeds "As each unwilling portal yields him way" (309); he forces "The locks between her chamber and his will" (302); he ignores that "The threshold grates the door to have him heard" (306). He rapes as he sees.

> Now is he come unto the chamber door
> That shuts him from the heaven of his thought,
> Which with a yielding latch, and with no more,
> Hath barr'd him from the blessed thing he sought.
>
> (337–40)

What he sees/rapes is nothing less than the patriarchically programmed, enclosed, inrushing space of the constructed feminine. Georgianna Ziegler[8] draws on Peter Stallybrass's useful analogy between Bakhtin's notion of the grotesque, and the Renaissance reading of female vision—the grotesque as transgressive, antihierarchical, unfinished, obscene.[9] Such potentiality within female space is normatively constrained by patriarchy—"her signs are the enclosed body, the closed mouth, the locked house."[10] Rape becomes a rending of gendered space; what undergoes pollution is not a body, but a patriarchal construction of female space her "body" occupies.

IV

What is our response upon viewing an effectively conceived and executed visual representation? Writing on narrative painting, Leonardo da Vinci states that if the work

> represents terror, fear, flight, sorrow, weeping, and lamentation; or pleasure, joy, laughter and similar conditions, the minds of those who *view* it ought to make their limbs *move* so that they seem to find themselves in the same situation which the figures in the narrative painting represent.[11] (italics mine)

As an *audience* before the Troy painting Lucrece herself does this, and more. We need to observe, however tritely, that she must have walked by this artwork, glanced at it, and doubtless viewed it at length on countless occasions during the years she lived at Collatium. Yet on this occasion she deliberately seeks it out. Faced by a representation-as-event, one that exerts a gradually intensifying, cathecting hold on her, she experiences herself mimicing and voicing the physiological and emotional states of its varied characters. In doing so she temporarily *steps into* the representation. Not surprisingly, the meaning she makes of herself in the painting is to a considerable degree determined by the remembered image of the violence of her rape—an image, some critics argue, unduly "stimulated" by her own language.

"Narratives," as R. Rawdon Wilson claims, can "catch, hold, illude, and frequently delude their narratees."[12] The painting-as-narrator tells Lucrece her own story. Moreover, being "caught" by an ostensible illusion can work no less genuine a transformation on a viewer/listener than that worked by a real sight. The Trojan figures she moves among open up and frame Lucrece's own narrative, that is the internal struggle between the two poles of violence she endures, rape and suicide. The gaze of the text-as-narrator at the painting (over Lucrece's shoulder) directs, constructs, and contains her (and our) gaze.

Let us take a brief, initial "wide-angle" look at the sweep of narration, Apostrophic address and prosopopoeic voice that speak in this scene of the "skillful painting." First the narrator throws his peripatetic, focalizing eye here and there over the painting in a cinematic manner—panning, cutting, tracking in and back, tilting—that gradually escalates. The linguistic effect of installing vision in this way intensifies the very reality (not the realism) of the representation, opening up a space in her own enclosed image of self.

It is during her first narration of (and address to) the painting that Lucrece, in effect, crosses over into what she sees, and also into herself as representation (Other). Indeed, the rhetorical features of her speech in this passage emphasize an emerging detachment from female space.

In the narrator's second passage, half the length of the first, Lucrece's impassioned response from within the painting is narrated. The text implements Simonides's aphorism mentioned earlier when Lucrece prosopopoeically gives language to the silent, painted figures, who in turn give to her her own movements and expressions. The narrator's language rearranges Lucrece's reality within her reading of the painting and herself. However, in her second passage, in which Lucrece responds emphatically to the artist's perjury of Sinon's face (linking Sinon to Tarquin), she takes control of her own seeing by the linguistic rearranging of what she sees.

In the narrator's third passage Lucrece is represented as having pulled back from her former rage, directed not only at Sinon/Tarquin, but also at the circumstances of her own (now oblique) "story."

The possibility of conferring worldhood on her own story, a place to which she returns from the embedded narrative of the painting, undergoes an anachronic shift. The space Lucrece's newly sighted eyes now project has little in common with her former world. At the moment of her death her language, actions, and seeing have a curious unity that allows us in, while holding back the males present in the scene.

V

Let us now "track in" for a closer look at the rhetorical, visual, and narrative components of each of these passages in the wall painting scene. In the narrator's first passage (1366–1463) we are gradually introduced to the "skillful painting." The narrator's initial, tentative address to the reader, "These *might* you see [. . .] / "

Lucrece's Gaze 217

(1380), "That one *might* see [. . .] / " (1386), and "You *might* behold [. . .] / " (italics mine) acknowledge the painting as "mere" representation, of which we are rightly to be skeptical. By the midpoint of this passage, however, by a grammatical shifting from the conditional to the simple past, the language inserts us into that representation.

This process is emphasized in the cinematic movement of narrative focus. Whom and what do we see? The most visual sequence within this passage directs our eye as follows: a "medium shot" on

> Ajax and Ulysses, O what art
> Of physiognomy might one behold!
>
> (1394);

CUT to a "close shot" on

> The face of either cipher'd either's heart
>
> (1396);

CUT to an 'extreme close' on

> Ajax' eyes blunt rage and rigor roll'd
>
> (1398);

PAN to

> the mild glance that smiling Ulysses lent.
>
> (1399);

CUT to a "medium" on Nestor; PULL BACK to a "long" to bring into frame the silent, listening faces of the soldiers; and follow with a slow "pan" among

> The scalps of many, almost hid behind,
> To jump up higher seem'd to mock the mind.
>
> (1413–14)

With this there is a shift back, in language, from what occurs in the painting-as-narrative to a look at the painter's technique itself. A subsequent description of the painterly device of *overlap* intensifies this:

> That for Achilles' image stood his spear,
> Grip'd in an armed hand, himself behind
> Was left unseen, save to the eye of the mind[:]
>
> (1424–26)

Space, in effect, is being constructed through an acknowledgement of what perception contributes—our learning to view the real in fragments. Fragments imply gaps; the text signals that what is "left unseen" is where the reader's role enters, to fill in such space. A whole is merely a consensus among the senses of a thing "they" willfully put together. From the poem's above-noted technical description of painterly special effects there is a further shift to the description of the Trojan mothers' contradictory spectatorship:

> And from the walls of strong-besieged Troy,
> When their brave hope, bold Hector, march'd to field,
> Stood many Troyan mothers, sharing joy
> To see their youthful sons bright weapons wield,
> And to their hope they such odd action yield
>   That through their light joy seemed to appear
>   (Like bright things stain'd) a kind of heavy fear.
>
> (1429–35)

We are compelled to read in both directions here. Our line of sight travels to the walls, and from there to the field, simultaneously reflected back from the "light" of the "bright weapons" to the mothers' eyes. Is vision an intersubjective agency, or an activity by which space invents itself between two sites of seeing? It would seem that we learn not to see how we have learned to see.

This progress of the first passage—a pull back from the painted representation as deep cinematic reality, to a framing of technique, and back again to a framing of the problematics of vision itself—leaves the reader at a considerable distance from Lucrece. We hear and see her identification with Hecuba, yet cannot follow her as she crosses over.

Escalating rhetorical density has a stroboscopic effect on the space this passage produces, as demonstrated in: the piling on of anaphora (1467–8) in her first stanza, the chiasmus (1475–6) in the second, an epanalepsis (1480) in the third, and the combined anaphora and assonance (1487–8) in the fourth, each involving variations on the strategic repetition of key words. Critical opinion has often tended to resist the reflexivity of rhetorical forms, arguing that rhetoric closes down the possibilities for the development of narrative and character otherwise present in a scene. All language, however, has a rhetorical dimension, of which audiences choose to be aware. Lucrece's rhetoricity can perhaps best be read as her awareness of her own transformation. She *knows* she can step outside her ideologically grounded female space, yet she also knows she cannot escape the similarly grounded expectations her social frame places on her.

The chiasmus of her second stanza warrants more specific attention.

> Thy eye kindled the fire that burneth here,
> And here in Troy, for trespass of thine eye[,]
>
> (1475–76)

It is Paris's inescapable, space-making eye that activates lust and destruction (of Helen and Troy), piercing, penetrating, fixing on its object: spatial absence as allotted the female. She sees that it is male envisioning that frames a woman's seeing and speech.

In the narrator's second passage Lucrece's intense sorrow over Troy's destruction is initially foregrounded. The literal sympathetic exchange between the silent painted figures and her rhetoricizing voice, "She lends them words, and she their looks doth borrow" (1498–9), removes her even further from our view. Her identification with the painting as embodying the Real, as being more than representation, reaches the stage where "Such signs of truth in his [Sinon's] plain face she spied" (1532) are such "That she concludes the picture was belied." (1533) She is seeing, in effect, two paintings—one she assembles in her mind (of which she is a part), and another she can designate as merely "the picture." The emphasis here on separating the painting (as embedded narrative) from Lucrece's viewing of it incites her to momentarily rescript Sinon's role in Troy's defeat. In the last stanza of this passage language rearranges both itself and Lucrece within what is (and is not) spoken.

> "It cannot be," quoth she, "that so much guile"—
> She would have said, "can lurk in such a look";
> But Tarquin's shape came in her mind the while,
> And from her tongue "can lurk" from "cannot" took:
> "It cannot be" she in that sense forsook,
> And turn'd it thus, "It cannot be, I find,
> But such a face should bear a wicked mind.
>
> (1534–40)

The active past tense is parried by the conditional past, what was spoken by what nearly was, the unspoken "can lurk" by the sense of the spoken "cannot." By the last two lines she recursively participates in the rearrangement of her own speech. With these spoken/unspoken phrases she gasps out her incredulity, her struggle with herself as narratee (after the spatial stroboscopy of the painting).

In her second narrative passage she responds directly to Sinon's treason, and commands herself to

> Look, look how list'ning Priam wets his eyes,
> To see those borrow'd tears that Sinon sheeds!
>
> (1548–49)

By the end of this passage she is no longer having her speech rearranged *for* her, she actively rearranges what she says and sees in a complex series of inversions:

> Such devils steal effects from lightless hell,
> For Sinon in his fire doth quake with cold,
> And in that cold, hot burning fire doth dwell;
> These contraries such unity do hold
> Only to flatter fools, and make them bold:
>   So Priam's trust false Sinon's tears doth flatter,
>   That he finds means to burn his Troy with water.
>
> (1555–61)

She takes a certain distracted enjoyment in her ability to manipulate the painting's reality.

In the narrator's third passage her language and sight collide, as

> She tears the senseless Sinon with her nails,
> Comparing him to that unhappy guest
> Whose deed hath made herself herself detest.
>
> (1564–66)

The violence of her action returns her to 'herself'; she collapses back into the world of *her* narrative. Space contracts as, with the arrival of Collatine, Lucretius, and Brutus, the narrator pulls back slightly. A period of time is elided, "But now the mindful messenger, come back" (1583), until Collatine "[. . .] finds his Lucrece clad in mourning black." (1585) When she speaks next, it is to address her husband and his guests.

She has stepped back into her former space, but with a difference. She looks ahead to her suicide from a vantage in which the text conflates the pagan Roman and Augustinian readings of her story.

> Though my gross blood be stain'd with this abuse,
> Immaculate and spotless is my mind;

> That was not forc'd, that never was inclin'd
> To accessary yieldings, but still pure
> Doth in her poison'd closet yet endure.
>
> (1655–59)

She has come to see her pollution in Augustinian terms, that her virtue is untouched, yet the text acknowledges that this is still governed, framed by, her society.

She does not escape through death; nor does she become a symbol of Chastity for others to follow; nor indeed does she become an ironized subject in the text. Her suicide is a reassertion of the differently constructed space she sighted within the painting, and from which she returns, transformed.

Notes

1. Marius von Senden, *Space and Sight* (London: Methuen & Co. Ltd., 1960).
2. Ibid., 109.
3. Ibid., 130.
4. Bice Benvenuto and Roger Kennedy, *The Works of Jacques Lacan: An Introduction* (New York: St. Martin's Press, 1986), 55.
5. Senden, *Space and Sight*, 130.
6. *A Select Library of the Nicene and Post-Nicene Fathers of The Christian Church*, Vol. II, "St. Augustin's [sic] City of God and Christian Doctrine" Philip Schaff, ed. (Grand Rapids, Mich.: Wm. B. Eerdmans Publishing Co., 1956), 13.
7. William Shakespeare, *The Riverside Shakespeare*, ed. G. Blakemore Evans (Boston: Houghton Mifflin, 1974), 1. 104. All subsequent references to the poem will appear in the text of the paper.
8. Georgianna Ziegler, "My lady's chamber: female space, female chastity in Shakespeare" *Textual Practice* 4.1 (1990): 73–90.
9. I partially concur with the position Ziegler argues with reference to Stallybrass, however in her conclusion regarding "these two female poles" she seems to essentialize the female grotesque as the authentic pole opposite female enclosure as a constructed normative. Rather, both "poles" are equally such constructions.
10. Peter Stallybrass, "Patriarchal territories: The body enclosed", in *Rewriting the Renaissance*, ed. Margaret W. Ferguson (Chicago: University of Chicago Press, 1986), 124.
11. Leonardo da Vinci, *Treatise on Painting*, trans. by A. Philip McMahon (Princeton, N.J.: Princeton University Press, 1956), 110.
12. R. Rawdon Wilson, "Shakespearean Narrative: *The Rape of Lucrece* Reconsidered," *Studies in English Literature* 28 (1988): 55.

REVIEWS

The Culture of Violence: Essays on Tragedy and History. By Francis Barker. Chicago: The University of Chicago Press, 1993.

Reviewer: Kiernan Ryan

In five interlocking essays this book lays siege to the latest kinds of critical theory and practice devised to obliterate history and their own collusion in the tales it has to tell. The implicit aim of *The Culture of Violence* is to demolish the humanist fantasy that works of art are uncontaminated by the cruelty and injustice of the societies they spring from. Shakespearean tragedy is therefore summoned, along with Milton's *Areopagitica* and Hobbes's *Leviathan*, to corroborate Walter Benjamin's less sanguine conviction that "There is no document of civilization which is not at the same time a document of barbarism." But the overt, prime targets of Barker's urgent polemic are the postmodern mentality and the new historicism in which he finds its most potent critical expression. For both stand accused of conspiring to dissolve the idea of history as an unfinished struggle for social justice, to suspend us in the depthless indifference of postmodernity. And in the end they emerge as more culpable than any of the literary texts arraigned for complicity with the violence of their times. Indeed Shakespeare's tragedies reveal by comparison an admirable readiness to sabotage their own coercive ploys and disclose the very historicity they would occlude.

Barker's critique of postmodernism and its disabling impact on cultural studies is convincing. In his second essay, "Nietzsche's Cattle," and again in the final essay on "Tragedy and the Ends of History," he supplies a shrewd diagnosis of the plight to which the likes of Lyotard and Baudrillard seem all too happy to consign us. By transmuting the reality of historical crisis into a post-historical condition, "a timeless absence of historicity" (100), postmodernism strives to induce in us that immediate state of bovine bliss ascribed by Nietzsche to the cattle as they graze, plagued neither by memory nor by expectation. It invites us to cultivate the art of amnesia, to forget the obligations and aspirations bequeathed us by the past, and surrender instead to the "rootless aesthetic of the momentary" (221) fostered by consumerism. In so far as postmodernism still speaks of history, it is a history reduced to one dimension and robbed of potentiality, a history manned by ghostly simulacra, adrift on the shoreless seas of textuality. If it celebrates transformation, it is "Transformation reified, as difference" (220); and "difference in and of itself will not do," because "oppressive societies thrive on difference, even when they are officially democratic" (227): the difference between poverty and wealth, for example, or between those who have power and those who do not.

The task of veiling such unpalatable realities from the critic's gaze and stifling their vulgar clamor in the text has been shouldered, Barker argues, by deconstruction and new historicism, whose apparent antagonism masks a mutual devotion to preaching the postmodern gospel. In the introduction to the account of Hobbes and Milton in his third essay, "In the Wars of Truth," he dismisses deconstruction's complacent idea of textual power as "self-subverting and therefore in need of no transformation other than that which it works upon itself by virtue of its nature as textuality;" while "the pessimistic and radical scepticism that will interminably question as metaphysical all positive strategies" (124) gets equally short shrift. But the brunt of Barker's wrath is reserved for the new historicists, the result of whose criticism "is often, in the name of studying at least the poetics of power, a practical denial of the fact and poignancy of domination, substituting notions of circulation for those of oppression, anxiety for terror" (124). The penultimate essay, "A Wilderness of Tigers," tracks this betrayal of history's harsh truths to its chief source in the anthropology of Clifford Geertz. A scrutiny of key texts by Stephen Greenblatt and Leonard Tennenhouse reveals "how the groundlessness of culture and cultural interpretation at work in Geertz leads to what in the critical practice of the new historicism is a signal de-realization of power in society, of its mechanisms and effects, and even of its representations" (160).

If criticism is to avoid such conniving in the occlusion of institutionalized violence, it needs to deploy a quite different idea of history and rethink its expectations of the literary text. Barker insists that "there were and are real social forces which contend for the past and present (and the future)" (104), and he looks to Benjamin for "a radical historicity" (106) capable of shuttling "between the history of the present and the difference of the past" (107) to accelerate the advent of social transformation. Notions of history as teleology, nostalgia, or timeless plenitude should be discarded in favor of that history which seeks to become "the memory of the future, the history that remains always to be made" (233). Indeed a truly effective political criticism, committed to releasing us from the difference of domination, should be powered by the same conflict that fuels the tragic drama of the early modern era: the conflict between how things have been and what they might become. Barker discerns the basis for that criticism in the "symptomatic" style of reading promoted by Pierre Macherey, who furnishes the epigraph of the book's closing essay: "it is possible to trace the path which leads from the haunted work to that which haunts it" (209). This means reading the work for its subconscious confession of guilty repressions and its involuntary flashes of dissidence.

Barker applies the Machereyan method in "The Information of the Absolute," the long, dense account of *King Lear*, *Hamlet* and *Macbeth* with which *The Culture of Violence* commences. But the results are far less persuasive than his subsequent critique of postmodern thought and contemporary criticism. Rewarding insights into a range of issues do crop up. Barker is especially illuminating on the political geography of the plays and the vital role of invasion in their symbolic economy. And he traces suggestive connections between these factors and crucial questions of sovereignty, identity, language and gender addressed by Shakespearean tragedy. But most of what he has to say about these matters disguises familiar ideas in the oppressively abstract, convoluted idiom in which too much of this book is cast. The location of mutinous implications in the licensed discourse of Lear's and Ophelia's madness, in the silent and the dispossessed, or in demonized female figures like Lady Macbeth, will startle few. Still fewer will be thrown by Barker's overall appraisal of "Shakespeare's art as very profoundly conservative" (70), yet compelled to unsettle and sometimes confound its endorsement of domination. There is manifest confusion, however, about the exact ratio of resistance to reaction in these plays. One moment their emphatically orthodox vision is seen as barely troubled by intrusions of otherness; the next, "we might almost be reading ... not so much an underwriting of sovereign power as its radical critique" (82), with Shakespeare forced to strike a last-minute compromise between his warring allegiances "to prevent the tragedy of crisis turning into the open-ended drama of revolution" (84). Barker is reluctant to wed himself to either view, and the whole problem remains vexingly unresolved.

Shakespeare's tragedies strike me a much keener to confirm a progressive modern reading than Barker is prepared to believe. That their ideological grain must be conservative is too readily taken for granted, and reading them against the grain too swiftly pounced upon as the sole means of securing their political salvation. Barker's shaky belief that "it would take massive rewriting to make this kind of tragedy radical" (49) concedes too much to the assumptions of the new historicists he so forcefully attacks. It also requires his own repression of those new historicists whose concept of Shakespeare is dramatically different from Greenblatt's. Both Annabel Patterson and Leah Marcus take a bow in the bibliography, but *The Culture of Violence* acknowledges neither the Bard of the people proposed by the one, not the Janus-faced playwright inferred by the other. The failure to absorb, if not refute, these powerful versions of Shakespeare, which bear so directly on Barker's case, weakens his political judgement of the tragedies and hobbles his otherwise acute critique of new historicism in "A Wilderness of Tigers."

The latter essay grafts onto that critique, however, the most arresting pages in the book. Haunted by the strange scene in *Titus Andronicus* (4.4) where the hapless Clown is dispatched to the hangman on the whim of an irate emperor, Barker amasses and scales an Everest of statistics to calculate how many human beings were actually put to death during the reigns of Elizabeth and James. The appalling, conservative estimate ("24,147.4 men and women hanged, 516.21 pressed to death, and 11,440.52 dead in gaol" [178]) prompts Barker to drop his usual opaque, portentous prose in favor of a plain statement of the atrocities neglected by Shakespeare and most of his modern critics:

> In defence of property and the established social order the Elizabethan and Jacobean crown killed huge numbers of the people of England. Their names not wholly unknown, the circumstances of their demise often recorded, the sheer number of them estimable, men, women and children in "Shakespeare's England" were strung up on permanent or makeshift gallows by a hempen noose. Sometimes the spinal cord was snapped at once; or they hung by their necks until they suffocated or drowned; until their brains died of hypoxeia, or until the shock killed them. Pissing and shitting themselves. Bleeding from their eyes. Thinking. (190)

Barker's complaint that "nothing of this is dramatized in *Titus Andronicus*" (190), whose spectacular, exotic violence is contrived to mask the routine slaughter and torture inflicted on the English populace by their own courts, is at one level absurd. For it rests on what Barker himself rejects earlier as the crude ambition "to reduce texts to reflections of a social reality elsewhere" (157). Shakespeare is blamed, in effect, for failing to deliver documentary realism, for an evasive preoccupation with other climes, other times, and other topics. But the blatant critical naivety of this charge does not dispose of the awkward questions posed by the forgotten dead for whom Barker feels impelled to speak. Neither Shakespearean tragedy nor our modern response to it is let off the hook. *The Culture of Violence* obliges us to reflect anew on Shakespeare's and our own complicity with structures of oppression then and now, and to realise that the fate of radical criticism may be riding on our conclusions.

Notorious Identity: Materializing the Subject in Shakespeare. By Linda Charnes. Cambridge: Harvard University Press, 1993.

Reviewer: Harry Berger, Jr.

"If A is the cause of B, then B is the cause of A is a cause; the effect is the cause of the cause; the cause is the effect of the effect." This simple, lilting paralogism, the paralogism of inverse causality, lies at the root of the most stimulating and influential criticism of the last few decades. It governs a hierarchy of structural flipovers ranging from the scheme of *hysteron proteron* and the trope of *metalepsis* to the larger structures of *genealogical* (re)construction. The procedure draws its inspiration from a mix of now canonical sources, of which Nietzsche's radicalization of the Hegelian *Aufhebung* variously mediated through Foucault, Derrida, and Lacan is one of the more familiar. It is a staple of the hermeneutics of suspicion, and it both presupposes and generates a skill of ironic reading. Thus it is that in the materializing precipitations of my preconscious imaginary the convergence of structural flipovers with ironic skill modulates into operations performed with an iron skillet and becomes The Pancake Maneuver in modern criticism. In Shakespeare criticism the most original and brilliant proponent of the maneuver is Patricia Parker, who has for some years been exploring the "preposterous" motions and events that energize the Shakespeare text and its context from the atomic to the molar level. *Notorious Identity* introduces a distinguished new practitioner of the Pancake Maneuver in a powerful study of *Richard III*, *Troilus and Cressida*, and *Antony and Cleopatra*. Since Charnes's approach in some respects overlaps Parker's, I shall preface my review with one of the latter's more compendious statements of the difference the maneuver can make.

Parker argues that the reversed ordering of Shakespeare's two tetralogies exposes their historical narrative as "forged" rather than "natural," a "retroactively constructed narrative" that is not very different from "the preposterous estate of a son who creates for a father, and hence for himself, the genealogy of an authorizing 'pedigree.'" From this generalization she generates the insight about *Richard III* that the play represents its protagonist as the product of the bad faith with which Tudor historiography demonized Richard and sanctified Henry VII: Richard's "unnatural" deformity and fiendishness are the creation of the official Tudor histories, their production after the fact of an authorizing villainy—the scapegoat that "a particular official construction of history might retroactively require."[1] This effect of citational disfigurement is what Charnes calls *notorious identity*, and her thesis is that Richard tries but ultimately fails to dissociate himself from the notorious identity the Tudors saddled him with, and that in different ways Cressida, Troilus, Antony, and Cleopatra unsuccessfully offer the same resistance to the identities constructed for them by the interests of official historiography and legend.

Charnes associates this resistance with the subjectivity effect: in the three plays she studies

> identity is aligned with the representational politics of narrative historiography and its policing role in the official technologies that consolidate "legitimate" authority. Identity is that which carves "characters" in stone, forcing them to correspond to earlier textual versions of themselves. Against this fixity, these figures express and enact a desire to be their own "originals"; a fantasy that uses "playing" and theater as a way to stage a subjectivity in which something "secret" about an overly known "self" might still materialize. (9)

"Subjectivity," in Charnes's lexicon, "means the subject's experience of his or her relationship to his or her identity,'" and in the space that opens up between subjectivity and identity "the possibility of indeterminacy, of dis-identification, as well as a fantasy of autonomous choice in thought, action, or emotion, becomes thinkable" (8–9). This is a crisp and usable distinction and it is maintained with consistency throughout the book, as she explores the lure, the pursuit, and the foreclosure of those possibilities. I find her interpretations of the plays for the most part exemplary in their attention to the text, the context, the criticism, and the relevance to her topic of a broad range of contemporary issues and practices. Each interpretive chapter unfolds in the light of brilliant formulations that allow her to get the most out of existing commentary on the plays while shifting the angle of illumination in such a way as make strange the familiar.

(1) The identity resisted by Richard III is the "putative physical and moral monstrousness" manufactured by Tudor myth to justify the overthrow of the last Plantagenet and the violent installation of the new regime (11). The inscription of monstrosity is displaced from official texts to the misshapen body, which Richard tries in effect to retextualize in an attempt "to be a monster of his own making" (11). Shakespeare thus makes "his project Richard's project: the task of producing another 'version' of Richard that will stand 'apart' from that of official Tudor historiography"—"Richard's Richard" over against "the play's Richard" (30, 32). And Charnes ingeniously unpacks the conflict between the two Richards from the ambiguity in the phrase "I am determined to prove a villain" (1.1.30): "Richard's determination of himself as villain is the literal realization of (and unwitting collusion in) the play's determination of Richard" (62). This formulation allows her to bring out the conflict and confusion of the two Richards in the final dialogical soliloquy on conscience in 5.3.

(2) In *Troilus and Cressida*, the figures' legendary status threatens to crush their representational viability as "subjects." Subjectivity in this play is posited as the disruptive effect of simultaneous resistance, and subjection, the determining force of famous names. The characters' names instantly convey the roles they are required to play. . . . Their very existence is authorized by these roles. Consequently, to attempt to avoid or subvert their "official" functions is to . . . "undo" their own conditions or existence and meaning. (74–75)

> Deeply exhausted and disillusioned by their own story even as the play begins, these figures must be tricked into continuing to fight, tricked into reproducing their notorious identities. Through the production of myths of "private" desire ... "legendary" behavior [is motivated] in figures who might otherwise want nothing so much as to roll over and play dead. (12)
>
> [I]n this play the subjectivity of the characters materializes in and through their "neuroses": through the return, in various forms, of what they attempt to repress. (75)

(3) Charnes approaches *Antony and Cleopatra* through a shrewd and imaginative critique of the technologies and ideologies of contemporary media coverage, especially television. This enables her to slide effortlessly from the coercive power of modern reporters to that of Shakespearean messengers and thus to focus her interpretation on the means by which the play "choreographs the representational technology of manufacturing legends" and probes "the relationship between staging spectacle and 'controlling the press'" (12). She demonstrates how the "war of competing strategies" between Cleopatra and Octavius is a kind of media war "staked out across the terrain of Antony's 'identity': the set of representations, images, and narratives he needs to recognize himself as 'Antony'" (110, 112). Caught between these conflicting attempts to colonize him, he "becomes like the land Roman imperialism seeks to conquer: vulnerable to continual remappings and reappropriations of his own subjective terrain" (113). Cleopatra's opposition to Octavius's "narrative imperialism" (110) is more securely based in "a theatrical principle of identity in which subjectivity is posited as a kind of theater" (199), an identity sustained "by the appropriateness of her performances to the theatrical space that Egypt represents in this play" (128). By continually performing herself as "theatrical effect," giving herself to be seen "in ways that disclose nothing so much as a *refusal* to disclose," she manages to take a reconnaissance activity that leaves Rome as voyeurism and translates it into something that returns to Rome only the strangely void "information" of spectacle" (128–29). But Octavius finally wins. In the stunning climax to her interpretation of the play, Charnes convincingly argues that the protagonists' cultural and critical reputation as partners in a "tragic yet transcendent" love affair— an affair that transports them beyond a world well lost—is the product not only of "their own investment in themselves as legends" (12–13) but also of Octavius's apparatus: "He swiftly trans-

lates them from rebellious figures who escaped his control and punishment into legendary lovers." This eliminates "any lingering threat" they "may still pose as exemplars of political rebellion" and freezes them "in the frame of a tragic 'story,' which is then excised from the political arena.... Thus Shakespeare's play ends where the history of its reception as a great tragedy begins: with the constructing and marketing of a legendary love story" (144–46).

Notorious Identity is more than an important first book. It's an important book. It unpacks a very strong, simple, and original idea with both consistency and flexibility so as to produce not merely new insights into the plays but also an exemplary model of programmatic ecumenicism in its deployment of the notorious discursive identities precipitated out of the theory wars. Charnes is forthright and independent if a little (as she puts it) "apotropaic" in "reorganizing insights" that pop up in all sectors of the embattled field of theoretical discourses, in "deterritorializing them" and converting them to moves in an "affirmative critical practice," and finally, in demonstrating how they may be variably mobilized to do justice to the different "manifestations of notorious identity in each play" (14–19). What makes this procedure successful and the book instructive, however, is that for the most part the appropriation of theory is determined in the last instance by the economy of close reading. For the most part, but not always, for there are moments when ecumenicism declines into an eclectic sequence of saccadic fixes on the formulations of one then another notorious authority (Bourdieu, Althusser, Zizek, Lacan, et al.) in such a way as to interrupt the flow of close reading without adding illumination. Yet there is a positive reason for the impression of over explanation or redundancy. Though Charnes's interpretive moves are sophisticated and complex, she articulates them with enough wit, sharpness, and lucidity to make them seem not only compelling but also deceptively simple. Occasionally, therefore, she draws out an explanation more than she needs to (e.g., the account of Antony on pp. 113–17) or adds a theoretical excursus that seems otiose or distracting. But this is a minor flaw in a major book, and I don't intend to make a big flapjack over nothing. Instead, I shall conclude with some comments on features of the book I found especially provocative and helpful.

1. *Notorious Identity* is—as a germinal notion and as a whole—deeply structured by the operations that comprise the Pancake Maneuver, but there are also many micropassages of analysis during which it surfaces with brilliant effect. Consider, for example, this

cluster dealing with the Trojan construction of Helen as a notorious signifier:

> [In a comparison with Cressida] Helen is used as that touchstone against which value is judged, but also as that which is curiously stripped of any inherent value, of any value that is not itself produced by the comparison. . . . Troilus . . . understands that Helen's "fairness" functions tropically as a *hysteron proteron:* a proleptic teleology for the war which reconstructs effects as causes. (82)

> Helen is first assigned her value . . . so that the attribution can then be "naturalized" and read back as something intrinsic to Helen herself. But in order for the fiction of "degree" to work in the play, the characters . . . must continually ward off their knowledge that they are the producers rather than the possessors of Helen's value. (83)

> The more Helen is *produced* as a rhetorical figure of and for "value," the more she is *reduced* as a mimetic figure, as a "presence" on the stage. The extent to which she is deployed as enabling fiction—for war, for comparison, for homo- and heteroeroticism, for identity itself—is equal to the extent to which she is theatrically and mimetically attenuated. (84)

I note in passing that throughout the book Charnes confidently and adeptly (but never polemically) avails herself of the resources of feminist critique and gender theory to show how the polarity between identity and subjectivity is crosshatched by the problematic inscriptions and performances we now associate, thanks to Judith Butler, with gender trouble.

2. From the basic polarity, Charnes generates a table of binary oppositions that are shaded a little differently for each play and that allow her to make trenchant correlations between ideological agendas and the forms of mediation through which they are imposed or resisted. Thus citationality, predetermination, narrative, and strategy correlate with identity; self-authorization, improvisation, theater, and tactics correlate with subjectivity. *Antony and Cleopatra* is framed by "a division between the compulsion to narrate . . . and the resistance of mimetic improvisation, or mimetic subversion" (107), which, in Cleopatra's case, involves exploiting the properties of theater to stage herself. Shakespeare's Richard challenges "the narrative reinscription . . . of Richard as monster" by trying to produce *in performance* something that will counter the cumulative textual weight of legend" (60–61). The ingenious correlation of narrative/text/document with identity and of theatri-

cal drama with subjectivity puts a metatheatrical spin on the latter pair: Charnes claims

> that in the Renaissance, drama is the dominate mode in which the provisional, performative, and contingent nature of subjectivity can be literally embodied. Alterity to textual identity is an inevitable condition of dramatic representation. The figures in these plays may be permanently "identified," insofar as their names encode their legends. But as dramatic figures, they exist as versions of themselves. (9)

> "Playing" opens up an aleatory space in which the "then" of narrative can be set against the "now" of drama. . . . As a consequence . . . there are always at least "two" of each character—the written character and the figure on the stage, the actor playing the role. (86)

3. Even on the rare occasions when Charnes does not, in my opinion, fully realize the possibilities she puts in play, her approach blazes a trail that makes it much easier for subsequent critics, who need only add a little paving. Thus although I was at times disappointed, in the chapter on *Richard III*, by a tendency to use specific readings as occasions for historical and theoretical reflections, I was struck by the way her account illuminates—and indeed all but expressly discusses—a major dramaturgical feature of the play, the frequency and distribution of Richard's soliloquies and asides: they provide the site of the oppositional performance in which Richard tries to "stand 'apart' from" the notorious identity he has been saddled with by "official Tudor historiography" (30). The fact that he talks (out loud) to himself more frequently, at greater length, and with considerably more brio and self-delight in the first part of the play than later bears out Charnes's thesis that he fails in his effort to execute The Pancake Maneuver: "the play's ultimate structural irony is that Richard's declaration of 'determination' leads him into actions that confirm his predetermination" and thus repeat the pattern that "reifies him into a monster" (62). At the end, Poor Richard is—or gets himself—flattened by what Nicholas Brooke calls the "gigantic machine" driving the Christian plot "on which the whole theory of Tudor history is built."[2]

4. Throughout the book Charnes makes judicious use of the modern-instance technique, most notably in the chapter on *Anthony and Cleopatra*, the conclusion, and the epilogue, the last of which extends the notorious identity thesis from the plays to Bardolatry and its recent fortunes on Capitol Hill (the Hill/Thomas affair). These contemporary analogies are more than window dress-

ing. They show that although the apparatus for producing and reproducing notorious identity may change with changing states of the culture, the economy, the prevailing media, etc., the apparatus itself displays a logic, a dynamic, a structure of agency, that may be a constant in the sense that one may find it anywhere in the historical record (the existence of which, of course, it presupposes). The problem of historicization is then to pick out the particular set of variables that give the apparatus its cultural specificity.

5. *Notorious Identity* is exemplary in its meticulous, generous, and discursive account of theoretical debts and commitments, on which the footnotes provide an extensive running commentary (see especially the long series of notes on pp. 166–70). I found both the tone and the exposition even-handed, critically discerning, and without any trace of contentiousness. In this respect Charnes's intertextual negotiations remind me very much of those of Janet Adelman, whose remarkable footnotes in *Suffocating Mothers* surely set the standard all footnote writers should try to meet.

Notes

1. Patricia Parker, "Preposterous Events," *Shakespeare Quarterly* 43 (1992): 202–203. See also Joel B. Altman, "'Preposterous Conclusions': Eros, Enargeia, and the Composition of *Othello*," *Representations* 18 (1987): 129–57. Altman, indeed, may be the pioneer investigator of early modern prototypes of the Pancake Maneuver in Tudor pedagogy and rhetoric. See his fundamental study, *The Tudor Play of Mind: Rhetorical Inquiry and the Development of Elizabethan Drama* (Berkeley: University of California Press, 1978).

2. Nicholas Brooke, *Shakespeare's Early Tragedies* (London: Methuen, 1968), 78–79. This underrated book contains wonderful passages of interpretation that anticipate many subsequent developments in the critical discourse about the early tragedies. Brooke's account of *Richard III* is the closest thing we have to the reading suggested by Patricia Parker and fully worked out by Charnes.

Hamlet versus Lear: *Cultural Politics and Shakespeare's art*. By R. A. Foakes. Cambridge: Cambridge University Press, 1993.

Reviewer: **Alexander Leggatt**

The main business of Professor Foakes's book is announced in its subtitle. The contest between *Hamlet* and *King Lear* for top spot in the Shakespeare canon is just one strand in the larger theme of the reception of Shakespeare, as exemplified through what criticism has made of these two plays. (For those who are keeping score, *Lear* overtook *Hamlet* some time in the 1950s, and is still in the lead.) Foakes surveys the reception of each play over the last few generations, questions a number of current critical practices, and finally offers his own readings of *Hamlet* and *King Lear* to exemplify the sort of criticism that is both possible and necessary in our time. The result is a timely and important book. The surveys of critical history are judicious and persuasive; the critique of current practices is not just curmudgeonly but identifies real problems; and the readings of the plays themselves show how what is best in current critical practice—particularly its awareness that a play takes on a life specific to the culture that reads it—can be used in the service of these texts.

The surveys illustrate what has happened in the past. In the nineteenth century and the early years of the twentieth, Hamlet the character, abstracted from the play, became a symbol of the over-sensitive, over-intellectual idealist, incapable of action in a world in which action was urgently required. It became possible to talk not just of Hamlet but of Hamletism, and Hamletism meant failure, uselessness, taedium vitae. The notion of Hamlet as a failure has persisted in the twentieth century, despite occasional attempts (such as the Olivier film) to reinstate him as a hero. At the same time, "The privatized Hamlet, abstracted from the play and turned into a projection of each of us as individuals ('I have a smack of Hamlet myself'; 'It is we who are Hamlet'), democratized criticism by opening up the possibility of any number of subjective interpretations" (37). *King Lear* has been privatized in a different way; according to Foakes, its reception "has to do for the most part with an evasion of political issues" (45). Nineteenth century readings ignored the political side of the play in order to emphasize its personal drama. In the early twentieth century, with Bradley as the key influence, that drama became a story of redemption. Yet for Foakes the play is inescapably political, and "resists being reduced and santizied into a universal allegory about the pilgrimage of Man" (57). The conjunction of "reduced" and "universal" catches the point nicely, and Foakes goes on to comment on the way the play creates in some critics "an addiction to capital letters" (58). Around 1960 the play became more political and the drama of redemption was succeeded by a drama of despair. Foakes attributes these developments to the cumulative effect of political horrors—Auschwitz, Hiroshima, and later Vietnam—in a world governed by tyrannical old men clinging to power.

The effect of this survey is clearly not to create a lost golden age of criticism in contrast to the follies of the present. It is rather to show that every age has its own agenda, creating its own distinctive insights, with blinkers to match. Our age is no different. The current development that Foakes particularly deplores is the denigration of the author and the text. He has no problem with revision theories as a way of studying the playwright's second thoughts; but he does not want to see the text disappear "into an endless series of reworkings and adaptations in ephemeral stage performances" (84) and he does not want the author reduced to a mere collaborator in those performances. He shifts the focus back on to the reading text, and he insists on the integrity of the text even if there are different versions of it. *King Lear*, for him, is not two different plays but one play in the process of revision. There is, he argues, a link between deconstruction and textual revisionism, in that "both reject external authority" (72). He goes on to see a further link (which he admits is impressionistic) between these developments in the realm of criticism and the growing disillusion with political authority in recent times in the United States and Great Britain. At the same time new historicism and cultural materialism have the effect of "marginalizing the text as a construct of the social and political order of the Elizabethan and Jacobean ages" (72). Since power abhors a vacuum, the authority lost by the author and the text is transferred to the critic, who becomes the center, even the subject of the enterprise. (I am reminded of the comment of a student of mine coming away from her first MLA convention; she complained that none of the speakers seemed interest in literature, but they all seemed mightily interested in themselves.)

Reviews 239

What then must we do? Foakes argues for appreciation, not just interpretation: "literature demands not merely to be understood, but to be appreciated as an experience, and as art" (7); "we need to be concerned with appreciation as well as understanding, and with the effect the plays have on us, not merely with what they mean. In other words, we need a way of talking about Shakespeare's artistry" (8). We do indeed, and it's not easy. The language we use to convey appreciation is liable to be soft-centered, and the attempt to convey appreciation in rigorous discursive prose is liable to turn it into interpretation. One passage may illustrate the difficulties Foakes runs into in formulating his key idea: "in experiencing *Hamlet* we enter imaginatively into the curve of the action, its shaping of characters and events, and so gain insight into, for example, clashes of value-systems, the problematics of revenge, the potential provocations to violence in human beings, the difficulty for those in power of matching ethical and political behavior, the controls that may be exercised over people by events in the past, and the cruelty that can emerge as the flip side of love. Such "knowledge" as is gained in this way may have little immediate relation to the ordinary lives of most readers or viewers, and will be interpreted differently by each in relation to his or other experience and mores" (142). In the first sentence, having immersed ourselves imaginatively in the play we suddenly find ourselves outside it again, contemplating general expediences in a way that sounds suspiciously like interpretation. The second sentence sends out contrary signals about the relation between the text and the reader or viewer's life.

However, as that theorist of the drama Bertolt Brecht was fond of saying, the proof of the pudding is in the eating. When it comes to demonstrating his approach in action, in readings of *Hamlet* and *King Lear*, Foakes makes his case. Certain principles inform each reading. Working from the Folio texts "as embodying the best reading versions we have of these plays" he aims at "a clarification of the dramatic design of the plays that is also necessarily partial and a product of the present time" (145). He looks at the total shape of each play, not just the bits and pieces that support a thesis. On the other hand, his chapter titles—"A design for *Hamlet*" and "A shaping for *King Lear*"—emphasize a provisional quality. Having resisted the notion that the text is purely a creation of the reader (i.e., the all-powerful critic) he also resists—indeed, his whole book resists—the notion of it as a timeless, immutable artifact.

Understandably, even Foakes's interest in shifting ideologies and the limitations of interpretation, Hamlet emerges as a text full of clashing values: the old heroic world of the elder Hamlet, the modern world of diplomacy, even democracy, presided over by Claudius; a ghost who comes from the Christian realm of Purgatory with an anti-Christian demand for revenge. Hamlet, who in older criticism failed in action, here fails in interpretation: he sees the dilemmas of the play less clearly than the audience does. He sees Claudius simply as a villain, while we see a skilled ruler and an affectionate husband, tainted by one black deed that gnaws at his conscience. If anything Claudius's conscience is more alert than that of Hamlet, who in the closet scene makes an "astonishing assumption of moral authority" that "allows him, here with the blood of Polonius fresh on his hands, to preach to [Gertrude] and claim 'virtue' for himself as an attribute of the male" (158–59). (Foakes has a refreshingly sympathetic view of Gertrude, who is allowed an independence and freedom of speech in the new reign that she seemingly did not have in the old one.) Hamlet admires the heroic code embodied in Fortinbras, though for the audience Fortibras embodies the absurdity of that code. It is unfortunate, given Foakes's choice of the Folio as his primary source, that the chief evidence for the play's denigration of the heroic is a Folio cut, but at least one can say that it is part of the total life of the play. The idea itself is one of the key factors in identifying Foakes's reading as a twentieth-century one, and I find it more convincing than his occasional attempts at specific contemporary analogies, such as the link between Claudius's private spiritual anguish and the public religious observances of contemporary political leaders (167). In general, Foakes's reading is alive to the many contradictions of the play, and provocative in the way it presents Hamlet as the first person to misread Hamlet.

His reading of King Lear is generally more straightforward (so is the play). He follows the curve of the action, tracing the escalating violence, the widening of focus, the growth of insight in Lear and of cruelty in his daughters, the intersection of the story lines. His account is written with a drive and energy that evoke the same qualities in the Folio text. He does, however, find some unexpected contradictions in Cordelia. While the Quarto presents her as "a saintly emblem of pity," the Folio "opens her part to interrogation, and makes it much more ambiguous" (212). She returns to Britain to bring healing and restoration, but her means of doing so is war; and she offers to Lear a kingship he has already seen through and rejected. As Lear matters more as a person, he matters less as a political figure; but this does not mean that the play itself ceases to be political in its later scenes, as some critics have claimed; rather, it "exposes the contradiction between, on the one hand, the importance our society places upon individual expression and fulfilment, upon the freedom and autonomy of each person, and on the other, the diminution of the individual to a nobody, another entry in the computer lists of the government, banks, police and advertisers, marking the social, economic and political insignificance of each person in a mass society" (213). That is one way of reading Albany's "Great thing of us forgot."

There is plenty of scope to argue with the details of Foakes's interpretations. What matters is the importance of his approach, with its call for a return to the text, not as a sacred document but as a living part of our culture and our experience, and its demonstration that to see aesthetic and political readings as incompatible is to impose a false dichotomy.

Women, "Race," and Writing in the Early Modern Period. Edited by Margo Hendricks and Patricia Parker. London and New York: Routledge, 1994.

Reviewer: Valerie Traub

A strong anthology can substantially influence the direction of an emerging filed of scholarship. *Women, "Race," and Writing in the Early Modern Period*, the first anthology to address the relations between "gender" and "race" in European literature of the sixteenth through eighteenth centuries, will effectively define the terms for future debate. Thoughtful essays by seventeen feminist (and female) critics collectively demonstrate the historically constructed nature of "race," its relation to an equally constructed female "gender," and the deployment of both in the texts of male and female writers of stage plays, poetry, novels, humanist and scientific essays and tracts, anatomies and travel narratives. Collectively, these essays range across geography, time, and subject: from the "simultaneity" of gender strategies of French and Iroquois women in the sixteenth century to imperialist discussions of African polygamy in the eighteenth century to postcolonial "Third Word" engagements with Shakespearean texts. What emerges from this diverse offering in historical terms is a sense of the instability of the category of "race" in the early colonialist period, and the consolidation in the eighteenth century of essentialist views of "race" and, correlatively, modern white racism.

The need for analysis of "race" is expressed astutely by Dympna Callaghan:

> In Renaissance studies, traditional scholarly resistance to the deployment of "race" as a category of analysis is based on its apparent invisibility in early modern England. This is wrong-headed ... because "white" is racially invisible only within the terms of the dominant ideology of white supremacy.... Further, the argument that there is no empirical justification for an analysis of racial difference is a line of reasoning that ignores the (empirically verifiable) imperialist ventures in Ireland and the New World in the sixteenth and seventeenth centuries, which produced "race" as a category of difference as never before. This production entailed dual processes: the racialization of the other and the concomitant de-racialization of the self. (165)

Most of the essays share an interest in these dual processes of cultural construction, through which, in the words of Jean Howard:

> a sense of English national [or European] identity took shape in relation to an emerging language of racial difference in which skin color and physiognomy became overdetermined markers of a whole range of religious and sexual and cultural differences by which the English [or Europeans] were distinguished from various non-European "others." (102)

In detailing textual discourses about various cultural "others"—the Irish, Jews, Africans, and North and South Americans—the contributors most often employ a methodology that derives from and contributes to what Laura Brown calls the "*new* new historicis[m]" (119, emphasis mine). Such a method involves analyzing the production of marginalized and dominant identities in the interest of gaining greater analytical purchase on those social processes that foster ideological complicity and those that circumscribe or enable resistance. A number of the essays critique previous (white) feminist work that has elided or ignored "race" as a central category of difference, and the best of these historicize this critical blindness with reference to the emergence of liberal feminism within the cultural imperialism of Enlightenment humanism.

This critique of feminist criticism is especially pertinent to scholarship on European women writers, where a celebration of female authorship is problematized by a recognition of women's multiple positioning within dominant ideologies. As Kim Hall writes:

> Given that these [European] women [writers] . . . were writing in the formative years of English nationalism and empire, perhaps it is incumbent on those of us studying them to investigate their multifaceted roles in the development of colonialism in order to understand more fully the ways in which they appropriate patriarchal, imperial values even as they resist domestic ideologies. (192–93)

In a far-reaching analysis of racialized tropes of beauty in Lady Mary Wroth's *Urania*, Hall demonstrates how thoroughly "[t]he language of aesthetics is constitutive of the language of race in early modern England" as well as how racialized tropes of blackness "function as markers of race which work to differentiate between women" (179). Hall argues persuasively that women writers' use of such tropes neutralizes the gender impropriety of authorship through a strategic alignment with privileged realms of authority: the upper class, whiteness, and Englishness.

This collection asks scholars, in the words of Margaret Ferguson, "to suspend their own assumptions about what a category like race means or meant to members of a different culture" (211), a caution reiterated by Lynda Boose as she resists superimposing the history of race relations in the United States onto the English sixteenth century. Suspending such assumptions enables Margo Hendricks to show the operations of a discourse of civility in Aphra Behn's *The Widow Ranter* which distinguishes between "noble" and "barbaric" Native Americans. Such analytical openness likewise informs Verena Stolcke's history of the conquest of Peru, as she demonstrates the gendered effects of the deployment of a racialized doctrine of purity of blood ("limpieza de sangre").

Just as awareness of the conquest of the Americas and the African slave trade informs many of the contributors' analyses, a number of essays implicate early modern "science" in provoking and maintaining the colonialist project. Juliana Schiesari discloses the role of physiognomy in promoting racialized systems of classification as well as the exclusion of women from the (Italian) public sphere. Stephanie Jed analyzes the formation of the "New World" as a "natural history museum," calling attention to how the impulse to classify "anomalies" structures the labeling of the "New World"

European woman writer as a supplemental "tenth Muse." And Patricia Parker intriguingly connects anatomy's ocular desire to "discover" female body parts to the development of a domestic English network of imperialist spies.

Those essays that integrate a high degree of methodological self-consciousness with close textual reading are particularly impressive, especially when they tackle the problem of "juggling," in the words of Ferguson, multiple categories of difference. Ferguson's own juggling of race, class, and gender in her discussion of Aphra Behn's *Oroonoko* comes to rest in a striking acknowledgment of the "*competiton* between the white English female author and the black female slave-wife-mother-to-be" (220)—a competition that the author/narrator necessarily wins. Within the dominant imaginary of a slave economy, the white woman's literary production—the book *Oroonoko*—displaces and substitutes for the black (slave) child that might have been born of the union of Oronooko and Imoinda. Callaghan's equally compelling examination of Jewish femininity in Elizabeth Cary's *The Tragedie of Mariam* demonstrates that "[t]he play's production of femininity, alternatively vilified as wanton and valorized as virtuous, is crucially dependent upon 'race.' That is, the cultural polarization of the category 'woman' is constructed via racial marking" (170). Jean Howard's essay on Thomas Heywood's *The Fair Maid of the West* and Laura Brown's analysis of the novels of Daniel Defoe likewise brilliantly theorize the interarticulations of race, gender, sexuality, and nationhood through precise textual interpretations.

Because *Women, "Race," and Writing* is likely to be influential, I want to explore some of the implications of the methodology most often in evidence in the "literary critical" essays in this volume: that is, the analysis of the construction of self-identity—of gender, status, nation—through a racialized politics of inclusion and exclusion. This emphasis on cultural "othering" or "abjection" is perhaps best exemplified in the contributions of Howard, Brown, Nussbaum, and Boose; their essays represent the very best of what a feminist/new historical approach has been capable of doing. In particular, the common structure of Howard's and Brown's essays provides a means of access into the conceptual difficulty involved in positioning race(s) in relation to gender(s) and vice versa. Focusing on a white female character (Bess of *The Fair Maid of the West* and Roxana of *Roxana*) who emblematizes "gender," both essays demonstrate how this gendered figure is racialized in reference to

England's "others." The justification of this method is articulated by Brown:

> This perspective inevitably places gender before race, because gender represents a category of difference constituted primarily within the geographical purview of the dominant culture, while race in this period remains mainly extrinsic, geographically foreign, a category of difference defined as an external object. (118)

Boose makes a similar critical move in a fascinating argument about the unrepresentability of the black woman within European frames of reference: "patriarchal culture's profound anxieties about gender ... spill over into a virulent system of racial anathema" (46).

As valuable as such analyses are in showing how racialized desires and anxieties structure gender relations, they also tend to reinscribe, as Brown acknowledges, the view of "the imperialist" (136). The interpretative focus remains fixed on how European women are racially "othered," and, in the work of Boose, how those excluded from European status (including those living in Europe) are ascribed gendered characteristics by Europeans. Such an approach leaves unasked the question of how non-Europeans racialize or gender themselves or *Europe*," and leads to some unwitting (or self-conscious) elisions of the "other" subject.

One instance of such an elision occurs in Browne's analysis of *Roxana*. In discussing exotic clothing as the spoils of an expansionist, imperialist market, Brown quotes Roxana saying that her dress is "the Habit of *a Turkish Princess; the Habit I got at Leghorn, when my Foreign prince bought me a Turkish slave.* ... and with this Turkish Slave, I bought the rich Cloaths too" (124). In addition to Brown's deft analysis of how Roxana is positioned within imperialism, I want to read more about this Turkish slavewoman—if not through the auspices of Defoe's text, then through the work of rendering visible the material history of Turkish peoples who were bought and sold.

Another common elision occurs when the European woman and the racial "other" become metaphors for one another. In her analysis of discourses of polygamy and Samuel Richardson's *Pamela*, Felicity Nussbaum argues that "[t]he Pamela of the sequel replays Otherness on the domestic rather than the African terrain" (149), thus collapsing the difference between gender and racial difference. Her assertion that "[t]he polygamous sensualized yet ugly African woman is produced *in order to make possible* the domestic Englishwoman" (154, emphasis mine) precludes analysis of the

African woman's material existence. And when Howard analyzes the "stunning act of displacement" whereby cultural anxiety is shifted "from the body of the woman onto the body of the racial other" (102), I wonder (as does Howard in her final sentence [117]) about the effect of such displacement on the African woman—is she not effaced through a kind of textual double exposure?

Within the logic of exposing the self-fashioning of "the English" and "the European," the category of "whiteness" would seem to be a useful object of analysis. And yet, few of the essays actually *explore* "whiteness" as a *racial* construction. For the most part, "whiteness" remains the racially unmarked term—if not self-evident in its naturalness, still not retrieved from its history of deracialization.

Nothing in Richardson, Defoe, or Heywood invites the kind of critical approach I am proposing. However, both feminist and new historical methods imply a resistance to (and revision of) the terms provided by history. I thus want to underscore the pertinence of Brown's own query: "how can we use a feminism that comes out of imperialism?" (136). As several of the contributors make clear, one way is to resist mapping racial "otherness" onto female "otherness," as if the historically changing relation between the two is adequately accounted for by analogy, metaphor, or metonymy. As Ania Loomba argues, the political "tensions between various 'others' serve as a crucial check against confusing intersections with parallels" (29). Similarly, Jyotsna Singh argues that the "neat elision—of categories like 'woman' and 'black man,' 'femininity' and 'blackness'—obscures the *specific* effects" of both racial and gender categories (290). In examining postcolonial revisions of *Othello*, Singh demonstrates that what is most at stake are the different *histories* of marginalized groups, histories that have positioned Indian men and white women, for instance, more in opposition than collaboration. The kind of specificity Singh and Loomba call for exists in nascent form in Ferguson's attention to "Imoinda's specificity as a *black wife*" (218) and Natalie Davis' admission that a necessary sequel to her analysis of the European tropes employed by Iroquois women would involve the counter-example of European women's use of "Iroquois tropes and frames" (244). Such specificity exists as well in Hall's discussion of the dependence of conceptions of "fairness" on rank: "whiteness" is produced not only through interpretations of skin color but through class hierarchy.

These moments suggest that it is possible to analyze the process of "othering" and yet resist reproducing the terms of that construction; to describe the white, English/European gaze while also detailing what might be seen when Africans, Celts, Jews, and Native Americans gaze at Europe; to shift relations of subject and object in order to demonstrate that nay process of cultural construction (no matter how asymmetrical the arrangements of power) is at least a two-way exchange. Interestingly, the most sustained effort in this volume to render the perspective of "others" comes from those trained in social anthropology and history—most intriguingly in Irene Silverblatt's description of native Andean women's appropriation of European discourses of witchcraft and virginity to resist colonization.

Each essay in *Women, "Race," and Writing* is a valuable contribution to critical debate. Brevity alone limits the effectiveness of two of the most provocative essays: Patricia Parker's positioning of *Othello* within eroticized discourses of anatomy and Carla Freccero's reading of gender in Montaigne's essays through representations of cannibalism and homophobia. Simply too gestural to be persuasive, they leave the reader longing for more. Yet, readerly longing is, in this instance, a good sign; I look forward to the forthcoming work of each contributor. Editors Patricia Parker and Margo Hendricks have compiled an excellent collection that will encourage and inspire more scholars to analyze the occlusion of "race" at the center of "the Renaissance" and "the Enlightenment."

The Stage and Social Struggle in Early Modern England. By Jean E. Howard. London and New York: Routledge, 1994.

Reviewer: Mary Beth Rose

Jean Howard's commanding new book makes good on the promises of new historicism, feminism, and cultural materialism in Renaissance studies. Neither ignoring the past uneasily nor attempting to recover it completely, Howard's analysis instead negotiates between the present and the past, revealing the complicated workings of ideology both in the material culture of English Renaissance theater and in its representations. Howard's engaged grasp of current critical discussion is motivated by a respect for the issues that is genuine and deep. She is intellectually and politically committed not simply to her own positions, which she clarifies with lucid elegance, but to the communal process of debate.

In this book she conjoins an exploration of the theater as a commercial institution and as the focus of particular discourses generated by theatricality with superb readings of several plays. Attempting to "achieve an understanding of Renaissance theatrical fictions at their original moment of production" (17), Howard concentrates on the struggles and contradictions that characterize theatrical discourses, positioning them as protagonists in the dramatically transforming relations of gender and class in Renaissance England. She outlines the possibility that, "in such a complex institutional setting, the ideological import of a dramatic fable and the ideological implications of the material conditions in which it was produced and consumed could conflict, interpellating subjects in contradictory ways that open space for change" (13). To demonstrate this argument, she joins in some familiar conversations: e.g., whether or not the drama, representing such class- and gender-based phenomena as monarchy or crossdressing, was subversive of networks of political power or recuperative of them; but, by insisting on the conjunction of ideological and representational complexities, Howard adds so much resonance and depth to existing discussions that she resolves them.

Her analysis of antitheatricalism, for example, places this urgently flamboyant discourse within a rich matrix of political and social self-interestedness, revealing it not simply as hysterical Puritanism, but as an embattled agent in processes of cultural change. Terming antitheatrical treatises a "genre of anxiety" (23), Howard agrees with previous commentators that those who vehemently inveighed against the theater traded in fear and nostalgia. In contrast to previous treatments of the subject, though, Howard provides an acute analysis of the ways in which antitheatrical discourse is embedded in the dynamics of social change in Renaissance England. Howard argues that the self-appointed, policing role of the tracts is to insist on a static and hierarchical conception of the world which, like misogyny, includes "an essentialist view of human identity as God-given, rather than as forged through participation in social processes." Also like misogyny, antitheatricalism embodies a mistrust of representation as falsifying the truth. Acknowledging the outraged naivete of the antitheatrical tracts, Howard views them searchingly as rooted in real anxiety about changing identities. Rather than scolding the antitheatricalists, she seeks to understand the reasons for their fears. As a result she is able to credit some of their actual perceptions, as well as to assess the particular self-interest behind their benighted pronouncements: "in general, the antitheatricalists were right that in Elizabethan England social relations were changing, that the expanding marketplace had something to do with the changes, and that the professional theater—urban, commercial, and new—was inseparable from the larger ensemble of new institutions and practices permeating the culture. Yet these pamphleteers regularly displaced the faint beginnings of an economic and social analysis with a moral one" (45).

In her chapter on antitheatricalism, Howard provides an acute analysis of Sidney's aristocratic defense of the theater which, she argues, despite its sophisticated mysitification of the poet, cloaks an attack on art as lying in the language of social disdain that implies a real fear about losing privilege. Thus she widens the sociology of participants in the peculiarly Elizabethan distrust of the theater. Howard also clarifies that, in its emphasis on the legitimacy of the semiotics that it believes are being distorted by theatrical representation (e.g., women or actors dressed as men or monarchs transgress the ways in which clothes encode gender and class), antitheatrical discourse ironically sanctions theatrical display for certain groups (e.g., artistocratic males and monarchs), thus speaking, as it were, "against itself." In a subsequent chapter she presents reading of Dekker's *The Whore of Babylon* and Shakespeare's *Much Ado About Nothing* as representing a distrust of visible signs, manifested in a concern with dramatic practices, that is identifiably antitheatrical. As she demonstrates with particular power in her analysis of *Much Ado*, the play acknowledges "the validity of much antitheatrical polemic and reproduc(es) its writing of the social order, especially its fear of the dangerous duplicity of women and of those who aspire beyond their station" (58).

Howard's reading of *Much Ado* seems to me to present a good example of the strengths of her method and technique. As she points out, traditional humanist readings of the play separate its preoccupations with fiction-making into "good" and "bad" theatricality. Howard argues that it is precisely this way of substituting moral for social categories of analysis that obscures the self-interested desire of the dominant group to retain power and naturalizes their authority as the culture's "common sense." That dominant group is, of course, "legitimate" aristocratic males; and the ideological effort of the play is to remove theatrical capacity from the hands of bastards, lower-class characters, and women. At the same time, Howard shows that the play does expose the arbitrariness of aristocratic male authority, precisely by its emphasis on the constructed, fictional nature of visible reality. In the recognition of authority's arbitrariness, the virtually "languageless" Dogberry and Verges come to embody "the utopian nature of the desire to escape discourse" (63).

The book also contains acute readings of women in the theater audiences, and of the ways in which Shakespeare's history plays can be viewed in the light of antitheatricality and its opposing discourses. All of these readings are thoughtful; but, to conclude, I would like to draw special attention to Howard's brilliant treatment of crossdressing. With considerable grace, Howard follows other scholars in analyzing the ways, both vivid and subtle, in which theatrical crossdressing provides a powerful representation of class and gender struggles in English Renaissance culture, presenting an opportunity to dramatize their peculiar interrelationship. But the real innovation in her treatment comes from the imaginative way in which she brings the theoretical distinction between gender and sexuality to bear on her readings of several plays featuring crossdressed female characters, including *Twelfth Night*, *As You Like It*, *The Merchant of Venice*, and *The Roaring Girl*.

She argues that "in the early modern period sexuality was less fully developed than gender as a site of social contestation ... While there was most definitely as subordinated gender, it is not so easy to say there was a subordinated sexuality in a culture in which the very idea that one had 'a' sexuality seems not to have been thinkable in a twentieth-century sense" (110). Although pointing out the dangers of romanticizing the multiple possibilities for representing erotic desire in the early modern period, Howard is able to show how erotic tensions and contradictions in the plays can run counter to the more conservative social resolutions centering on heterosexual marriage that are conveyed in comic structures.

Howard insists throughout her book on the complexity of political, social, and gendered power struggles in English Renaissance culture and, particularly, their representation in the public theater. While the drama could work both to complicate gender subordination and to destabilize the social hierarchy, or to bolster traditional narratives of cultural legitimacy, its power rested in its ability to participate in the articulation of conflict and change. "Wrong about many things," Howard writes in conclusion, "the antitheatricalists were thus right about the potential power of the upstart institution in their midst" (153).

Elizabeth I. By Wallace T. MacCaffrey.
London and New York: Routledge, 1993.
Elizabeth I. By Susan Frye. New York:
Oxford University Press, 1993.

Reviewer: Maurice Lee, Jr.

Queen Elizabeth I of England is one of the most scrutinized of all historical figures. She has been the subject of innumerable biographies and studies of various aspects of her rule; the only other ruler of England who has come close to attracting so much attention is the man who temporarily put an end to kingship there, Oliver Cromwell. The two are obviously very different, yet in one way they resemble each other: at the core of the personality of each there is something mercurial and elusive. About their rivals we can be far more certain. We know why Mary Queen of Scots, Philip II, and Charles I behaved as they did. But with Elizabeth and Oliver the mystery remains. Hence their fascination for historians.

Wallace MacCaffrey, recently retired from his chair at Harvard, has spent the last thirty years on the problems of Elizabethan government and politics. The result was a magisterial three-volume study, the first part of which appeared in 1968, the third in 1992. Now he has given us a biography of the queen that summarizes his great work, and at the same time modifies it, especially with respect to the first fourteen years of the reign, the subject of the 1968 volume. But his approach has not changed. The topics covered before are covered again; what found no place in the previous three volumes finds no place here.

MacCaffrey wries history in the manner of his great predecessors of the mid-twentieth century, Sir John Neale and Conyers Read. This is history as high politics: religion, finance, relations with parliament, above all, foreign affairs. There is very little about the economy, scarcely a mention of the court or the culture of the age—Shakespeare does not figure in the index, which is embarrassingly inadequate—and the common people do not make an appearance, even as spectators of the queen's numerous "progresses." More serious is the absence of any discussion of local government, which was the subject of MacCaffrey's first book, Exeter 1540–1640, since local considerations so heavily influenced the attitudes of the members of parliament with whom Elizabeth had to deal.

The picture of Elizabeth that emerges in these pages is nuanced, judicious, and in most respects convincing to this reviewer. What drove the queen, says MacCaffrey, were tow considerations: first, "the establishment of the regime laid down in the 1559 settlement of religion;" second, "to keep her realm at peace" (445). Behind these two public objectives lay three facts that Elizabeth did not want people to talk about but that were never far from anyone's mind. The first was the fact that she was a woman; John Knox was by no means the only person who believed that female rule was monstrous and against nature. Second, she was unmarried, and remained so, which was also against nature, save for those brides of Christ whom the new religious dispensation had obliterated. As the queen once remarked in some exasperation, "There is a strong idea in the world that a woman cannot live unless she is married or at all events if she refrains from marriage she does so for some bad reason" (93). Third, no one knew who would succeed her, and Elizabeth resolutely refused to name a successor. MacCaffrey believes that in 1579 Elizabeth genuinely wanted to marry the duke of Anjou, but if she did, the chances of her having a child were very remote—she turned forty-six that year. The succession question was further complicated by the fact that until the execution of Mary Queen of Scots in 1587 all those nearest in blood to the queen, the heirs by both primo-geniture and Henry VIII's will, were female. Uncertainty as to the succession was a pall that hung over the whole of the reign, and contributed to the atmosphere of crisis that persisted even after 1588. MacCaffrey might have made the point that it was an atmosphere that was in some ways helpful to Elizabeth: she was the only sovereign Englishmen had. Not until the mid–1590s, the point at which the discontented and ambitious earl of Essex began to deal with James VI, was it possible even to think in terms of a reversionary interest.

MacCaffrey gives high marks to Elizabeth's religious policy; in his view the church of England was her most permanent legacy to her country. She was, he says, "a convinced Protestant," (49), but he is not at all clear about the nature of those convictions. His earlier comment, that "The beacon which guided her actions was not one of religious or political principle but, first of all, survival and, beyond that, the pursuit of power," (28) seems much nearer the truth. He elsewhere comments on her "temperamental coldness to the passionate politico-religious convictions of her contemporaries" (187). There is no doubt, however, that she was determined not to alter the settlement of 1559 once it was made. In his earlier work MacCaffrey had accepted Neale's view, first published in 1950, that in 1559 Elizabeth was forced to swallow a more radical settlement than she wanted; now he follows the argument of Norman Jones, in *Faith by Statute* (1982), that the settlement was what Elizabeth had wanted from the beginning. Certainly she was stubborn and rigid about defending it, while at the same time following a policy of looting her bishoprics which deprived her principal ecclesiastical agents of a large part of the resources they might have used to support her. She left behind her, in consequence, an impoverished church and a great deal of subterranean discontent among those Protestant who wished further reform. MacCaffrey does not discuss this. He makes no use of Christopher Hill's *Economic Problems of the Church from Archbishop Whitgift to the Long Parliament* (1956), nor of Patrick Collinson's *The Religion of Protestants* (1982), which points to the success of King James in defusing the tense and difficult situation Elizabeth left behind her. Most admirers of the great queen are uncharitable to her successor.

MacCaffrey is by no means an uncritical admirer of the queen, however. This is clear from his discussion of Elizabeth's foreign policy. MacCaffrey argues that the queen's desire to remain at peace was driven by financial considerations. His chapter on finance, "An Economical Queen," though too reliant on the old work of F. C. Dietz, is one of his best, a neat and concise summary marred only by some inconsistency in the figures he gives on the size of the debt she left to her successor (388). He asserts that Elizabeth was able to break down the old idea that direct taxation was only for existing emergencies. Taxation was voted in peace-time, but only, as her chancellor of the exchequer said in 1576, in anticipation of "the dangers that may come" (386). The atmosphere of crisis was very helpful here; with the end of the crisis, after 1604, the old distinction rapidly reappeared.

Elizabeth's pocketbook approach to policy decisions sometimes cost her dearly. Not, to be sure, in Scotland—she refused to subsidize the Protestant party there because she knew that it had no one else to turn to, though military expeditions were occasionally necessary to preserve its position. She was niggling with King James, knowing that his ambition would keep him in line, though she had to stage the charade of pretending fury at the execution of his mother in order to help him cope with his outraged subjects. In Ireland, however, her cheeseparing approach turned out, in the end, to be very costly indeed in terms of money. MacCaffrey follows received wisdom in his discussion of this point, though his judgment that the conquest of Ireland "was the greatest of Tudor enterprises and (apart from the Reformation) the most long-lasting in its consequences" (432) might raise some eyebrows. The only alternative to conquest was abandonment, unthinkable in the circumstances: conquest it had to be. It is arguable that the really fateful decision in Ireland was not Elizabeth's but James's: the colonization of Ulster.

Pocketbook considerations also dictated Elizabeth's decisions in the Netherlands, which presented the great foreign-policy issue of her reign. She misread the situation there, and persisted in believing that compromise was possible long after it should have been apparent that it was not. "She consistently failed to understand both Philip's ineradicable determination to exterminate heresy and to reassert his power in (sic) its fullest and the conviction of the Prince of Orange and his colleagues that this was an all-or-nothing fight for survival" (212). This, coupled with her woeful overestimation of the abilities of her suitor Anjou and her willingness to do anything to earn the confidence of the rulers of France, caused her to follow a line which, in the end, left her to face the Spanish colossus virtually alone. MacCaffrey does not go as far as Charles Wilson, who in *Queen Elizabeth and the Revolt of the Netherlands* (1970), another work MacCaffrey does not cite, argued that Elizabeth's failure to intervene in full force in 1576, when the unity of the Netherlands might have been preserved and Spanish power permanently wrecked, was a blunder that was both enormous and inexcusable. But MacCaffrey clearly feels that the queen, had she known of it, would have endorsed the observation of the late, great Lefty Gomez: "I'd rather be lucky than good." Thanks to her fleet and her sailors, England survived.

MacCaffrey's scholarship is, as always, of a very high order. There are very few factual slips, and only a very occasional typo. There are a few odd judgments that reflect MacCaffrey's strictly Tudor focus—for example, that "Under the Stuarts the monarchs, faced by judicial checks on their will, were driven to heavy-handed intervention" in the law courts (355). Judicial checks were precisely what the Stuarts did *not* face. it was parliament which thwarted them, and when parliament did, it was their habit to turn to the courts, as, for example, in the case of the *post-nati*. This reviewer, an historian of Scotland by trade, must mention that MacCaffrey knows far more about Scotland than do most historians of England, although his account of the York-Westminster conference, the hearing Elizabeth arranged on the question of Mary Queen of Scots' responsibility for the premature demise of that dangerous ninny, her husband, does not do justice to all of its complexities. The style is straightforward and very readable, though hardly exciting. If the book disappoints—as, in some measure, it does—it is because it is so very much a recapitulation of MacCaffrey's earlier work. He might have taken the opportunity to explore some topics not discussed in those three massive volumes; he does not. His judgments are mainstream—though on some matters, such as the transmogrification of Robert Dudley from courtier-lover to politician, it is MacCaffrey himself who, as it were, created the channel into which the waters have flowed. This is a sound and solid book. MacCaffrey had never been a scholar given to surprises. But he always provides value for money and food for thought.

From time to time MacCaffrey touches on a subject of considerable importance to Elizabeth, her public image. She was concerned that all of her subjects, the humble as well as the great, hold her in awe, and she was enormously successful in doing this. Her public appearances, in London and in the countryside on her famous progresses, her splendidly stylized portraits, her speeches in and out of parliament, the decorum of her court and the deference she required from her courtiers, the famous appearance before her soldiers at Tilbury in the Armada year—all were calculated to impress upon the world that she was the child of Henry VIII, and no less entitled than he to their obedience.

Child of Henry she certainly was—female child, which fact presented a special set of problems with respect to that public image. This is the subject of Susan Frye's book. The "competition" in Frye's title *Elizabeth I* is that between Elizabeth and the masculine world around her for control of her image. The men wished her to be portrayed as female: essentially passive and weak, and in need of protection from assault, sexual and other; the queen insisted on appearing as an active figure, in control of her own destiny. In discussing this question Frye focuses on three episodes: the queen's official entry into London for her coronation in 1559, the famous entertainments at Kenilworth in 1575, and—rather less precisely—the 1590s, with emphasis on *The Faerie Queene*.

Frye is a professor of English whose work is described on the jacket as providing a "feminist historicist reading" of Elizabeth's reign. This approach is bound to provide difficulties for the mere historian, and, indeed, the need to provide feminist interpretations of what happened leads to a certain amount of silliness. For example, Frye describes the gift by the city of London of a purse of gold to Elizabeth during her coronation procession thus: "I is an allegory at once financial—a gift of gold to a sovereign who will always need money—and sexual—a kind of inseminated vessel" (42). Does anyone really suppose that London officialdom and the queen were thinking in sexual terms on that occasion? This is theory run amok.

The most interesting section of the book is that on Kenilworth, since it involves the only occasion on which, Frye argues, the queen intervened in the presentation of her image: she vetoed two pieces of entertainment that the earl of Leicester, her host, had planned. One, the masque of Diana and Iris, argued in favor of the queen's marriage; the other, the rescue of a maiden (Elizabeth) by an heroic knight (Leicester) from the clutches of a would-be rapist, was an argument in favor of military intervention in the Netherlands. The latter was rewritten to portray the rescue of a maiden, the Lady of the Lake, by "sovereign maiden's might," i.e., by Elizabeth herself. The first was simply not performed, as its author discreetly says, for "lack of opportunity and seasonable weather" (71); it seems likely that the real reason was that it referred to the worst moment of Elizabeth's life, her imprisonment in the Tower of London during her sister's reign. She did not care to be reminded of this episode, and it was certainly tactless, as well as untrue, to suggest that Mary released Elizabeth because of her marriageability. Frye declares that "Elizabeth censored the masque and skirmish" and "replaced them with her own apotheosis as the rescuer of Chastity . . ." (92) but she gives no evidence for this. It is at least as likely that Leicester himself had second thoughts about the appropriateness of the original texts. To sustain her interpretation Frye has to argue that both the queen's marriage and intervention in the Netherlands were live options in 1575. They were not. During the governorship of the conciliatory Requesens, who replaced the duke of Alva as Philip's viceroy in the Netherlands in 1573, the whole thrust of Elizabeth's policy was conciliation and negotiation. As for marriage: Leicester had long since given up hope of the queen's hand for himself, and the only person who could in any sense be described as a "suitor" in 1575, the duke of Anjou, was in bad odor with his brother the new king of France, and actually joined the French rebels later in the year.

Some of Frye's arguments thus rest on a dubious reading of the historical record. But that does not mean that her book, though uncomfortably jargon-filled and containing far too many long, discursive theoretical footnotes, is not both interesting and suggestive. For example, she makes some perceptive comments on the feminization of the courtier implicit in Castiglione's famous book, available in English by 1561 and frequently reprinted. She might have added that, confronted with a female prince, the courtier becomes bisexual, combing the deferential behavior recommended by Castiglione with the knight-errant qualities of the older tradition of courtly love. Frye's arguments are not, in the end, altogether convincing. But she has grappled with an important problem: how does a female prince persuade a male-chauvinist society to take her seriously as a ruler? Elizabeth was the only such ruler of her era to succeed—indeed, one of the few in any era of western civilization until the elected royalty of our own day, such as Margaret Thatcher and Golda Meir. The contrast with her predecessor and her cousin of Scotland is striking. And the mystery endures.

The Politics of Tragicomedy: Shakespeare and After, edited by Gordon McMullan and Jonathan Hope. London and New York: Routledge, 1992.

Reviewer: Jill L. Levenson

This collection of essays originated in a 1988 conference on "The Politics of Drama 1610–1650." Focusing on a single dramatic genre in relation to politics and romance, it measures a significant gap in the study of early modern theater. Over the dozen years leading to its publication, only a handful of books, a dissertation, and fewer than two dozen articles have confronted what Annabel Patterson calls the "edgy" genre of Renaissance tragicomedy (ix). Eleven of the articles appear in Nancy Klein Maguire's substantive book *Renaissance Tragicomedy: Explorations in Genre and Politics* (New York: AMS Press, 1987), a more general project which extends beyond England and ranges between the Middle Ages and the Restoration.

McMullan and Hope present essays which advance on the same well-defined subject from different angles. While that subject gives the volume coherence, cross-referencing among the papers makes it dynamic: each author seems aware of the others' views, and critical engagement within the arguments reflects what must have been a lively conference. Several topics recur—intertextuality, utopian features, masterial conditions of performance, women's roles on and off the stage—but their contexts invariably change. As a whole this book offers nine highly individual and densely packed analyses which fulfill the editors' intentions, representing "a series of exploratory approaches to the tragicomedy of the period." McMullan and Hope agree with Walter Cohen that "the explorations and the conflict *en route* to tragicomedy's resolutions, rather than the edgy certainties of the plays' conclusions, . . . offer the primary possibilities for valuable political criticism of the genre" (7).

In their introductory first essay the editors define the terms of their volume. Like all of the papers theirs is divided into sections, each division a signal that the argument is moving in a new direction. The first aim to marginalize Fletcher's "To the Reader" in the apparatus to his pastoral tragicomedy *The Faithful Shepherdess*. Usually read out of context, this influential document has narrowed the conception of tragicomedy for modern scholars. After showing its limitations in context, McMullan and Hope describe how the critics in their volume occupy the space just freed. In particular they locate their contributors with reference to new historicism ("aims are at times shared, but strategies can differ" [8]) and the time frame 1610–1650 (it controls Shakespeare's presence and allows consideration of plays traditionally ignored because they appeared after 1642 [10]). Finally they alert their audience to questions that reappear despite the contributors' divergent attitudes toward tragicomedy of the period: "To what extent does culture predetermine the artistic production of individuals and groups? Is it possible to see in the tragicomedy of the period in question the enactment of issues other than those subsumed and legitimated by the dominant culture?" (16). What is the relationship between literature and history, between gender and genre? What does collaboration reveal about the tensions within this political drama? (16–17).

The next two essays deal with Shakespearean plays. In his discussion of "Language and Utopia in *The Tempest*," David Norbrook demonstrates how irony attaches to the utopian ideals expressed through Gonzalo, Prospero, and Caliban: "As several critics have noted, it is not so much that the play is a romance as that it stages, and in the process distances itself from, the romance scenario of dynastic redemption that Prospero is staging" (26). Norbrook's persuasive argument includes a close original reading of the intertextuality between Gonzalo's utopian speech and Montaigne's "Of Cannibals"; an interpretation of Prospero's betrothal masque and its collapse as a parody of courtly formulas of power; and a survey of Caliban's discourse which complicates this figure's role as a natural man. In her consideration of "Political Service and Professional Liberty in *Cymbeline*," Erica Sheen examines the subliminal presence of Seneca's *Hercules furens* at crucial moments in the play. Applying theoretical modes from Quentin Skinner and H. P. Grice, Sheen finds in this subtle intertextuality shifting and oppositional perspectives on Imogen, Posthumus, and even Jupiter. Both of these papers challenge orthodoxies of Shakespearean criticism; and both liberate Shakespeare, through his professional repertory company, to articulate unorthodox views. With the concluding section of her essay Sheen isolates the latter issue: "Officially and ideologically under direct court patronage, but financially and materially independent to a remarkable extent, Shakespeare was in an unprecedented position to use theatre to make present within the discourses of his culture relations between political and professional mastery which he was himself helping to unsettle" (73).

Making a transition from Shakespeare to other dramatists, Lois Potter writes about *The Two Noble Kinsmen* between its first performance c. 1613 and its publication in 1634. She deals with its topicality as a play of death and renewal, as well as the political implications of the interconnected plots. In light of the various uncertainties that generate uneasiness with this tragicomedy, she asks whether collaborative authorship too disturbs modern critical sensibilities:

This is the result of our own politics, which demand commitment and distrust pluralism. To suspend judgement is felt to be irresponsible: we must interpret, and this means discriminating between Shakespeare and Fletcher; it means finding a meaning in the play or, if there are more possible meanings than one, giving priority to the one belonging to the dramatist who long since won the trial by combat. (90)

Kathleen McLuskie concentrates on the other combatant, Fletcher, along with his non-Shakespearean collaborators, in an essay first published as part of her *Renaissance Dramatists* (Hemel Hempstead: Harvester, 1989). Working her way carefully through more than half a dozen texts, she shows how theatrical play with dramatic conventions both contains and flouts sexual decorum; how Fletcherian theater created its own audience by the 1630s; and how it negotiated its treatment of sex and heroines not only with the urbane young men in that audience but with the women addressed by its prologues, epilogues, and commendatory verses.

Walter Cohen contributes the volume's farthest-reaching essay, outlined by its initial complex sentence:

> To what extent might one argue that the English Revolution constitutes the crucial reception of the tragicomedies composed between 1610 and 1642, that the plays are prerevolutionary in more than the obvious chronological sense, that they are shaped by the forces that led to civil war and that they often anticipate many of the conflicts of the revolutionary era? (122)

He first sets out his rationale and method, efforts to discuss the links between gender and class (as part of a Marxist-feminist project) and to support the prerevolutionary nature of Stuart drama as a whole (122–23). In the next two sections he surveys tragicomedy for particular analogies: family/women and the state (128–31); class and the state (131–41). His conclusion summarizes these findings and identifies two problems remaining in his method, which can seem to recover a radicalism that has never existed or to subordinate issues of gender to those of class. Difficult to condense, this explorative study reads evolving history into tragicomedies preceding the Revolution, suggesting a variety of ways in which drama can prefigure crisis (143, 127).

The last three essays cover less expansive but valuable terrain. Also concerned with prerevolutionary drama, Margot Heinemann demonstrates how plays expressed discontent and protest in the popular theaters. She draws on "Elect Nation plays" based primarily on Reformation history and Foxe, and on works by Dekker which represent drama anxious about economic adversity. Martin Butler successfully challenges revisionist views of Jonson's "dotages" (by Anne Barton, David Norbrook, and himself) with a different revision. If recent criticism argues "a tentative double-edged late Jonsonian radicalism" (167), Butler finds evidence in Jonson's patrons, friends, and dramatic texts of continuity in his ideological presumptions about the court's social/political hegemony. Sophie Tomlinson tracks the woman-actor from her first appearance on the stage with Henrietta Maria's pastoral of 1626 through her career until 1643 in the theater and in discourse (as a trope and then a topic). Appropriately this collection of essays ends in medias res, just as it seems to set off in yet another new direction.

Cross-Cultural Performances: Differences in Women's Re-Visions of Shakespeare. Edited by Marianne Novy. Urbana and Chicago: University of Illinois Press, 1993.

Reviewer: Barbara E. Bowen

"Is to invoke Shakespearean drama always to reproduce Shakespearean ideology?" asks Valerie Traub in her essay on African American women's uses of Shakespeare. "Is the ideology of Shakespearean texts so self-evident as to admit no room for alternative response, interpretative negotiation? Is the cultural power of the bard so absolute as to obviate all revision, all subversion?" (150). These are the questions that animate Marianne Novy's collection of twelve new essays on women's revisions of Shakespeare and place the book within important debates on the possibility of oppositional culture and the nature of political resistance. One major contribution the volume makes is in identifying as readings of Shakespeare a rich array of cultural works—ranging from novels and poem sequences to individual performances and alternative theater companies—whose interventions in Shakespeare criticism and in larger questions about oppositional culture might otherwise be missed. *Cross-Cultural Performances: Differences in Women's Re-Visions of Shakespeare* implicitly makes the point that the critical canons of a racist patriarchal culture, no less than the literary ones, need to be fractured—not only because of whom they don't represent, but because they tend, as Eve Sedgwick has argued, "to insulate and deform the reading of politically important texts." Marianne Novy's fine collection lifts the insulation too often surrounding women readers and rewriters of Shakespeare and argues for the importance of women's fictive texts as sources of Shakespeare commentary and cultural criticism. Thus such diverse "performances" as a Zora Neale Hurston short story, the craze for restaging *Hamlet* in northeastern India, the history of women's alternative theater companies in England, a lesbian novel from Canada, and Aphra Behn's *Oroonoko* emerge here as significant engagements with Shakespeare—and complex cultural productions in their own right.

The volume would be valuable if only for the wealth of material it brings together (the footnotes to the articles on theater alone make the book worth owning), but its most lasting significance may lie in its collective attempt to theorize the practice of revision or appropriation itself. Recognizing revision as a flash point in postmodern and postcolonial cultural politics as well as a central issue in literary feminism, the most ambitious of the essays urge a move beyond the binary model of alliance/resistance as an explanation of women's stances towards Shakespeare. "Cultural 're-visions' and appropriations—in fact all seizures of the book, all processes of 'unlearning' and formulating alterative cultures," writes Ania Loomba, "are especially vulnerable to . . . circularity in conceptualizing resistance" (229); this collection at its best escapes that circularity and reimagines appropriation as a polysemous, historically defined encounter between cultures—and one whose political potential we cannot know in advance.

The collection has its roots in the studies from the mid-eighties that became part of Marianne Novy's 1990 anthology, *Women's Re-Visions of Shakespeare: The Responses of Dickinson, Woolf, Rich, H. D., George Eliot and Others*. The present collection, as Novy explains in the Introduction, builds on the first while addressing some of its limitations: *Women's Re-Visions*, she comments, "stayed within the world of white women, particularly Anglo-American women, and it paid very little attention women of the theater" (2). *Cross-Cultural Performances* is itself, then, something of a revision (a point delicately suggested by Margaret Ferguson's opening out of Novy's 1990 Introduction in the first essay of this volume). Benefitting from the exposure of racism within feminism in the eighties and the recent flourishing of feminist performance theory, the new volume seeks to correct the omissions of the first with a twofold emphasis: on women's appropriations of Shakespeare in the theater and across racial or cultural lines. Both, Novy observes, are "performances"; both cross cultures.

While Novy's willingness to revise and extend her own work is in the best tradition of feminist practice, her division of the essays into these two volumes somewhat undermines her purpose. The individual essays in both volumes go beyond the oversimplifications of "women" on the one hand and "cross-culturals" on the other, but the decision to treat white women first and women of color in a separate volume threatens to reify the boundaries Novy wants to dissolve. Novy's tendency to rely on binary oppositions even when her stated purpose is to complicate them appears again when she describes her subject as the "uses of Shakespeare by black women, mainly in the U. S., and women of the theater, mainly in England" (4). "Women of the theater" means, almost exclusively, *white* women of the theater; thus the volume misses the chance to consider how even its own two categories overlap. Although the essay on *Hamlet* in India touches on some of these convergences, the book would be strengthened by more interaction between the different areas of criticism it represents and by consideration of African-American, Caribbean, European, or African women in the Shakespearean theater. Without the signs of intense collaboration among the contributors or the shared theoretical agenda that characterized collections like *The Woman's Part, Rewriting the Renaissance, Shakespeare Reproduced* or *Political Shakespeare* (volumes to which Peter Erickson compares this one in his afterword), *Cross-Cultural Performances* does not position itself as a manifesto for a new direction in Shakespeare studies or feminist criticism. Rather, in subtle and often groundbreaking essays it offers a powerful example of cultural materialist criticism that is alive to issues of gender, sexuality and nation; at the same time it advances a new analysis of the way women and other marginalized subjects "negotiate the plots, conventions, and politics of Anglo-European cultural traditions" (150).

Margaret Ferguson's "Transmuting Othello: Aphra Behn's *Oroonoko*," the first and longest essay in the book, sets the tone for much of what follows by cracking open the alliance/resistance model for revision. Arguing for *Oroonoko* as a sensationalized and partially critical appropriation of *Othello*, Ferguson makes clear how complex a relation to the Shakespearean subtext a woman writer could have. This essay is part of an unfolding critical argument about *Oroonoko* that is also a meditation on the origins of racism; Ferguson's engagement with the novel derives at least in part from its position as a pivotal text in the invention of white womanhood. Behn "deliberately sought to capitalize on *Othello*'s popularity during the Restoration era" (23), Ferguson tells us; on the one hand she exaggerated "precisely that aspect of Othello's relation to a metropolitan state which we might call 'the Aaron potential'—the possibility ... that a black male slave will seize any chance to usurp the white leader's political and erotic places" (29), on the other she included references to her own implication in "the imperial project that caused Oroonoko's death" (30). The result is a narrative that "oscillates between criticizing and profiting from a 'system' of circulation which includes both bodies and words" (33). From this analysis of Behn's position Ferguson derives a new paradigm of European colonialism: a triangulation based on "relations of sameness and difference" among an African male slave, a white English woman and native American men and women. Enabling the triangle is the silenced figure of Imoinda, and African woman; the essay is concerned finally to examine the "advantage" Behn takes as a white metropolitan woman of the silence of nonwhite women in England's colonized periphery.

The questions Ferguson raises about the political complexity of white women's alliances, even critical alliances, with Shakespeare resonate throughout the book, and are taken up in two essays that concentrate on the importance of nineteenth-century ideologies of (white) womanhood for Shakespearean revision. In "Helen Faucit and Shakespeare: Womanly Theater," Julie Hankey argues that the phenomenal success of this Victorian actress depended on her alignment of herself with Shakespeare and the culture's alignment of Shakespearean women with "that utterly private and virtuous person, the 'womanly woman'" (51). The trick of Faucit's Shakespearean women was their apparent *lack* of theatricality, their embodiment of private virtue on the public stage; yet Hankey suggests that some roles revealed the limits of this "autobiographical Shakespeare" (64) and that even the actress herself began to be restless within the confines of ideal womanhood. In a fine essay that recovers Lillie Wyman's novel *Gertrude of Denmark*, Martha Tuck Rozett shows Victorian ideologies of womanhood still at work in 1924, though here they are embodied in a fascinating hybrid text: an almost genteel romance (by the daughter of a feminist, abolitionist mother) followed by an epilogue that directly contradicts the Bradleian critical establishment. A retelling of the *Hamlet* narrative from Gertrude's point of view, the novel "interrogates the 'maleness' of *Hamlet* as a sacrosanct canonical text" (81) and offers significant challenges even to recent feminist criticism of the play.

Judith Lee analyzes Isak Dinesen's 1958 collection of tales, *Anecdotes of Destiny*, as a "dialogue with" *The Tempest*. Unlike George Lamming, who was writing *The Pleasures of Exile* in the same year, and other writers of the African diaspora who followed him, Dinesen suppressed the colonial politics of the play and concentrated on the potential subversiveness of Ariel (whom she made female) rather than Caliban. Lee does not claim for Dinesen the capacity for self-critique Margaret Ferguson found in Aphra Behn; instead she cites Dinesen's "insistence upon subordinating the political to the poetical and . . . ignoring the cultural determinants in all behavior, her own included" (88). If Dinesen's *Tempest* could profitably be read against the Caribbean rewritings of the same period, it could also be seen as the first in a series of *women's* appropriations of the play, eight more of which are discussed in this book. Rewriting *The Tempest* emerges as almost a subplot of *Cross-Cultural Performances*; the book suggests that there may be a feminist *Tempest* tradition that both rewrites the male tradition and reveals its gendered, heterosexist basis. For both Toni Morrison and Gloria Naylor *The Tempest* has been a central text: Morrison, according to Malin LaVon Walther, uses the play to think through the connection between aesthetics and colonialism; and Naylor, Valerie Traub argues, invokes *The Tempest* in *Mama Day* "to assert the irreducible fact of historical and political difference" (154). These two important essays cannot be easily summarized—they include discussion of Morrison's involvement with *criticism* of *The Tempest*, Zora Neale Hurston's feminist critique of *Hamlet* in "Spunk," Naylor's distance from her own characters' "universal Shakespeare"—but they are crucial in demonstrating the multiple positions on Shakespeare available to contemporary black women writers. Like Ferguson, Ania Loomba, and Diana Brydon in a superb essay on Canadian Mirandas, Walther and Traub are working towards a more nuanced and capacious model of textual appropriation than we have seen so far in Shakespeare studies. The model as Traub articulates it includes the possibility of political agency against hegemonic culture; yet it acknowledges that as much as Shakespeare speaks *against* "us," "we are drawn to deconstruct only that which also speaks *to* us" (162).

Diana Brydon shares Traub's sense that the comedic in Shakespeare can be reclaimed for a politics of social regeneration; she dares to imagine a future in which "Miranda seizes the initiative to work for change and then surrenders her control to make room for others" (180). The importance of recent Canadian *Tempests*, including Suniti Namjoshi's poem "Snapshots of Caliban" (1984) and Sarah Murphy's novel *The Measure of Miranda* (1987) lies in their ability to suggest "the ways in which postcolonial and feminist critiques overlap, differ, and may inform one another" (166). Brydon's concern is with the *limits* of "certain kinds of African-nationalist postcolonial reading" and of "international white feminism"; she sees the Canadian Miranda-figure as useful in dramatizing both. The limits of white feminism can be addressed in part by reimagining silence; in a move that almost answers Margaret Ferguson's essay, Brydon imagines an "enabling" silence, in which white women make a priority of "listening to Caliban, rather than solely to Prospero" (181).

The openness Brydon exhibits in desiring political change and being willing to envision it is evident in several of the essays on women in the theater. Starting with a rich account by Margaret Drabble of how Shakespeare became entwined for her with the ideology of female obedience and domesticity (she spent her wedding night alone, watching, "ominously," *The Taming of the Shrew*), the four articles on modern British theater document the efforts of women to appropriate the power of the theater for social transformation. The essays—by Dympna Callaghan, Joyce Green MacDonald and Lizbeth Goodman in addition to Drabble—are remarkable for their detail and uniformly strong in their attention to the material conditions of theatrical performance. Callaghan and Goodman chronicle the work of women who resisted the hegemonic national theater companies, while MacDonald concentrates on a single production within the Shakespeare establishment, Deborah Warner's *Titus Andronicus* for the Royal Shakespeare Company in 1987. Warner proved wrong generations of "genteel exception" to the play when she repudiated the theatrical tradition that saw Lavinia's rape and mutilation as "either too violent or too absurd to be performed as written" (198); she insisted on making Lavinia's "unbearable pain" and her rapists' desire to degrade her present on stage. Faced with a theatrical establishment that institutionalized both patriarchy and gentility, many British women of the theater sought alternatives to Shakespeare, either refusing to play him, as Tilda Swinton does ("Rosalind, Viola, Portia... I don't think that those roles should be played by women at all" [212]), or transforming his works and the conditions of theatrical production in feminist companies. Lizbeth Goodman documents the struggles of women in the 1970s and '80s to create feminist theater and invent a feminist Shakespeare, while Dympna Callaghan calls for a reexamination of Joan Littlewood's Theater Workshop, a "rigorously oppositional" (109) class-identified company of the fifties, as a model for future feminist performance and analysis. Both essays are instructive in their commitment to investigating marginalized cultural practices as sources of social transformation; one strength in particular of Callaghan's article is its discussion of how a class politics that often equated radicalism with virility might still be useful to feminism.

Ania Loomba's "*Hamlet* in Mizoram" is beautifully placed as last article in the volume. Her investigation of the "political unconscious" of *Hamlet-drama*, a touring version of the play in remote eastern India, is a major statement on the issue at stake in both of Marianne Novy's collections on revision. How can we think about the power/resistance dialectic without seeing disempowered groups as either doomed to reproducing their own oppression or positioned totally outside the structure of power? "Surely Caliban's curse is made possible by more than Prospero's language," Loomba writes. "Is to probe this 'more' necessarily to resurrect a romantic notion of oppositional culture?" (230) Loomba's strategy is to connect the issue of appropriating literary texts across cultures to theories of colonial discourse and "their repeated debates over what constitutes subaltern agency" (235). Under such an analysis, the categories of subversion and containment, of subalternity itself, become fluid (245); both dominant and resistant cultures are revealed to be heterogeneous:

> Prospero is not the whole of Caliban's history or identity—it is also Sycorax (among other factors), who, even though absent, shapes his curse. But no precolonial culture is merely precolonial; it is also permeated by its own hierarchies and oppressions. . . . Thus we are enabled to think of resistance as entirely bounded by specific cultural and historical parameters, and yet as being more than the effect of power it contests. (230–31)

The brilliance of Loomba's formulation is in seeing that this postmodern analysis of political power offers more, not less scope for feminist and other liberatory movement. Because they represent negotiations between texts and cultures already in themselves heterogenous, appropriations (and Loomba would stretch this term to its widest meaning) are "especially rich sites" for those who want to mark the "limits of otherness" and open a "'genuine dialogue' between the 'ex-coloniser and the ex-colonised,'" (the terms are from the anthropologist S. P. Mohanty). We are at the edge here of what a study of Shakespearean appropriation can hope to achieve; if postcolonial feminist criticism can go on from here to begin the dialogue Loomba envisions—while always asking why this historical moment so often limits discussions of political resistance to questions of cultural revision—*Cross-Cultural Performances* will have made a profound contribution to feminist thought.

Private Matters and Public Culture in Post-Reformation England. by Lena Cowen Orlin. Ithaca: Cornell University Press, 1994.

Reviewer: Richard Helgerson

I first heard of Lena Orlin two summers ago in the little Kentish town of Faversham. I had gone there to begin work on a book I thought I might write about *Arden of Faversham* and the event on which that anonymous play was based, the 1551 murder of Thomas Arden by his wife, her lover, and a host of accomplices. But no sooner had I arrived than a local antiquary asked me if I knew the other American who had been hanging around. I didn't, but I was soon to hear more. Before I left Faversham, another of the locals slipped me the draft of a preliminary essay Orlin had written on the Arden murder, and in the next few months, as I worked more on this material, her name kept cropping up. Now her book has appeared, and I must acknowledge that I have been thoroughly scooped. The whole first chapter and a good part of the second are about Arden. But I can't be too unhappy about it. Orlin has done such fine job that she clearly deserves the good fortune of having gotten there first. Not only does she brilliantly illuminate both the play and the event, but she sets both in relation to many other plays and many other events with the result that her book succeeds in mapping a broad new territory for literary historical investigation.

It is no accident that Orlin and I should both have been attracted to Faversham. Just a few months before publishing Orlin's book,

Cornell brought out Frances Dolan's *Dangerous Familiars*, with another lengthy discussion of *Arden*, and still other *Arden* essays have either recently appeared or are now in the works. How are we to explain this sudden interest in a play whose previous chief claim was its occasional and quite improbable appearance on the list of Shakespeare apocrypha? At least this time Shakespeare has little to do with it. Nor do motives like those that prompted earlier critics to propel this anonymous play into the transcendent realm of High Art, where Shakespeare reigns supreme. No, instead of Culture with a capital "C," lower-case culture, *culture* in the anthropologists' sense, is laying its claim on *Arden*. The Arden story now finds itself, along with a number of other stories of a similar sort, at the crossroads where the once marginalized interests of popular history, the history of crime, local history, women's history, domestic history or the history of private life, socioeconomic history, and material history converge.

Others working in these expanding fields—history-department historians—have masses of printed and, especially, manuscript documents on which to base their conclusions. For literary historians the archive is not as full. We still need a poem, play, of fiction to ground our work, and there are not all that many that respond to the new concerns. In this awkward situation, *Arden* has proved extraordinarily valuable. Not only does it provide literary scholars with a work of some aesthetic standing (old habits die hard!) that addresses the historical issues that now interest us, but it also opens the way to whole categories of evidence of which it is a distinguished member or toward which it conspicuously points. English domestic tragedy, a dramatic subgenre that seems to have got its start with *Arden*, is only the most obvious of these. Others are: the chronicle histories, crime pamphlets, and popular ballads that shared with plays the work of making such events known to a wide public; the deeds, leases, land transfers, marriage contracts, inventories, and other legal documents that describe the often hidden economic setting of domestic crime; admonitory tracts on marriage, the family, and household government that suggest orthodox values the plays variously test, undermine, and reaffirm; letters, diaries, account books, and other records of actual domestic practice; the physical structures, starting with Arden's own house in Faversham, in which domestic life and domestic crime took place; and, finally, the plethora of material objects that filled sixteenth-century houses. All these and more appear along the way of someone who takes off from *Arden* with the objectives of a cultural historian. Many of them would, of course, also lie in the path of the more conventional social historian. What distinguishes an approach that begins with a play is an inclination to regard all the evidence as participating in systems of cultural representation—that and a related curiosity about the social and political function of such representations. As Orlin puts it, "My particular interest is not in how post-Reformation men and women conducted their private lives"—the social historian's usual aim—"but, rather, in how they conceptualized their private lives and, especially, in their own awareness of how these conceptualizations both served and sometimes failed the community" (4).

At the center of the sixteenth-century conceptualizations that most engage Orlin is the house. Indeed, she defines her topic as "a cultural history of the house: its notional structures, prescribed activities, prevailing assumptions, and persistent conflicts" (4). After centuries of castle-building and church-building, post-Reformation England experienced an enormous surge of house-building, a surge accelerated by the massive expropriation of monastic lands and the resultant expansion of the real-estate market. All over England, "new" men were both building new houses—the physical structures that provided the setting for domestic life—and establishing new houses—the lineal structures through which property and status passed from generation to generation. Thomas Arden was just such a new man. Though of obscure social and geographic origin, Arden ended life as the richest man in Faversham, the king's customs agent for the town's busy port, the owner of virtually all the lands and tenements once held by the town's important abbey, the landlord of many of the town's most prominent inhabitants, including the former abbot. And by the time he died, Arden also owned, as a preeminent sign of his arrival, the largest house in town, the former gatehouse and guesthouse of the expropriated abbey.

How Arden achieved this position is the subject of Orlin's first chapter. In a fascinating survey of the large cache of surviving documents, she traces Arden's progress from his earliest appearance as clerk to Sir Edward North, who was then parliamentary secretary and was soon to be treasurer and eventually chancellor of the new Court of Augmentations, the institution set up to handle the vast properties that came to the crown from the dissolution of the monasteries. As Orlin shows, Arden's connections served him well. Not only did he gain an insider's knowledge of the burgeoning land market, but he also secured his position by marrying his patron's stepdaughter. Nor was North Arden's sole benefactor. In a marked departure from earlier accounts, Orlin shows that Arden's career also depended on the patronage of Thomas Cheney, the lord warden of the Cinque Ports and one of the most powerful men in Kent. But Orlin does more than this. Out of her reading of the archives, she constructs a counternarrative of Arden's murder, one in which Cheney himself emerges as a leading suspect.

This last suggestion is admittedly speculative. But it and the more solidly grounded story of the suspicion and animosity produced by a new man like Arden both in the neighborhood he so suddenly dominated and in the political center from which he had moved throws into high relief the more familiar accounts of Arden's murder, including the one that was first staged in London sometime around 1591. Though not all those accounts wholly efface the memory of Arden's spectacular and bruising rise—on this score Orlin exaggerates just a bit—they do shift responsibility away from Arden and the sociopolitical system he represented to put it squarely on a figure who hardly appears in the public archive, Arden's adulterous wife, Alice. In the place of Arden's hard dealings and the retribution they may have provoked, we have (to echo the title of Catherine Belsey's well-known essay) "Alice Arden's crime."

Now, there probably was such a crime. Neither Orlin nor anyone else has suggested that Alice had no hand in her husband's murder. But why did that part of the story become the whole story? Orlin's answer goes to the heart of the early modern construction of the domestic: "Alice served the cultural function of giving definition to the shape of domestic evil by marking its extreme" (68). By making Arden's murder so exclusively Alice Arden's crime, sixteenth- and seventeenth-century commentators and redactors drew a firm line around the domain of the private. This was, as Holinshed put it, "but a private matter"—though a "private matter" that was made central, by Holinshed among others, to the "public culture" of early modern England. Alice's deadly violation of domestic order helped make that order a subject of general concern, one that eclipsed even the wholesale transfer of wealth and property on which it was founded. Nor did the public/private construction of Arden's murder, with Alice as prime target, have to await the intervention of Holinshed and the many others who retold the story. In a "coda" to her first chapter, Orlin retrieves a hitherto unremarked reference to the Arden story, John Ponet's "chilling" (the word is Orlin's) claim in his 1556 *Short Treatise of Politic*

Power that, after Arden's murder and before her execution, Alice ("the wicked woman in Faversham in Kent, that not long since killed her husband") was laid "open free to every man" who would take his "liberty" of her (80). Transgressing the private through adultery and murder, Alice had made herself common ground, common ground on which posterity has continued to exercise its retributive will.

The Arden story—this time only in its staged version—makes a return appearance in Orlin's second chapter where she takes up the vexed issue of early modern Patriarchalism. Seen from this perspective, domestic tragedy justifies itself by analogy with the more familiar tragic story of the fall of kings. Arden is monarch in the little kingdom of his household. His murder is thus a kind of rebellion—"petty treason," as the law that led to Alice's burning had it. And just as royal protagonists suffer from their own blindness and misjudgment, their own failures of rule, so Arden's fall results as much from his abdication as from his wife's rebellion. But still more interesting is the discovery in other plays of contradictions in the very structure of analogy on which patriarchalism depended. Patriarchal ideology could produce divided loyalties, particularly in the women who were most subject to it. As Orlin shows in three of her most sensitive readings, Mistress aSnders in *A Warning for Fair Women*, Merry's sister Rachel in Robert Yarington's *Two Lamentable Tragedies*, and Jane Shore in Thomas Heywood's *Edward IV* are all destroyed not by their Alice-like rebellion against patriarchal control but rather by their submission to it: Anne Sanders by the transfer of duty from her living husband to the man she is assured is to be her husband; Rachel by her devotion to her household patriarch, her murderous brother, rather than to the abstract law; and Jane Shore by her submission to the national patriarch, the king himself, when he usurps the place of her husband. Such rethinking of ideology through the dramatic representation of actual experience was, as Orlin argues, the theater's special contribution to the construction and deconstruction of early modern domesticity. By its very nature, its appetite for conflict, the theater could not help exposing rifts in the orthodoxy it claimed only to be supporting.

Furthering her claim for the role of the theater in the social construction of the house and for the use of plays as historical evidence is the work of Orlin's last two chapters. Chapter 3 centers on Heywood's *Woman Killed with Kindness* and the conflict that emerges in that play between the classical ideal of friendship and the more recent demands of householding, while chapter 4 examines "domestic abdications" in *Othello* and the anonymous *Yorkshire Tragedy*. In the breakdown of one social ethic, the ethic of friendship and hospitality, *Woman Killed with Kindness* finds another. As Orlin puts it in her conclusion to the chapter, virtue now "inheres in domestic duty, in the right ordering of the individual's household commonwealth and the careful supervision of its associated powers" (180). Failure to fulfill such domestic duty is what brings about the destruction of Frankford's marriage and the death of his wife in *Woman Killed*, as it exposed Arden to the rebellion that overthrew him in *Arden of Faversham*. And something like it also underlies the fatal events that mark *Othello* and *A Yorkshire Tragedy*.

In Orlin's view, Othello's great fault is his failure to establish a house of his own. Where early modern marriage usually meant the emergence of a new "house," Othello takes his bride to the oddly named Venetian "Sagittary," an inn or public residence of some sort. Faced with this tantalizing anomaly, Orlin temporarily switches from her usual "diagnostic" reading to what (following Clifford Geertz) she calls a "cryptographic" reading. She deciphers this "sign"—the sign of the Sagittary—to get at its meaning and, through it, at the meaning of the play. It would be impossible here to follow all the wanderings of Orlin's wonderfully intricate argument. Suffice it to say that Othello has lodged Desdemona in what amounts to an ill-fated astrological "house," the house of the centaur/archer, Sagittarius—a figure variously associated with Iago. By eloping to the Sagittary, Othello has put his marriage under the influence of its eventual destroyer. From such a beginning, the loss of control that leads to Othello's murder of his innocent wife follows naturally—presuming, of course, that we identify, as we are meant to do, domestic ideology with nature. And when this play is placed next to *A Yorkshire Tragedy*, Orlin can return to the diagnostic mode to define the common ailment that runs through both: "Male collapse under the burdens of oeconomic"—that is, *domestic*—"responsibility" (195). Despite his marriage, Othello, who had talked of his reluctance to put his "unhoused free condition . . . into circumscription and confine," never does establish a house and ends by destroying all prospect of one, while the Yorkshire husband, who is obsessed with the damage his "riotous courses" have done his ancient lineal house, tries to remedy his fault by murdering (or attempting to murder) his wife and three sons.

These plays suggest an early-seventeenth-century shifting in dramatic attention from husband-killing wives, like Alice Arden and

Anne Sanders, to wife-killing husbands, a shift that transformed the husband himself from a petty king in a household realm to a sometimes violent intruder in what had become essentially a woman's space. Here we see the first sign of the modern regendering of the house from male to female, and with it the passing of the patriarchal analogy that had likened family to state. All this was of course not accomplished in the few years that separate *A Warning for Fair Women* from *Othello* and *A Yorkshire Tragedy*. The chronological ordering of these few plays cannot be made to bear so heavy a burden of historical significance. But there is additional evidence—including some that Orlin surprisingly neglects—that by the early decades of the seventeenth century the patriarchal construction of the household was under increasing attack. In still another version of the Sir Walter Calverley story that supplied the plot of *A Yorkshire Tragedy*, the 1607 *Miseries of Enforced Marriage*, the Calverley character's alienation from his wife and children is made the fault of his overbearing guardian, who insisted on this marriage rather than another the young man had contracted for himself. And fourteen years later, in the Frank Thorney plot of *The Witch of Edmonton*, a very similar pattern recurs. These husbands kill or attempt to kill their wives not out of an unwillingness to accept the burdens of oeconomic responsibility, but rather in reaction to the defeat of their domestic ambitions by a father or father-surrogate. But this additional evidence only strengthens Orlin's larger argument. The early modern house was being forcibly redesigned, and the theater participated actively in the change.

Can a cultural history of the early modern house be written? And can playtexts serve as the prime evidence in such a history? Before reading Orlin's book, one might have been inclined to answer "no" to both questions. After reading it, one can say with some confidence not only that it can be done but that it has been done. How does Orlin manage it? In part by bringing so much other evident to her playtexts—including the kind of evidence she picked up visiting Arden's house in Faversham and lots of other houses all over England. Again and again—in her description of the actual houses of Thomas Arden and Sir Walter Calverley, in her discussion of the domestic structures imagined by speeches and stage directions in *A Woman Killed with Kindness* and *Othello*, in her third-chapter coda on the locked studies of early modern houses, in her concluding meditation on the sixteenth-century proliferation of household objects—she wonderfully links the materiality of houses to the ideological functions they served. But her success comes too from a nice combination of interpretive daring and critical tact. As should by now be clear to any reader of this review, Orlin is not afraid to speculate. But—and this a review cannot so easily represent—she is also very good at framing her speculations in a broader and finely nuanced argument of considerable complexity and sophistication. What finally emerges from this remarkably rich and compelling book is a sense of the multiple and often contradictory construction of the early modern house, of the troubling paradoxes, as well as the ideological force, of sixteenth;- and seventeenth-century English householding. It was worth a trip to Faversham just to be able to appreciate the accomplishment.

Faultlines: Cultural Materialism and the Politics of Dissident Reading. By Alan Sinfield. Berkeley: University of California Press, 1992.

Reviewer: Terence Hawkes

Shakespeare's name lends authority to any viewpoint. This is the wisdom of the centuries and, despite the charges of some their more indignant detractors, cultural materialists were by no means the first to use the Swan of Avon as a weapon, enlisting his plays in the service of a larger political program. The criticism of Hazlitt and of Coleridge involves a crucial exchange of salvos to exactly that effect and, amongst many others, T. S. Eliot, E. M. W. Tillyard, even G. Wilson Knight were not averse to the occasional canny mobilization of the Bardic militia against the alien hordes. Cultural Materialism's open acknowledgment of its purposes, whilst not disarming, may nonetheless have some claim to be unique. Its bold discarding of aesthetic camouflage, its spirited unleashing of the contents of those iambic caissons, might even appear a refreshing novelty, if not a saving grace.

Faultlines begins, appropriately enough, with the meticulous sifting of an advertisement proclaiming the virtues of the Royal Ordnance Company. The confidence with which weapons manufacturers use Shakespeare and his theater to symbolize the values their products supposedly protect ("After 400 years, Royal Ordnance still plays the Globe. All of it.") presents a prime target for Alan Sinfield's well-aimed scorn. What he has in his sights is a "faultline."

Faultlines appear at those moments when the project of ideology remains not altogether completed; when its aim, which is to smooth over conflicts and contradictions, to assure us that everything in the garden is, if not lovely, then at least under control, hasn't quite been achieved. No society can ever be perfectly true to the sense of itself that it seeks publicly to endorse. Faultlines (Shakespeare, symbol of art, "culture," wisdom, and beauty suddenly appearing to promote the engines of maiming, death, and destruction) are inevitable. Indeed, since the social order cannot but generate them, they offer the most fruitful point of departure for dissident readings of it. Faultlines, in short, constitute the points at which a "dissident perspective" may be able to obtain a decisive purchase on a way of life. And since it is likely that literary texts will address controversial aspects of society, their "faultline stories" are usually the ones that yield most productively to close and deliberately transgressive scrutiny.

This effectively announces a program of rigorous and politically committed rereading and realignment in which "the awkward, unresolved issues, the ones in which the conditions of plausibility are in dispute" will be firmly brought to the fore. Applied to Shakespeare's plays, as here, with an appealing vigor and, occasionally, a nicely calculated perversity, it turns out to be bracingly unsettling. A lively interrogation of *Julius Caesar* considers the ways in which the play drew upon and contributed to notions of legitimacy in its own time, and proposes for it in ours the sort of argumentative restructuring, or "creative vandalism" promoted by Brecht. This involves a novel redeployment of the tribunes on stage as part of a tragedy aimed at checking the play's tendency to authorize reactionary discourses. In *Macbeth*, a crucial "faultline" emerges in a narrative which allows the protagonist to be praised at the beginning of the play for exactly the kind of violence for which he turns out to be condemned at the end. As Sinfield argues, this highlights an important question which our own response to the play needs to confront: what precisely is the difference between Macbeth's detested rule in Scotland and that of any other contemporary European monarch?

Predictably, in this context, the cloudy realms of "Englishness" find themselves scoured with a zealous rigor. A perceptive account of *Henry V* brings into sharp critical focus some of the nationalist presuppositions currently inhabiting—and inhibiting—the play. The callous "Englishing" of Britain, perhaps as corrupting a process today as it was in the early modern period, emerges as a crucial topic, and Ireland's by now almost traditional role as the suppressed, yet defining English other—the bad conscience of an English state that sees itself as the divine agent of peace and justice—is tellingly assessed. The play's construction of various masculinities also receives careful probing. Against Henry's determinedly "English" wooing of Katherine, climaxing in his winsomely brisk kissing of her lips, Sinfield neatly sets the no less English lovedeath of Suffolk and York:

> Suffolk first died; and York, all haggled over,
> Comes to him, where in gore he lay insteep'd,
> And takes him by the beard, kisses the gashes
> That bloodily did yawn upon his fact . . .
> . . . .
> So did he turn, and over Suffolk's neck
> He threw his wounded arm, and kiss'd his lips;
> And so espous'd to death, with blood he seal'd
> A testament of noble-ending love.
>   (4.6.11–32)

Despite the occluding operations of convention, a disturbing "emotional weight" inhabits these lines, and its evident, almost structured, absence in the later scenes of heterosexual wooing—and kissing—forces another faultline to the surface.

Essays on Sidney's *Acadia* and *Defence of Poetry*, on Marlowe's *Dr. Faustus* and *Tamburlaine*, as well as on the broader sweep of intellectual history serve as a helpful and revealing foil to those on Shakespeare, with their precision continuing and augmenting the range of the analysis. Amongst other matters, they discuss the paradoxical role taken by early modern Protestantism and Puritanism in fostering both a sense of personal inwardness and a commitment to bonding and affiliation on the basis of shared moral and social beliefs, which can be said to be the origin both of modern party politics, and of oppositional subcultures. Questions of subjectivity and control occupy the foreground here without inhibiting the scope. Finally, a lengthy, slightly meandering chapter reprises the book's initial concerns in its discussion of "the cultural and institutional roles of Shakespeare in the United States, interactions between Britain and North America, and the structures of professional Englit."

It is here that Sinfield engages with some of the major distinctions between the cultural materialist enterprise and that that of its American cousin, new historicism. Certainly much more is involved than the simple possibility (stated here tongue-in-cheek) that a professionalized notion of literary research now prevails in the United States whereas in Britain there remain residual, amateur concerns with "the question of what it is all for." After all, both new historicism and cultural matrialism maintain an abiding interest in those moments when an ideological veil seems momentarily to slip, to reveal uglier and contradictory possibilities boiling away beneath the surface. But where new historicism seems content finally to regard such lapses almost as safety-valves, or stratagems endorsed by an authority whose ultimate aim is containment and the preservation of a status quo, cultural materialism persists in seeing in them and in their careful explication the potential for genuine revolutionary enquiry and perhaps change.

And there's the rub. At his most pessimistic, Sinfield offers us a new historicism shackled to a North American academy which, itself ruthlessly marginalized, effectively conspires to muzzle the scholars to whom it seems to offer a platform. The new historicists' obsession with potential "entrapment" by an authority that seems to them to lurk within every ideological lapse perhaps springs from a deep-seated sense of their own betrayal. Unable effectively to intervene in the society that gives them house-room, they end by sharing the suspicions and frustrations of their generation: one for whom Woodstock might well appear as a sophisticated stratagem of containment entirely similar in its "carnival-festival" role to those which characterize state policies from the early modern period on.

On the other hand, cultural materialists, whose—largely British—institutions have yet (perhaps) to be so marginalized, feel correspondingly less shackled and less betrayed. However, it's also true that British academic life, operating within a still-powerful classstructure, detaches its participants from prior, alternative, subcultural allegiances, and encourages the abandonment of older loyalties. Much of Raymond Williams's work focuses on this culture of deracination and its political consequences: his finest novel, *Border Country*, takes that as its central concern. In arguing that we should retain those affiliations, and should even make them the basis of a new materialist stance, Sinfield finally calls for what, in British terms, would be a social and political realignment of almost heroic proportions. That its model, and indeed its major inspiration, derives form a kind of literary analysis attests to the energy that cultural materialism is capable of harnessing.

The question that energy will address is ultimately one of power and empowerment. It is appropriate that Sinfield's book finally comes to dwell on such matters since the major contribution of both cultural materialism and new historicism clearly lies in a number of judgments both schools have reached concerning the workings of political structures. Significant amongst them is the conclusion that whether it is being reinforced or interrogated, any power that shows itself to be susceptible to either operation can never, by that fact, have been totally embracing or entirely dominant. Power is never a seamless garment, and it can only partly cover the body politic. Resistance to it is therefore always theoretically and usually practically possible, even inevitable, and indeed is obviously presupposed by the very existence of strategies of containment.

A text's interrogation of power will in turn require it both to draw upon and adjust its own resources to match whatever forms of subjection it encounters. The early modern drama's own inherited practice of gender cross-dressing, and indeed the broad nature of its art at large, which required commoners to dress as nobility, even royalty, was bound systematically to conflict with existing modes of enforcing gender and class distinctions. The drama's very presentation of these distinctions as alterable, and so the product of culture, rather than unchangeable, and so the result of God's will, or nature, brought them into question and, ultimately, to the point of crisis. The drama thus found itself inescapably engaged with political domination in a material form and, as a result, could hardly avoid questioning its authority.

A historicist criticism capable of recognizing the complexities of this kind of contestation of meaning both in the past and in the present, cannot and does not, unlike traditional criticism, pretend to be politically neutral. This, perhaps, most clearly marks the final distinction between new historicism and cultural materialism. For the latter, as Sinfield insists, the recognition that all cultural practices have a political dimension must bring with it the implication that this principle finally applies to literary criticism itself. Committed to the study of the involvement of literary texts in material history, that is, to a politics of reading, cultural materialism is thus ultimately obliged to challenge a social order whose politics it rejects. In consequence, it cannot but see its own culture as an arena, a site of struggle where, in the name of this obligation, battle must be joined. The conflict evidently continues. To some, *Faultlines* — may rank as one of the more strident bugle calls to rise above the melee. But when Royal Ordnance commands the field, perhaps it needs to be.

Shakespeare the Actor and the Purposes of Playing. By Meredith Anne Skura. Chicago and London: University of Chicago Press, 1993.

Reviewer: Lois Potter

Meredith Skura has a good story to tell. The hero is Shakespeare. He has the kind of background which traditionally makes an actor: an absent or inadequate father and a dominant mother—at least, a mother who had lost two daughters shortly before he was born and who perhaps secretly wanted a child in her own image. Thanks to these pressures and his own exceptional sensitivity to them, he develops a life-long habit of self-denial—and of dramatizing that self-denial; an ability to occupy multiple viewpoints; a few of commitment to the active experience of loving, and a remarkable willingness to make himself contemptible or ridiculous in order to be loved and applauded.

When he creates actor-type characters in his plays, he replicates versions of this life experience. So Richard III, whose mother has rejected him perhaps simply because his monstrosity was "maleness misunderstood" (68), needs to win Lady Anne for reasons that have nothing to do with political advantage (this is essentially the interpretation that Ian McKellen so memorably embodied in the 1991 National Theatre production). On the other hand, Bottom, who is adopted by a nurturing substitute mother, the fairy queen, has a flexibility that makes him willing to play all the parts, male and female. Falstaff, in a nightmare reversal of this situation, rejects the fairy queen, Doll Tearsheet (is Skura confusing her with Jonson's Doll Common, the real fairy queen impersonator?), and, in

Merry Wives, meets another fairy queen who creates a rival performance to mock him.

Like modern actors, who create a substitute authority figure in the director, Shakespeare and many of his characters project their longing for the missing paternal authority onto an aristocratic patron: the Lord in The Taming of the Shrew; Theseus; Navarre, with whom Armado fantasizes himself to have an intimate relationship; Hamlet; Prince Hal; the recipient of the Sonnets. The reality of the situation—the actors are beggars, not friends—is hinted at in several references to the ballad of the Beggar and the King and epitomized in the act of kneeling (like the speaker of the Epilogue to 2 Henry IV). Actors also project their fears of rejection onto the audience surrounding them, seen as the dogs that bait the bear or hunt down Acteon, the crowd mocking Jesus Christ in the passion play, or the suffocating mother in her most terrifying form. Since the lord, being an aristocrat, is also identified with the hunter, the actor is thus caught in an ambivalent relationship with those he seeks to please: "We cannot help running with the hare when we hunt with the hounds" (28). Falstaff at the end of Merry Wives is perhaps the epitome of the unsuccessful actor. Parolles and Patroclus are still more disturbing: given to mindless mimicry and suspected of homoerotic designs on his aristocratic patron, each embodies the worst accusations that had been leveled at the whole profession. The theater also has a therapeutic side: Hamlet and Edgar escape into it. But, at least in Edgar's case, this escape is also part of the pattern that Stanley Cavell has made famous as "the avoidance of love." The self-abnegating Antonios of Merchant and Twelfth Night are Christ-figures manqué, longing to display their wounds and receive recognition for playing their role.

It is characteristic of our age that the same careful analysis of imagery which led Caroline Spurgeon to detect a well-balanced and healthy Shakespeare who loved the open air has, in Skura's hands, come up instead with this complex neurotic. Returning to the famous dog-candy-melting image cluster, she complicates it, showing that the dogs evoke hunting, while the melting is part of a configuration of glass-sun-mirrors: Shakespeare did not just hate flattery, as Spurgeon thought—he also recognized the flatterer as the mirror of his own relation to his audience. It is this analysis of the attraction of the victim's role—very much a message for our time—that differentiates Skura's approach from the analysis of the family by Barber and Wheeler in The Whole Journey (Berkeley and Los Angeles: University of California Press, 1986), though they too find "an exceptional capacity in Shakespeare for identification with women" (7). They are aware of one aspect of Shakespeare's professional life, as they show in their comment on *Timon of Athens*:

> Timon, in his giving himself to his countrymen, in involving himself in the lives of others, is in a sense like Shakespeare creating parts for his whole company, sharing in a brotherly enterprise for which he provides the words, the nurturant substance. (305)

By way of comparison, one might take Skura's comment on Shakespeare the actor, whose plays

> suggest not only that princes—Elizabeth as well as Richard II—are like actors, but also that an actor can feel like a prince when he pleases the audience and like a savaged god when he doesn't. We have considered that it was Shakespeare's play which prompted Queen Elizabeth to say, 'I am Richard II.' But we tend to forget the significance—wider than we may so far have guessed—of the player who also said, 'I am Richard II.' (169)

I should have liked to quote more: Skura's book is as enjoyable to read as a novel, which, in a way, it is. It is obviously not for anyone who feels that the whole argument is vitiated by our inability ever to know what Shakespeare's mother and father were "really" like. But it is about two great topics, acting and Shakespeare, and it creates a consistent and compelling world on the basis of its reading of the plays. If the opening chapter, a brief and rather superficial look at the early lives of some actors, makes it sound as if they all have the same basic personality, by the end of the book I suspect that most readers will feel that the book is really about them. Academics, like actors, are instinctively led to professions where flexibility and creativity are highly valued, while aggression and authority are usually masked.

Unfortunately, the book badly needed at least one authority figure of its own: a painstaking copyeditor. The absence of acknowledgements to anyone at the University of Chicago Press presumably means that this is yet another of the presses that now expect the author to do all the editorial work. Authors are still learning what this means in terms of the time they must be prepared to spend in the latter stages of a book. Perhaps just one more careful reading would have made a great difference. There is repetition of the same material from one page to another (sometimes even the next page), as well as between text and footnotes; there are confusions of name:

"the shrewish Aemilia in *Comedy of Errors*" (264, n.3), "Edward [IV]'s proposal to Lady Jane" (69), a line of Cassius attributed to Brutus (210), misinterpreted lines ("the disgrace of death" in *Love's Labor's Lost* [quoted on 89] means exactly the opposite of the line with which it is paired, "death's dishonorable victory" in *1 Henry VI*; other lines, like "a soldier is better accommodated than with a wife" (*2 Henry IV* 3.2) correctly interpreted but quoted in the wrong context. Names are too often mispelled, and sometimes I even got the feeling that the author was working from old notes. These are maddening and unnecessary blemishes in a work that is genuinely exciting and thought-provoking.

I don't wish to end on that note, but with a suggestion. It's a pity that Skura doesn't extend her approach to non-Shakespearean material, or at least to Shakespeare's collaborations. As someone who is currently completing an edition of *The Two Noble Kinsmen*, I can see how perfectly it would fit the paradigms described in her book. Hunting is central to the plot, for example; it is full of the glass-sun-mirror image clusters that she discusses so interestingly, not to mention twins, Narcissus, some highly Freudian language, and even a doctor who prescribes sex as therapy. The fact that some of this language can be confidently attributed to John Fletcher, Shakespeare's co-author, seems to me all the more reason to extend the approach to him. We have a large body of material, collaborative and noncollaborative, on which to base a psychoanalytic study of this writer. We also know more about his childhood than we do about Shakespeare's, and when it comes to strong mothers, inadequate fathers, and an awful adolescence, he can probably beat Shakespeare any day. He came originally from the class that patronized actors (or preached against them), not the class form which actors themselves usually came. But his family was plunged into poverty through the death of his father (through chain-smoking, according to one story) immediately after the latter had fallen out of favor with Queen Elizabeth I because of his second marriage. This sounds like the classic background for the passive aggressive type and, by all accounts, Fletcher was at least as "gentle," in both senses, as Shakespeare is supposed to have been. Their collaboration must have been a case of the resistible force meeting the moveable object. Considering that the human psyche is itself a collaborative work, I don't see why it can't be studied in a collaborative play.

Appropriating Shakespeare: Contemporary Critical Quarrels. By Brian Vickers. New Haven: Yale University Press, 1993.

Reviewer: **Robert S. Miola**

Astonishingly learned and fiercely argumentative, this is a book of major importance. It is not primarily about Shakespeare, announcing no revelations about sources, texts, contexts, productions, or the like; instead, it is about Shakespeare studies today, particularly those grounded in Current Literary Theory, Vickers's contemptuous term, for the contradictory complex of attitudes and assumptions deriving from that now canonized group of intellectuals: Lévi-Strauss, Lacan, Barthes, Althusser, Foucault, and Derrida. Associated with structuralism and poststructuralism, this group rejected several traditional principles of philosophy and criticism: "the notion of a subject or individual producing language and making sense of the world by a free, intentional act; the notion of an author as the originator of a literary work; the idea of language as a medium by which human beings reliably communicate with each other (despite misunderstandings, which can usually be overcome); the notion that an argument, or larger systems of thought, should be built up on coherent reasoning, citing evidence; the sense of history as having been made by human actors in a sequence of actions and reactions which can be chronicled and interpreted by language but remain independent of it" (xii). Vickers offers a historical description and critique of this iconoclastic movement and these principles; then he analyzes the assimilation of the movement into literary studies, dividing his targets into separate schools—deconstructionist, new historicist, psychoanalytical, feminist, Christian, Marxist. With wide erudition and clear reasoning, Vickers demonstrates how confused and self-contradictory is much contemporary critical writing, ignorant of its primary sources (normally cited, in translation), uncritical of its assumptions and their implications. Time and again, he notes with trenchant irony how contemporary criticism proclaims independence from received traditions only to become enslaved to newer orthodoxies, falling into predictable stances and routines, systematizing various and complex literary experiences into turgid prose with mind-numbing monotony.

The book begins with a dense and illuminating discussion of Saussure, Lévi-Strauss, Lacan, Barthes, Foucault, and Derrida. Assembling these diverse figures under the rubric "The Diminution of Language," Vickers examines the original texts in the original languages and reviews them in light of current philosophical and linguistic thinking. The rigor of his mind and method earn serious attention. The discussion of Saussure, for example, pays due respect to the linguist's brilliance but observes that the seminal *Cours de linguistique générale* derives from copious notes taken by students from three lecture courses, that the editors who published the book drastically rearranged these notes, adding and compressing material, that some editions do not use all the manuscript material available, and that the standard English translation is misleading. This by way of prefatory admonition to those innocents who cite Saussure (and other European authors) without knowing the original languages and primary sources. Analyzing further, Vickers notes Saussure's unreconciled claims for language as self-contained and for its inherently social nature as the interplay between *langue* and *parole*. Drawing on diverse scholars like Clark, Timpanaro, Harris, and Holdcroft, who have contributed devastating critiques, Vickers traces the fragmentation of Saussure's ideas in later theories: on the one hand, in Foucault's denial of individual meaning, his dispersal of the subject into discontinuity, and, on the other, in Derrida's perception of discontinuity not in the subject but in discourse itself, in the gaps, uncertainties, and deferrals that make language radically unstable. With a sharp sword, Vickers has at such large claims, exposing their ignorance of empirical evidence, their oversimplification of complex ideas and traditions, their logical fallacies and inconsistencies, their facile dichotomies that privilege one pole and dismiss the other, their self-congratulatory exclusionism, and their expression in self-referential jargon and evocative but empty metaphor. Against them and the fashionably "free play of the signifier," in the formidable company of recent child psychologists, semanticists, comparative linguists, and philosophers of language, he boldly proposes the countertheory—namely, that language is intentional and communicates meaning.

This is not a book against theory but against the uncritical acceptance of fashionable attitudes. Once one looks beyond the outmoded 60s French connection, Vickers argues, one can find fascinating theoretical possibilities. The vogue for post-structuralism faded in France in the '70s, replaced by "nouvelle philosophie," a resurgence of interest in Kant, a revival of phenomenology, and hermenuetics. Why haven't these areas been explored? More recently, fields like the philosophy of art, speech-act theory, and discourse analysis have opened up interesting possibilities for literary criticism. (Vickers uses speech-act theory for an analysis of Othello, by way of demonstration.) The point here is that literary critics need to take theory more, not less, seriously, to subject it to serious skepticism, to pay attention to the advances that have been made in the last thirty years. They also, Vickers declares, need to use common sense. Can individual authors continue to trumpet the death of other authors, replacing them with anthropomorphized texts that validate preconceived ideologies? Can we continue to entertain the notion of a radically incoherent text, impossible of interpretation, when this notion runs counter to both the cognitive and affective experience of writing and reading?

The second and longer part of the book devotes itself to current critical practices. Vickers takes aim at deconstruction, first, at theorists like Derrida and De Man, and then at various well-known Shakespearean practitioners, among them Hawkes on Bradley, Miller on *Troilus and Cressida*, Felperin on *The Winter's Tale*, and Evans on the comedies. He deplores in such work the uncritical acceptance of poststructuralist cliché, the ignorance (intentional or not) of some twenty or more serious critiques of deconstruction, written from a wide variety of fields and approaches. Simply put, Vickers argues, deconstruction mechanically flattens and reduces dramatic experience to linguistic indeterminacy. It cannot cope with drama as interaction between characters with clear goals and values; it cannot address performance, neither the actor's art nor the audience's reaction. The influential movement known as new historicism, as practiced by Montrose, Greenblatt, and Goldberg, shows different but equally serious defects. Vickers subjects Greenblatt's celebrated essays—"Fiction and Friction," "Shakespeare and the Exorcists," "Learning to Curse," "Invisible Bullets," and others—to thorough examination. Throughout, he finds carelessness in the use of sources, a partial and selective use of evidence under the guise of anecdote, a disregard for context, the old fallacy of biographical criticism, the ascription of political motives to Shakespeare outside the plays themselves—all served up in a mesmerizing, overtly politicized prose. Greenblatt's inaccuracies have been noted before, but the analysis here has a cumulative effect. Even if one sides with him against Vickers on a particular point or essay (as I do on "Learning to Curse," which has opened up exciting vistas on *The Tempest*), one cannot easily overlook outright omissions and distortions. The analysis of "Invisible Bullets," for example, proceeding by a review of Harriot's original text and context, seriously undermines this seminal essay and its methods.

Vickers next turns to two allied schools of criticism—psychocriticism and feminism. Both subscribe to a kind of essentialism, assuming that all characters of all times and places, even fictional ones, exhibit the same neuroses. Focusing on the overlooked or the marginal, relying on free associative play instead of literary context, splitting characters into constituent selves to be freely identified with other characters, psychocritics confidently diagnose sexual dysfunctions and generalize about the cultures that produce them. The problems in method are compounded by the specific choice of Freud as high priest of the hidden mysteries; for a substantial body of scholarship (Vickers provides a dozen or more references) proves him sham as well as shaman, documenting his unacknowledged indebtedness to predecessors like Fliess, his misleading accounts of cures, glaring omissions of information, his projection of theory onto individual cases. Psychocritics, of course, can make up their own minds about such issues, but they ought at least to be aware of them and the controversy. Feminists have made more substantial contributions than the other schools, according to Vickers, who appreciates, for example, the work of Neely and Woodbridge. Yet, even at this late date feminist critics adopt the crudest gender stereotypes, i.e., woman as good, nurturing, creating, flexible, life-giving, man as power-mad, lusty, fearful, destructive, inflexible, and lethal. Moreover, too many easily assume that literature provides raw material for sociohistorical analysis and too many adopt Lawrence Stone as intellectual patriarch. Few seem aware that male and female historians have assembled a substantial (Vickers, indeed, thinks "unanswerable" [333]) case against Stone. Again, at the very least, critics who follow a leader ought to show some awareness of his demonstrated and alleged deficiencies.

Vickers next castigates Christian and Marxist critics, interpreters who ignore "theatrical experience, dramatic structure, aesthetic properties" (373), who subordinate action to preconceived paradigms, and who reduce characters to representatives. In my view, Christian interpreters, however, do not play a significant role in contemporary critical quarrels; the argument would have been better served had it focused on Marxists and cultural materialists, instead of dismissing the latter group as a minor and eccentric variation of the former. Turning to Marxists, Vickers goes on to criticize Weimann, Althusser, Macherey, and Jameson, again drawing on an impressive range of primary and secondary materials, again protesting the reduction of complex interactions to simply-conceived models, in this case, a two-level system featuring the dominant versus a subordinate ideology.

Appropriating Shakespeare is a learned, well-argued study that sharply challenges the orthodoxies regnant in professional conferences, graduate schools, some leading journals, and university presses. It forcefully argues the contrary case, demanding a fair hearing for the other side, denouncing the cloying self-righteousness of Current Literary Theory as so much blather. (Teaching at a school where two-thirds of the students spend significant time working with the aged, the handicapped, the poor, volunteering time to soup kitchens, at orphanages and the like, I have always found suspect the moral pretensions of literary critics.) Yet, it is a pity that Vickers, who knows well the Ciceronian dictum defining the duty of an orator, *dicere ad persuadendum accommodate,* "to speak in a style fitted to convince," chose to present his arguments in a tone of high outrage; the rhetoric will offend many readers, who will simply dismiss the writer as an arrogant patrician. Moreover, the frequent appeals to the educated reader or playgoer are, at times, unnecessarily prescriptive; and Vickers's own interpretations of Shakespeare seem intended to close off discussion, to settle matters once and for all rather than to invite the consideration of respected colleagues. (They are, by the way, the least interesting parts of the book.) Not destined to persuade everyone, or perhaps even many of its adversaries, *Appropriating Shakespeare* still may have three salutary effects on the field: 1) It puts into circulation an enormous bibliography of pertinent material, drawn from various disciplines, that can spark discussion and reconsideration of accepted beliefs. 2) The book makes a strong case for the study of languages, philosophy, history, and linguistics as opposed to the currently fashionable reliance on technique, translations, and the uncritical adoption of a template or master-thinker. 3) The book invites serious consideration of aesthetics, a subject now maligned, ignored, and marginalized. It is an impressive achievement.

Index

Adams, Clement, 45
Adelman, Janet, 92n, 93n, 95n, 96n, 99n, 177n, 206n, 236
Aesop, 132
Afer, Publius Terentius, 117n
Alberti, Leon Battista, 46, 50, 52, 54, 60
Alexander VI, Pope, 40
Allen, William, 175
Alpers, Paul, 177n
Althusser, Louis, 233, 284, 288
Amussen, Susan Dwyer, 194, 201, 203, 205, 206n, 207n
Annesley, Brian, 175
Arden of Faversham, 268–75
Aristotle, 126, 131, 132, 136
Armin, Robert, 21
Ascham, Roger, 106, 118n
Auerbach, Erich, 179n
Augustine, St., 212, 220

Bachelard, Gaston, 105
Bacon, Francis, 158, 179n
Bakhtin, M. M., 214
Baldwin, T. W., 106, 109, 118n
Barber, C. L., 147, 177n, 281
Barber, Peter, 69n
Barish, Jonas A., 178n
Barker, Francis, 99n, 122, 124, 125, 141n, 142n, 143n, 179n, 225–29
Barthes, Roland, 284, 285
Barton, Anne, 260
Baudrillard, Jean, 225
Behn, Aphra, 243, 244, 262, 263–64, 265
Belsey, Catherine, 179n
Benevenuto, Bice, 221n
Benjamin, Walter, 110, 119n, 225, 226
Berger, Harry, Jr., 177n
Binns, J. W., 106
Boas, Frederick, 114, 119n
Boccacio, 24, 25
Bodin, Jean, 187
Boose, Lynda, 243, 244, 245

Booth, Stephen, 94n, 98n, 177n, 184n
Borch-Jacobsen, Mikkel, 92n
Bordwell, Percy, 179n
Bourdieu, Pierre, 151, 152, 180n, 233
Braden, Gordon, 130, 131, 144n
Bradley, A. C., 176n, 238, 264, 286
Brecht, Bertolt, 239
Breight, Curt, 121, 124, 141n, 142n, 144n
Brennan, Teresa, 61
Brooke, Nicholas, 235
Brown, Laura, 242, 244, 245, 246
Brown, Lloyd, 57
Brown, Paul, 121–22, 124, 141n, 142n, 144n
Brundage, James A., 209n
Brunelleschi, Filippo, 46
Brydall, John, 193, 202, 207n
Brydon, Diana, 265, 266
Bullough, Geoffrey, 116n
Burckhardt, Jacob, 179n
Burckhardt, Sigurd, 178n
Burke, Kenneth, 177n
Burton, Robert, 92n
Butler, Martin, 260, 261

Cabot, Sebastian, 45
Calderwood, James, 98n, 178n
Callahan, Dympna, 242, 244, 266, 267
Carroll, William C., 177n
Cartelli, Thomas, 121, 125, 141n, 142n, 143n, 144n
Cary, Elizabeth, 244
Castiglione, Baldessar, 257
Cavell, Stanley, 84, 96n, 165, 177n, 184n, 282
Cecil, William, 177n
Charnes, Linda, 229–36
Chaucer, Geoffrey, 24, 25
Cheney, Thomas, 271
Chettle, Henry, 37n
Cheyfitz, Eric, 122, 141n, 142n
Chudleigh's Case, 149, 158, 179n

Cicero, 126, 127, 131, 132, 135, 136, 139, 143 n, 144 n, 145 n, 288
Clark, Simon, 285
Cobler of Canterbury, 24–26, 28, 33
Coddon, Karin S., 94 n
Cohen, Walter, 258, 260
Coke, Edward, 155, 158, 179 n, 182 n
Coleridge, Samuel Taylor, 171, 180 n, 184 n, 275
Colie, Rosalie, 176 n
Collinson, Patrick, 253
Columbus, Christopher, 40
Cook, Ann Jennalie, 132, 144 n
Crashaw, Richard, 95 n
Cromwell, Oliver, 251
Cutts, John, 142 n

Danson, Lawrence, 178 n
Dante, 23
da Vinci, Leonardo, 215, 221 n
Davis, John, 39, 43
Davis, Natalie, 246
de Dinteville, Jean, 54
Dee, John, 39, 46, 48, 56
Defoe, Daniel, 244, 245, 246
Dekker, Thomas, 249, 250, 260
Delany, Paul, 178 n
de Man, Paul, 286
Derrida, Jacques, 229, 284, 285, 286
Decartes, Rene, 39
de Selve, George, 54
Dickens, Charles, 128
Dinesen, Isak, 265
Dolan, Frances, 269
Dollimore, Jonathan, 147, 149, 150, 178 n, 184 n, 208 n
Donne, John, 33
Drabble, Margaret, 266
Drake, Francis, 43, 46, 47, 48
Dudley, Robert, 255
Dusinberre, Juliet, 119 n
Dyer, Chief Justice, 158, 181 n
Dyer, Richard, 36 n

Eagleton, Terry, 206 n
Eden, Richard, 48
Edgerton, Samuel, 46, 68 n
Elaide, Mircea, 91 n
Eliot, T. S., 71, 132, 144 n, 275
Ellis, Henry, 35 n
Elton, William R., 144 n
Elyot, Thomas, 126, 132, 134, 136, 137, 138, 143 n, 144 n, 145 n

Elizabeth I, 34, 47, 54, 183 n, 228, 251–57, 283
Empson, William, 176 n
Engle, Lars, 96 n
Epicetus, 139, 145 n
Erasmus, 92 n, 111, 132
Erickson, Peter, 95 n, 188, 205 n, 263
Erlich, Avi, 93 n, 94 n, 95 n, 96 n
Euclid, 46
Evans-Pritchard, E. E., 129
Everest, George, 68
Everett, Barbara, 177 n

Faucit, Helen, 264
Felperin, Howard, 286
Ferguson, Margaret, 91 n, 98 n, 243, 244, 246, 262, 263–64, 265
Fineman, Joel, 97 n, 179 n
Fitzwilliam's Case, 158
Fletcher, John, 258, 260, 283
Florio, John, 125–26
Foakes, R. A., 237–41
Foucault, 120, 178 n, 190, 229, 284, 285
Foxe, John, 260
Freccero, Carla, 247
French, Marilyn, 91 n
Freud, Sigmund, 92 n, 94 n, 97 n, 140, 173, 190, 207 n, 287
Frowike, Chief Justice, 157
Frye, Northrup, 176 n
Frye, Susan, 184 n, 251–57
Fuller, Thomas, 33–34
Fumerton, Patricia, 179 n

Garber, Marjorie, 90 n
Gascoigne, George, 101, 102, 108, 117 n
Geertz, Clifford, 226
Girard, René, 96 n
Goddard, Harold C., 177 n
Goethe, Johann, 91 n
Goldberg, Jonathan, 69 n, 179 n, 286
Golding, Arthur, 132
Gomez, Lefty, 254
Goodman, Lizbeth, 266
Graham, Kenneth J. E., 178 n
Greenblatt, Stephen, 54, 69 n, 120, 122, 140, 141 n, 147, 149, 150, 177 n, 178 n, 183 n, 226, 228, 286
Greene, Robert, 37 n
Greenhut, Deborah, 114, 119 n
Grice, H. P., 259
Grinstein Alexander, 96 n
Gronovious, J. F., 132

Index

Habermas, Jurgen, 128, 130, 143 n
Hakluyt, Richard, 39, 43, 48, 53
Hall, Joseph, 35, 126, 138, 145 n
Hall, Kim, 243
Hamer, Mary, 70 n
Hankey, Julie, 264
Hansby, Ralph, 175
Hanson, Elizabeth, 179 n
Harriot, Thomas, 287
Harvey, Gabriel, 22, 36 n, 37 n
Hawkes, Terrence, 68 n, 286
Hazlitt, William, 275
Hedrick, Donald, 118 n
Hegel, G. W. F., 229
Heidegger, Martin, 151, 152, 178 n, 180
Heilbrun, Carolyn, 91 n
Heilman, Robert B., 177 n
Heinemann, Margot, 260
Helgerson, Richard, 36 n, 70 n, 268–75
Henderson, Katherine Usher, 188
Hendricks, Margo, 241–47
Henrietta Maria, 261
Henry III, 191, 197
Henry VII, 230
Henry VIII, 45, 252
Heywood, Thomas, 244, 245, 272
Hill, Christopher, 253
Hobbes, Thomas, 225, 226
Holbein, Hans, 39, 50, 54, 62
Holdcroft, David, 285
Holland, Norman, 99 n
Homer, 112, 113
Hope, Jonathan, 257–61
Horace, 100
Hosley, Richard, 119 n
Howard, Jean, 242, 247–51
Howard, Thomas, 114
Howell, Thomas Bayly, 184 n
Hulme, Peter, 70 n, 122, 124, 125, 141 n, 142 n, 143 n
Hurston, Zora Neale, 262, 265
Hyde, Lewis, 129, 143 n

Ingram, Martin, 207 n

Jaffa, Harry V., 178 n, 182 n
James I, 126, 132, 135, 136, 143 n, 144 n, 228, 252, 253–54
Jameson, Fredric, 288
Jed, Stephanie, 243
Jones, Ann Rosalind, 179 n
Jones, Ernest, 90 n, 95 n

Jones, Norman, 253
Jonson, Ben, 260, 261
Jung, Carl, 140

Kahn, Coppélia, 83, 95 n, 177 n, 206 n
Kant, Immanuel, 131, 167, 286
Kelly, Joan, 187, 192, 207 n
Kelso, Ruth, 130, 131, 143 n, 144 n
Kempe, William, 21
Kenilworth, 256
Kennedy, Roger, 221 n
Kermode, Frank, 143 n
Kernan, Alvin B., 177 n
Kerrigan, William, 130, 144 n
Kind Harts Dreame, 28, 29, 30
King, Barry, 27, 37 n
Knight, G. Wilson, 275
Knights, L. C., 177 n
Knox, John, 252
Kristeller, Paul Oskar, 144 n
Kwakiutl society, 130

Lacan, Jacques, 39, 41, 50, 51, 52, 54, 58, 61, 92 n, 211, 229, 233, 284, 285
Lamming, George, 265
Laqueur, Thomas, 206 n
Laslett, Peter, 127, 143 n, 203, 209 n
Latini, Brunetto, 131
Lee, Judith, 265
Legate, John, 102
Leicester, Earl of, 256
Leininger, Lori, 121, 125, 141 n, 143 n, 144 n
L'Estrange, Roger, 132
Leverenz, David, 91 n
Levin, Richard, 143 n
Levin, David, 208 n
Lévi-Strauss, Claude, 284, 285
Lewis, Cynthia, 199, 208 n
Linville, Susan E., 185 n
Lipsius, Justus, 132
Littlewood, Joan, 267
Lodge, Thomas, 132
Longstreth, Sven, 128, 143 n
Loomba, Ania, 246, 265, 267
Lupton, Julia Reinhard, 93 n
Lupton, Kenneth, 93 n
Lyotard, Jean, 225

MacCaffrey, Wallace T., 251–57
MacDonald, Joyce Green, 266
Macfarlane, Alan, 194, 195, 202, 207 n, 209 n

Macherey, Pierre, 227, 288
Mack, Maynard, 171, 185 n
Macluskie, Kathleen, 187, 205 n, 260
Maguire, Nancy Klein, 258
Maitland, F. W., 198
Manning's Case, 158
Marcus, Leah, 228
Marlowe, Christopher, 42, 48, 276
Marx, Karl, 127, 128 143 n
Maus, Katharine Eisaman, 179 n
Mauss, Marcel, 129, 143 n
McFarland, Thomas, 177 n
McKellen, Ian, 280
McManus, Barbara F., 188
McMullan, Gordon, 257–61
McQuail, Dinis, 36 n
Meir, Golda, 257
Merleau-Ponty, Maurice, 180 n
Mercator, Gerard, 39, 42–43, 45, 47, 50, 53, 54, 57, 65
Mildmay's Case, 158
Milton, John, 225, 226
Miseries of an Enforced Marriage, 274
Mohanty, S. P., 268
Montaigne, 125, 126, 132, 139, 141 n, 143 n, 145 n, 259
Montrose, Louis, 120, 286
Morris, Brian, 116 n, 119 n
Morrison, Toni, 265
Muir, Kenneth, 182 n
Mullaney, Steven, 98 n, 120, 140

Namjoshi, Sarah, 266
Nashe, Thomas, 34, 35
Naylor, Gloria, 265
Neale, John, 251, 253
Neely, Carol Thomas, 98 n, 287
Nevo, Ruth, 177 n
Newman, Karen, 119 n
Nietzche, Friedrich, 102, 225, 229
Norbrook, David, 259, 260
Norden, John, 56, 61
North, Edward, 270
Novy, Marianne L., 103, 117 n, 147, 149, 150, 178 n, 184 n, 261–68
Nussbaum, Felicity, 244, 245

Oliver, H. J., 110, 118 n, 119 n
Ong, Walter J., 106, 118 n
On the Privileges of Parliament, 33
Orgel, Stephen, 122, 125, 141 n, 142 n, 143 n

Orlin, Lena Cowen, 104, 117 n, 118 n, 268–75
Ortelius, Abraham, 39, 42, 66
Orwell, George, 177 n
Ovid, 100, 101, 109, 111–15

Pace, Richard, 118 n
Pagnol, Marcel, 90 n
Pandit, Lalita, 99 n
Parker, Patricia, 91 n, 92 n, 94 n, 96 n, 118 n, 230, 241–47
Pascal, 39
Patterson, Annabel, 228, 257
Peacham, Henry, 132, 144 n
Pearson, D'Orsay, 143 n
Peat, Derek, 177 n
Pechter, Edward, 143 n
Philip, Ranjini, 93 n
Phillipi, Patricia, 118 n
Plato, 131, 132, 135, 140
Plowden, Edmund, 184 n
Plutarch, 132
Pocock, J. G. A., 150, 151, 153, 180 n, 181 n
Polyani, Karl, 128, 129, 143 n
Ponet, John, 271
Popham, Chief Justice, 149
Porter, Carolyn, 120, 121, 140 n
Potter, Lois, 259
Prosser, Eleanor, 125, 132, 143 n
Prynne, William, 119 n
Ptolemy, 43, 45, 46, 47, 52, 54

Queen Elizabeth's Men, 19, 21

Rabasa, José, 57
Raleigh, Walter, 47
Rambuss, Richard, 95 n
Read, Conyers, 251
Richardson, Samuel, 245, 246
Riefer, Marcia, 203, 209 n
Roberts, Jeanne Addison, 117 n
Roche, Thomas P., Jr., 177 n
Rorty, Amélie Oksenberg, 178 n
Rose, Jacqueline, 71
Rosenberg, Marvin, 90 n
Rozett, Martha Tuck, 264

Sahlins, Marshall, 129, 143 n
Saint German, Christopher, 181 n, 185 n
Salter, Katherine, 191
Saussure, Ferdinand, 285

Index

Saxton, Christopher, 55
Schanzer, Ernest, 207n, 208n
Schiesari, Juliana, 93n, 94n, 243
Scott, Margaret, 195, 207n
Scottowe, John, 35n, 36n
Seaton, Ethel, 42
Sedgwick, Eve, 262
Seneca, 126, 127, 129, 131, 132, 133, 134, 135, 136, 139, 143n, 144n, 145n
Seronsy, Cecil C., 119n
Shakespeare, William, 21, 36n, 127, 131, 132, 149, 158–59, 162, 164, 170, 172, 183n, 258, 262, 275, 276, 280–83
Shakespeare, William (plays): *All's Well That Ends Well*, 190, 194, 195; *Antony and Cleopatra*, 56, 57, 59–60, 64, 192–93, 230, 232, 234, 235; *As You Like It*, 250; *Comedy of Errors*, 283; *Coriolanus*, 60, 61, 133; *Cymbeline*, 51, 52, 53, 55, 61, 196; *Hamlet*, 71–99, 160, 227, 237–41, 264–65, 267, 282; *1 Henry IV*, 41, 58, 133, 281, 283; *2 Henry IV*, 58, 66; *Henry V*, 61, 66–67, 101, 276; *1 Henry VI*, 55; *Julius Caesar*, 49, 54–55, 59, 276, 283; *King John*, 47, 62–64, 65, 70n; *King Lear*, 40, 42, 48, 51, 52, 60, 133, 146–47, 148, 149, 150, 157, 158–76, 194, 227, 237–41; *Love's Labours Lost*, 281, 283; *Macbeth*, 133, 227, 276; *Measure for Measure*, 187–209; *Merchant of Venice*, 132, 250, 282; *Merry Wives of Windsor*, 101, 106, 281; *Midsummer Night's Dream*, 56, 195, 281; *Much Ado About Nothing*, 188, 249; *Othello*, 48, 129, 133, 193–94, 247, 264, 273–74, 286; *Richard II*, 48, 49, 58; *Richard III*, 55, 80, 230, 231, 234, 280; *Romeo and Juliet*, 191, 194, 195; *Taming of the Shrew*, 100–119, 192, 195, 266, 281; *Tempest*, 56, 120–25, 127, 133, 134–35, 136, 137, 138, 139, 140, 265, 266, 267, 287; *Timon of Athens*, 133, 282; *Titus Andronicus*, 100, 228, 229, 266; *Troilus and Cressida*, 190, 230, 231, 234, 286; *Twelfth Night*, 43, 45, 250; *Two Noble Kinsmen*, 259, 283; *Winter's Tale*, 286
Shakespeare, William (poems): *Rape of Lucrece*, 210–21; Sonnets, 85, 282

Shanker, Sidney, 177n
Sheen, Erica, 259
Showalter, Elaine, 94n
Shudofsky, Maurice M., 90n
Sidney, Philip, 38n, 249, 276
Simonini, R. C., Jr., 105, 118n
Simpson, A. W. B., 179n
Sinfield, Alan, 275–80
Singh, Jyotsna, 246
Sisson, Charles Jasper, 185n
Skelton, R. A., 65
Skinner, Quentin, 259
Skura, Meredith Anne, 140n, 280–83
Sommerville, J. P., 180
Speed, John, 66
Spurgeon, Carolyn, 281
Stallybrass, Peter, 179n, 208n, 214, 221n
Stanhope's Case, 158
Statute of Uses, 157–58
Steinmo, Frank, 128
Stern, Daniel N., 180
Stolcke, Verena, 243
Stone, Lawrence, 191, 193, 194, 195, 198, 207n, 287
Stowe, John, 19, 20, 33, 34
Strachey, Lytton, 141n
Stuart, Mary, 34, 251, 252, 255
Stubbes, Philip, 102–3, 117n
Summers, Joseph, 143n
Swetnam, Joseph, 188, 189, 206n
Swinburne, Henry, 193, 194, 197, 207n, 208n
Swinton, Tilda, 266

Tarlton's Jests, 31, 33
Tarlton's Newes Out of Purgatory, 23–26, 28, 33
Tarlton's Tragical Treatises, 22
Teichman, Jenny, 193, 207n
Tennenhouse, Leonard, 226
Terence, 102, 107
Thatcher, Margaret, 257
Thelen, Kathleen, 128
Thompson, Ann, 116n
Thorne, Robert, 45
Tilney, Edmund, 187, 201, 208n
Tillyard, E. M. W., 275
Timpanaro, Sebastiano, 285
Tomlinson, Sophie, 261
Traub, Valerie, 95n, 97n–98n, 261, 265
Tubervile, George, 113–14

Underdown, David, 201, 209n

Vaughan, William, 106, 118n
Vawter, Marvin, 144n
Veeser, H. Aram, 141n
Vergil, 107, 129
Vickers, Brian, 284–88
Vining, Edward P., 91n
Vives, Juan, 111, 116, 119n
von Senden, Marius, 210, 221n

Waingrow, Marshall, 178n
Walsingham, Francis, 38n
Walther, Malin LaVon, 265
Warner, Deborah, 266
Warning for Fair Women, 272, 274
Watson, Robert, 189, 190, 206n
Wayne, Valerie, 187, 189, 205n, 209n
Weber, Max, 128, 143n
Weimann, Robert, 36n, 70n, 288
Wheeler, Richard, 188, 206n, 281
Whitney-Brown, Carolyn, 206n

Whyttynton, R., 132
Wikander, Matthew M., 144n
Wiles, David, 36n
Williams, Raymond, 278
Willoughby, Sir Hugh, 45
Wilson, Charles, 254
Wilson, R. Rawdon, 215, 221n
Winnicott, D. W., 93n
Witch of Edmonton, 274
Wittgenstein, Ludwig, 180n
Woodbridge, Linda, 287
Wright, Edward, 39, 43, 45, 46, 51
Wrightson, Keith, 208n
Wroth, Mary, 243
Wyman, Lillie, 264

Yarington, Robert, 272
Yates, Frances, 70n
Yorkshire Tragedy, 273–74

Ziegler, Georgianna, 214, 221n
Zizek, Slavoj, 233